Service Innovations in Tourism:

Metaverse, Immersive Technologies, and Digital Twin

Surabhi Singh
G.L. Bajaj Institute of Management and Research, India

A volume in the Advances in Hospitality, Tourism, and the Services Industry (AHTSI) Book Series

IGI Global
PUBLISHER of TIMELY KNOWLEDGE

Published in the United States of America by
IGI Global
Business Science Reference (an imprint of IGI Global)
701 E. Chocolate Avenue
Hershey PA, USA 17033
Tel: 717-533-8845
Fax: 717-533-8661
E-mail: cust@igi-global.com
Web site: http://www.igi-global.com

Library of Congress Cataloging-in-Publication Data

Names: Singh, Surabhi, editor.
Title: Service innovations in tourism : metaverse, immersive technologies, and digital twin / Edited by Surabhi Singh.
Description: Hershey, PA : Business Science Reference, [2024] | Includes bibliographical references and index. | Summary: "The book aims to introduce the facets of innovative models of services in tourism that can form the profitability quotient of organizations in the VUCA world"-- Provided by publisher.
Identifiers: LCCN 2023050934 (print) | LCCN 2023050935 (ebook) | ISBN 9798369311035 (hardcover) | ISBN 9798369311042 (ebook)
Subjects: LCSH: Tourism--Technological innovations. | Tourism--Management. | Metaverse--Economic aspects. | Service industries--Technological innovations.
Classification: LCC G156.5.I5 .S47 2024 (print) | LCC G156.5.I5 (ebook) | DDC 910.68/4--dc23/eng/20231222
LC record available at https://lccn.loc.gov/2023050934
LC ebook record available at https://lccn.loc.gov/2023050935

This book is published in the IGI Global book series Advances in Hospitality, Tourism, and the Services Industry (AHTSI) (ISSN: 2475-6547; eISSN: 2475-6555)

British Cataloguing in Publication Data
A Cataloguing in Publication record for this book is available from the British Library.

Advances in Hospitality, Tourism, and the Services Industry (AHTSI) Book Series

ISSN:2475-6547
EISSN:2475-6555

Editor-in-Chief: Maximiliano Korstanje, University of Palermo, Argentina

MISSION

Globally, the hospitality, travel, tourism, and services industries generate a significant percentage of revenue and represent a large portion of thc business world. Even in tough economic times, these industries thrive as individuals continue to spend on leisure and recreation activities as well as services.

The Advances in Hospitality, Tourism, and the Services Industry (AHTSI) book series offers diverse publications relating to the management, promotion, and profitability of the leisure, recreation, and services industries. Highlighting current research pertaining to various topics within the realm of hospitality, travel, tourism, and services management, the titles found within the AHTSI book series are pertinent to the research and professional needs of managers, business practitioners, researchers, and upper-level students studying in the field.

COVERAGE

- Customer Service Issues
- Leisure & Business Travel
- Sustainable Tourism
- Travel Agency Management
- Service Management
- Casino Management
- Health and Wellness Tourism
- Destination Marketing and Management
- Hotel Management
- Service Design

IGI Global is currently accepting manuscripts for publication within this series. To submit a proposal for a volume in this series, please contact our Acquisition Editors at Acquisitions@igi-global.com or visit: http://www.igi-global.com/publish/.

The Advances in Hospitality, Tourism, and the Services Industry (AHTSI) Book Series (ISSN 2475-6547) is published by IGI Global, 701 E. Chocolate Avenue, Hershey, PA 17033-1240, USA, www.igi-global.com. This series is composed of titles available for purchase individually; each title is edited to be contextually exclusive from any other title within the series. For pricing and ordering information please visit http://www.igi-global.com/book-series/advances-hospitality-tourism-services-industry/121014. Postmaster: Send all address changes to above address.

Titles in this Series

For a list of additional titles in this series, please visit:
http://www.igi-global.com/book-series/advances-hospitality-tourism-services-industry/121014

Mountain Tourism and Ecological Impacts Himalayan Region and Beyond
Soumendra Nath Biswas (Assam University, Silchar, India) and Pradip Kumar (Assam University, Silchar, India)
Business Science Reference • copyright 2024 • 320pp • H/C (ISBN: 9798369308233) • US $250.00 (our price)

Career Pathways and Professional Identities for Front-Line Workers in the Service Industries
Mark Peter Vitale (University of Phoenix, USA)
Business Science Reference • copyright 2024 • 370pp • H/C (ISBN: 9781668425282) • US $255.00 (our price)

Experiences, Advantages, and Economic Dimensions of Pilgrimage Routes
Vítor João Pereira Domingues Martinho (Agricultural School, CERNAS-IPV Research Centre, Polytechnic Institute of Viseu, Portugal) João Augusto Guerra da Rocha Nunes (School of Education, Polytechnic Institute of Viseu, Portugal) Maria Lúcia de Jesus Pato (Agricultural School, CERNAS-IPV Research Centre, Polytechnic Institute of Viseu, Portugal) and Liliana Andrade de Matos Castilho (School of Education, Polytechnic Institute of Viseu, Portugal)
Business Science Reference • copyright 2023 • 367pp • H/C (ISBN: 9781668499238) • US $240.00 (our price)

Exploring Culture and Heritage Through Experience Tourism
Yashwant Singh Rawal (Parul Institute of Hotel Management, Parul University, India) Rupa Sinha (Amity Institute of Travel and Tourism, Amity University, India) Sankar Kumar Mukherjee (Amity Institute of Travel and Tourism, Amity University, India) and Debasish Batabyal (Amity Institute of Travel and Tourism, Amity University, India)
Business Science Reference • copyright 2023 • 348pp • H/C (ISBN: 9781668499573) • US $240.00 (our price)

Sustainable Development Goal Advancement Through Digital Innovation in the Service Sector

For an entire list of titles in this series, please visit:
http://www.igi-global.com/book-series/advances-hospitality-tourism-services-industry/121014

IGI Global
PUBLISHER of TIMELY KNOWLEDGE

701 East Chocolate Avenue, Hershey, PA 17033, USA
Tel: 717-533-8845 x100 • Fax: 717-533-8661
E-Mail: cust@igi-global.com • www.igi-global.com

Editorial Advisory Board

List of Reviewers

Table of Contents

Detailed Table of Contents

The Metaverse is a ground-breaking technology development that has the potential to fundamentally alter how tourism is managed and promoted. Its capacity to provide immersive encounters across both the virtual and physical domains, successfully bridging the gap between the digital and material worlds, is what is driving this transition. Users now have a wide range of options thanks to this ground-breaking idea, which makes it simple for them to move between the physical and digital worlds. People can travel through time in this fully immersive digital environment, where they can virtually experience historical events, go on space expeditions, or even come across dangerous natural phenomena. Users can explore virtual settings for work, education, commerce, following their interests, and engaging with people in this world in addition to sating their wanderlust. Players interact naturally inside this virtual world, demonstrating the Metaverse's influence on the gaming industry and laying the groundwork for its greater potential.

The Metaverse represents a revolutionary force in transforming religious tourism, demonstrating its versatile applicability in reinforcing visit intentions, advancing research, expanding resources sustainably, and transforming hospitality experiences. It serves as a catalyst for immersive education, virtual pilgrimages, community building, and facilitating religious events, transcending boundaries. However, challenges such as maintaining sacredness, preventing commercialization, ensuring authenticity, addressing ethical concerns, overcoming inclusivity issues, managing security, and navigating global regulatory compliance require careful consideration to fully harness the Metaverse's potential in religious tourism.

The world of innovation and innovative technologies is rapidly proving its scope and benefits across the business sector featuring business intelligence tools. The traditional way of searching data sources, visualizing those data, and arriving at business decisions has transformed with tools of computational intelligence. Here the role of virtual reality (VR) and augmented reality (AR) comes into the picture. The current work looks into the possibilities of VR and AR in business, which support predictive analytics, customer analytics, business analytics, and data visualization aspects through systematic literature review and content analysis. In this paper, a systematic analysis of associations and features of both VR and AR has been done by detailing the outline, organization, management, and devices for business and industry intelligence. The objective of the current work is met with the insights and understanding of VR and AR in relation to business intelligence.

This research will study the effective use of technology in employee programmes in County Clare (Ireland). A strong onboarding programme with the assistance of emerging technology can decide a firm's success. This research explores the new technological advancements made in automation and artificial intelligence as well as data analytics and its application to the onboarding experience. The research objectives were established to facilitate the direction of the examination. In order to achieve the objectives, primary and secondary research was conducted. The analysis of the findings interprets data by comparing and contrasting results between participants and current literature to measure synergy between current knowledge and current practitioners' opinions. The research has shown a deep enthusiasm for new efficient technological advancements for the HR department in businesses.

In the travel business, metaverse tourism symbolises a revolutionary paradigm change that reshapes how people discover, interact with, and connect with places. This in-depth chapter examines the revolutionary potential of metaverse tourism and considers how it may affect travel businesses, customer experiences, and the overall exploration environment. The chapter starts out by presenting the idea of the metaverse and highlighting how important it is becoming to modern travel. It moves through the metaverse's history of tourism, stressing the immersive and endless experiences it promises. Key themes influencing metaverse tourism

customer needs. Practical recommendations are provided for organizations to embark on their digital innovation journey, including strategic planning, talent acquisition, and fostering an innovative culture. Overall, the chapter offers a roadmap for businesses to leverage digital technologies and revolutionize customer experiences in today's digital era.

Metaverse tourism is an emerging concept that refers to the practice of exploring and experiencing virtual worlds and digital environments. It offers a wide range of immersive experiences, social interactions, and exploration opportunities. In the metaverse, tourists can visit and interact with various virtual destinations, which can be designed to replicate real-world locations, historical periods, fantasy realms, or entirely new and imaginative landscapes. Tourists can embark on virtual adventures, solve puzzles, or participate in multiplayer games with people worldwide. It is important to note that the metaverse concept is still evolving, and the extent of its development and adoption may vary over time. However, as technology advances and virtual experiences become more immersive, metaverse tourism will likely become an increasingly popular and accessible form of travel and exploration. Based on the above, the authors intend to systematically review the bibliometric literature on tourism in the metaverse using the Scopus database with the analysis of 75 academic and/or scientific documents

Blockchain technology is an emerging technology useful to provide innovative solutions in various sectors. The real world uses cases of blockchain technology such as faster cross-border payments, identity management, crypto currencies, smart contracts, and supply chain-blockchain technology are here to stay and have become the next innovation just like internet. There have been attempts to formulate and introduce digital money, but they have not been successful due to security and trust issues. Blockchain has moved past crypto currency and discovered implementations in other real-life applications; this is where we can expect blockchain technology to be simplified and not remain a complex concept. Blockchain technology's desirable characteristics are decentralization, integrity, immutability, verification,

Foreword

In an era where the boundaries between the physical and digital worlds are increasingly blurring, the tourism industry stands on the cusp of a revolutionary transformation. The advent of service innovations involving the metaverse, immersive technologies, and digital twins heralds a new age of exploration, not just geographically but within the vast, untapped expanse of virtual realms. This book, *Service Innovations in Tourism: Metaverse, Immersive Technologies, and Digital Twin*, arrives at a critical juncture, offering a comprehensive exploration of how these technologies are reshaping the landscape of tourism.

The chapters within this book delve into a variety of topics, each a testament to the transformative potential of digital innovations in tourism. From the exploration of ecotourism as a burgeoning business opportunity to the intricate examination of automation in human resource practices, the range is both broad and deep. It addresses the pivotal role of the metaverse in promoting religious tourism, the application of virtual and augmented reality in enhancing industrial and business intelligence, and the innovative use of blockchain technology in the tourism and hospitality industry. Furthermore, it provides insightful analyses on navigating the opportunities and challenges that these technologies present, emphasizing their impact on operational efficiency, customer experience, and sustainable tourism practices.

This pioneering work does more than just chronicle the current state of digital innovations in tourism; it serves as a beacon for future explorations, highlighting the immense potential for creating more resilient and inclusive tourism ecosystems. The contributions from various authors offer a multi-faceted view, ensuring a clear understanding of the subject matter for readers across the spectrum, from industry stakeholders to academic researchers.

As we stand at the threshold of this new digital dawn, the importance of such a work cannot be overstated. It is not only timely but also fascinating, providing both a theoretical framework and practical insights into the application of these technologies. The editor deserve commendation for their foresight in bringing together this collection of works that illuminate the path forward for the tourism industry.

I extend my heartfelt congratulations to the editor for this significant contribution to the field of tourism studies. It is an honor to contribute a foreword to this book, and I eagerly anticipate the advancements and discussions it will inspire. Here's to the success of *Service Innovations in Tourism: Metaverse, Immersive Technologies, and Digital Twin*, a guidepost for navigating the future of tourism in an increasingly digital world.

Yogesh K Dwivedi
Digital Futures for Sustainable Business and Society Research Group, School of Management, Swansea University, UK

Yogesh K. Dwivedi *is a Professor of Digital Marketing and Innovation and Founding Director of the Digital Futures for Sustainable Business & Society Research Group at the School of Management, Swansea University, Wales, UK. In addition, he holds a Distinguished Research Professorship at the Symbiosis International (Deemed University), Pune, India. Professor Dwivedi is also currently leading the International Journal of Information Management as its Editor-in-Chief. His research interests are at the interface of Information Systems (IS) and Marketing, focusing on issues related to consumer adoption and diffusion of emerging digital innovations, digital government, and digital and social media marketing particularly in the context of emerging markets. Professor Dwivedi has published more than 600 articles in a range of leading academic journals and conferences that are widely cited (more than 70 thousand times as per Google Scholar). He has been named on the annual Highly Cited Researchers™ 2020, 2021 and 2022 lists from Clarivate Analytics. Professor Dwivedi is an Associate Editor of the Journal of Business Research, European Journal of Marketing, and Government Information Quarterly, and Senior Editor of the Journal of Electronic Commerce Research.*

Preface

Welcome to *Service Innovations in Tourism: Metaverse, Immersive Technologies, and Digital Twin*. This edited reference book, spearheaded by Surabhi Singh from GLBIMR Greater Noida, India, embarks on a journey through the cutting-edge realms of service innovations that are reshaping the landscape of the tourism industry.

In an era marked by rapid technological advancements, the tourism sector stands at the forefront of transformative change. This book ventures into the emerging areas of metaverse, digital twins, and immersive technologies, exploring how these innovations are poised to revolutionize services and redefine the very essence of the tourism experience. As the world moves towards the era of Industry 5.0, it becomes imperative for businesses to not only adapt but also innovate to ensure sustainability in the long run.

The study presented within these pages introduces varied applications of technological innovations synonymous with Industry 5.0. The book not only explores the present impact of metaverse applications but also delves into the futuristic perspectives that these technologies hold for the tourism industry. It addresses the key role of automation in achieving success across industries and emphasizes the transformative power of metaverse applications in the hospitality and tourism sector.

Metaverse applications have become the catalyst for change, offering virtual experiences that transcend physical boundaries. This book elucidates how virtual hotels, destinations, and tours within the metaverse are reshaping the ways in which people engage with travel—from selecting lodging and destinations to making bookings and attending virtual concerts. The immersive nature of virtual reality experiences provides travelers with a tangible sense of what to expect from a particular destination, influencing their decisions and inspiring bookings.

Our aim is to present innovative models of services in tourism that serve as the profitability quotient for organizations navigating the VUCA (Volatile, Uncertain, Complex, Ambiguous) world. This book highlights the emerging trends of Metaverse Tourism, setting the stage for sustainable business practices in Industry 5.0. The incorporation of digital twins and immersive technologies in service innovations is not just altering the tourism industry; it is redefining how businesses operate in an ever-evolving environment.

For readers seeking a comprehensive understanding of service innovations in tourism, this book covers a spectrum of topics, including metaverse experiences in travel, virtual travel, service innovations with immersive technology, digital twin models, augmented reality in tourism, and the role of Industry 5.0 in driving service innovations. The chapters explore how these innovations contribute to the sustainability of businesses and provide a roadmap for industry stakeholders to navigate the changing landscape effectively.

Our target audience spans academics, researchers, students, practitioners, and professionals in the tourism industry. The curated topics include Metaverse Tourism, Service Excellence with Metaverse Tourism, Service Technologies in Tourism, Emerging Trends of Metaverse Tourism, and much more. Each chapter is crafted to deliver valuable insights, facilitating a deeper understanding of how service innovations are reshaping the tourism industry.

As editor, I extend my gratitude to the contributors who have shared their expertise and research, making this book a comprehensive resource for anyone interested in the intersection of technology and tourism. We hope this volume inspires further exploration and discussion in the dynamic field of service innovations in tourism.

Ecotourism: A New Business Opportunity in the Tourism Industry

Authored by Uttapal Kumar and Shiv Yadav from Bennett University, India, this chapter navigates the realms of sustainable business strategies within the tourism industry, focusing on the substantial growth of ecotourism. Delving into the premium yet responsible travel experiences, the authors explore the integration of technology to enhance environmental and cultural awareness, emphasizing the challenges posed by mass tourism. The chapter also sheds light on the role of governments in actively promoting sustainable tourism, emphasizing the need for global collaboration.

Understanding the Unpredictable: Technological Revolution's Transformative Impact on Tourism Management and Marketing

In this chapter by Ankit Garg, Himanshu Sharma, Anubhav Singh, Nikhil Sharma, and Sakhi Aneja from Ajay Kumar Garg Institute of Management, India, the focus is on the transformative impact of the Metaverse on tourism management and marketing. The authors highlight the Metaverse's groundbreaking potential in providing immersive experiences across virtual and physical domains. The chapter explores the historical context of the Metaverse and its influence on the gaming industry, setting the stage for its broader applications in tourism.

Exploring the Role of Metaverse in Promoting Religious Tourism

Authored by Munir Ahmad from Survey of Pakistan, Pakistan, this chapter explores the revolutionary force of the Metaverse in transforming religious tourism. The Metaverse's versatile applicability in reinforcing visit intentions, facilitating virtual pilgrimages, and community building is discussed. While highlighting the transformative potential, the chapter addresses challenges such as maintaining sacredness, preventing commercialization, and ensuring authenticity in religious tourism within the Metaverse.

Virtual Reality and Augmented Reality for Industrial and Business Intelligence

The chapter by Karishma Desai, Dileep M, Mohamed Khairi, Normala Govindarajo, and Vinod Sharma from various institutions explores the role of virtual reality (VR) and augmented reality (AR) in business intelligence. Through systematic literature review and content analysis, the authors examine how VR and AR support predictive analytics, customer analytics, and data visualization. The chapter aims to provide insights into the applications and features of VR and AR concerning business and industry intelligence.

Examination of Automation in Human Resource Practices: A Study of Effective Use of Technology in Employee Induction Programmes in County Clare (Ireland)

Authored by Dawid Glowski, June O'Byrne-Prior, and Noelle O'Connor from Technological University of the Shannon, Ireland, this chapter explores the effective use of technology in employee induction programs. Focusing on technological advancements in automation, artificial intelligence, and data analytics, the authors investigate the impact on onboarding experiences. The findings showcase a keen interest in technological advancements for HR practices, revealing a significant enthusiasm for new and efficient technological solutions.

Tourism in the Metaverse What's Next? Building Immersive Experiences

Dr. Preeti Mehra and Amit Dutt from Lovely Professional University, India, contribute a chapter that delves into the revolutionary paradigm change brought about by metaverse tourism. The authors explore the historical context of metaverse tourism, emphasizing immersive experiences and endless possibilities. Key themes, including the growth of NFTs, digital mementos, virtual places, and personalized adventures, are examined, highlighting the transformational potential of metaverse tourism.

Navigating the Metaverse: Opportunities and Challenges in Tourism

Dr. Arpita Srivastava, Dr. Nidhi Srivastava, and Sunetra Saha from various institutions in India investigate the metaverse's potential in the tourism industry. Utilizing a systematic review of scholarly literature, media articles, and industry reports, the chapter establishes a comprehensive definition and conceptual framework for the metaverse ecosystem within the context of tourism and travel. Opportunities and challenges are discerned, providing insights into the future development of the metaverse in tourism.

Digital Innovation in the Service Sector: Transforming Customer Experiences

Authored by Viana Hassan, Shakeel Basheer, Faizan Mir, and Simon Abou Fayad from various institutions, this chapter explores digital innovation in the service sector and its impact on customer experiences. Covering drivers and enablers such as AI, data analytics, and mobile apps, the authors emphasize a customer-centric approach. The chapter offers practical recommendations for organizations to leverage digital technologies and revolutionize customer experiences in the digital era.

Tourism in the Metaverse: Opportunities and Challenges

Albérico Rosário and Joana Dias from institutions in Portugal investigate the emerging concept of metaverse tourism. The chapter explores the wide range of immersive experiences, social interactions, and exploration opportunities offered by metaverse tourism. The authors aim to systematically review the bibliometric literature on tourism in the metaverse using the Scopus database, analyzing 75 academic and/or scientific documents.

Service Innovation Through Blockchain Technology in the Tourism and Hospitality Industry: Applications, Trends, and Benefits

Authored by Amrik Singh and Shuaibu Hassan from Lovely Professional University, Punjab, India, and Isa Kaita College of Education, Nigeria, respectively, this chapter delves into the applications, trends, and benefits of blockchain technology in the tourism and hospitality industry. The authors explore real-world use cases and discuss the desirable characteristics of blockchain technology, emphasizing decentralization, integrity, immutability, and transparency.

Exploring Enlarged Perceptions of Value: The Utilization of Virtual Reality in Indian Tourism

In this chapter by Ankit Garg, TR Pandey, Ritesh Singhal, Himanshu Sharma Sharma, and Anubhav Singh from Ajay Kumar Garg Institute of Management, India, the focus is on how virtual reality (VR) technology has been used in Indian tourism. The authors introduce a framework considering perceived advantages, sacrifices, and overall perceived value to examine how users view VR as valuable. The findings highlight the significant influence of perceived telepresence and usefulness on judgments of VR's value. Trade-offs related to perceived health risk and physical risk also play a crucial role in determining how much people value VR usage.

In an era characterized by rapid technological evolution, the tourism sector emerges as a crucible of transformative change. This edited reference book ventures into the forefront of innovation, focusing on the burgeoning domains of metaverse, digital twins, and immersive technologies. It delves deep into how these innovations are not just altering services but redefining the very essence of the tourism experience. In the backdrop of Industry 5.0, the imperative for businesses to innovate becomes paramount for sustainability in an ever-changing environment.

The contributions within these pages offer a glimpse into the diverse applications synonymous with Industry 5.0. The book not only explores the current impact of metaverse applications but also provides futuristic perspectives. Automation takes center stage as a key driver of success, and the transformative power of metaverse applications in the hospitality and tourism sector is underscored.

The overarching goal of this book is to present innovative service models in tourism that serve as the bedrock for profitability in a VUCA world. It brings into focus the emerging trends of Metaverse Tourism, laying the groundwork for sustainable business practices in Industry 5.0. The incorporation of digital twins and immersive technologies in service innovations is not just altering the tourism industry; it is redefining how businesses operate in an ever-evolving environment.

For readers seeking a comprehensive understanding of service innovations in tourism, this book covers a spectrum of topics, including metaverse experiences in travel, virtual travel, service innovations with immersive technology, digital twin models, augmented reality in tourism, and the role of Industry 5.0 in driving service innovations. The chapters collectively explore how these innovations contribute to the sustainability of businesses and provide a roadmap for industry stakeholders to navigate the changing landscape effectively.

Our gratitude extends to the contributors who have shared their expertise and research, making this book a comprehensive resource for anyone interested in the intersection of technology and tourism. We hope this volume inspires further exploration and discussion in the dynamic field of service innovations in tourism. May it serve as a beacon guiding academics, researchers, students, practitioners, and professionals in the tourism industry toward a future where innovation and sustainability coalesce for unparalleled experiences.

Surabhi Singh
G.L. Bajaj Institute of Management and Research, India

Chapter 1
Ecotourism:
A New Business Opportunity in the Tourism Industry

Uttapal Kumar
Bennett University, India

Shiv Kumar Yadav
Bennett University, India

ABSTRACT

Tourism participation hinges on key determinants such as leisure time and disposable income, acting as facilitators that either enable or hinder travel engagement. Ecotourism is experiencing substantial growth of 7% to 30%. This chapter explores a sustainable business strategy in tourism, particularly emphasizing ecotourism. Sustainable tourism businesses, though premium, prioritize responsible travel experiences. Technology integration enhances environmental and cultural awareness but poses challenges like mass tourism. Business service management in ecotourism emphasizes e-service quality for enduring consumer relationships. Governments, as demonstrated in the G20 summit, actively promote sustainable tourism, highlighting the need for global collaboration. Sustainable tourism, balancing environmental, cultural, and economic aspects, fosters positive travel experiences and supports the ethical future of the industry.

INTRODUCTION

The tourism industry, characterized by its expansive and dynamic nature, holds a pivotal position in the global economy. Beyond its contributions to governmental

DOI: 10.4018/979-8-3693-1103-5.ch001

interests, this sector serves as a significant source of employment generation for local populations, thereby influencing the demographic dynamics of the respective regions. According to the survey, 81% of global travelers believe that ecotourism is important. The report says that the tourism market size increased by 41% and there were 295 million jobs in 2022 compared to the previous year, and it will be projected that by the end of 2023, the economic growth will be 2.29 trillion dollars and there will be 320 million jobs in 2023 (Statista, 2023). Ecotourism has grown their importance as a source of revenue in natural tourist areas around the world (Drumm et al., 2002). Eco-tourism business model focuses on all the services that they provide to consumers i.e. recycling of biodegradable products, use of renewable sources of energy, etc. Responsible travelers expect the services from tour operators to be full of green tourism services, which will evoke eco-travel. The purpose of this constructive business model is to educate the reader and tour operator about the value of local cultures and biodiversity conservation while enabling them to witness potent expressions of nature and culture. It is a new economic model known as the "green economy" that is market-driven, built on the foundations of the traditional industrial economy, and aims to balance the needs of the environment and the economy. It is a type of development state that the industrial economy generates and demonstrates to satisfy the demands of human health and environmental preservation (Chen, 2023). Ecotourism word was introduced forty years ago. When the concept of sustainable tourism initially emerged at the beginning of the 1980s, it provided a means for tourists to lessen the environmental harm they caused while visiting far-off places (Ecotourism World, 2021b). Based on thought Ceballos-Lascurain provided the first description of ecotourism in 1987 His definition of ecotourism is "tourism that consists in travelling to relatively undisturbed or uncontaminated natural areas with the specific object of studying, admiring and enjoying the scenery" (Ceballos-Lascurain, 1987, p. 13). After that, there are so many definitions given by Authors and environmental organizations Since 1990, the International Ecotourism Society (TIES), a non-profit organization, has worked to advance ecotourism. "Responsible travel that preserves the environment, supports local people, and involves interpretation and education for both staff and guests" is how they define ecotourism (What Is Ecotourism - the International Ecotourism Society, 2019). Overall, the ecotourism market size was valued at USD 37,365 million in 2021 and is expected to reach an estimated value of USD 1,29,402 million by 2030. This growth can be attributed to a projected CAGR of 14.8% during the forecast period (2022–2030) (Research, n.d.). For businesses like new SMEs in tourism, it is important to understand how much sustainability is required for the development of economic, social, and government (ESG), as it ensures a viable and profitable business idea that benefits the environment and communities. As per the government requirement on sustainability in tourism, Ecotourism business is defined as the appreciation and observation of nature along with their local traditional culture that motivates the traveler to visit the place through a tourism operator. Technology is also changing the way that tourism is organized and has a great deal of promise for growth in the future. (Huang et al., 2016; Werthner & Klein,1999). Digitalization has expanded the horizons of travelers, affording them the opportunity to explore novel and undiscovered destinations. Before digitalization, people were limited in their knowledge of places they could visit. Nowadays, with the help of technology, there are many hidden gems waiting to be explored. Immersive technology has made ecotourism even more appealing, as it allows prospective tourists to get a virtual preview of their destination. From testing out rustic accommodations in beautiful landscapes to experiencing local customs and traditions firsthand, this novel approach helps visitors gain an insight into what they can expect from their trip before setting foot on the ground. It has huge potential benefits for SMEs. It facilitates enhanced efficiency, liberates temporal and resource constraints for concentrating on pivotal tasks, and augments the capability to formulate innovative business models, penetrate new markets, or globalize operational endeavors. The development of digital technology aided in the involvement of tourists in numerous online and mobile apps. Through this business, tourism organizations promote the sustainable growth of people, renewable and non-renewable natural resources, and the environment to ensure long-term development. As per the government's agenda, this new form of tourism is a necessity. It has been found that 5.3 billion people around the world were using the internet, which means 65.7% out of these 4.95 billion individuals (61.4%) had active social media accounts (Internet and Social Media Users in the World 2023 | Statista, 2023).After the integration of digital media in business, researchers accept that demand is high and continues to grow, regardless of the market's size or actual economic worth. These demands also promote the niche segment of tourism. It's a fantastic way to see the world and contributes to its preservation for coming generations. Ecotourism is an essential component of the tourism industry, as it encourages sustainable practices. A fresh chance for business in the tourism sector could benefit people and communities greatly. Ecotourism businesses in Florida manifest diverse ownership models, encompassing private ownership, public agency ownership, and public-private partnerships, each providing a spectrum of services or products. Each model provides different benefits that can help you choose the best option for your business.

1. HOLISTIC MODEL OF ECOTOURISM SUSTAINABILITY

According to Hendricks (2023) "A business model that prioritizes sustainability is one that, at a minimum, considers all stakeholders, assesses and addresses environmental impacts, and is transparent and thorough in its reporting". A holistic model of ecotourism sustainability acknowledges the interdependence of environmental, social, and economic aspects and attempts to establish a balanced and responsible approach to tourism that benefits both the destination and its residents. Organizations must adapt the way they produce, transmit, and embody values from social, economic, and environmental standpoints (Shakeel et al. 2020). In order to operate their firm in accordance with sustainability policies, they must establish a sustainable business model (SBM) (MuñozTorres et al. 2019). Geissdoerfer et al. (2016) A sustainable business model is defined as a "simplified representation of the elements, the interrelationship between these elements, and the interactions with its stakeholders that an organizational unit uses to create, deliver, capture, and exchange sustainable value." Regular review and adaptation of practices in response to feedback and changing conditions is critical to the long-term viability of ecotourism sustainability initiatives. Public and private investment drive job and income growth in a green economy. These eco-friendly investments boost the economy and encourage the construction of green energy infrastructure, which lowers carbon emissions, increases energy and resource efficiency, and safeguards ecosystems and biodiversity. Sun et al. (2020) This paradigm centers on the corporation's dedication to generating enduring value for both itself and the broader community. It emphasizes a harmonious equilibrium between profitability and constructive impacts on both individuals and the environment. Through this model, the tourism industry gains up with competitive edge by reducing costs, enhancing reputation, and fostering innovation.

Figure 1. Conceptual model for ecotourism

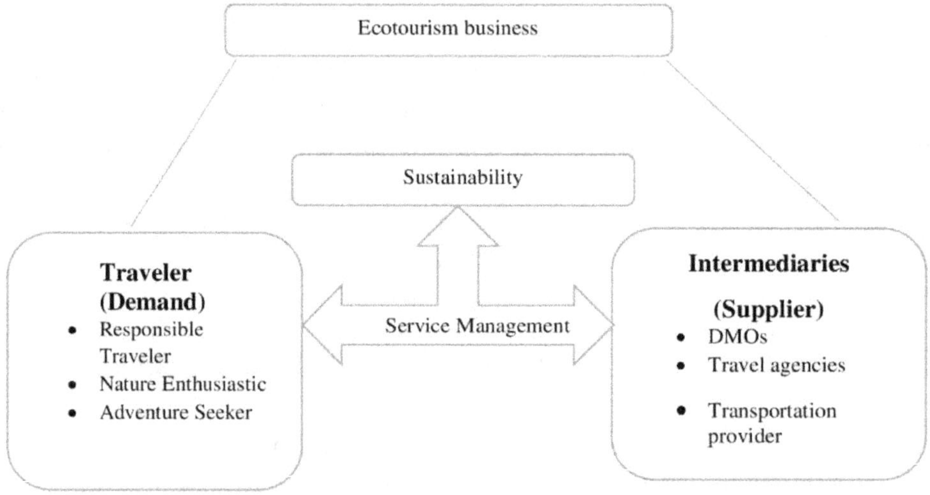

In the model of ecotourism enterprises, shows the relationship between tourists, traveler intermediaries, and sustainability is a dynamic and complicated, including various interactions, interdependencies, and impacts among the players and variables that define the ecotourism phenomena. The nexus between stakeholders in ecotourism is contingent upon the extent to which they adhere to and invest in the principles and objectives of ecotourism. This connection clarifies how travelers contribute to the demand for ecotourism experiences that are sustainable. Moreover, it underscores the cognizance among travelers regarding the adverse impacts of tourism on both societal and environmental aspects. Notably, a substantial number of these tourists proactively seek out vacation alternatives that align with sustainability and ethical considerations. The Concept of making this model is to define the relationship between supply, demand, and sustainability which is very impactful in the long-term business of Ecotourism. Traveler intermediates, (tour operators, travel agencies, guides, hotel providers, and transportation providers) are organizations that facilitate travel and tourism activities. These middlemen positively influence travelers' decisions by providing eco-friendly goods and services. The fact that these travelers influence others by endorsing the services provided by travel firms makes it potentially beneficial in the future. Travel intermediaries are accountable for following ecotourism guidelines and best practices, guaranteeing the caliber and security of services, enlightening and educating guests and hosts, and collaborating with partners to manage resources sustainably. It may help to ensure sustainability by providing tours that follow ethical practices, benefit local people, and have a low environmental effect. The fundamental aim and benchmark of ecotourism lies in achieving sustainability, denoting an equilibrium and consonance among the economic, environmental, and social dimensions of tourism development. The attainment of sustainability mandates the active involvement and collaboration of a diverse array of stakeholders in the formulation, execution, and evaluation of ecotourism initiatives. These stakeholders encompass visitors, traveler intermediaries, local communities, government bodies, non-governmental organizations (NGOs), academic institutions, among others. Moreover, sustainability in ecotourism necessitates the continuous monitoring and enhancement of operational performance and impact. This process relies on comprehensive metrics and reporting mechanisms to evaluate economic, environmental, and social outcomes.

1.1 Demand of Ecotourism

According to Cunha (2003) Tourism demand may be described as a "quantity of goods and services acquired by people to complete their journeys" (Cunha, 2003). According to the author (Wight,1993) an enlightening nature travel experience that contributes to conservation of the ecosystem, while respecting the integrity of host communities. It is sufficient to state that the ecotourism industry contributes significantly, and many. Travelers are demanding to visit ecotourist places in their leisure time because these places give them inner peace. There are various groups of individual travellers (nature lovers, wildlife enthusiasts, cultural explorers, and responsible travellers) who have a similar interest in ethical and sustainable travel, a love for nature, and a desire to have meaningful and real experiences. Individuals who prioritize conservation, community involvement, and sustainable practices in their travel choices are drawn to ecotourist destinations that emphasize conservation, community engagement, and sustainable practices. Now people are becoming more ecologically concerned and seeking meaningful vacation experiences, which has increased interest in ecotourism. According to the author's research on ecotourism, there is an increase in ecotourism growth compared to the tourist sector as a whole, with estimates ranging from 7% to 30%. (Fennell, 2003; Page & Dowling,2002; Wight, 2001). Ecotourism demand also depends on the services provided by the tourist operator. Growing global awareness of environmental issues is also a factor in environmental sustainability. Increasing the demand for ecotourism also motivates the government to focus on national parks and so many other private protected areas, ostensibly to help protect their environmental functions and their biological diversity. Moreover, the incentives for ecotourism experiences are the feelings of the traveler, as opposed to those of conventional experiences. It also contains ecotourism-related items. Digital technology integration has democratized travel information, enabled customers to make educated decisions, and established a worldwide community of ecologically concerned travelers. As a result, demand for ecotourism has increased. With the aid of technology, consumers can travel at any time, and it also helps tour operators meet the demand for destinations. Digitalization holds the inherent capacity to stimulate innovation, yield economic and environmental efficiencies, and enhance productivity, especially within the context of the extensively globalized tourism sector. This transformative process involves the integration of digital technologies and platforms, contributes to the evolution of operational paradigms, and fosters advancements in various facets of the tourism industry. IoT is a strategic technology trend that would tremendously impact business opportunities. (Gartner, 2015). Tourists are increasingly using the Internet to research and purchase travel components, discover new places, and get new experiences. The Internet is a great tourism partner since it allows for knowledge sharing and the dissemination of tourist products. It also shows that the larger the number of Internet users, the greater the likelihood of increased tourism demand.

1.2 Role of Supplier in Ecotourism

Suppliers are invaluable partners in the ecotourism industry, playing a key role in promoting responsible growth and the long-term sustainability of tourism destinations. Without their support, ecotourism would not be able to thrive. According to Boon et al. (2002), ecologists might play an important role in supplying crucial environmental information to tour operators' planners and managers in the temperate, marine, and coastal habitats of south-eastern Australia. To fulfill the supply side, information regarding firms, tourist preferences, intermediaries, rivals, and tourism market trends must be produced. According to Weiler and Ham (2001), tour guides can help tourists understand natural phenomena by ensuring that interpretation is enjoyable for visitors, relevant for visitors, follows a theme, has a high level of organization in presentation, and avoids taking an overly academic approach. Several other industries worked with sustainable tourism and formulated the concept of being environmentally friendly. Travel agencies help connect travelers with sustainable and responsible travel experiences. To explore how ecotourism is conceived and packaged for international tourists. After the adoption of digitalization at the level of the tourism industry, a society formed new forms of communication, interactions, and relationships between producers and consumers, including in the field of tourism service operators and other tourism services that spread quickly. Social media plays an important role in increasing consumer happiness. Tour operators use social media to communicate with consumers, create relationships, and deliver a more tailored and pleasurable travel experience. Within the tourist industry, businesses use these technological innovations to set themselves apart from other travel companies by implementing AR and VR technologies. The utilization of AR/VR holds the potential to augment the physical travel experience by recreating historical locales or events, thereby rendering museums, attractions, and historical sites more interactive and, in certain instances, more immersive. This technological integration contributes to a heightened level of engagement and realism, enriching the overall tourism experience and redefining the ways in which travelers interact with and perceive cultural and historical landmarks. Tourist operators, travel agencies, and DMOs use marketing technologies that influence travelers to visit unseen places. These tourist players also help in providing job openings to the locals and making business partners. Different types of homestays, hostels, and hotels are tied up with these tourist operators, which also shows a win-win situation.

1.3 Ecotourism From a Services Perspective

Service management approaches organizational transformation holistically and addresses several issues that arise in companies. Klungseth, N. J., & Danivska, V. (2021, August 2). An important determinant of a company's success or failure in the online marketplace and e-commerce platforms is the quality of its e-services. To make ecotourism a sustainable way of traveling that can be beneficial for organizations and consumers alike. It involves providing customers with an unforgettable experience that is not only enjoyable but also educational and meaningful. The chapter focuses on three service management domains that have been significantly impacted by sustainable tourism: consumer-provider communication, customer relationship management (CRM), and service recovery processes. Ecotourism can provide customers with the opportunity to assess the value and quality of services they receive from travel agents and tour operators, as well as their impact on local communities. In relation to tourist operators and tourist people Service management can be identified in various ways. Academics studying tourism and hospitality have looked at the relationship between the quality of the service experience and the customer-provider interaction as it relates to service management.

2. SUSTAINABILITY IN ECOTOURISM BUSINESS

A useful foundation for implementing "system changes" that move organizations towards sustainability is provided by business models (Bocken et al. 2015). According

Figure 2. Sustainable ecotourism business model
Source: Adapted from Geissdoerfer et al (2018)

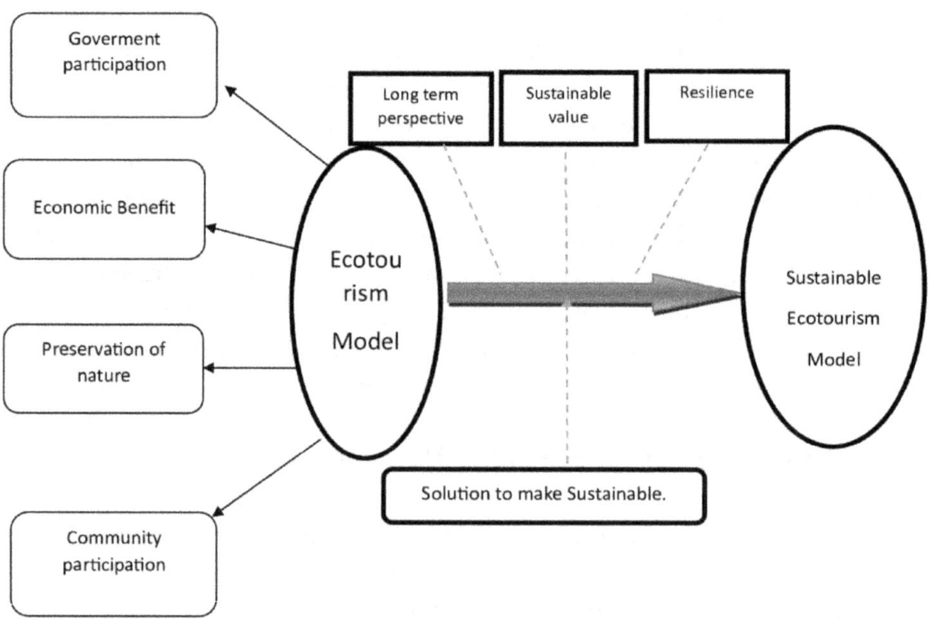

to Colabello, "every business leader aspires to achieve a sustainable business model and a company that will make money quickly and endure over the long term." "A business model that prioritizes sustainability is one that, at a minimum, considers all stakeholders, assesses and addresses environmental impacts, and is transparent and thorough in its reporting (Hendricks, 2023)." The tourism sector plays a significant role in achieving certain Sustainable Development Goals (SDGs). The business model aims to discover novel approaches that assist companies in managing their operations by boosting revenue and adding value (Bagheri et al. 2019). The company seeks to not only grow economically but also create positive change in communities and the environment. This approach will find a healthy balance between the needs of tourists and future generations of tourism. Tourism companies explore the sector to promote sustainable development while driving economic growth (Muthukumar, 2023). The concept of ecotourism is reshaping the tourism industry, with an emphasis on balancing people's profit and protecting nature. This model requires careful oversight from governments to ensure that its principles are followed. People have visited these natural places for the past many years but now it has become a trend. Many tourism operators practice greenwashing in the name of ecotourism, which has the potential to exacerbate conflicts in the community and permanently deteriorate natural areas. We can see that there is a need to safeguard the environment and make the most of existing natural attractions. It is possibly an opportunity for the tourism industry to explore or open up its dimension in the ecotourism sector. The tourism industry can be sustainable by applying eco-marketing practices.

Nature tourism has the potential to not only reach new audiences and garner support for conservation efforts but also educate people on the value of wild ecosystems. It encourages visitors to use wilderness areas without taking anything from them, which benefits populations that rely on these regions. Additionally, it provides a temporary escape from the hustle and bustle of urban life as well as smog-filled cities. Today's successful businesses are those that consider not only financial value but also social and environmental impacts, embrace digital innovation, and adapt to changing customer and societal expectations. Businesses that can navigate this complex landscape and continuously evolve their business models to meet new challenges and opportunities will be the most resilient and successful. According to the Deloitte report, 67% of participants were willing to pay up to 41% more for sustainable products, and this preference was stronger among the younger age group (Grundmann et al., 2022). Travelers are now looking to visit places where they can find themselves in peace, where they can find a pollution-free environment, and where eco-tourism is suited to the tourism industry, where they also take care not to increase mass tourism, environmental impact, and customer satisfaction. The success of the ecotourism industry in any region is largely determined by the number of tourists who visit it. For ecotourism to thrive, adequate facilities and infrastructure must be provided so that visitors can make optimal use of tourist destinations. With proper utilization, the local ecotourism industry will have a greater chance of succeeding and progressing over time. From a business perspective, it's a win-win situation; ecotourism could be the leading financial gain and a good initiative for environmental concern. To make the tourism industry sustainable, the organization came in front of society and the government in the form of CSR practices.

3. OPPORTUNITIES AND CHALLENGES OF ECOTOURISM BUSINESS

We all noticed that there is a continuous announcement by the tourism companies to make new climate commitments, with asset managers announcing their plans for ESG integration or regulators proposing additional disclosures or expanding producers' duties (Young & Gerard, 2023). These decisions demonstrate the company's agenda as well as the fact that they are now venturing into new areas of industry where retaining a competitive advantage necessitates organizations transforming their business models for sustainability.

3.1 Challenges

The biggest challenges have to be faced by consumers in the name of green hotels (sustainable practices by hotels); they are making a fool of consumers and also discourage others who are focused on operating sustainably. Companies are not practicing ethics in the context of sustainability, which shows the negative impact on the environment and also affects consumer decisions. Nowadays, we can see that there is a huge individual tourism footfall in regular tourist places, which also promotes mass tourism (Williams, 2010).

This situation is faced by every part of the country like Indonesia (Bali), Costa Rica, and India (Uttarakhand). The biggest detrimental consequence of mass tourist development has been noted as cultural dilution (Altinay, Var, Hines, & Hussain, 2007). Sezgin and Yola (2012) have identified three key factors that are driving the growth of mass tourism in today's world: technology, production, and management.

Technology has enabled easier access to travel destinations around the globe; production is increasing the availability of accommodations, services, and attractions, while management helps ensure efficient operations for a successful tourist experience. People need to understand why there is a need to protect natural places. They are aware of the degradation of the environment and global warming, but due to a lack of conscious decision-making, they intentionally or sometimes unintentionally impact

Figure 3. Challenges and opportunity of ecotourism business

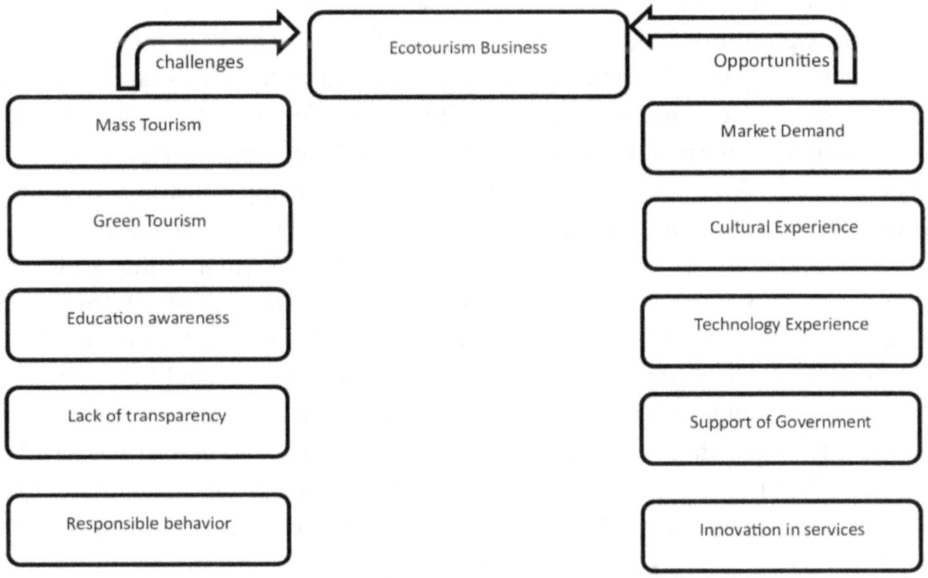

these places. According to a recent study on the habits of travellers, global emissions from tourism could be four times higher than originally estimated (Harrisson, 2020). This research illustrates just how much impact tourists have on our environment and emphasizes the need for more sustainable travel practices. Transparency is essential for establishing confidence with visitors, local communities, and other stakeholders. It also conceals unsustainable practices, with the result being the destruction of environmentally vulnerable places. Tourists who select ecotourism activities frequently have certain expectations involving environmental conservation and community participation, which are not always delivered. Tourists and travellers can demonstrate their responsibility when visiting natural or protected areas by following the "Leave No Trace" principles. This includes avoiding littering, staying on designated trails, and not disturbing wildlife. Responsible behavior is essential for the success of ecotourism initiatives, as it helps preserve natural and cultural heritage while also supporting local communities. By embracing these practices, tourists can ensure that their travel experiences have a positive and lasting impact on the environment.

3.2 Opportunities

Nowadays people are demanding to travel to natural places so that they can take the vibe of nature as well as for their own mental peace. The growth of tourism

GDP also shows how much people are demanding of these kinds of places. In tourism travelling to hilly areas, beaches, and green places is trending which has created an opportunity for tourism businesses who are focused on this only. Many SMEs come into the field, and they use this demand of tourist as an opportunity in their business. Companies are tied up with travel influencers to create a positive impact from a business point of view and also make people curious to visit that untouched part. SME also responds in their business by implementing sustainable practices into their operations. Customers can have individualized and customized ecotourism experiences because of digital innovation. Virtual reality (VR) and augmented reality (AR) technologies allow for virtual destination discovery and preview, assisting customers in making consistent, well-informed decisions. There are various marketing strategies and steps to increase the demand to visit natural places as compared to other historical or any other tour. Influencer plays a crucial role as we all know that social media has become an integral part of modern life, with 4.8 billion users worldwide representing 59.9% of the global population and 92.7% of all internet users (Nyst, 2023). Companies use this platform as a key tool in marketing strategy and showcase those places that people haven't visited. E-marketing strategy gives a boost to the ecotourism sector and motivates people to visit all-natural places and take pleasure. In May 2021, India hosted the first Global Tourism Investors Summit in New Delhi. The goal of this summit was to showcase the Indian travel and tourism industry as an attractive investment destination while providing a platform for central and state governments to discuss potential investments in the flourishing sector. By bringing together investors from around the world, India hoped to attract more international capital into its burgeoning tourism industry. The G20 summit presented a significant opportunity for investors, and India had the unique chance to showcase its tourism, culture, and heritage to the 19 most powerful nations plus the EU. By leveraging its G20 presidency, India can make meaningful progress in developing its tourism sector while promoting sustainable, responsible, and inclusive tourism within the country. Tourists visiting a new place don't just appreciate the atmosphere and environment, but they also learn about the culture. to meet the demands of visitors and make their journey operators make them stay in the natural and cultural region of origin easier. They consist of lodging (hotels, guesthouses, rural homes, vacation apartments, etc.) and catering businesses. Together with supplemental services (tourist information offices, tourist guides, trip planning, and air, land, and sea transportation), it also comprises these elements. Experiencing authentic cultural connections and positively impacting the regions they visit are key benefits of ecotourism that attract tourists. Supporting local communities is an essential part of this type of tourism, allowing travelers to enjoy a more meaningful travel experience. Not only can ecotourism provide enjoyment in a particular location, but it also provides a means of understanding the lives of local communities. Services are increasingly concentrating on providing environmentally friendly transportation choices such as electric vehicles, biofuel-powered transportation, and even cutting-edge solutions.

4. DISCUSSION

Ecotourism has grown in popularity in recent years as a result of its emphasis on responsible and sustainable travel. The principle of ecotourism is to emphasize environmentally conscious practices. The perspective of designing an ecotourism model is to make society aware of the natural places, and when travellers visit those places, they should try to make less use of non-biodegradable products. There are lots of tour operators who claim that they fulfil the needs of tourists by providing all the recyclable products, but in reality, they are doing nothing like this. Due to this, they came under greenwashing. There are also so many start-ups that came in the lame light that travel the tourists to natural places, but these companies indirectly promote mass tourism, and due to this, the localities of that region have to face the negative impact of this. Innovation in digitalization is an advantage for sustainable tourism businesses, where sustainability is showcased in different forms on the metaverse platform. Ecotourism, or sustainability in tourism, is a premium service delivered by a tourism company. These companies focus only on niche customers, i.e., responsible travelers or hard-core nature lovers who are environmentalists. The motive for designing this model is to inform the reader about the business that is profitable as a social business because it encourages every tourist to participate in ecotourism and encourages them to minimize their environmental impact and save our natural beauty, which is endangered. Numerous researchers have authored articles on ecotourism from an ESG (environmental, social, and governance) perspective. Nonetheless, this business model's focus is on addressing the issue of mass tourism and greenwashing as it relates to other travel agencies. within the provided figure. The issues associated with "mass tourism" are closely linked to market demand and opportunities. The statistics for the sustainable tourism market indicate a growth rate of 33.3% by 2022. The FMI report projects that by 2022, the size of the sustainable tourism sector will exceed US$1.0 trillion. It is crucial to keep in mind that culture is an integral part of every place. Investing some time in familiarizing yourself with the regional practices and traditions can make your trip more memorable. The process of promoting environmentally friendly goods and services is the most challenging aspect of "green marketing," as seen in Figure 2. It enables companies to show their dedication to social responsibility and sustainability. Using sustainable transit options, eschewing single-use plastic, and booking eco-friendly lodging are a few examples. Ecotourism is a win-win situation for travellers and the environment.

By encouraging environmentally friendly travel methods, ecotourism can have a direct impact on preserving threatened species' habitats. putting best practices to lessen disruptions to the environment, society, and culture into practice. Sustainable tourism also makes it easier to have enjoyable travel experiences that promote respect for local culture and the environment. Tourism may contribute significantly to preserving the balance of the environment, culture, and economy if it is handled responsibly. This establishes a moral and sensible basis that will help the tourism sector grow in the future.

5. CONCLUSION

This chapter delves into the burgeoning realm of ecotourism as a new business opportunity within the tourism industry. We focused on sustainability and the growing demand for ecotourism. Travellers are also looking for genuine and peaceful experiences from tour operators who oppose the damaging effects of mass tourism. SMEs also use these nature-centric ideas in their businesses to fulfil the requirements of a responsible traveler. Through this conceptual model, the chapter also addresses the impact of ecotourism, such as mass tourism and greenwashing. A digital tool is the mode that gives more hands to improve the business in terms of awareness and growth among tourists. The conclusion highlights the necessity for continuous evaluation and improvement of operational performance across economic, environmental, and social aspects. Ecotourism creates a revolution in the travel industry by promoting sustainable tourist practices that support both environmental preservation and economic growth.

REFERENCES

Altinay, L., Var, T., Hines, S., & Hussain, K. (2007). Barriers to sustainable tourism development in Jamaica. *Tourism Analysis*, *12*(1–2), 1–13. doi:10.3727/108354207780956690

BBC News. (2022, January 23). *What is greenwashing?* BBC News [Video]. YouTube. https://www.youtube.com/watch?v=0XGAMJsm6Tg

Bocken, N. M. P., Rana, P., & Short, S. W. (2015). Value mapping for sustainable business thinking. *Journal of Industrial and Production Engineering*, *32*(1), 67–81. doi:10.1080/21681015.2014.1000399

Boon, P. I., Burridge, T. R., & Fluker, M. (2002). A case for supply-led nature-based tourism within the marine and coastal temperate systems of south-eastern Australia. *Journal of Ecotourism*, *1*(2-3), 93–103. doi:10.1080/14724040208668117

Chen, W. (2023). Developing a Sustainable Business Model of Ecotourism in Ethnic-Minority Regions Guided by the Green Economy Concept. *Sustainability (Basel)*, *15*(2), 1400. doi:10.3390/su15021400

Colors, C. I. (2023, October 18). *In Bali, "sea-sun-sand" tourists threaten ancient rainforest*. Eco-Business. https://www.eco-business.com/news/in-bali-sea-sun-sand-tourists-threaten-ancient-rainforest

Cunha, L. (2003). *Introdução ao Turismo*. Editorial Verbo.

Drumm, A., Moore, A., & Conservancy, N. (2002, January 1). *Ecotourism Development: The business of ecotourism development and management*. Academic Press.

Ecotourism World. (2021b, April 19). *What is Ecotourism? The Evolution of Ecotourism in Recent Years*. https://ecotourism-world.com/what-is-ecotourism-the-evolution-of-ecotourism-in-recent-years/

Evans, J. R., & Lindsay, W. M. (2013). *Managing for quality and performance excellence*. Cengage Learning.

Fennell, D. A. (2003). *Ecotourism: An Introduction* (2nd ed.). Routledge.

Gartner. (2015). *Gartner says the Internet of things installed base will grow to 26 billion units by 2020*. Retrieved May 30, 2019, from https://www.mcit.gov.sa/en/media-center/news/91424

Global Tourism Investors Summit 2023 | Tourism Investors Meet Delhi, India. (n.d.). https://www.gtistourism.in/

Goni, F. A., Gholamzadeh Chofreh, A., Estaki Orakani, Z., Klemeš, J. J., Davoudi, M., & Mardani, A. (2021). Sustainable business model: A review and framework development. *Clean Technologies and Environmental Policy*, *23*(3), 889–897. doi:10.1007/s10098-020-01886-z

Grundmann, G., Klein, F., & Josten, F. (2022, December 21). Sustainability in business: Staying ahead of the curve. *Deloitte Insights*. https://www2.deloitte.com/xe/en/insights/topics/strategy/sustainability-in-business-staying-ahead-of-the-curve.html

Harrisson, T. (2020, August 27). *Tourism responsible for 8% of global greenhouse gas emissions, study finds*. Carbon Brief. https://www.carbonbrief.org/tourism-responsible-for-8-of-global-greenhouse-gas-emissions-study-finds /-

Hendricks, D. (2023, March 1). *How to Create a Sustainable Business Model*. business.com. https://www.business.com/articles/how-to-create-a-sustainable-business-model

Higham, J. (2007). Ecotourism: Competing and conflicting schools of thought. *Critical issues in ecotourism: Understanding a complex tourism phenomenon*, 1-19.

Internet and social media users in the world 2023. (n.d.). Statista. Retrieved November 29, 2023, from https://www.statista.com/statistics/617136/digital-population-worldwide /

Kim, J., & Fesenmaier, D. R. (2015). Measuring emotions in real time: Implications for tourism experience design. *Journal of Travel Research, 54*(4), 419–429. doi:10.1177/0047287514550100

Klungseth, N. J., & Danivska, V. (2021). Service management – focus on customer experience. In Routledge eBooks (pp. 205–219). doi:10.1201/9781003128786-18

Muthukumar, T. I. D. P. (2023). *Role of ecotourism in sustainable development: An overview*. www.pnrjournal.com

Nyst, A. (2023, July 17). 134 Social Media Statistics You Need To Know For 2023. *Search Engine Journal*. https://www.searchenginejournal.com/social-media-statistics/480507 /

Page, S. J., & Dowling, R. K. (2002). *Ecotourism*. Pearson Education.

Research, S. (n.d.). *Ecotourism Market Size, Share and Forecast to 2030*. StRAiTs Research. https://straitsresearch.com/report/ecotourism-market

Sezgin, E., & Yolal, M. (2012). Golden age of mass tourism: Its history and development. In M. Kasimoglu (Ed.), *Visions for global tourism industry-creating and sustaining competitive strategies*. IntechOpe. doi:10.5772/37283

Shakeel, J., Mardani, A., Chofreh, A. G., Goni, F. A., & Klemeš, J. J. (2020). Anatomy of sustainable business model innovation. *Journal of Cleaner Production, 261*, 121201. doi:10.1016/j.jclepro.2020.121201

Statista. (2023c, November 7). *Travel and tourism employment worldwide 2019-2033*. https://www.statista.com/statistics/1268465/number-of-travel-and-tourism-jobs-worldwide /

Sun, Y., Chen, L., Sun, H., & Taghizadeh-Hesary, F. (2020b.) *Low-carbon financial.* . doi:10.1016/j.frl.2020.10149

Sustainable Tourism market. (2022, June 17). https://www.futuremarketinsights.com/reports/sustainable-tourism-sector-overview-and-analysis

Times of India. (n.d.). Mass tourism hits Hallstatt in Austria; locals protest. *Times of India Travel*. https://timesofindia.indiatimes.com/travel/travel-news/mass-tourism-hits-hallstatt-in-austria-locals-protest/articleshow /103173755.cms

Tussyadiah, I. (2020). A review of research into automation in tourism: Launching the annals oftourism research curated collection on artificial intelligence and robotics in tourism. *Annals of Tourism Research, 81*, 102883. doi:10.1016/j.annals.2020.102883

Volo, S. (2017). Emotions in tourism: from exploration to design. In D. R. Fesenmaier & Z. Xiang (Eds.), *Design science in tourism* (pp. 31–40). Springer. doi:10.1007/978-3-319-42773-7_3

Weiler, B., & Ham, S. H. (2001). Tour guides and interpretation. In *The encyclopedia of ecotourism* (pp. 549–563). CABI publishing. doi:10.1079/9780851993683.0549

Werthner, H., & Klein, S. (1999). *Information technology and tourism: a challenging ralationship*. Springer-Verlag Wien. doi:10.1007/978-3-7091-6363-4

What Is Ecotourism. (2019, January 11). The International Ecotourism Society. https://ecotourism.org/what-is-ecotourism /

Wight, P. (1993). Ecotourism: Ethics or eco-sell? *Journal of Travel Research, 31*(3), 3–9. doi:10.1177/004728759303100301

Wight, P. A. (2001). Ecotourists: Not a homogeneous market segment. In D. B. Weaver (Ed.), *The Encyclopedia of Ecotourism* (pp. 37–62). CAB International. doi:10.1079/9780851993683.0037

Williams, A. M. (2010). Mass tourism, culture, and the historic city: Theoretical perspectives. *Rivista di Scienze del Turismo Ambiente Cultura Diritto Economia, 1*(2), 9–29.

Xiang, Z., & Fesenmaier, D. R. (2017a). Big data analytics, tourism design and smart tourism. In Z. Xiang & D. Fesenmaier (Eds.), *Analytics in smart tourism design. Tourism on the Verge* (pp. 299–307). Springer. doi:10.1007/978-3-319-44263-1_17

Young, D., & Gerard, M. (2023, August 9). *Four Steps to Sustainable Business Model Innovation*. BCG Global. https://www.bcg.com/publications/2021/four-strategies-for-sustainable-business-model-innovation

Zeithaml, V. A., Parasuraman, A., & Malhotra, A. (2002). Service quality delivery through web sites: Acritical review of extant knowledge. *Journal of the Academy of Marketing Science*, *30*(4), 362–375. doi:10.1177/009207002236911

Chapter 2
Understanding the Unpredictable:
Technological Revolutions' Transformative Impact on Tourism Management and Marketing

Ankit Garg
Ajay Kumar Garg Institute of Management, India

Nikhil Sharma
Ajay Kumar Garg Institute of Management, India

Himanshu Sharma
Ajay Kumar Garg Institute of Management, India

Sakhi Aneja
Ajay Kumar Garg Institute of Management, India

Anubhav Kumar Singh
Ajay Kumar Garg Institute of Management, India

ABSTRACT

The Metaverse is a ground-breaking technology development that has the potential to fundamentally alter how tourism is managed and promoted. Its capacity to provide immersive encounters across both the virtual and physical domains, successfully bridging the gap between the digital and material worlds, is what is driving this transition. Users now have a wide range of options thanks to this ground-breaking idea, which makes it simple for them to move between the physical and digital worlds. People can travel through time in this fully immersive digital environment, where they can virtually experience historical events, go on space expeditions, or even come across dangerous natural phenomena. Users can explore virtual settings for work, education, commerce, following their interests, and engaging with people in this world in addition to sating their wanderlust. Players interact naturally inside this virtual world, demonstrating the Metaverse's influence on the gaming industry and laying the groundwork for its greater potential.

DOI: 10.4018/979-8-3693-1103-5.ch002

INTRODUCTION

The Metaverse, which provides users with a seamless passage between the physical and digital domains, is essentially the union of the two worlds. The Metaverse promises to transform how we interact with different facets of life, whether it's for jobs, education, training, health, following personal interests, or engaging with others. When digital environments can give hyper-realistic virtual interactions, experiences, and transactions, they will reach their full potential and open up new horizons of possibility. We predict a totally interconnected society by 2030, where any physical object may communicate digitally, obliterating the distinction between the physical and digital worlds. The Metaverse, an interconnected environment, includes a variety of technologies like cloud computing, AI, blockchain, IoT, VR, AR, and digital twins. It is not just confined to virtual reality headsets.

The Metaverse, which is becoming more and more popular in the gaming sector, has the power to alter customer behavior and business procedures. It comprises of two distinct populations: metaverse colonists who prefer the actual world and metaverse natives who were reared in the world of interactive online gaming (Disztinger et al., 2017). While its commercial potential is frequently discussed in studies, little is known about how it will affect customer behavior and corporate procedures.

The potential for tourism in the metaverse, which provides access to a wealth of virtual resources, is acknowledged by the World Economic Forum. By offering immersive previews and enhanced content for destinations, it improves passengers' experiences. The creation of metaverse tours allows for complete immersion and avatar embodiment. The Metaverse provides access to virtual resources during physical visits, increasing the visitor experience. Extended Reality (XR) devices give consumers the chance to experience historical moments or natural occurrences, which promotes loyalty and return visits.

With the goal of defining the Metaverse's function in the tourism industry, this study intends to arm practitioners with the basic information they need to incorporate this technology into their operations. The Metaverse is a parallel virtual world where people work and interact utilizing immersive technologies like MR/VR headsets and smart glasses, according to Neal Stephenson, who coined the phrase in "Snow Crash" (1992). By enabling face-to-face interactions across many virtual environments, it simulates real life.

With MR/VR headsets, haptic gloves, and sensory clothing, the Metaverse magnifies sensory experiences and encourages imagination and creativity. Major corporations including J.P. Morgan, Gucci, and McDonald's have recognized the possibilities of the Metaverse. By 2030, SITA projects that Metaverse operations will be commonplace at airports, streamlining procedures and boosting passenger control. Travel planning has been altered by the metaverse, which provides tools for creativity and decision-making. User Generated Content (UGC) timeliness and the absence of haptic cues are problems, though.

Digital twins are supported by Metaverse, allowing customers to digitally visit locations and picture experiences before making a reservation. This enables more individualized travel planning and thorough destination knowledge (Cho et al., 2002)

The Metaverse offers voice commands for interactivity and increased travel personalization. Tourism providers can advertise their products in online shops and personalize the experiences for customers. The Metaverse enriches the traveler's experience by providing knowledge about locations and historic landmarks. It also allows for time travel and the preservation of records.

After a trip, the Metaverse aids users in recalling memories, sharing user-generated content (UGC), learning more, and making new friends. It promotes return trips and can take the place of travel, particularly when there are travel limitations (Dubé-Rioux, 1990). In summary, the Metaverse has the potential to transform tourism by offering individualized and immersive experiences. Tourism management and marketing can be done on a dynamic digital platform called the Metaverse. With the help of immersive involvement and co-creation with customers, it highlights travel locations, attractions, and services. In order to encourage real-world visitation, destinations can recreate digital doubles in the Metaverse. Along with describing travel behavior, it supports virtual event experiences and market intelligence. The Metaverse does, however, bring difficulties, such as technological, financial, moral, and legal issues. To address concerns including privacy, security, and intellectual property, care must be taken. In order to use the Metaverse for value co-creation rather than destruction, leadership is essential. The development of strategies must take advantages and costs into account. The Metaverse era brings improvements to suppliers and customers, yet there are still many unanswered questions. An effective Metaverse ecosystem requires networking infrastructure, enablers, and platform interoperability.

This paper describes the changes and openings the Metaverse has created in the tourist ecosystem and offers suggestions for practitioners and scholars in the field. It seeks to deepen comprehension and encourage more tourism-related investigation of the Metaverse.

We predict a totally interconnected society by 2030, where any physical object may communicate digitally, obliterating the distinction between the physical and digital worlds. The Metaverse, an interconnected environment, includes a variety of technologies like cloud computing, AI, blockchain, IoT, VR, AR, and digital twins. It is not just confined to virtual reality headsets (Falk, R.F. and Miller, N.B. (1992).

The Metaverse, while has grown more and more popular in the gaming sector, has the power to alter customer behavior and business procedures. It comprises of two distinct populations: metaverse colonists who prefer the actual world and metaverse natives who were educated in the world of interactive online gaming. While its commercial potential is frequently discussed in studies, little is known about how it will affect customer behavior and corporate procedures.

The potential for tourism in the metaverse, which provides access to a wealth of virtual resources, is acknowledged by the World Economic Forum. By offering immersive previews and enhanced content for destinations, it improves passengers' experiences. The creation of metaverse tours allows for complete immersion and avatar embodiment.

The Metaverse provides access to virtual resources during physical visits, increasing the visitor experience. Extended Reality (XR) devices give consumers the chance to experience historical moments or natural occurrences, which promotes loyalty and return visits. With the goal of defining the Metaverse's function in the tourism industry, this study intends to arm practitioners with the basic information they need to incorporate this technology into their operations (Fornell, C. and Larcker, D.F. (1981).

The Metaverse is a parallel virtual world where people work and interact utilizing immersive technologies like MR/VR headsets and smart glasses, according to Neal Stephenson, who coined the phrase in "Snow Crash" (1992). By enabling face-to-face interactions across many virtual environments, it simulates real life.

With MR/VR headsets, haptic gloves, and sensory clothing, the Metaverse magnifies sensory experiences and promotes imagination and creativity.

Large companies including J.P. Morgan, Gucci, and McDonald's have recognized the possibilities of the Metaverse. By 2030, SITA projects that Metaverse operations will be common at airports, streamlining procedures and boosting passenger control.

Travel planning has been altered by the metaverse, which provides tools for creativity and decision-making. User Generated Content (UGC) timeliness and absence of haptic cues are problems, though (Gautam, 2012).

Digital twins are supported by Metaverse, allowing customers to digitally visit locations and picture experiences before making a reservation. This enables more personalized travel planning and thorough destination knowledge.

The Metaverse offers voice commands for interactivity and increased travel customization. Tourism providers can advertise their products in online shops and personalize the experiences for customers. The Metaverse enriches the traveller's experience by offering knowledge about locations and historic landmarks. It also allows for time travel and the preservation of records. After a trip, the Metaverse aids users in recalling memories, sharing user-generated content (UGC), learning more, and making new friends. It promotes return trips and can take the place of travel, especially if there are travel limitations.

Research Gaps by Literature Review

A number of research gaps are brought to light by the chapter's literature assessment in relation to the Metaverse and how it affects the travel and tourism sector. These areas of research deficiency comprise:

1. Insufficient Knowledge of Customer Behaviour: The chapter notes that although the Metaverse's commercial potential is frequently discussed, little is understood about how it will impact customer behaviour and business policy. To gain a deeper understanding of the effects of the Metaverse on traveller behaviour, it is imperative to fill this important study gap.
2. Unresolved Issues and the Need for Further Research: The chapter highlights the fact that there are still a lot of unsolved problems and unanswered questions regarding how the Metaverse will affect the travel and tourism sector. This emphasises the need for more research to fill up these knowledge gaps and examine the ways in which the Metaverse may affect tourism marketing and management (Gefen & Straub, 1997).
3. Inadequate Knowledge of Metaverse Technology: Although the chapter gives a general overview of the Metaverse's technological components, more in-depth study is necessary to fully comprehend the range of technologies at play and how they specifically affect the travel and tourism sector.
4. Limited Knowledge of Economic Impact: Although the chapter discusses the possible financial effects of Metaverse operations at airports by 2030, it also notes that little is known about the Metaverse technologies' larger financial effects on the travel and tourist sector. This indicates a research void that needs to be filled (Gupta, S. and Kim, H.W. (2010).

Future research endeavours can enhance our grasp of the Metaverse's implications for tourist management and marketing by filling in these research gaps. This will help practitioners and policymakers make better informed decisions about how best to use this technology.

Research Objective

This study's main goal is to thoroughly examine how the Metaverse affects the travel and tourism sector and consider how it can revolutionize both consumer behaviour and business practices. The study specifically seeks to accomplish the following scientific goals:

Analyze the Integration of Technologies from the Metaverse

Examine the ways in which a range of technologies, including as blockchain, IoT, cloud computing, AI, VR, AR, and digital twins, are influencing the creation of the Metaverse.

Examine how these technologies contribute to the creation of a linked environment in ways that go beyond virtual reality headsets (Guttentag, 2010).

Recognize the Metaverse Tourism Adoption

Examine how the Metaverse is being embraced by the travel and tourism industry, paying particular attention to both Metaverse colonists and locals.

Analyze the Metaverse's commercial potential and the effects it may have on consumer behavior and business operations (Hair, J. F., Anderson, R. E., Tatham, R. L., & Black, W. C. (1995).

Analyze the Effect on Experiences With Tourism

Analyze the ways in which metaverse tours, improved content, and immersive previews can improve tourism experiences.

Examine the ways in which Extended Reality (XR) technology enhances visitor engagement, loyalty, and repeat business.

Examine How Travel Planning and Decision-Making Have Changed

Examine how the Metaverse has changed the way that people plan their travels by giving them more creative and decision-making tools.

Talk about issues including the timeliness of User Generated Content (UGC) and the lack of haptic indications when it comes to travel planning (Hair, J.F., Black, W.C., Babin, B.J. and Anderson, R.E. (2010).

Evaluate the Significance of Digital Twins in Tailored Travel Arranging

Examine how the Metaverse helps customers use digital twins to virtually visit places and see experiences before making bookings.

Analyze the effects on destination awareness and customized trip planning.

Analyze the Application of Personalization and Voice Commands

Examine how voice commands can improve the Metaverse's personalization and interactivity for the travel and tourism sector.

Examine the ways in which travel agencies use internet stores to market to and customize travel experiences for clients (Hanafizadeh, P., Behboudi, M., Koshksaray, a. a., & Tabar, M. J. S. (2014).

Examine the Engagement in the Metaverse Following a Trip:

Examine the ways in which the Metaverse helps people learn, connect, share UGC, and recollect memories after a journey.

Examine the Metaverse's ability to encourage recurrent visits and act as a substitute for actual travel, especially in the event of travel restrictions.

Handle Issues and Difficulties

Determine and evaluate the technological, economical, ethical, and legal difficulties that the tourism industry faces with the Metaverse (Di Milano Milano Italy, n.d.).

Provide solutions for issues like intellectual property, security, and privacy to ensure that the Metaverse is used responsibly.

Analyze the Metaverse Ecosystem's Development

Examine the advantages that the Metaverse era has given to vendors and buyers.

Examine the necessary networking architecture, enablers, and platform compatibility for a functioning Metaverse ecosystem.

Give Scholars and Practitioners Recommendations

Provide actionable advice on how tourist industry professionals can integrate Metaverse technologies into their daily operations.

Promote additional academic research on the Metaverse's effects on travel with the goal of improving understanding and addressing open-ended issues (Hillmann, 2019).

By achieving these goals, the study hopes to add insightful knowledge to the expanding body of research on metaverse-related topics, particularly as they relate to tourism.

Conceptual Framework of the Chapter

The metaverse's revolutionary effect on the travel and tourism sector forms the core of the chapter's conceptual foundation. It includes a number of important components, such as user behavior, technology components, business practices, and possible ramifications for marketing and administration of tourism. The structure of the framework is as follows:

1. A Brief Overview of the Metaverse
    - Definition: A parallel virtual environment that incorporates immersive technology such as smart glasses, haptic gloves, MR/VR headsets, and sensory clothing is called the Metaverse.
    - Historical background: originally used by Neal Stephenson in "Snow Crash" (1992) and has since evolved in the video game industry.
2. Technological Components: - Synopsis: Digital twins, cloud computing, blockchain, IoT, VR, and AR are all essential components of the Metaverse.
    - Not just virtual reality goggles: Highlight the various technologies that are a part of the linked environment.
3. User Behavior in the Metaverse: - Differentiating between individuals who were raised in interactive online gaming environments and those who prefer the real world as metaverse colonists or natives.
    - Commercial potential: investigating how corporate policies and consumer behavior may be affected by the Metaverse.
4. Tourism in the Metaverse: - The World Economic Forum has identified the following potential: virtual resource access, immersive previews, and improved destination material.
    - Metaverse tours: They offer total immersion and avatar embodiment, enhancing the traveler experience in general.
    - Extended Reality (XR) gadgets: Encouraging recurrent visits and loyalty by facilitating historical and natural experiences.
5. Repercussions for Marketing and Management of Tourism:
    - Digital twins: Facilitating detailed destination knowledge and individualized travel planning.
    - Voice commands for more customizable travel and interaction.
    - Promotion and customization: Possibilities for travel service providers to highlight goods and improve traveller experiences.
6. Difficulties and Fears: - Legal, ethical, financial, and technological issues: security, privacy, and intellectual property concerns.

Headship position: highlighting the importance of strong leadership in overcoming obstacles and guaranteeing value co-creation.

7. Impact on Travel Behavior: - Altered travel planning: Tools for creativity and decision-making.
   - The lack of haptic cues and the timeliness of user-generated content (UGC) are issues that require attention.
8. Investment Return (ROI) and Upcoming Changes:
   - Corporate recognition: Prominent businesses that have acknowledged the possibilities include McDonald's, Gucci, J.P. Morgan, and McDonald's.
   - SITA's estimate for airport Metaverse operations by 2030.
9. Creating a Metaverse Ecosystem: - Platform interoperability, enablers, and networking infrastructure are crucial elements.
   - Unresolved issues and the requirement for continued research in the travel and tourist industry.
10. Conclusion: - An overview of how personalized and immersive experiences offered by the Metaverse have the potential to revolutionize travel.
    - An appeal for researchers and practitioners to do further research on how the Metaverse affects the tourism industry.

This conceptual framework addresses both opportunities and difficulties by offering an organized method for investigating the different ways in which the Metaverse is influencing the travel and tourism sector (Hirunyawipada, n.d.).

Implications

A few of the Metaverse's ramifications for tourism are discussed in the chapter you supplied. Based on the information given, the following are some important implications:

1. Transformation of Tourism Experience: - By providing customized and immersive experiences, the Metaverse has the potential to revolutionize the travel and tourism sector.
   . Digital twins, virtual tours, and immersive technologies encourage innovation and improve sensory experiences while giving people an advance look at places before they visit.
2. Shift in Travel Planning and Decision-Making: - By offering resources for creativity and judgment, the Metaverse has changed the way that travel planning is done.

- Customers can virtually visit places and see activities before making reservations because to digital twins, which makes trip planning more individualized.

3. Improved Customer Engagement and Customization: - Voice commands within the Metaverse facilitate heightened engagement and tailored travel encounters.
   - Travelers can enhance their experience by learning about regions and landmarks by advertising and customizing their products in online stores within the Metaverse.
4. Impact on Customer Behavior: - There are two different groups within the Metaverse: those who are native to the metaverse and those who are colonists who prefer the real world. The chapter makes the argument that although the Metaverse's commercial potential is regularly mentioned, little is known about how it will affect consumer behavior and company policies.
5. Changes in Business Procedures: - Notable companies, like McDonald's, Gucci, and J.P. Morgan, have acknowledged the potential of the Metaverse and the possibility for changes in business practices across a range of industries.
6. Potential Disruptions and Challenges: - The Metaverse age offers benefits to suppliers and consumers alike, but it also poses obstacles, including legal, ethical, financial, and technological problems.
   - To ensure appropriate usage of the Metaverse, privacy, security, and intellectual property concerns must be carefully considered.
7. Integration with Emerging Technologies: - Cloud computing, artificial intelligence, blockchain, the Internet of Things, virtual reality, augmented reality, and digital twins are just a few of the technologies that are included in the Metaverse.
   - By integrating these technologies, it becomes easier to move between the digital and physical realms, making the lines between them even more hazy.
8. Potential for Economic Impact: - According to the chapter, metaverse operations at airports might become standard by 2030, simplifying processes and possibly improving passenger control. Technologies from the Metaverse may have a big economic impact on a lot of industries, including tourism (Scholars@Duke Publication: Reliability and Validity of a Brief Measure of Sensation Seeking, n.d.)
9. Requirement for Strategic Planning and Leadership:
   - It is believed that strong leadership is necessary to overcome obstacles and guarantee that the Metaverse is used to co-create value rather than destroy it.
   - When making strategic plans, keep in mind the benefits and drawbacks of Metaverse technologies.

10. Request for Additional Research: - The chapter ends by highlighting the need for additional research on the Metaverse in the context of tourism, noting that there are still a lot of unsolved issues and areas that might need more study.

SCOPE OF THE CHAPTER

This chapter's focus is on the Metaverse's effects on the travel and tourism sector, as well as the possible advantages and difficulties of implementing it. An overview of the Metaverse, its origins in history, and the several technological elements that comprise it are given in this chapter (Stejskal et al., 2021). It also talks about how the tourism sector may profit from the Metaverse, citing enhanced consumer interaction, personalisation, and immersive experiences as some of the advantages.

The chapter also discusses the difficulties in implementing the Metaverse, such as issues with security, privacy, and intellectual property. It highlights the necessity of leadership and strategic planning to guarantee that value is co-created rather than destroyed when using the Metaverse. The chapter also points out a number of research gaps regarding the effects of the Metaverse on the travel and tourism sector, such as the need for more research on consumer behaviour and the wider economic implications of Metaverse technology.

All things considered, the chapter offers a thorough analysis of the Metaverse's possible effects on the travel and tourism sector and identifies the advantages and disadvantages of its implementation (Web 3D Simulation-based Application in Tourism Education: A Case Study With Second Life | Scholars Portal Journals, n.d.). Policymakers, practitioners, and scholars interested in investigating the possibilities of the Metaverse for tourist management and marketing will find it to be a useful resource.

Managerial Implications

Policymakers can use the management implications presented in this chapter to better align the Metaverse with the needs of the tourism sector. Among them are:

1. Strategic Planning and Leadership: In order to make sure that the Metaverse is used to co-create value rather than destroy it, policymakers must assume a leadership position. This calls for meticulous strategic planning that weighs the advantages and disadvantages of metaverse technologies.
2. Integration with Emerging Technologies: When integrating emerging technologies into the Metaverse, policymakers should take into account the use of blockchain, cloud computing, artificial intelligence, the Internet of Things,

virtual and augmented reality, and digital twins. The distinctions between the digital and physical worlds will become increasingly blurred as a result of this easier transition between them.

3. Privacy, Security, and Intellectual Property Issues: When utilising the Metaverse, policymakers must give serious consideration to privacy, security, and intellectual property issues (Jepkorir et al., 2022). By doing this, the Metaverse will be used appropriately and any detrimental effects on the travel and tourism sector will be avoided.
4. Investment Return (ROI) and Future Developments: Decision-makers must acknowledge that the Metaverse could have a financial influence on the travel and tourism sector. They ought to promote investment in Metaverse technologies and get ready for impending market shifts.
5. Establishing a Metaverse Ecosystem: Platform interoperability, enablers, and networking infrastructure comprise the Metaverse ecosystem that policymakers should concentrate on building. This will guarantee that the tourism sector makes effective use of the Metaverse.

Policymakers can guarantee that the Metaverse is employed in the tourist sector in a way that offers travellers personalised and immersive experiences while simultaneously fostering economic growth and development by considering these management implications.

Limitations of the Chapter

The following list identifies the chapter's limitations:

1. Absence of In-depth Analysis: Although the chapter gives a general overview of the Metaverse and its possible effects on the travel and tourism sector, it does not analyse particular case studies in-depth or offer actual data to back up its assertions (Huang, Backman, Backman, & Chang, 2016). This limits the breadth of comprehension and real-world application for practitioners and policymakers, which adds to the chapter's ineffectual elements.

Recommendation for Improvement: To better illustrate the real-world effects of the Metaverse on tourism management and marketing, the chapter should include particular case studies or empirical research (Jackson, Chow, & Leitch, 1997). This would give readers more tangible proof and useful insights.

2. Limited Discussion of Ethical and Legal challenges: Although the chapter recognises the privacy, legal, and ethical challenges related to the Metaverse,

it does not go into great detail about possible fixes or best practices for dealing with these problems. This restricts the chapter's ability to advise practitioners and policymakers on how to use the Metaverse responsibly.

Recommendation for Improvement: The chapter needs to go into further detail about the moral and legal dilemmas that the Metaverse raises, as well as offer concrete solutions. Examining current frameworks or policies for the appropriate use of immersive technology in the travel and tourism sector may fall under this category.

4. Limited Practical Advice for Practitioners: Although the chapter covers the possible advantages and difficulties of the Metaverse for marketing and management of tourism, it does not provide practitioners with any useful advice on how to successfully incorporate Metaverse technology into their daily operations.

Recommendation for Improvement: For practitioners wishing to take use of the Metaverse in the tourism sector, the chapter should contain more useful advice in the form of best practices, case studies, or implementation methodologies (Jennett et al., 2008). This would improve the chapter's usefulness for professionals in the industry.

The chapter can enhance its efficacy in offering significant perspectives and recommendations to policymakers, practitioners, and researchers who are intrigued by the convergence of the Metaverse and the tourist sector by tackling these shortcomings and executing the proposed enhancements.

Strengths of the Chapter

The chapter's strong points are as follows:

Detailed Overview of the Metaverse: This chapter gives a thorough explanation of the Metaverse, covering its definition, context in history, and technological aspects. By providing readers with a strong framework for comprehending the idea of the Metaverse and its possible ramifications for the travel and tourism sector, this enhances the chapter's worth and quality.

Application for Enhancement: The thorough synopsis of the Metaverse can be used as a springboard for deeper exploration and real-world implementation, which will strengthen the chapter's weak points (Jiang, 2016). Building on this solid base, the chapter can solve the flaw of a lack of in-depth research by delving into particular case studies and empirical data to back up its assertions.

2. Identification of Research Gaps: The chapter does a good job of pointing out areas that require more research in order to fully understand how the Metaverse

is affecting the travel and tourism sector(Jun, Cho, & Park, 2018). By indicating to scholars and practitioners the areas that need focus and investigation, this adds to the chapter's usefulness.

Application for Improvement: By offering a road map for filling in these gaps, the discovered research gaps can be used to strengthen the chapter's weak points. The chapter might direct future research efforts in a more focused and significant way by providing particular recommendations for filling up the research gaps and carrying out more study.

3. Emphasis on Ethical and Legal Concerns: The chapter recognises the privacy, ethical, and legal issues surrounding the Metaverse, indicating an understanding of the possible obstacles in using Metaverse technology in the travel and tourism sector.

Application for Improvement: By offering detailed suggestions for resolving these matters, the chapter's weak points can be strengthened by drawing attention to the ethical and legal considerations (Jung et al., 2018). The chapter can help prepare practitioners and policymakers to appropriately integrate Metaverse technologies into the tourist industry by providing best practices and practical guidance for navigating moral and legal quandaries.

4. Potential Economic Impact: The chapter discusses how Metaverse technology may affect the travel and tourism sector economically. It also projects how many airports will have metaverse operations by 2030. This prospective viewpoint gives value by indicating the possibility of economic expansion and advancement.

Application for Improvement: By offering practitioners useful advice on utilising Metaverse technology for financial gain, the possible economic impact can be used to strengthen the chapter's weak points. The chapter can be made more useful to industry professionals by providing particular implementation plans and approaches for maximising the Metaverse's economic potential.

Policymakers, practitioners, and scholars interested in the effects of the Metaverse on the tourist industry can benefit from the chapter's significant insights and suggestions, which can be further enhanced by capitalising on its strengths and using them to remedy its weaknesses.

Suggestions

Here are some suggestions for researchers, practitioners, and policymakers who want to learn more about the Metaverse's potential for tourism marketing and management:

1. Conduct Additional Research: The chapter identifies a number of research gaps about the influence of the Metaverse on the travel and tourism sector. To fill in these knowledge gaps and develop a more thorough grasp of the implications of the Metaverse for tourist management and marketing, policymakers, practitioners, and scholars should carry out additional research.
2. Create Strategic Plans: Considering the advantages and disadvantages of Metaverse technology, policymakers and practitioners should create strategic plans. The main goal of these strategies should be to establish a Metaverse ecosystem with networking infrastructure, enablers, and platform interoperability.
3. Handle Privacy and Security Concerns: When utilising the Metaverse, policymakers and practitioners should give great consideration to privacy, security, and intellectual property issues. They ought to guarantee proper Metaverse usage and guard against any detrimental effects on the travel and tourism sector.
4. Promote Investment: In order to get ready for impending changes in the industry, policymakers should promote investment in Metaverse technologies. By doing this, the travel and tourism sector will be in a strong position to benefit from the Metaverse's possible economic effects.
5. Examine the Potential of Digital Twins: In the travel and tourism sector, policymakers and practitioners ought to investigate the possibilities presented by digital twins. Travellers can enjoy personalised, immersive encounters with digital twins that also foster economic development.

Policymakers, practitioners, and researchers may harness the Metaverse's potential to revolutionise the tourism sector and provide travellers cutting-edge, immersive experiences by considering these recommendations.

CONCLUSION

The Metaverse has the potential to transform tourism by offering individualized and immersive experiences. Tourism management and marketing can be done on a dynamic digital platform called the Metaverse. With the help of immersive involvement and co-creation with customers, it highlights travel locations, attractions, and services.

In order to promote real-world visitation, destinations can recreate digital doubles in the Metaverse. In addition to describing travel behavior, it supports virtual event experiences and market intelligence. The Metaverse does, however, bring difficulties, such as technological, financial, moral, and legal issues. To address concerns including privacy, security, and intellectual property, care must be taken. In order to use the Metaverse for value co-creation rather than codestruction, leadership is essential. The formation of strategies must take advantages and costs into account.

The Metaverse era brings improvements to suppliers and customers, yet there are still many unanswered questions. An effective Metaverse ecosystem requires networking infrastructure, enablers, and platform interoperability (Venkatesh, Morris, & Ackerman, 2000). This paper examines the changes and openings the Metaverse has created in the tourist ecosystem and offers ideas for practitioners and scholars in the field. It seeks to deepen understanding and encourage more tourism-related investigation of the Metaverse.

Future Directions

The following are potential future avenues for investigation into how the Metaverse affects the travel and tourism sector:

1. Empirical Research: Performing empirical research to determine the true influence of metaverse technologies on traveller behaviour, destination preferences, and travel experiences in general. This might entail gathering information from Metaverse platform users and examining their interactions and decision-making techniques.
2. Case Studies: Researching extensively cases of travel agencies and locations that have effectively incorporated Metaverse technologies into their operations. These case studies may offer insightful information on best practices, obstacles encountered, and the results of Metaverse adoption in the travel industry.
3. Ethical and Legal Frameworks: Creating frameworks that are especially suited to the application of metaverse technologies in the travel and tourism sector. Concerns around intellectual property rights, privacy, and the responsible application of immersive technologies in travel and tourism may all be part of this.
4. User Experience Design: Investigating how to improve travel options by designing and implementing user experiences inside the Metaverse. This could entail developing engaging and educational interactive experiences, historical reenactments, and immersive virtual tours.

5. Industry Collaboration: To establish norms and guidelines for the ethical and efficient integration of Metaverse technologies in the tourist sector, legislators, technology developers, and travel businesses should work together.
6. Economic Impact Assessment: Carrying out thorough evaluations of the possible economic effects of Metaverse technologies on the travel and tourism industry, encompassing changes in consumer purchasing habits, income production, and employment creation.
7. Education and Training: Creating educational materials and training courses to help tourist industry professionals comprehend and use Metaverse technologies in their operations. Upskilling in fields like consumer engagement tactics, digital marketing in the Metaverse, and virtual experience design may be necessary for this.
8. Long-Term Societal Implications: Examining how the tourism industry's widespread use of the Metaverse may affect community participation, cultural preservation, and sustainable tourism practices over the long run.

Through the pursuit of these future directions, scholars, professionals, and legislators can acquire a more profound comprehension of the advantages and difficulties posed by the Metaverse within the travel and tourism domain. This will ultimately result in better-informed choices and inventive implementations within the sector.

REFERENCES

Cho, Y. H., Wang, Y., & Fesenmaier, D. R. (2002, October 1). Searching for Experiences. *Journal of Travel & Tourism Marketing*, *12*(4), 1–17. Advance online publication. doi:10.1300/J073v12n04_01

Di Milano Milano Italy, M. C. P. (n.d.). *Emotion Tracking in Virtual Reality Fashion Shows | Extended Reality*. Guide Proceedings. https://dl.acm.org/doi/abs/10.1007/978-3-031-43401-3_31

Disztinger, P., Schlögl, S., & Groth, A. (2017, January 1). *Technology Acceptance of Virtual Reality for Travel Planning*. Springer eBooks. doi:10.1007/978-3-319-51168-9_19

Dubé-Rioux, L. (1990). *The Power of Affective Reports in Predicting Satisfaction Judgments*. https://www.semanticscholar.org/paper/The-Power-of-Affective-Reports-in-Predicting-Dub%C3%A9-Rioux/be71ecf2e6e96da73faeab2c78775a10fb484998

Falk, R.F., & Miller, N.B. (1992). *A Primer for Soft Modeling*. University of Akron Press. https://www.scirp.org/reference/ReferencesPapers?ReferenceID=1323343

Fornell, C., & Larcker, D.F. (1981). Evaluating Structural Equation Models with Unobservable Variables and Measurement Error. *Journal of Marketing Research, 18,* 39-50. https://www.scirp.org/reference/ReferencesPapers?ReferenceID=1927929

Gautam, V. (2012). *An empirical investigation of consumers' preferences about tourism services in indian context with special reference to state of Himachal Pradesh*. https://ideas.repec.org/a/eee/touman/v33y2012i6p1591-1592.html

Gefen, D., & Straub, D. W. (1997, December 1). Gender Differences in the Perception and Use of E-Mail: An Extension to the Technology Acceptance Model. *Management Information Systems Quarterly*, *21*(4), 389. Advance online publication. doi:10.2307/249720

Gupta, S., & Kim, H.W. (2010). Value-Driven Internet Shopping The Mental Accounting Theory Perspective. *Psychology and Marketing, 27*, 13-35. https://www.scirp.org/reference/referencespapers?referenceid=2503340

Guttentag, D. A. (2010). *Virtual reality: Applications and implications for tourism*. https://econpapers.repec.org/article/eeetouman/v_3a31_3ay_3a2010_3ai_3a5_3ap_3a637-651.htm

Hair, J. F., Anderson, R. E., Tatham, R. L., & Black, W. C. (1995). *Multivariate data analysis*. Prentice-Hall. https://www.scirp.org/reference/referencespapers?referenceid=435421

Hair, J.F., Black, W.C., Babin, B.J., & Anderson, R.E. (2010). *Multivariate Data Analysis*. Pearson. https://www.scirp.org/reference/ReferencesPapers?ReferenceID=1841396

Hanafizadeh, P., Behboudi, M., Koshksaray, A. A., & Tabar, M. J. S. (2014). Mobile-Banking Adoption by Iranian Bank Clients. *Telematics and Informatics, 31*, 62-78. https://www.scirp.org/reference/referencespapers?referenceid=2915106

Hillmann, C. (2019, January 1). *The VR Ecosystem and What to Expect in the Years to Come*. Apress eBooks. doi:10.1007/978-1-4842-4360-2_1

Hirunyawipada, T. (n.d.). *Consumer Innovativeness and Perceived Risk: Implications for High Technology Product Adoption*. eCommons. https://ecommons.udayton.edu/mgt_fac_pub/66/

Huang, Y. C., Backman, K. F., Backman, S. J., & Chang, L. L. (2016). Exploring the implications of virtual reality technology in tourism marketing: An integrated research framework. *International Journal of Tourism Research, 18*(2), 116–128. doi:10.1002/jtr.2038

Jackson, C. M., Chow, S., & Leitch, R. A. (1997). Toward an understanding of the behavioral intention to use an information system. *Decision Sciences, 28*(2), 357–389. doi:10.1111/j.1540-5915.1997.tb01315.x

Jennett, C., Cox, A. L., Cairns, P., Dhoparee, S., Epps, A., Tijs, T., & Walton, A. (2008). Measuring and defining the experience of immersion in games. *International Journal of Human-Computer Studies, 66*(9), 641–661. doi:10.1016/j.ijhcs.2008.04.004

Jepkorir, C., Mose, T., & Mwalili, T. (2022, October 14). Factors affecting adoption of internet of things in selected greenhouse farms in Kenya. *International Journal of Technology and Systems*. doi:10.47604/ijts.1668

Jiang, S. (2016). Purchase intention for electric vehicles in China from a customer-value perspective. *Social Behavior and Personality, 44*(4), 641–656. doi:10.2224/sbp.2016.44.4.641

Jun, J., Cho, I., & Park, H. (2018). Factors influencing continued use of mobile easy payment service: An empirical investigation. *Total Quality Management & Business Excellence, 29*(9–10), 1043–1057. doi:10.1080/14783363.2018.1486550

Jung, T. H., Lee, H., Chung, N., & Tom Dieck, M. C. (2018). Cross-cultural differences in adopting mobile augmented reality at cultural heritage tourism sites. *International Journal of Contemporary Hospitality Management, 30*(3), 1621–1645. doi:10.1108/IJCHM-02-2017-0084

Scholars@Duke publication: Reliability and validity of a brief measure of sensation seeking. (n.d.). https://scholars.duke.edu/publication/777353

Stejskal, J., Hájek, P., & Prokop, V. (2021, July 5). The role of library user preferences in the willingness to read and pay for e-books: Case of the Czech Republic. *The Electronic Library, 39*(4), 639–660. Advance online publication. doi:10.1108/EL-01-2021-0001

Umrani, F., & Ghadially, R. (2008). Gender and decision-making in technology adoption among youth. *Psychology and Developing Societies, 20*(2), 209–227. doi:10.1177/097133360802000204

Venkatesh, V., Morris, M. G., & Ackerman, P. L. (2000). A longitudinal field investigation of gender differences in individual technology adoption decision-making processes. *Organizational Behavior and Human Decision Processes*, *83*(1), 33–60. doi:10.1006/obhd.2000.2896 PMID:10973782

Web 3D simulation-based application in tourism education: A case study with Second Life | Scholars Portal Journals. (n.d.). https://journals.scholarsportal.info/details/14738376/v11i0002/113_w3saitacswsl.xml&sub=all

Chapter 3
Exploring the Role of Metaverse in Promoting Religious Tourism

Munir Ahmad
https://orcid.org/0000-0003-4836-6151
Survey of Pakistan, Pakistan

Muhammad Akram
https://orcid.org/0000-0002-5739-4456
Preston University Kohat, Islamabad, Pakistan

Saadia Ureeb
https://orcid.org/0009-0001-4195-8720
Zarai Taraqiati Bank Ltd., Pakistan

ABSTRACT

The Metaverse represents a revolutionary force in transforming religious tourism, demonstrating its versatile applicability in reinforcing visit intentions, advancing research, expanding resources sustainably, and transforming hospitality experiences. It serves as a catalyst for immersive education, virtual pilgrimages, community building, and facilitating religious events, transcending boundaries. However, challenges such as maintaining sacredness, preventing commercialization, ensuring authenticity, addressing ethical concerns, overcoming inclusivity issues, managing security, and navigating global regulatory compliance require careful consideration to fully harness the Metaverse's potential in religious tourism.

INTRODUCTION

Religious tourism derives its primary momentum from spiritual motivations, representing one of the oldest manifestations of travel (Rinschede, 1992). Termed as

DOI: 10.4018/979-8-3693-1103-5.ch003

"Faith Tourism," this phenomenon encompasses journeys undertaken by individuals to express their religious convictions and immerse themselves in centers of faith, distinct from their routine lives, work commitments, and everyday requirements (Demircioğlu, 2020). Religious tourism has the potential to facilitate both individual and societal transformation by placing a strong emphasis on spirituality (Tomljenović & Dukić, 2018). Those engaged in religious tourism seek to fortify their faith, seek spiritual experiences, connect with their religious heritage, and participate in sacred ceremonies and traditions (Tsironis, 2022). Kim et al., (2020) noted that perceptions of religious tourism have broadened to go beyond mere pilgrimage, now incorporating the significance of a destination.

Promoting religious tourism faces many challenges that require innovative solutions to unleash its full potential. One prominent issue lies in the traditional marketing methods employed, which often fall short of capturing religious destinations' unique and profound experiences. The challenge extends to effectively communicating the spiritual and cultural richness inherent in these places, as conventional promotional strategies may inadvertently oversimplify or misrepresent the essence of the religious journey (Štefko et al., 2015). Additionally, the evolving landscape of technology and communication demands new approaches (Haq, 2013) such as video marketing (Lemmi, 2020), with a crucial need to harness the power of digital platforms and social media to reach a wider audience (M. Ahmad, 2023). Striking a balance between modern promotional tools and respecting the sacred nature of these destinations is paramount. Moreover, addressing concerns related to inclusivity, accessibility, and sustainable practices becomes integral for fostering a positive image of religious tourism (Cugini, 2021; Sica et al., 2021; Trono & Castronuovo, 2023; UNWTO, 2016). By navigating and resolving these challenges, we can pave the way for a more nuanced, authentic, and globally embraced promotion of religious tourism.

The integration of the metaverse into the realm of tourism heralds a groundbreaking era marked by immersive and transformative experiences. This digital frontier offers a paradigm shift in how individuals can explore and engage with destinations, transcending the limitations of physical travel. In the metaverse, travelers can navigate virtual replicas of iconic landmarks, participate in culturally enriching simulations, and even forge connections with fellow explorers from around the globe (Gaafar, 2021; Jo, 2023; Liu et al., 2023). The potential extends beyond mere entertainment, with the metaverse becoming a powerful tool for pre-travel research and planning, enabling tourists to preview destinations in unprecedented detail (Bale et al., 2022; Hutson & Hutson, 2023).

Furthermore, this digital evolution brings a heightened sense of accessibility, making tourism experiences more inclusive for individuals with physical limitations or financial constraints. However, as we embrace the metaverse's potential, ethical considerations, such as data security and the preservation of authentic cultural experiences, must be carefully navigated to ensure a harmonious integration that enhances rather than diminishes the essence of travel (Y. Huang et al., 2023; Kaddoura & Al Husseiny, 2023). In the convergence of the metaverse and tourism, a new frontier of exploration emerges, promising to redefine the very nature of our journeys.

The concept of the metaverse presents numerous dimensions for exploration within the tourism industry. While its potential has been widely discussed across various sectors, one area that remains relatively underexplored is its integration into religious tourism. Therefore, this chapter is dedicated to examining the metaverse's potential as a strategic tool for overcoming the challenges hindering the advancement of religious tourism. It embarks on a comprehensive exploration of how the metaverse can bring about transformative changes in religious tourism and contribute to promoting sustainable tourism development. The chapter is structured into various key sections to effectively pursue this objective.

METAVERSE IN TOURISM

The Metaverse, aiming to construct a fully immersive, hyper spatiotemporal, and self-sustaining virtual shared space for humans to play, work, and socialize (Wang et al., 2023), holds the potential to bring about significant transformations across various domains of human activity. As Momtaz (2022) pointed out, it may give rise to novel products, services, job profiles, and business models, expanding the horizons of human engagement. It is even having the potential to be integrated with information management systems (M. Ahmad & Ali, 2023).

In diverse industrial applications, the Metaverse could foster convergence, spanning digital twins, telehealth care, connected vehicles, virtual education, social networks, and financial applications (Bhattacharya et al., 2023). The Metaverse, often referred to as a 3D version of the internet, is revolutionizing industries like tourism, providing virtual platforms, and content services, and shaping consumer and business behavior for brand presentation and communication (Hollensen et al., 2022). The metaverse is recognized as a transformative influence on digital commons and tourism content creation (Yang & Wang, 2023).

The integration of the Metaverse into the tourism industry is a burgeoning area of research, exploring potential impacts, disruptions, and transformative effects on travel experiences. Koo et al. (2023) proposed research propositions for metaverse tourism, identifying core technologies that lead to transformative effects. Meanwhile, Go & Kang, (2023) focused on defining metaverse tourism and exploring its potential for sustainable tourism development, offering a viewpoint and research agenda within the context of sustainability. Examining current trends and future research directions in the hospitality and tourism industries, Gursoy et al. (2022) provided valuable insights into the role of the Metaverse in shaping customer experiences and transferring real-life experiences to virtual environments.

The integration of NFTs in tourism, as highlighted by Folgieri et al. (2023), presented an avenue to promote tourist destinations, exhibitions, art, and products in a tokenized, digital form. Additionally, the case study titled "Travel Incheon as a Metaverse," Um et al. (2022) focused on the development of smart tourism cities in Korea, intertwining the concepts of the Metaverse and smart tourist cities. This study shed light on the synergy between tourism and the Metaverse within the current context of smart tourism city development. Moreover, Buhalis et al. (2023) delved into the disruptive potential of the Metaverse in tourism management and marketing, outlining the essential building blocks of metaverse tourism. Volchek & Brysch, (2023) contributed to the discourse by covering consumer behavior, virtual commerce, and investor interest in Metaverse hardware, providing a comprehensive view of the evolving landscape of the Metaverse in tourism.

Expanding beyond its core functionalities, an Extended Metaverse framework, as proposed by Guan et al. (2022), can seamlessly integrate interoperable agents between virtual and physical environments, particularly enhancing connected experiences in tourism. Virtual worlds, as Cruz-Lara et al. (2011) suggested, could become a vital tool for touristic areas to enhance services, incorporating multilingual tools for a more captivating tourist experience. However, this progression towards a metaverse-centric world is not without its nuances. While the metaverse strengthens visual experiences, it weakens tactile, taste, and auditory sensations, leading to a homogeneous experience within the simulated world (Jiang, 2022).

In the hospitality and tourism industries, VR technology holds the potential to enhance customer value by addressing issues and creating pleasant sensations, as evidenced by a study in the Sri Lankan context (Muwandeniya & Eranda, 2022). However, challenges persist, as guests in Egyptian hotels lack sufficient information about metaverse technology, potentially hindering its marketing in the country (Abass & Zohry, 2022). Despite these challenges, the Metaverse has demonstrated its immersive and experiential potential in marine tourism, as exemplified by the development of a virtual metaverse surfing village at Song-Jeong Beach in South Korea (Yoon et al., 2022).

Envisioning an immersive virtual space for diverse human activities, the Metaverse holds transformative potential across various domains. This technological paradigm extends its influence to the tourism sector, fostering convergence in digital applications and reshaping the industry landscape. Despite challenges, such as a lack of awareness in certain contexts, the Metaverse exemplifies its immersive potential through virtual experiences to shape consumer behavior and redefine business paradigms underscoring its crucial role in the evolution of virtual experiences and human engagement.

CHALLENGES OF RELIGIOUS TOURISM

Religious tourism entails journeying for religious reasons to explore sacred centers, locations, or events. Terms such as pilgrim tourism, pilgrimage, and faith-based tourism are interchangeably employed to refer to religious tourism (Mercadal, 2017). Religious tourism manifests in diverse ways, motivated by spiritual incentives and encompassing brief visits to sacred pilgrimage hubs, devout conventions, as well as extended journeys to both domestic and international pilgrimage destinations (Rinschede, 1992). Its significance spans across urban and rural areas, with Mafudi et al., (2021) identifying four potential opportunities for educational visits related to religious experiences in rural settings, including simulated pilgrimage routes, designated facilities for Muslim rituals, prayer spaces, and venues for archery activities. This form of tourism involves individuals or groups traveling for purposes such as pilgrimage, missionary work, or leisure, categorized into two primary types: active participation in pilgrimages and seeking insights into religious practices and visiting locations associated with faith (Ramos & Mafé-García, 2018).

Pilgrimage, a distinctive category within religious tourism, involves journeys to sacred sites or shrines of profound religious importance, exemplified by Islam's Hajj directed towards Mecca (Luz, 2020). This practice extends beyond Islam, including Judaism, Christianity, Buddhism, Hinduism, and Sikhism (Almuhrzi, 2020). Pilgrimage tourism entails individuals or groups journeying to specific religious or sacred locales, driven by religious reverence, the pursuit of spiritual encounters, or the fulfillment of religious duties. These sacred sites encompass religious temples, shrines, sacred cities, or locations associated with revered religious figures. Pilgrims often engage in rituals, prayers, and religious observances during their visits, embodying profound historical and cultural significance as an age-old mode of exploration (Di Giovine Michael A.and Elsner, 2016).

Despite its rich cultural and spiritual dimensions, religious tourism confronts intricate challenges. The challenges of managing large-scale religious tourism events, such as the hajj in Saudi Arabia, involve demand and provision issues (Henderson, 2011). Similarly, in Uganda, challenges of religious tourism include policy, planning, and institutional perspectives (Ayorekire et al., 2020). Stampedes, terrorist attacks, and health hazards present risks that require careful mitigation during religious events while respecting the specificity and importance of religious rituals (Butler, 2020). Construction of infrastructure, managing mass influx, and preparing for large-scale events are challenges faced globally in religious tourism as noted by Idris (2019). Balancing spirituality with cultural concerns and aligning economic benefits with community involvement poses additional challenges (Fernández-Álvarez et al., 2022).

Religious tourism in Pakistan faces challenges such as below-par performance of agencies, non-development of tourist spots, inadequate infrastructure, sub-standard transportation, and poor health services (N. M. Ahmad et al., 2022). Similarly, Irfan & Ali (2020) noted political tensions, visa unavailability, and limited accessibility for citizens of neighboring countries as additional challenges in Pakistan. Challenges to religious tourism development in Ethiopia include thefts, robbery, insufficient land, lack of infrastructure, parking problems, loss of spirituality, unskilled experts, and unity and coordination problems (Daricha, 2019). Conflict environments like Jerusalem grapple with legal status and political instability (Pipia & Pipia, 2020). Social media usage for marketing religious tourism in India presents both opportunities and challenges as underscored by (Singh & Dhankhar, 2020).

Ezenagu et al. (2021) noted that Nigeria's major challenge is overcrowding, which can be mitigated by proper management measures. Spiritual tourism promotion and development in Iran requires innovative methods, such as incorporating religious rituals, theatrical performances, and national religious semi-theatres into tourism programs as underpinned by Zareei & Namjoo (2018). In Mexico, managing large visitor populations is crucial for security in religious tourism (Cárdenas & Puente, 2017). Shinde (2020) argued that factors like town size, pilgrimage economy, and land use influence environmental challenges in religious tourism destinations. The greatest challenge in managing living religious heritage is reconciling heritage protection, tourism development, and maintenance of religious function as noted by Poulios (2019). Figure 1 shows the challenges of religious tourism. Most of the challenges mentioned under the country-specific exist in many parts of the world such as management of large crowds, inadequate infrastructure, tourist site development, and lack of coordination.

APPLICABILITY OF THE METAVERSE IN RELIGIOUS TOURISM

The Metaverse, a sprawling digital cosmos where virtual and augmented realities converge, has emerged as a transformative force across various domains. This section explores the applicability of metaverse in religious tourism. The summary is depicted in Figure 2.

Figure 1. Challenges of religious tourism

Reinforce Visit Intention

Metaverse tours represent a powerful catalyst in reinforcing the genuine intent to visit tourism destinations. By immersing potential visitors in virtual experiences that prioritize holistic presence, social engagement, and a profound sense of self-presence, these tours go beyond conventional promotional methods. The immersive nature of metaverse experiences taps into the psychological aspects of travel desires, creating a more visceral and enticing connection with destinations (Tsai, 2022). For individuals engaged in virtual reality (VR), the impact of spiritual experiences played a more pronounced role in shaping the inclination to persist in using virtual platforms for accessing content pertaining to religious cultural heritage sites and visiting real religious heritage sites compared to participants utilizing the web as noted by Hwang et al. (2023).

Tool for Tourism Research

The Metaverse emerges as a groundbreaking tool in the realm of tourism research, offering unparalleled opportunities for virtual collaboration and interdisciplinary projects. Monaco and Sacchi (2023) underscore the transformative potential of the Metaverse, not just as a platform for simulating travel experiences but as a robust environment for conducting research (Monaco & Sacchi, 2023).

Expand Tourism Resources

The Metaverse introduces a new frontier in expanding tourism resources, presenting a transformative avenue for destinations to support sustainability and bolster profitability. In alignment with the UNWTO Sustainable Development Goals, the innovative products and experiences crafted within the Metaverse have the potential to revolutionize the tourism industry (Go & Kang, 2023).

Transform Hospitality Experience

Metaverse has the capability to transform hospitality customer experience and value co-creation, enabling engagement with organizations and customers before, during, and after their visit (Buhalis et al., 2023). This transformation could lead to a new sector in hospitality, offering flexible travel options, customized consumer services, and improved entertainment (Ampountolas et al., 2023). The metaverse in the hospitality and tourism industry can be applied by creating experiences, understanding consumer behavior, and implementing marketing and operations strategies (Gursoy et al., 2022). The extended metaverse can foster user satisfaction and smart tourism experiences in destinations, supporting sustainability (Suanpang et al., 2022).

Site Maintenance and Conservation

A cultural heritage metaverse can offer more effective solutions for tourism guidance, site maintenance, and heritage object conservation (Zhang et al., 2022). Virtual reality can be used to create accurate and detailed replicas of historical religious sites, helping to preserve cultural and religious heritage. This ensures that future generations can experience and appreciate these sites even if they undergo physical changes over time.

Marketing and Brand Storytelling

The metaverse, a threedimensional virtual world inhabited by avatars of real people, has the potential to revolutionize advertising, with its potential to revolutionize the way we interact with brands and products (J. Kim, 2021). In the rapidly evolving landscape of tourism, the integration of immersive technologies, particularly within the metaverse, marks a profound shift in the way businesses articulate and convey their brand narratives. This transformation is a response to the distinctive preferences of Generation Z, a cohort known for its digital fluency and inclination towards novel, engaging experiences (Rancati & D'Agata, 2022).

Virtual Tourism Spatial Situations

Virtual tourism spatial situations significantly impact participants' comfort, including environmental temperature and audio-visual conditions (X. T. Huang et al., 2023). In the realm of virtual tourism, the spatial design and ambiance of digital landscapes directly influence participants' perceptions and engagement. The temperature of the virtual environment, whether it simulates a tropical paradise or a snowy retreat, can impact the users' sense of presence and immersion. Likewise, the quality of audio-visual elements contributes to the overall authenticity and realism of the virtual experience.

Metaverse-Based Education

Metaverse-based education can benefit real-time communication and dynamic interactions with digital artifacts (Mustafa, 2022). Religious teachings and moral values can be imparted through interactive educational experiences within the Metaverse. Users can engage in scenarios that present ethical dilemmas and explore how religious principles guide decision-making.

Virtual Pilgrimages

Pilgrimages are an essential aspect of many religious traditions. The metaverse aims to build a fully immersive, hyper-spatiotemporal, and self-sustaining virtual shared space for human activities such as play, work, and socializing (Cheng et al., 2022; Wang et al., 2023). The Metaverse could provide a virtual pilgrimage experience, allowing individuals to visit sacred sites, participate in rituals, and engage in spiritual practices from the comfort of their homes. This could be particularly valuable for individuals who are physically unable to make a traditional pilgrimage.

Community Building

Metaverse aims to create a shared virtual space where users can communicate and collaborate as if they were in the physical world (Cheng et al., 2022; Wang et al., 2023). Virtual spaces within the Metaverse can facilitate the formation of online religious communities. People from different parts of the world can come together to share their faith, discuss spiritual topics, and engage in virtual religious events. This can create a sense of global unity among believers. Virtual environments have the potential to integrate multilingual tools, facilitating engagement with diverse language groups (Cruz-Lara et al., 2011).

Religious Events and Ceremonies

Religious organizations can host virtual events and ceremonies within the Metaverse which is a shared virtual space (Cheng et al., 2022; Wang et al., 2023). This can include virtual worship services, religious festivals, and other communal activities. Participants can attend these events in real-time or access recordings, fostering a sense of inclusivity and accessibility.

Interfaith Dialogue

The Metaverse being a shared virtual space (Cheng et al., 2022; Wang et al., 2023) can also serve as a platform for fostering interfaith dialogue and understanding. Pilgrims from diverse backgrounds can come together in virtual spaces, sharing their beliefs and experiences. This not only promotes tolerance and unity but also facilitates a global exchange of cultural and spiritual insights. Virtual worlds can help to incorporate multilingual tools to engage multiple language groups (Cruz-Lara et al., 2011).

Management of Large Crowds

The Metaverse can provide a strategic solution for managing large crowds in religious tourism through its virtual landscape. It can support the implementation of crowd management strategies within the virtual realm first, followed by the physical realm. Virtual simulations and advanced crowd control mechanisms can be employed to regulate the congregation, ensuring a seamless and orderly religious tourism experience.

Planning for Infrastructure Development

In the context of infrastructure development for religious tourism, the Metaverse can serve as a versatile platform. Virtual replicas of sacred sites can be meticulously crafted, allowing for the exploration of provision of infrastructural facilities such as roads, and accommodation. Planners and developers can collaborate within the Metaverse to simulate and refine infrastructure plans, considering factors such as accessibility, crowd flow, and the overall visitor experience. This collaborative virtual environment can provide a testing ground for innovative infrastructure solutions, ensuring that physical spaces are designed to accommodate the needs of a diverse and global audience engaging in religious tourism.

Planning for Tourist Site Development

The integration of the Metaverse, along with the concept of digital twins, can play a pivotal role in the meticulous planning of tourist site development, particularly in the context of religious destinations. This innovative approach can offer a dynamic and interactive space for stakeholders, including architects, urban planners, and religious authorities, to collaboratively immerse themselves in virtual simulations of proposed developments, creating a digital twin of the physical site. This can facilitate a thorough evaluation of the site layout, architectural aesthetics, and visitor experience, allowing for informed decision-making in the planning phase.

CHALLENGES OF INTEGRATING THE METAVERSE INTO RELIGIOUS TOURISM

This section explores the challenges associated with metaverse use for religious tourism. The summary is depicted in Figure 3.

Maintaining Reverence and Sacredness in the Metaverse

The Metaverse enables the creation of a virtual universe, transcending natural and social constraints, fostering free ideological innovation, and potentially reshaping cosmology, body and mind, creation, cognition, and ethics (X. Huang, 2021). It is imperative to instill a sense of awe and respect akin to physical religious sites, guarding against inadvertent diminishment of sacredness. Designing virtual experiences that faithfully represent diverse religious practices is challenging, as misrepresentation can lead to offense and compromise authenticity.

Preventing Commercialization of Sacred Experiences

The Metaverse economy, driven by digital currency, digital legal currency, and new production and business models around digital assets, establishes diverse economies and expands the global economy (Yuan & Yang, 2022). As religious tourism goes digital, preventing the commercialization of sacred experiences is vital. Safeguards are necessary to protect against exploitation and uphold the integrity of religious practices.

Figure 2. Applicability of Metaverse for religious tourism

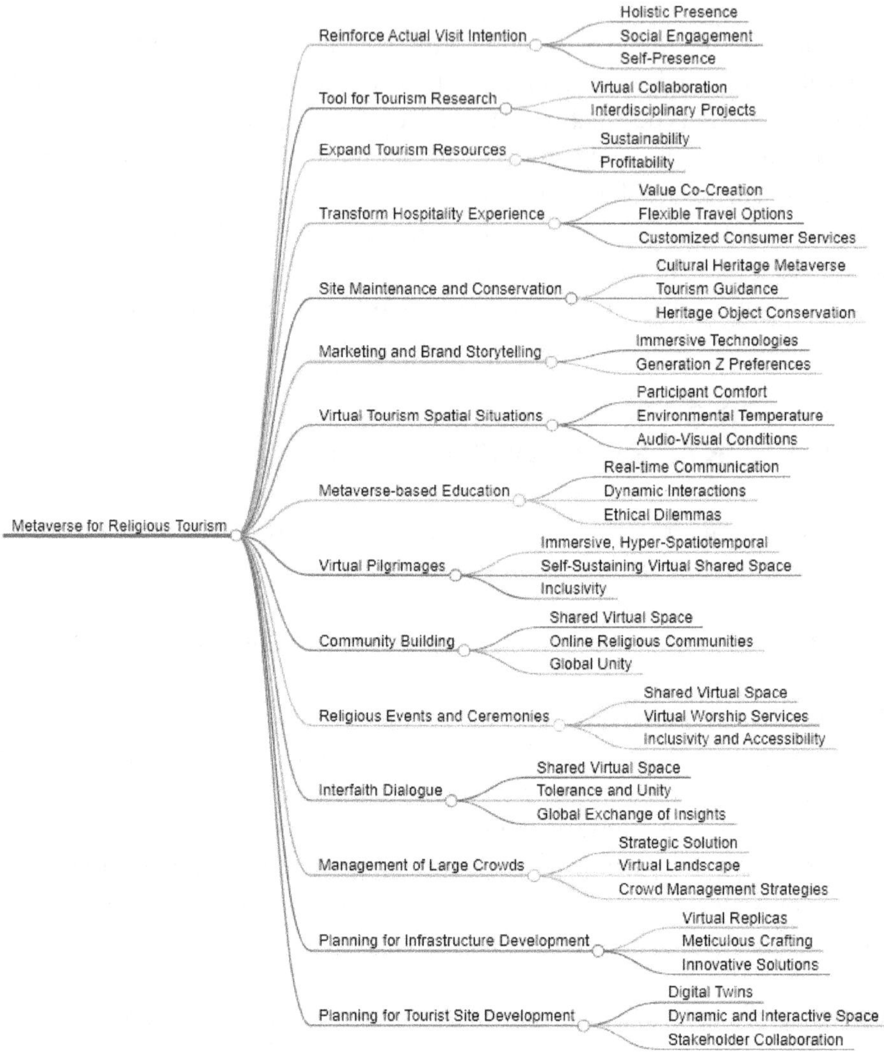

Authenticity Concerns in Virtual Representations

The Metaverse faces challenges such as social acceptance, affordability, environmental sustainability, and the accurate simulation of real experiences (Monaco & Sacchi, 2023). Ensuring virtual representations capture the essence of religious sites and practices requires balancing technological advancement with preserving historical, cultural, and spiritual significance.

Ethical Considerations in Virtual Environments

Virtual environments involving religious figures, objects, or rituals raise ethical questions. Developers must avoid controversies and conflicts, and businesses using the Metaverse should establish transparent policies to foster ethical practices, preventing violations or misuse of user data (Anshari et al., 2022).

Inclusivity and Accessibility Challenges

While the Metaverse enhances accessibility, there is a risk of excluding certain demographics. Addressing the digital divide and disabilities is crucial for ensuring inclusivity. The Metaverse must tackle accessibility challenges to enable people with disabilities to access immersive Virtual Reality platforms (Fernandes & Werner, 2022).

Security and Privacy Concerns

While the Metaverse offers advantages, privacy concerns, and early-stage development require further research and enhancement (Al-Ghaili et al., 2022). Safeguarding the personal and private nature of religious experiences in virtual environments is essential. Addressing data protection and unauthorized access is crucial for building user trust.

Global Regulatory Compliance Challenges

The Metaverse may introduce new products, services, job profiles, and business models, but challenges in building and operating it persist (Momtaz, 2022). Compliance with international regulations related to virtual experiences, data storage, and content distribution can pose a complex challenge for Metaverse developers.

Technical Barriers in Metaverse Implementation

The Metaverse for healthcare combines multiple enabling technologies, but implementation in higher education institutions faces barriers such as limited bandwidth and computing power (Chengoden et al., 2023; Kshetri et al., 2022). The digital divide and technology access limitations may restrict the reach of virtual religious tourism experiences.

Community Engagement and Acceptance

User satisfaction is crucial for users' intention to use the Metaverse in medical education (Almarzouqi et al., 2022). Convincing religious communities to embrace virtual experiences demands careful engagement and education, particularly addressing concerns about the compatibility of technology with traditional practices.

IMPLICATIONS OF USING METAVERSE FOR RELIGIOUS TOURISM

The exploration of the metaverse within the context of religious tourism carries profound implications that transcend conventional boundaries. First and foremost, the proposition of metaverse technology as a solution to authentically present the ambiance and natural essence of religious locations (Ratnawati et al., 2023), suggests a transformative potential for spiritual journeys. This could revolutionize the way pilgrims and tourists engage with sacred sites, offering a virtual experience that captures the sacredness and cultural richness of religious destinations.

The positive influence of virtual reality (VR) experiential value on tourists' cultural dissemination behavior (Zeng et al., 2022) underscores the potential for the metaverse to become a powerful tool for cultural exchange within religious tourism. The metaverse could facilitate a more immersive and engaging exploration of religious traditions, rituals, and historical contexts, fostering a deeper understanding and appreciation among diverse global audiences.

Figure 3. Challenges associated with metaverse for religious tourism

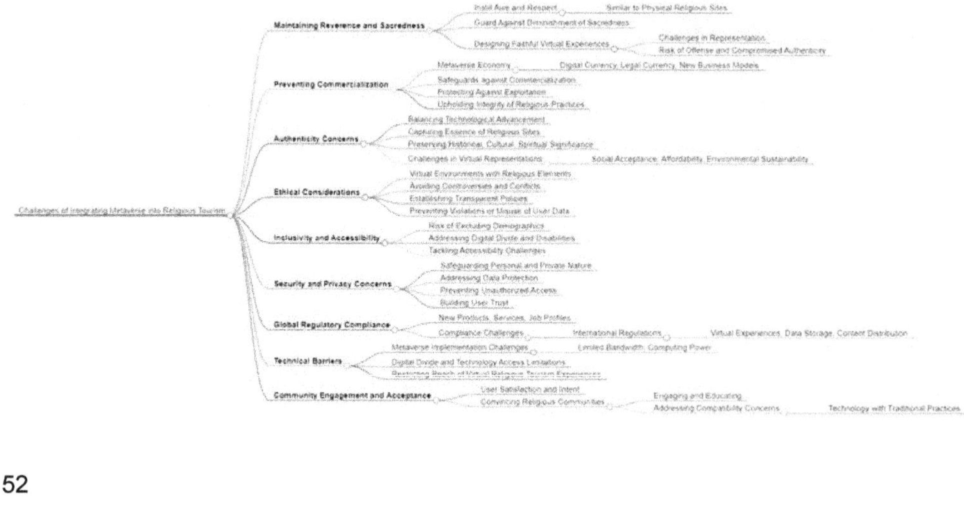

The examination of the influence of VR on tourists' quality of experience (González-Rodríguez et al., 2020) suggests that the metaverse's incorporation into religious tourism has the potential to significantly enhance the overall quality of the pilgrims' virtual journeys. By prioritizing a positive and immersive virtual encounter, the metaverse can effectively elevate the satisfaction and engagement levels of users, ensuring that the digital experience mirrors the richness and authenticity of physical pilgrimages.

Furthermore, considering the impact of VR experience quality on destination visit intention and VR travel intention (Yersüren & Özel, 2023), it becomes evident that the metaverse holds the promise of not only shaping perceptions but also influencing the actual decision-making process of potential pilgrims. A high-quality VR experience could serve as a compelling catalyst, inspiring individuals to transform their virtual exploration into concrete plans for physical visits to religious sites. This suggests that the metaverse has the potential not just to augment the digital experience but to actively drive and shape the pilgrimage journey itself.

The study by Lee (2017) emphasizes the importance of VR-guided tours in determining the usability of head-mounted displays, such as Oculus or Gear VR. Applying this insight to religious tourism, the metaverse could offer guided virtual pilgrimages, providing an interactive and immersive experience that goes beyond static representations. Pilgrims using VR headsets could engage in rituals, explore sacred sites, and participate in religious ceremonies, creating a dynamic and personalized journey that transcends physical limitations.

Additionally, Telepresence, as highlighted by Ouerghemmi et al. (2023), contributes to shaping positive attitudes toward tourist destinations even before physical visits occur. In the context of religious tourism, the metaverse could play a pivotal role in fostering a sense of spiritual connection and anticipation, allowing pilgrims to virtually immerse themselves in the sacred aura of their chosen destination. The metaverse thus becomes a tool for pre-travel engagement, heightening the significance of religious experiences and deepening the emotional connection before embarking on the actual pilgrimage.

However, it's crucial to consider the potential challenges unveiled by Merkx & Nawijn (2021), who identified addiction and temporary isolation as new themes in VR analysis. In the context of religious tourism, striking a balance between immersive experiences and the preservation of genuine, physical pilgrimages becomes paramount. The metaverse should enhance, not replace, the authenticity of spiritual encounters, mindful of the risk of isolating individuals from the tangible aspects of their faith.

CONCLUSION

Metaverse unfolds as a revolutionary frontier in reshaping the landscape of religious tourism. Its profound applicability is evident in reinforcing visit intentions, advancing tourism research, expanding resources sustainably, transforming hospitality experiences, preserving cultural heritage, and fostering new avenues for marketing and brand storytelling. The Metaverse not only enriches virtual tourism but also serves as a catalyst for immersive education, virtual pilgrimages, community building, and facilitating religious events, transcending geographical boundaries and cultural differences.

However, the integration of the Metaverse into religious tourism is not without its challenges. Maintaining reverence and sacredness, preventing commercialization, ensuring authenticity in virtual representations, addressing ethical concerns, overcoming inclusivity and accessibility challenges, managing security and privacy, and navigating global regulatory compliance issues pose significant obstacles. These challenges necessitate careful consideration and strategic planning to safeguard the integrity of religious experiences while harnessing the potential of the Metaverse.

Looking ahead, future endeavors in the realm of Metaverse-driven religious tourism hold promising avenues. Research can focus on enhancing virtual pilgrimages through advanced technologies, ensuring inclusivity for diverse demographics, establishing comprehensive ethical frameworks, promoting sustainable Metaverse tourism, developing robust regulatory frameworks, and fostering cultural integration within virtual communities. The journey into the Metaverse for religious tourism is poised for exciting innovations, promising a more connected, inclusive, and sustainable exploration of spirituality and cultural heritage in the digital age.

REFERENCES

Abass, M., & Zohry, M. (2022). Mixed Reality Drama Towards Metaverse Technology in Smart Hotels: An Exploratory Study on Egyptian Hotels Evidence from Guests' Perspectives. *Journal of Association of Arab Universities for Tourism and Hospitality*, *23*(2), 130–154. Advance online publication. doi:10.21608/jaauth.2022.177500.1411

Ahmad, M. (2023). Exploring the Role of OpenStreetMap in Mapping Religious Tourism in Pakistan for Sustainable Development. In V. João Pereira Domingues Martinho (Ed.), *Experiences, Advantages, and Economic Dimensions of Pilgrimage Routes*. IGI Global. doi:10.4018/978-1-6684-9923-8.ch002

Ahmad, M., & Ali, A. (2023). Integrated Geospatial Information Management in the World of Metaverse. In P. Lekhi & G. Kaur (Eds.), *Concepts, Technologies, Challenges, and the Future of Web 3* (pp. 248–270). IGI Global. doi:10.4018/978-1-6684-9919-1.ch013

Ahmad, N. M., Sohail, R., & Ahmad, M. M. (2022). Impact of Religious Tourism on the Development of Smokeless Industry in Pakistan. *Global Social Sciences Review*, *7*(2), 77–89. Advance online publication. doi:10.31703/gssr.2022(VII-II).08

Al-Ghaili, A. M., Kasim, H., Al-Hada, N. M., Hassan, Z. Bin, Othman, M., Tharik, J. H., Kasmani, R. M., & Shayea, I. (2022). A Review of Metaverse's Definitions, Architecture, Applications, Challenges, Issues, Solutions, and Future Trends. In IEEE Access (Vol. 10). doi:10.1109/ACCESS.2022.3225638

Almarzouqi, A., Aburayya, A., & Salloum, S. A. (2022). Prediction of User's Intention to Use Metaverse System in Medical Education: A Hybrid SEM-ML Learning Approach. *IEEE Access : Practical Innovations, Open Solutions*, *10*, 43421–43434. Advance online publication. doi:10.1109/ACCESS.2022.3169285

Almuhrzi, H. (2020). Islamic tourism: Management of travel destinations. *Journal of Heritage Tourism*, *15*(4), 480–482. Advance online publication. doi:10.1080/1743873X.2019.1658351

Ampountolas, A., Menconi, G., & Shaw, G. (2023). Metaverse research propositions: Online intermediaries. *Tourism Economics*. Advance online publication. doi:10.1177/13548166231159520

Anshari, M., Syafrudin, M., Fitriyani, N. L., & Razzaq, A. (2022). Ethical Responsibility and Sustainability (ERS) Development in a Metaverse Business Model. *Sustainability (Basel)*, *14*(23), 15805. Advance online publication. doi:10.3390/su142315805

Ayorekire, J., Obua, J., Mugizi, F., & Byaruhanga, B. M. (2020). Opportunities and challenges of religious tourism development in Uganda: Policy, planning and institutional perspectives. In International Journal of Religious Tourism and Pilgrimage (Vol. 8, Issue 3).

Bale, A. S., Ghorpade, N., Hashim, M. F., Vaishnav, J., & Almaspoor, Z. (2022). A Comprehensive Study on Metaverse and Its Impacts on Humans. In *Advances in Human-Computer Interaction* (Vol. 2022). Hindawi Limited. doi:10.1155/2022/3247060

Bhattacharya, P., Saraswat, D., Savaliya, D., Sanghavi, S., Verma, A., Sakariya, V., Tanwar, S., Sharma, R., Raboaca, M. S., & Manea, D. L. (2023). Towards Future Internet: The Metaverse Perspective for Diverse Industrial Applications. *Mathematics*, *11*(4), 941. Advance online publication. doi:10.3390/math11040941

Buhalis, D., Lin, M. S., & Leung, D. (2023). Metaverse as a driver for customer experience and value co-creation: Implications for hospitality and tourism management and marketing. *International Journal of Contemporary Hospitality Management*, *35*(2), 701–716. Advance online publication. doi:10.1108/IJCHM-05-2022-0631

Butler, R. (2020). Risk and safety challenges for religious tourism and events. *Current Issues in Tourism*, *23*(3), 388–390. Advance online publication. doi:10.1080/13683500.2018.1502860

Cárdenas, R. M., & Puente, O. T. (2017). The perception of security of the tourists in a site of religious tourism. *International Journal of Scientific Management and Tourism*, *3*, 255–274.

Cheng, R., Wu, N., Chen, S., & Han, B. (2022). Will Metaverse Be NextG Internet? Vision, Hype, and Reality. *IEEE Network*, *36*(5), 197–204. Advance online publication. doi:10.1109/MNET.117.2200055

Chengoden, R., Victor, N., Huynh-The, T., Yenduri, G., Jhaveri, R. H., Alazab, M., Bhattacharya, S., Hegde, P., Maddikunta, P. K. R., & Gadekallu, T. R. (2023). Metaverse for Healthcare: A Survey on Potential Applications, Challenges and Future Directions. *IEEE Access : Practical Innovations, Open Solutions*, *11*, 12765–12795. Advance online publication. doi:10.1109/ACCESS.2023.3241628

Cruz-Lara, S., Cabello, J. M., Osswald, T., Collado, A., Franco, J. M., & Barrera, S. (2011). Tourism in virtual worlds: Means, goals and needs. In Handbook of Research on Practices and Outcomes in Virtual Worlds and Environments (Vol. 1). doi:10.4018/978-1-60960-762-3.ch009

Cugini, A. (2021). Religious tourism and Sustainability: From Devotion to Spiritual Experience. In Tourism in the Mediterranean Sea. doi:10.1108/978-1-80043-900-920211006

Daricha, D. N. (2019). Religious Tourism Development in Ethiopia: Challenges and Opportunities at Adyame Yordanos Wonkshet St. Gabriel Monastery. *Journal of Tourism, Hospitality and Sports*. doi:10.7176/JTHS/40-02

Demircioğlu, A. (2020). Introducing the cities of Ghazali in the context of religious tourism. In Global Development of Religious Tourism. doi:10.4018/978-1-7998-5792-1.ch003

Di Giovine Michael, A., & Elsner, J. (2016). Pilgrimage tourism. In H. Jafari Jafar and Xiao (Ed.), Encyclopedia of Tourism (pp. 722–724). Springer International Publishing. doi:10.1007/978-3-319-01384-8_146

Ezenagu, N., Okpoko, P. U., & Okpoko, C. (2021). Faith-based activities and religious tourism in southwestern Nigeria: Challenging factors. *Ikenga*, *22*(3), 1–25. Advance online publication. doi:10.53836/ijia/2021/22/3/006

Fernandes, F., & Werner, C. (2022). *Accessibility in the Metaverse: Are We Prepared?* doi:10.5753/waihcws.2022.226618

Fernández-Álvarez, Ó., González-González, M., & Ouali-Fernández, S. (2022). Religious Heritage: Reconciliation between Spirituality and Cultural Concerns. *Rupkatha Journal on Interdisciplinary Studies in Humanities*, *14*(4). Advance online publication. doi:10.21659/rupkatha.v14n4.29

Folgieri, R., Gricar, S., & Baldigara, T. (2023). NFTs: What opportunities and challenges in tourism? *Tourism & Hospitality Industry 2022, Congress Proceedings*. 10.20867/thi.26.3

Gaafar, A. A. (2021). Metaverse In Architectural Heritage Documentation & Education. *Advances in Ecological and Environmental Research, 6*.

Go, H., & Kang, M. (2023). Metaverse tourism for sustainable tourism development: Tourism Agenda 2030. *Tourism Review*, *78*(2), 381–394. Advance online publication. doi:10.1108/TR-02-2022-0102

González-Rodríguez, M. R., Díaz-Fernández, M. C., & Pino-Mejías, M. Á. (2020). The impact of virtual reality technology on tourists' experience: A textual data analysis. *Soft Computing*, *24*(18), 13879–13892. Advance online publication. doi:10.1007/s00500-020-04883-y

Guan, J., Irizawa, J., & Morris, A. (2022). Extended Reality and Internet of Things for Hyper-Connected Metaverse Environments. *Proceedings - 2022 IEEE Conference on Virtual Reality and 3D User Interfaces Abstracts and Workshops, VRW 2022*. 10.1109/VRW55335.2022.00043

Gursoy, D., Malodia, S., & Dhir, A. (2022). The metaverse in the hospitality and tourism industry: An overview of current trends and future research directions. *Journal of Hospitality Marketing & Management*, *31*(5), 527–534. Advance online publication. doi:10.1080/19368623.2022.2072504

Haq, F. (2013). Islamic spiritual tourism: An innovative marketing framework. *International Journal of Social Entrepreneurship and Innovation*, *2*(5), 438. Advance online publication. doi:10.1504/IJSEI.2013.059320

Henderson, J. C. (2011). Religious tourism and its management: The hajj in Saudi Arabia. *International Journal of Tourism Research*, *13*(6), 541–552. Advance online publication. doi:10.1002/jtr.825

Hollensen, S., Kotler, P., & Opresnik, M. O. (2022). Metaverse – the new marketing universe. *The Journal of Business Strategy*. Advance online publication. doi:10.1108/JBS-01-2022-0014

Huang, X. (2021). The technological essence and philosophical significance of the Metaverse. *Metaverse*, *2*(2), 10. Advance online publication. doi:10.54517/met.v2i2.1786

Huang, X. T., Wang, J., Wang, Z., Wang, L., & Cheng, C. (2023). Experimental study on the influence of virtual tourism spatial situation on the tourists' temperature comfort in the context of metaverse. *Frontiers in Psychology*, *13*, 1062876. Advance online publication. doi:10.3389/fpsyg.2022.1062876 PMID:36687952

Huang, Y., Li, Y. J., & Cai, Z. (2023). Security and Privacy in Metaverse: A Comprehensive Survey. *Big Data Mining and Analytics*, *6*(2), 234–247. Advance online publication. doi:10.26599/BDMA.2022.9020047

Hutson, J., & Hutson, P. (2023). Museums and the Metaverse – Emerging Technologies to Promote Inclusivity and Engagement. In *Application of Modern Trends in Museums*. IntechOpen. doi:10.5772/intechopen.110044

Hwang, K., tom Dieck, M. C., Jung, T., & Kwon, O. (2023). The influence of virtual reality on the experience of religious cultural heritage content. *Internet Research*. Advance online publication. doi:10.1108/INTR-08-2022-0669

Idris, J. (2019). Spiritual motivation for religious tourism destinations. In Spiritual and religious tourism : motivations and management. doi:10.1079/9781786394163.0059

Irfan, E., & Ali, Y. (2020). Religious tourism in Pakistan: Scope, obstacles & strategies. *Journal of Convention & Event Tourism*, *22*(2), 134–154. Advance online publication. doi:10.1080/15470148.2020.1852990

Jiang, J. (2022). Metaverse: Homogenization experience and cultural illusion. *Metaverse*, *3*(1), 8. Advance online publication. doi:10.54517/met.v3i1.1811

Jo, H. (2023). Tourism in the digital frontier: A study on user continuance intention in the metaverse. *Information Technology & Tourism*, *25*(3), 307–330. Advance online publication. doi:10.1007/s40558-023-00257-w

Kaddoura, S., & Al Husseiny, F. (2023). The rising trend of Metaverse in education: Challenges, opportunities, and ethical considerations. *PeerJ. Computer Science*, *9*, e1252. Advance online publication. doi:10.7717/peerj-cs.1252 PMID:37346578

Kim, B., Kim, S., & King, B. (2020). Religious tourism studies: Evolution, progress, and future prospects. *Tourism Recreation Research*, *45*(2), 185–203. Advance online publication. doi:10.1080/02508281.2019.1664084

Kim, J. (2021). Advertising in the Metaverse: Research Agenda. In Journal of Interactive Advertising (Vol. 21, Issue 3). doi:10.1080/15252019.2021.2001273

Koo, C., Kwon, J., Chung, N., & Kim, J. (2023). Metaverse tourism: conceptual framework and research propositions. In Current Issues in Tourism (Vol. 26, Issue 20). doi:10.1080/13683500.2022.2122781

Kshetri, N., Rojas-Torres, D., & Grambo, M. (2022). The Metaverse and Higher Education Institutions. *IT Professional*, *24*(6), 69–73. Advance online publication. doi:10.1109/MITP.2022.3222711

Lee, K.-S. (2017). A study of the impacts of virtual reality guided tours' affordances on user experiences. *International Journal of Tourism and Hospitality Research*, *31*(3), 105–118. Advance online publication. doi:10.21298/IJTHR.2017.03.31.3.105

Lemmi, E. (2020). Heritage and new communication technologies: development perspectives on the basis of the Via Francigena experience. *Hthic*, 43–62. https://www.academia.edu/42977285/Heritage_and_new_communication_technologies_development_perspectives_on_the_basis_of_the_Via_Francigena_experience

Liu, Z., Gong, S., Tan, Z., & Demian, P. (2023). Immersive Technologies-Driven Building Information Modeling (BIM) in the Context of Metaverse. *Buildings*, *13*(6), 1559. Advance online publication. doi:10.3390/buildings13061559

Luz, N. (2020). Pilgrimage and religious tourism in Islam. *Annals of Tourism Research*, *82*, 102915. Advance online publication. doi:10.1016/j.annals.2020.102915

Mafudi, M., Sugiarto, S., & Praptapa, A. (2021). Emerging Opportunities for Halal Tourism in Rural Areas: Insights from Indonesia. *Fokus Bisnis : Media Pengkajian Manajemen Dan Akuntansi*, *20*(1), 16–26. Advance online publication. doi:10.32639/fokusbisnis.v10i1.726

Mercadal, T. (2017). Religious Tourism. In L. L. Lowry (Ed.), *The SAGE International Encyclopedia of Travel and Tourism*. SAGE Publications, Inc. https://doi.org/https://doi.org/10.4135/9781483368924

Merkx, C., & Nawijn, J. (2021). Virtual reality tourism experiences: Addiction and isolation. *Tourism Management*, *87*, 104394. Advance online publication. doi:10.1016/j.tourman.2021.104394

Momtaz, P. P. (2022). Some Very Simple Economics of Web3 and the Metaverse. SSRN *Electronic Journal*. doi:10.2139/ssrn.4085937

Monaco, S., & Sacchi, G. (2023). Travelling the Metaverse: Potential Benefits and Main Challenges for Tourism Sectors and Research Applications. *Sustainability (Basel)*, *15*(4), 3348. Advance online publication. doi:10.3390/su15043348

Mustafa, B. (2022). Analyzing education based on metaverse technology. *Technium Social Sciences Journal*, *32*, 278–295. Advance online publication. doi:10.47577/tssj.v32i1.6742

Muwandeniya, W. A. K. C. B., & Eranda, B. A. N. (2022). Virtual Reality for Enhancing Customer Value in Sri Lankan Hospitality and Tourism Industry: Perspective of Industry Experts. *Sri Lanka Journal of Marketing*, *8*(2), 64–83. Advance online publication. doi:10.4038/sljmuok.v8i2.102

Ouerghemmi, C., Ertz, M., Bouslama, N., & Tandon, U. (2023). The Impact of Virtual Reality (VR) Tour Experience on Tourists' Intention to Visit. *Information (Basel)*, *14*(10), 546. Advance online publication. doi:10.3390/info14100546

Pipia, S., & Pipia, S. (2020). Challenges of religious tourism in the conflict region: An example of Jerusalem. Global Development of Religious Tourism. doi:10.4018/978-1-7998-5792-1.ch009

Poulios, I. (2019). On the greatest challenge in the management of living religious heritage: Linking the authenticity of heritage and the authenticity of tourist experiences to the authenticity of religious tradition. *Communications in Computer and Information Science*, *962*, 262–271. Advance online publication. doi:10.1007/978-3-030-12960-6_17

Ramos, C. M. Q., & Mafé-García, A. (2018). Analysis of the contribution of ICT to cultural and religious tourism: In communicating religious heritage to visitors and tourists. In Handbook of Research on Socio-Economic Impacts of Religious Tourism and Pilgrimage. doi:10.4018/978-1-5225-5730-2.ch010

Rancati, E., & D'Agata, A. (2022). Metaverse in Tourism and Hospitality: Empirical Evidence on Generation Z from Italy. *European Scientific Journal, 18*(34), 122. Advance online publication. doi:10.19044/esj.2022.v18n34p122

Ratnawati, I. I., Prasetyo, A. R., & Sidyawati, L. (2023). *Using Virtual Reality Video Development as Educational and Tourist Promotional Media*. KnE Social Sciences. doi:10.18502/kss.v8i15.13933

Rinschede, G. (1992). Forms of religious tourism. *Annals of Tourism Research, 19*(1), 51–67. Advance online publication. doi:10.1016/0160-7383(92)90106-Y

Shinde, K. A. (2020). Managing the environment in religious tourism destinations: a conceptual model. In Religious tourism and the environment. doi:10.1079/9781789241600.0042

Sica, E., Sisto, R., Bianchi, P., & Cappelletti, G. (2021). Inclusivity and responsible tourism: Designing a trademark for a national park area. *Sustainability (Basel), 13*(1), 13. Advance online publication. doi:10.3390/su13010013

Singh, L., & Dhankhar, D. (2020). Use of social media by tourists at religious tourism destinations in India. In Global Development of Religious Tourism. doi:10.4018/978-1-7998-5792-1.ch015

Štefko, R., Kiráľová, A., & Mudrík, M. (2015). Strategic Marketing Communication in Pilgrimage Tourism. *Procedia: Social and Behavioral Sciences, 175*, 423–430. Advance online publication. doi:10.1016/j.sbspro.2015.01.1219

Suanpang, P., Niamsorn, C., Pothipassa, P., Chunhapataragul, T., Netwong, T., & Jermsittiparsert, K. (2022). Extensible Metaverse Implication for a Smart Tourism City. *Sustainability (Basel), 14*(21), 14027. Advance online publication. doi:10.3390/su142114027

Tomljenović, R., & Dukić, L. (2018). *Religious Tourism - from a Tourism Product to an Agent of Societal Transformation*. doi:10.15308/Sitcon-2017-1-8

Trono, A., & Castronuovo, V. (2023). Pilgrimage Tourism, Accessibility and Local Communities in Western Countries. The Camino de Santiago de Compostela and the via Francigena for All. In Perspectives on Asian Tourism: Vol. Part F191. doi:10.1007/978-981-19-9677-1_9

Tsai, S. P. (2022). Investigating metaverse marketing for travel and tourism. *Journal of Vacation Marketing*. Advance online publication. doi:10.1177/13567667221145715

Tsironis, C. N. (2022). Pilgrimage and Religious Tourism in Society, in the Wake of the COVID-19 Pandemic: A Paradigmatic Focus on 'St. Paul's Route' in the Central Macedonia Region, Greece. *Religions*, *13*(10), 887. Advance online publication. doi:10.3390/rel13100887

Um, T., Kim, H., Kim, H., Lee, J., Koo, C., & Chung, N. (2022). Travel Incheon as a Metaverse: Smart Tourism Cities Development Case in Korea. In Information and Communication Technologies in Tourism 2022. doi:10.1007/978-3-030-94751-4_20

UNWTO. (2016). *World Tourism Day 2016 "Tourism for All-promoting universal accessibility" Good Practices in the Accessible Tourism Supply Chain*. World Tourism Organization (UNWTO).

Volchek, K., & Brysch, A. (2023). *Metaverse and Tourism: From a New Niche to a Transformation*. Springer Proceedings in Business and Economics. doi:10.1007/978-3-031-25752-0_32

Wang, Y., Su, Z., Zhang, N., Xing, R., Liu, D., Luan, T. H., & Shen, X. (2023). A Survey on Metaverse: Fundamentals, Security, and Privacy. *IEEE Communications Surveys and Tutorials*, *25*(1), 319–352. Advance online publication. doi:10.1109/COMST.2022.3202047

Yang, F. X., & Wang, Y. (2023). Rethinking Metaverse Tourism: A Taxonomy and an Agenda for Future Research. *Journal of Hospitality & Tourism Research (Washington, D.C.)*. Advance online publication. doi:10.1177/10963480231163509

Yersüren, S., & Özel, Ç. H. (2023). The effect of virtual reality experience quality on destination visit intention and virtual reality travel intention. *Journal of Hospitality and Tourism Technology*. doi:10.1108/JHTT-02-2023-0046

Yoon, T. H., Do, J. K., & Jeong, S. C. (2022). Developing Songjeong Metaverse Surfing Village: Development of Metaverse-based Platform Specialized for Marine Tourism. *Proceedings - 2022 IEEE/ACIS 7th International Conference on Big Data, Cloud Computing, and Data Science, BCD 2022*. 10.1109/BCD54882.2022.9900793

Yuan, Y., & Yang, Y. (2022). Embracing the Metaverse: Mechanism and logic of a new digital economy. *Metaverse*, *3*(2), 15. Advance online publication. doi:10.54517/m.v3i2.1814

Zareei, A., & Namjoo, A. (2018). *The Role of Theatre, Rituals and Religious Ceremonies in Improving the Concept of Spiritual Tourism (Case Study: Iran)*. doi:10.22133/IJTS.2018.69312

Zeng, Y., Liu, L., & Xu, R. (2022). The Effects of a Virtual Reality Tourism Experience on Tourist's Cultural Dissemination Behavior. *Tourism and Hospitality*, *3*(1), 314–329. Advance online publication. doi:10.3390/tourhosp3010021

Zhang, X., Yang, D., Yow, C. H., Huang, L., Wu, X., Huang, X., Guo, J., Zhou, S., & Cai, Y. (2022). Metaverse for Cultural Heritages. *Electronics (Basel)*, *11*(22), 3730. Advance online publication. doi:10.3390/electronics11223730

Chapter 4
Virtual Reality and Augmented Reality for Industrial and Business Intelligence

Karishma Desai
Atlas University, Mumbai, India

M. Dileep Kumar
Nile University, Nigeria

Mohamed Omar Khairi
College of Administrative Sciences, Bahrain

Normala Govindarajo
Xiamen University, Malaysia

Vinod Sharma
https://orcid.org/0000-0002-0815-8502
Symbiosis Centre for Management and Human Resource, Symbiosis International University, Pune, India

ABSTRACT

The world of innovation and innovative technologies is rapidly proving its scope and benefits across the business sector featuring business intelligence tools. The traditional way of searching data sources, visualizing those data, and arriving at business decisions has transformed with tools of computational intelligence. Here the role of virtual reality (VR) and augmented reality (AR) comes into the picture. The current work looks into the possibilities of VR and AR in business, which support predictive analytics, customer analytics, business analytics, and data visualization aspects through systematic literature review and content analysis. In this paper, a systematic analysis of associations and features of both VR and AR has been done by detailing the outline, organization, management, and devices for business and industry intelligence. The objective of the current work is met with the insights and understanding of VR and AR in relation to business intelligence.

DOI: 10.4018/979-8-3693-1103-5.ch004

INTRODUCTION

Industry 4.0-initiated technology changes are conquering every realm of engineering, business, and trade in contemporary days. Some of the terms frequently used by industrial and business leaders in decision-making include virtual reality (VR) and augmented reality (AR). Industries like manufacturing, communications, and services are rapidly improving their operations with AR and VR. AR, as computing technology is metamorphosing has enabled the widespread availability of stimulated reality technologies like AR and VR. VR and AR are recognized worldwide as technologies prominent in the 21st Century and are crucial to support businesses and industries. A wide range of disciplines that have been used with AR and VR include military, aviation, healthcare, marketing, advertising, and sales. The use of novel technologies in industrial manufacturing has its virtues and brings substantial process enhancement. The technological wave is gaining momentum across sectors like gaming, entertainment, education, tourism, financial services, sports, etc.

Industry 4.0 and digital technology growth are imperative to improve the productivity and suppleness of the manufacturing process of products. The technology integration contributes a high-quality range, which makes use of optimum time and less cost ensuring competitive advantage. (RuBmaan et al, 2015). As a part of this digital technology growth, VR is fetching more hindrance-free with dedicated hardware and software domains. VR provides immersive 3D visualization, authentic rendering material, interactions with natural gestures, collaborations with functionalities, and swift navigational devices in wide areas. VR programs imitate real-world virtual interaction and cooperation, accordingly offering near to better life experiences (Berg & Vance, 2017), Marzan et al, 2015, Galambos et al, 2015). Businesses have now to work on value creation and modification for customer communication by making use of AR and VR platforms. Industries have to examine technology-oriented strategies for value creation towards all their stakeholders and internal influencers who are driving the B2C and B2B VR markets (Anouk de Regeter et al, 2020). As contemporary businesses are geared toward technological innovations, an intelligence business is the new order of industrial society. VR and AR are undoubtedly going to be indispensable and provides new interactive domains to customers and business, which are aimed at enhancing the overall consumer experience. Hence is hypothesized that there is an urgent need to adopt preemptive strategies by defining VR and AR roles in the ecosystem to stay relevant and resilient by capitalizing on opportunities and navigating through unforeseen complexities. The current work is a conceptual paper exploring the market trends, applications, and technologies of AR and VR in manufacturing, business, and service sectors, in the industrial 4.0 for better intelligent business responses.

LITERATURE REVIEW

Internet of Things (IIoT)

IoT or the Internet of Things has turned out to be the life and blood of several organizations which support them with analytical tools, applications, and services in certain domains. IoT enables smart technologies to be developed, tested, and applied in several functional processes. Major functions IoT and AI-integrated applications perform are sensing and actuating, data across the platforms through a unified structure, and enabling innovative applications. IoT makes use of data analytics and information interpretation using state-of-the-art technologies for sensing and cloud computing (Verma et al., 2019). Basically, IoT involves three components a) Hardware, which includes sensors, actuators, and entrenched communication hardware b) Middleware, which includes on-demand storage and computation techniques for data analytics and c) Presentation, which includes visualization and interpretation techniques that can be widely accessed on different platforms and can be planned for diverse application (Sethi & Sarangi, 2016)

Virtual reality and augmented reality*

Virtual reality (VR) is described as “a computer-generated digital milieu that can be networked with as if that setting were real” (Jerald, 2015, p. 9). VR is collaborative know-how that overlays the virtual 3D model of a commodity into the real world to adapt the physical environment, where users can manipulate the 3D model, for example, revolving, moving, and zooming in and out” (Poushneh and Vasquez-Parraga, 2017). Augmented reality (AR) is where virtual stuff and settings are mixed with the real world. The user views his/her actual environment alongside computer-generated perceptual data. AR overlaps digital data with real-world elements. AR improves real-world familiarity with other digital particulars, layering a new layer of insight, and incorporating the user’s veracity or environment by possessing the real domain dominant.

Difference Between AR/VR/XR and MR

Extended reality (ER) is an umbrella term that covers all stimulation-based technology such as AR, VR MR, and holography. VR is the visualization and concurrent observation of veracity and its physical characteristics in a collaborating virtual event that is made do a computer in real time. The intelligence of immersion annexed over a virtual 3-D environment deals plentiful advantages especially photo visualization and communication, based on real-time geographical facts and figures that have been portrayed conventionally in 3D maps or 3D models. While AR is a computer-ordered extension of discernible reality over a mixture of virtual reality. In simple terms, AR is assumed as a visual illustration of supplementary data as a stratum over the type of image of reality. (Farshid, Paschen, Eriksson, & Kietzmann, 2018).

One of the major features of VR is its appropriate interaction with an immersive and entirely virtual application. AR presents a stratum of virtual content over a layer of real-world imageries caught in real-time. AR and VR have tremendous potential to metamorphose consumer interaction and the ways businesses operate. They have evolved over a period of time. With the advent of technological innovations, their presence has yielded to the next big platforms after PC, Net, and Mobile. VR immerses in an imagined or replicated world as AR overlays digital imagery into the real world. VR allows consumers to have unique experiences in many businesses ranging from healthcare, tourism, retail, and entertainment. It does this by creating a sense of presence that is invigorated by computer-generated stimulation. However, AR allows people to simultaneously exist in their physical and digital worlds by facilitating seamless access to digital information in their real-world environments (Chawla et al, 2018).

MR covers the notion of AR with features to notice deviations in the real world permitting virtual features to acclimatize and respond e.g., by stimulating the clatter of a virtual ball with a real wall. It is external to note that MR carries the two ends of the range together i.e. reality and virtuality. The three conceptions are congregated together in the overall notion of extended reality (XR), this carries them all collectively. VR tolerates the handler to intermingle with an immersive and completely virtual use. A layer of real-world images is gathered by the AR as a part of the strata of virtual content. It is significant to understand that AR is more encouraging than VR for raising a strong point to Industry 4.0, nearer association with reality. Although VR is often used for tanning sessions it becomes almost difficult to comprehend VR uses for real working sittings as it requires interactions with real objects.

The advantage of AR over VR is that it is named AR technology, and has a higher reduction of images. It is significant to understand that AR is more promising than VR for fostering strength to industry 4.0 closer connection with reality Although VR is often used for tanning sessions it becomes almost impossible to conceive VR applications for real working sessions as it requires interactions with real objects. Mixed reality denotes to amalgamation of real-world paradigms with computer-produced concepts that are either real or not conceivable. Mixed reality is also alternatively termed as hybrid reality which combines what is possible and real. But with the supremacy of virtual reality, also combines the actual reality.

Figure 1. Striking prospects in virtual reality market (Markets and Markets, 2020)

Attractive Opportunities in Virtual Reality Market

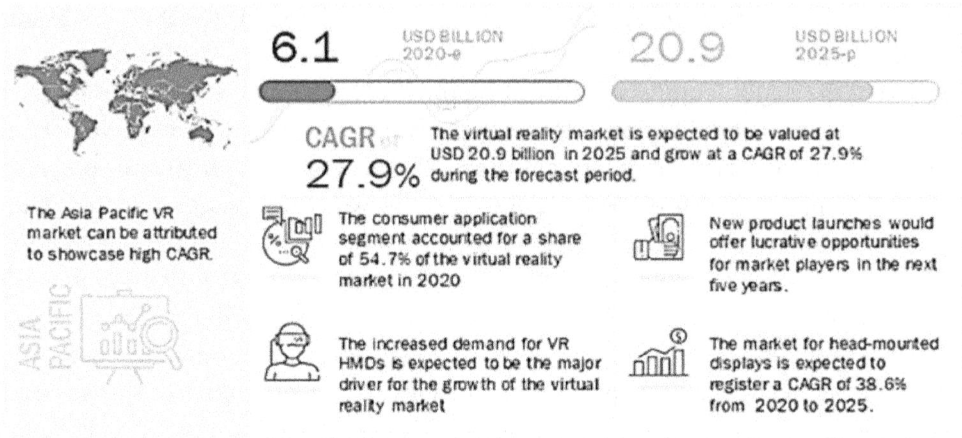

e-estimated, p-projected

Growth Statistics

The Covid19 pandemic is expected to support growth of VR marketing. The main companies operating in the market place are concentrating on increasing the sale of their products. Most of the economies of the world at present are focusing on expanding their healthcare facilities. The virtual reality market is predictable to be appreciated at USD 20.9 Billion in 2025 and develop at CAGR of 27.9% throughout the predicted period.

The world-wide augmented reality market-size was prised at USD 17.67 billion in 2020. It is projected to develop at a composite yearly growing rate (CAGR) of 43.8% from 2021 to 2028. The increasing response for distant support and co-operation from varied firms which contribute in operational workflow direction and optimization, that is predictable to drive market development. Businesses are making use of Augmented Reality (AR) grounded applications for tracking, identifying, and decisive technical aspects as well as for everyday jobs, such as retrofitting, assembling, manufacturing, and repairing production lines. Henceforth, businesses are mainly reconnoitring the potential of AR know-how to offer a custom-made and collaborating involvement to consumers.

The major players in the AR and VR market comprise of Intel corporation (US), Microsoft corporation (US), QUALCOMM incorporated (US), Apple Inc (US), Sony Corporation (Japan), Magic leap (US) Jaunt Inc (US), Avegant corporation (US) and Atheer INC(US).

Figure 2. Attractive opportunities in virtual reality market (Grand View Research, 2020)

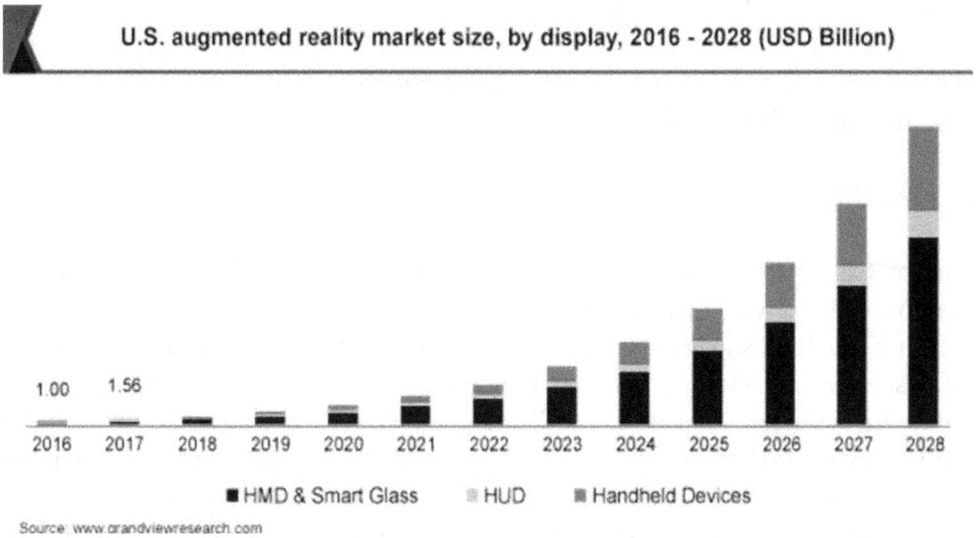

Figure 3. Top players in the augmented reality (Grand View Research, 2020)

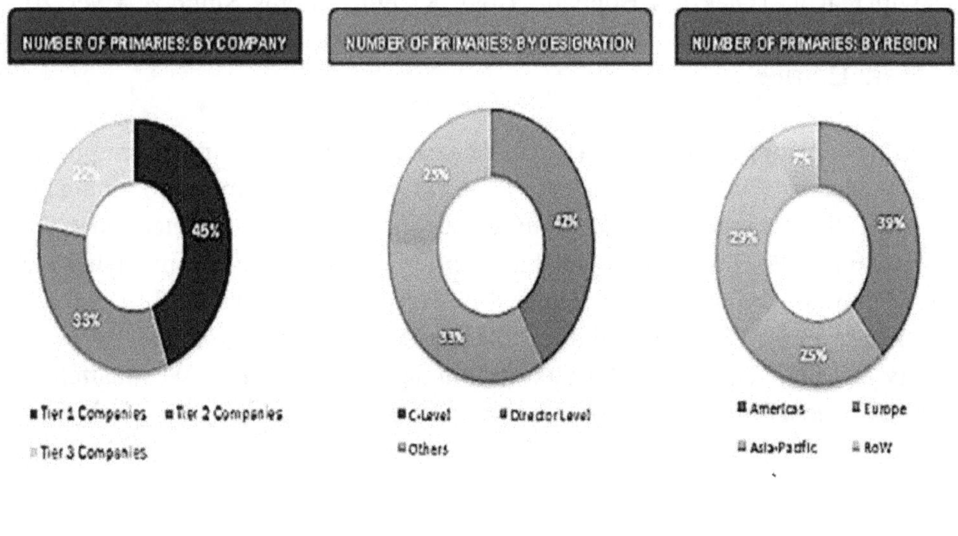

Theories and AR and VR

It is essential to understand theoretical implications of VR and AR as it is imperative to consider theories surrounding VR and AR while designing VR and AR tools and solutions. For VR applications some approaches like CASA (Computers and Social Action) theory, Immersion, Cognitive load, presence and construct theory. Linking these theories will facilitate in designing lucrative solutions at an individual level by highlighting the relevance of immersion, existence and load in the design of VR solutions. (Khandelwal & Upadhyay, 2021)

Application and Adaption of Augmented Reality and Virtual Reality

a. Healthcare

Virtual Reality is an art of creating on virtual assessments of multiple and anatomical regions of the body union arms to in diagnosis, planning and surgical training. When it comes to AR its super imposition of a 3D context specific to an entity in patient on to surgical and adopting semi-transparent glasses in order to enhance the visual scene. Virtual Reality access to profile in a safe, flexible and standard platform for the valuation of different primitive regions of the body with respect to diagnosis and surgical planning. So VR specifies 3D Corporation developed environment which could readily be employed and interfaced by person. Whereas AR combine Virtual reality 3D environment limited to individual patient. The aim is to process a practical registering procedure to achieve an vital image that reinforce the virtual act with real one (Diekfuss, Bonnette, Hogg, Riehm, Grooms, Singh, & Myer, 2021)

b. Real Estate

Building information modelling (BIM) is a new technique that is used in engineering, architecture and construction industry aimed at enhancing seamless communication between all the stakeholders, scheduling, design, and error clash detection. Current smartphones HMD technology enable mobile IVR is limited in immersing a user completely in computer -mediated reality. However it doesn't enable everyone's experience in VR. It is essential to note that VR technology can alter a sense if reality and interaction played a vital role under this construct. (Westmattelmann, Grotenhermen, Sprenger, Rand, & Schewe 2021).

c. Tourism

It is interesting to note trends of immersive virtual environments in which upcoming technologies are used statistically by operators in tourism for stimulating their clients before, during and after they experience VR – AR. It may be used to attract towards booking a destination package or to eventually submerge the customers in a challenge and new leisure experience when virtual reality is used to enhance tourist experience, it abstracts the users from their secondary environment and presents them with audio and visual stimuli which makes them feel they are in a completely different setting (telepresence). While in AR tourist observe the world and virtual objects overlaid on the real world and usually by interacting with the use of digital camera or smartphone. VR and AR are undergoing a huge metamorphosis over time and these include improvements in immersion and feelings of telepresence. VR and AR technologies are making a revolution in enhancing tourist travel experience and also such as spatial- aligned wall projections commonly known as 3D video mapping. Customer engagement can be enhanced by the customer experience and creating memorable memories. VR and AR are playing instrumental notes in tourism managers to enhance tourist satisfaction.

d. Sports

VR and MR applications used in sports application permits multiple tasks like training, competition, health-orientation, socializing to be performed which is extremely beneficial. Several literature emphases on health applications and smart phones apps which focus on health and fitness of the user. MR sports platforms such as ZWIF represents a way to exercise physical sports with them or in contradiction of each other in a virtual sphere which has worked exceptionally well especially during times of COVID 19 (Ozdemir, 2021).

Augmented Reality Applications

There is enough literature comparing software developments. AR tools which are marker-based tool kits are accessible in markets which manipulate black and white marker, to bring back the position of cameras required to structure the extraneous

Figure 4. Augmented reality and tourism (gettecla.com, 2018)

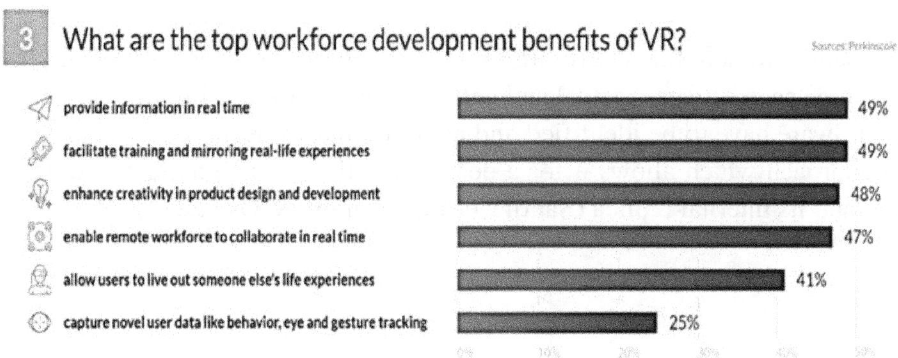

world and attribute correctly to multiple systems in reference to it (Santi, Ceruti, Liverani, & Osti 2021).

a. Video-See-Through Devices

The VST tools depends on the purpose of a camera that captures the outside scenes. HMDs are not broadly associated to VST as they do not require to implement the coverage and procedure the pictures on display built up by customary pixels. VST HDM has potential to breakthrough in MR environment as they set a powerful nature of Virtual Reality and Augmented Reality perception (Santi, Ceruti, Liverani, & Osti 2021).

b. Optical-See-Through Devices

The OST device works in a peculiar way projecting synthetic VMs on to semi-transparent lenses OST can analyse a set of know-hows evolved to upkeep air need the importance given to projection technology is considered to be the heart of OST HMD's (Santi, Ceruti, Liverani, & Osti 2021).

c. Embedded Tracking Systems and Tools

These equipment's have undergone software development and are of a former period embedded helmets. The gesture algorithms take support of the learning attained through leap motion device which is primarily framed for object interaction on hand recognition. The device has been designed by integrating the data from three IR sensors and two cameras, hence it can identify each of the finger of a human being's hand correlating job to each one of the program. (Santi, Ceruti, Liverani, & Osti 2021).

d. Hardware Limitations

It is essential to note that the future swing of evolvement of AR hardware aims to bridge the space between virtual and authentic world. Hence, limitations related to AR hardware have to be identified and attention has to begin to follow the digital twin approach which allows it for a decent real time switch amidst absolute real object and its internal replica (Santi, Ceruti, Liverani, & Osti 2021).

Applications of AR

AR is a well build up computer graphics technique with respect to research applications there is a constant need for technological innovation and improvement, born from an s/w and h/w perspective to enhance industrial operations. AR also is utilized in industrial environmental surroundings for backing maintenance and it is advantageous for AR as highly noticeable symbols be in the firm are used as markers. The efficient and effective profiteering of AR potential in the industrial environment can be made feasible once adequate reality- virtuality continuation will be applied. Shadows, blockage applied in an efficient way, accomplished virtual simulations, immense capability-human machine interface are few of the technologies that must be made feasible to bridge the gaps pertaining to absolute and natural. AR is disrupting functions across industries. It is expected by the leaders from Technology arena that AR will exceed VR in the next 3-5 years (Coie, 2019). Majority business entities are making use of AR to improve their processes in application oriented software.

a. AR in Mobile Services

AR in mobile services is gaining momentum especially with the tech savvy younger generation. Snapchat was the first application to use AR through filters and soon followed by Pokémon Go. IKEA enhances customer experience using AR by assisting them to visualize the furniture which they wish to purchase before actually purchasing it.

b. AR in Shopping Services

AR in shopping services is disrupting consumer shopping experience and research shows that a whopping 61% modern consumers prefer using AR (Hacker Noon) and 46% retailers are ushering in a new transition by enabling AR and VR shopping experiences.

c. AR and COVID-19 Disruptions

As COVID -19 disrupted the regular functioning of workspaces the Work from Anywhere Culture became the byproduct of the VUCA changes. Before the pandemics only 4% employees worked remotely while as of September 2020 post the early quarantine constraints, nearly a whopping 40% are still working from home. (Gallop, 2020). AR adds value to both external

d. Intelligent Display Technology

According to multiple research studies is proven that more than 65% of information which is attained by human beings are from their own vision which also additionally becomes an intuitive response in interacting in a real surroundings with the initiation of the Intelligent Display technology which has resulted into innovation of a new array of display devices based on the premise of intelligent display technology (Chenetal, 2019).

e. Helmet Display (HMD)

Helmet Display was initiated in 1968 and Prof. Ivan Sutherland developed the optical perspective helmet display which made it thinkable to super impose simple graphics fabricated by computers on real scenes in real time (Chenetal, 2019).

f. Handheld Device Displays

Handheld device displays utilizes AR technology and the handheld device display is very small and light. In the PC desktop display the camera captures a 3D virtual model which matches the real -world scene. The 3D registration know-how permits virtual images to be overlaid in a real environment (Chenetal, 2019).

g. 3D Registration Technology

3D registration technology is based on hardware tracking computer vision, mixed registration technology and wireless network. There is a surging need for online platform enabled by AR. It may post multi fold obstacles to share vision for ambitious projects in a Work from home set up. However, 3D enabled by AR could be alternatively used to bring out clarity regarding concepts and for better visualizations of projects. There are collaborative tools which by means of life like Avatars assist remote work which make the team members feel each other's presence during the meeting. Augmented Reality combines virtual info to the real world by using 3D modelling, intelligent interactions, multimedia tracking and registration, which are instrumental in the growth and development of AR. AR has modified customer experience completely and seamlessly bridges the gap between the digital and the real world. AR has extensive industry application and is no more at a nascent stage (Chenetal 2019).

h. Intelligent Interaction Technology

It is closely related to cognitive psychology, ergonomics etc. AR technology is gaining momentum owing to intelligent interactions which unlike traditional AR not only superimpose virtual data to real scenes but also realize that the intelligent collaboration between people and virtual objects in real life scenes . The more evolved is AR cloud which is the digitization of the whole world in which the whole world will become a pooled space. Whereas current AR experiences is stand- alone nature (Chenetal 2019). Some studies highlights how AR technology can be used to enhance customer experiences and attend to their customized needs like using AR technology consumers can without opening the packaging of the product see everything about it by scanning the product picture with the rise of customers who are inadvertently making lifestyle choices and increased veganism, allergen alerts, AR cloud could be strategically used to enhance experience .Use of AR in healthcare where innovative technology will assist to remind patients to take their medicines on time. (Chenetal 2019). It is reported by finance online (2020) that AR and VR reality supported business organisations to have better collaborations, increased efficiency, generating new business models and better marketing.

Key Challenges of AR/VR Adoption

There are multiple challenges in AR and VR adoption. It is essential to note that VR are in their infancy and represent basic structure 360 degrees recording which can cause nausea and dizziness in some individual costs involved in the purchasing. As a technology, is at nascent stage it is also takes time select equipment in specially to convert the images to AR format equipment. The challenge is that security of the data that stems from the consumer behaviour, while using such environment. The challenges with respect to transmitting, storing and presenting VR technology implementation are enormous and organisations are focusing on developing standards for captivating media events to ease innovation and advance. However, there are also rising concerns with respect to security in AR and VR adoption. It is not as easy as they are not reliable enough and robust, especially when compared to actual industry concern. The additional challenges were security-related, lack of apps in this technology, enormous time-commitment for its implementation of AR-VR and apprehensions in accepting a real substitute (Elnikety, Badr & Abdelaal, 2021).

a. Cost

The financial costs involved in using AR and VR are very high, although there are multi-fold benefits of them, with advancement of technology AR and VR applications are widespread however they are still not cost effective. For example: in the healthcare sector it's indeed very expensive to train surgeons to adapt to technologies involving VR and AR (Elnikety, Badr & Abdelaal, 2021)

b. Computing Power and Speed

It is known that there are some pre-existing challenges in VR adoption and industry performance. Industry professional and Academics are trying hard to bridge the gap. The Virtual Reality terminal's comprehensive effect is unsatisfactory providing simple and limited experience. The processing latency of Virtual Reality is determined by computing power, comparing notes and volume of computing tasks. Despite the fact that few remote cloud servers can release computerised presence, it is to not possible to guarantee latency performance (Mahmoud, Amer & Ismail, 2021)

c. Security

The challenges with respect to transmission: Storing and presenting VR technology implementation are excessive and organisations now focus to develop standards to ease innovation and progress for immersive media events. However, there are also rising concerns with respect to security in AR and VR adoption. It is not as easy as they are not reliable enough and robust, specially to cater to actual industry demands. The additional challenges are security related, lack of familiarity of technology, substantial time-commitment for application of AR and VR and apprehensions in accepting a real substitute (Ruan and Xie, 2021).

Benefits of VR-AR

AR - VR applications are most relevant in entertainment, gaming, tourism, sports, etc. For example, UPSA parcel delivery to Navy UR trainings in safety of drivers and for Boeings, works is an aerospace company while using AR – VR, recorded 40% productiveness in electrical wing installation. Some research report stated that about the purpose of use of AR and VR which includes knowledge enrichment, training facilitation and experience enhancement (Jing et al. 2016, Kounans et. al. 2012).

a. Personalised Services

The innovations in AR - VR are needed for personalised services like tourism. Even tourists with disabilities experience the tourist place in same way as the ones without any disability. Personalising digital technology to suit the younger generation of tourists thus enhancing their customer experience and making information easily accessible.AR and VR help enhance the attractiveness of specific destinations and tourist products. Many of them personalised based on customer's requirements for accommodations, food and beverages, ancient cities, festivals, museums, activities, etc. (Ozdemir, 2021)

b. Reduced Customer Support

AR is also an interactive kind of technology which overlays the 3D model of product into real world to adjust the physical environment by doing this the end user can operate the 3D model by revolving and zooming in and out. This allows them to dynamically reach out to their commodities with less effort just like trying a dress or lip-stick or glasses suiting their face using the virtual mirror. This consequently results into reduced customer support (Hu, Luo, Chen, Lee, Zhou, & Wu, 2021).

c. Cross Selling Opportunities

VR & AR technology have profound impact on marketing practices and provide cross selling prospects cross vending is a strategy where a vender suggests complementary or improved products based on their needs past behaviour. Mobile AR apps are used in order to reduce friction in the buying process allowing consumers to try products at home by enabling virtual aimed at reducing online reducing costs (Hu, Luo, Chen, Lee, Zhou, & Wu, 2021).

Supporting evidences coming from varied sources indicates that VR and AR support the industry and organisations in providing real-time access to information, facilitate upskilling and reflecting real life involvements, enhance ingenuity in product design and improvement, allows distant employees to cooperate with one another (Finance online 2020).

Figure 5. Benefit of AR and VR reality: Survey report 1 (Finance Online, 2020)

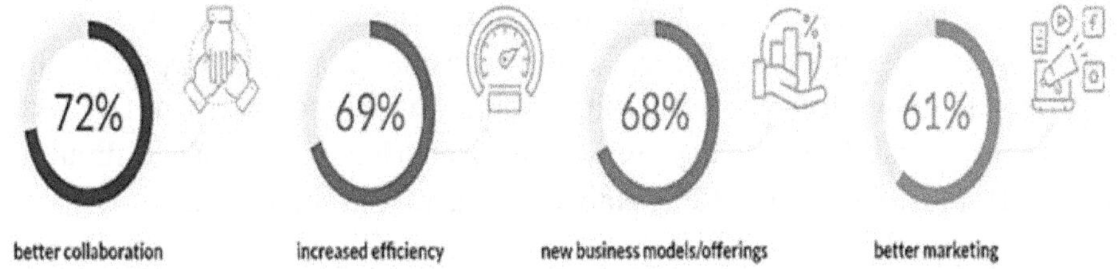

Figure 6. Benefit of AR and VR reality survey report 2 (Finance Online, 2020)

Usability Limitations

AR is an upcoming technology which is typically used to enhance stakeholder experience by providing digital content and feedback over the depiction of an actual scenario. Undoubtedly, VR technology had tremendous practical usability, was dependable and acknowledged worldwide. However, VR systems are not used extensively, as they are not cost-effective, complex, lack accessibility and maintainability of the application system. Since technology is into transformation, there is a need to improve the system applications. Further, this could be initiated as the VR system has evolved with use of smartphones and tablets that comes along with specially designed wearable technologies aimed to enhance users experience immersive VR. With the advent of disruptive technologies, there are still pertinent usability limitations and occurrence of system issues only to high prices complexity in development, limited accessibility to content, and unfamiliar feature and functionality. There are some common usability limitations of VR which include motion sickness, rendering speed and underestimated depth feel caused by software, hardware, human physical and perceptual limitations. MR and VR can be utilized for gaming and also in entertainment composite contents as VR apps are wired for operations on interactivity is not strong enough, which poses as limitations in the interactivity, portability of VR systems in the scenarios like remote communication (Ribeiro, Ramos, Safadinho, Reis, Rabadão, Barroso & Pereira, 2021).

Research Evidence on VR and AR Benefits

People often take advantage of AR and VR attractions when travelling and select locations based on these experiences. Using augmented reality (AR), you can add an artificial "virtual" object (CAD model, picture, symbol, and writing) to the external environment. Santi et al. (2021) note that AR is a computer graphic technique that is comprised of a real-time video streaming of the environment being augmented with artificial objects. AR (assisted robotics) is a key component of Industry 4.0, a movement whose goal is to increase production by introducing newer and more sophisticated technologies. Defining mixed reality as the link between actual and virtual is more in-depth and specific than just defining it as a blend of the two. Mix reality technology, a mix of virtual and actual content, help bring the two worlds together.

Research report which is related to AR Platforms for Radiology Teaching and Up skilling, Communication, and Medical Care, clearly details how the three departments of imaging have explored virtual reality and augmented reality for radiology. In the paper the authors first give an overview on virtual and augmented reality. Then the authors define the applications of VR and Arin various fields of radiology. They start with the applications of VR-AR for education in the field of diagnostic radiology, in which they discuss how AR and VR provide various opportunities for educating students and engaging patients. Towards the next part, the authors explain the application of AR and VR in interacting with radiology colleagues, citing patients and clinicians. The authors discuss how 2D and 3D imaging is helpful interacting with the clients and suggesting clinicians and patients. The most accurate and effective way to guide catheters, needles and/or wire from the skin entry site to the desired location is a technological problem for all interventional radiology treatments. And so, in the next part the authors discuss the purpose of AR - VR for helping in interventional radiology procedures. In conclusion the authors consider both AR and also VR have clinical potential in patient preoperative education preparation. In addition, technological advancements that enable further hardware minimization and improved image registration reliability will approve these technologies to revolutionise procedural outlining and patient interaction (Uppot, Laguna, McCarthy, De Novi, Phelps, Siegel, & Courtier, 2019).

Another research report on AR and VR states that VR - AR applications developed for tourism, present the most important studies emerging from this literature this literature was extracted from web of sciences and Scopus online libraries. This paper helps in discussing the overall studies that have been conducted over time on the application of VR and AR in tourism. It makes a citation network analysis of the main journal papers and their references uncovered in the literature, to find the most influential papers so far. The paper uses a text mining technique to find correlated patterns among discussions in the use of VR and AR in tourism and it recommends areas for further research, such as how VR and AR may be utilised to better understand customer behaviour or how different types of VR and AR adaptations can be more effective based on the consumers' age, gender, and other socio-psychological characteristics. (Loureiro, Guerreiro, & Ali, 2020)

AR and VR Applications and Hardware

The essential driver in the choice of hardware for AR operations is the score for final applications. HMD's are divided into VST (Vide-See-Through) and OST (Optical-See-Through) (Rolland & Fuchs, 2000). Using this VST hardware the user can see the real world in the device show. For example: applications in smart phones. In order to bridge the gap between AR and industry needs AR hardware can be carried by excruciating hardware into groups based on stand- alone devices in the processing unit.VST is based on the concept of seeing the world through cameras for example mobile phone based AR systems. When a user uses video see through devices through AR displays, they always see the world as represented in the camera and they don't see the physical world directly. This has a few advantages as well as disadvantages. The advantage being that as the information is usually merged in camera – image space, visually coherent representation is easy whereas while using video see through AR displays the user may get disengaged from reality and social issues and consequently may result into disabling mutual eye contact. Spatial Augmented reality or prognosis plotting is the use of projectors to supplement a real environment with the help and assistance of virtual information. AR experiences can also be create using optical -see-through displays which are semi-transparent in the users view. Optical-see-through displays resemble normal glasses which allows the user to see the real environment undeterred biotechnical limitations, thus making them more suitable for multiple scenarios (Langlotz et al, 2021).

In order to experience AR it is pivotal to have the right tools for it, especially as consumer spending accounts for 15% on AR hardware. Social media prevalence and increased use of smart phones has resulted into consumers' awareness with respect to AR hardware. The demand for AR headsets is steadily increasing and consumers are purchasing them for work as well as entertainment. Other than Google glass which was launched in 2013 many other hardware's such as smartphones and tablets are extremely popular with the consumers. Thus there are fewer concerns with respect to seamless utilization and privacy when it comes to hardware. As technological innovations are expedited AR hardware will consequently get a significant boost. In 2015, only 0.17 million units of AR headsets were sold and it is projected that by 2025, AR and VR headset consignments worldwide are expected to reach 43.5 Million (Statista, 2020). AR hardware can be utilized as a strategic tool to enhance customer experience and even business can improvise the quality of their process, it should not be looked upon just as a gaming tool.

c. Software

For tracking industrial applications depending on symbols like road signs, simultaneous localization and mapping (SLAM) technology may be used to perceive the environment for self-governing applications without any operator. Currently for this purpose Laser-guided vehicle technology is being used. It is important to bridge gaps between AR and industry needs by allowing reverse engineering of objects by advanced software packages framed by cameras, real and virtual objects shall be absolutely interchangeable.

CONCLUSION

This paper presented provides the reader an in-depth understanding of VR and AR fostering strength to Industries 4.0. We discussed the difference between the AR, VR, MR and XR .The work also highlighted VR and AR with relevant and contemporary statistical information in terms of growth, user and market share. The paper incorporated an in-depth review of the augmented reality software which includes video see through devices, optical see-through devices, embedded tracking systems and tools. The paper has well comprehended and analysed the applications and adoption of VR and AR in the sectors of health-care, real estate, tourism, sports. Along with understanding the key challenges in AR/VR adoption. The current work thus ensure the advancement of the body of knowledge and henceforth extending theoretical implications.

REFERENCES

Alizadehsalehi, S., Hadavi, A., & Huang, J. C. (2021). Assessment of AEC Students' Performance Using BIM-into-VR. *Applied Sciences (Basel, Switzerland)*, *11*(7), 3225. doi:10.3390/app11073225

Ayoub & Pulijala. (2019). The application of virtual reality and augmented reality in Oral & Maxillofacial Surgery. *BMC Oral Health*, *19*(1), 1-8.

Birt, J., & Vasilevski, N. (2021). Comparison of single and multiuser immersive mobile virtual reality usability in construction education. *Journal of Educational Technology & Society*, *24*(2), 93–106.

Carbone, M., Domeneghetti, D., Cutolo, F., D'Amato, R., Cigna, E., Parchi, P. D., Gesi, M., Morelli, L., Ferrari, M., & Ferrari, V. (2021). Can Liquid Lenses Increase Depth of Field in Head Mounted Video See-Through Devices? *Journal of Imaging*, *7*(8), 138. doi:10.3390/jimaging7080138 PMID:34460773

Chen, Y. (2020). An overview of augmented reality technology. *Journal of Physics: Conference Series* (Vol. 1237, No. 2, p. 022082). doi:10.1088/1742-6596/1575/1/012027

Cipresso, P., & Giglioli, I. A. C. (2018). The Past, Present, and Future of Virtual. *Frontiers in Psychology*.

Colley, A., Suoheimo, M., & Häkkilä, J. (2020). Exploring VR and AR Tools for Service Design. *19th International Conference on Mobile and Ubiquitous Multimedia*, 309-311. 10.1145/3428361.3432074

De Ponti, R., Marazzato, J., Maresca, A. M., Rovera, F., Carcano, G., & Ferrario, M. M. (2020). Pre-graduation medical training including virtual reality during COVID-19 pandemic: A report on students' perception. *BMC Medical Education*, *20*(1), 1–7. doi:10.1186/s12909-020-02245-8 PMID:32977781

de Reget, A. (2020). The Virtual Reality Chain. *Business Horizons*, *63*(6), 737–748. doi:10.1016/j.bushor.2020.08.002

Diekfuss, J. A., Bonnette, S., Hogg, J. A., Riehm, C., Grooms, D. R., Singh, H., Anand, M., Slutsky-Ganesh, A. B., Wilkerson, G. B., & Myer, G. D. (2021). Practical training strategies to apply neuro-mechanistic motor learning principles to facilitate adaptations towards injury-resistant movement in youth. *Journal of Science in Sport and Exercise*, *3*(1), 3–16. doi:10.1007/s42978-020-00083-0

Farshid, M., Paschen, J., Eriksson, T., & Kietzmann, J. (2018). Go boldly! Explore augmented reality (AR), virtual reality (VR), and mixed reality (MR) for business. *Business Horizons*, *61*(5), 657–663. doi:10.1016/j.bushor.2018.05.009

Gettecla. (2018). *Augmented Reality and Accessibility.* https://gettecla.com/blogs/news/augmented-reality-and-accessibility

Grandviewresearch. (2020). *Augmented Reality Market Size, Share & Trends Analysis Report By Component, By Display (HMD & Smart Glass, HUD, Handheld Devices), By Application, By Region, And Segment Forecasts, 2021 – 2028.* https://www.grandviewresearch.com/industry-analysis/augmented-reality-market

Havard, V., Jeanne, B., Lacomblez, M., & Baudry, D. (2019). Digital twin and virtual reality: A co-simulation environment for design and assessment of industrial workstations. *Production & Manufacturing Research*, *7*(1), 472–489. doi:10.1080/21693277.2019.1660283

Imoize, A. L., Adedeji, O., Tandiya, N., & Shetty, S. (2021). 6G Enabled Smart Infrastructure for Sustainable Society: Opportunities, Challenges, and Research Roadmap. *Sensors (Basel)*, *21*(5), 1709. doi:10.3390/s21051709 PMID:33801302

Ji, Q., Deng, H., Zhang, H., Jiang, W., Zhong, F., & Rao, F. (2021). Optical See-through 2D/3D Compatible Display Using Variable-Focus Lens and Multiplexed Holographic Optical Elements. *Photonics*, *8*(8), 297. doi:10.3390/photonics8080297

Jones, P. R., Somoskeöy, T., Chow-Wing-Bom, H., & Crabb, D. P. (2020). Seeing other perspectives: Evaluating the use of virtual and augmented reality to simulate visual impairments (OpenVisSim). *NPJ Digital Medicine*, *3*(1), 1–9. doi:10.1038/s41746-020-0242-6 PMID:32195367

Kersten, T. P., & Edler, D. (2020). *Special issue "methods and applications of virtual and augmented reality in geo-information sciences". Deutsche Gesellschaft für Photogrammetrie, Fernerkundung und Geoinformation*. DGPF.

Khandelwal, K., & Upadhyay, A. K. (2021). Virtual reality interventions in developing and managing human resources. *Human Resource Development International*, *24*(2), 219–233. doi:10.1080/13678868.2019.1569920

Khandelwal, K., & Upadhyay, A. K. (2021). Virtual reality interventions in developing and managing human resources. *Human Resource Development International*, *24*(2), 219–233. doi:10.1080/13678868.2019.1569920

Küçük, S., Kapakin, S., & Göktaş, Y. (2016). Learning anatomy via mobile augmented reality: Effects on achievement and cognitive load. *Anatomical Sciences Education*, *9*(5), 411–421. doi:10.1002/ase.1603 PMID:26950521

Kumar, A. M., & Dutta, R. (2021). Development of an augmented reality-based scaffold to improve the learning experience of engineering students in embedded system course. *Computer Applications in Engineering Education*, *29*(1), 244–257. doi:10.1002/cae.22245

Loureiro, S. M. C., Guerreiro, J., & Ali, F. (2020). *20 years of research on virtual reality and augmented reality in tourism context: A text-mining approach* (Vol. 77). Tourism Management.

Mahmoud, H. H. H., Amer, A. A., & Ismail, T. (2021). 6G: A comprehensive survey on technologies, applications, challenges, and research problems. *Transactions on Emerging Telecommunications Technologies*, *32*(4), e4233. doi:10.1002/ett.4233

Markets and Market. (2020a). *Virtual market reality. Online Document.* https://www.marketsandmarkets.com/Market-Reports/reality-applications-market-458.html

Markets and Market. (2020b). *Augmented Reality and Virtual Reality – M&A Private Equity Investment, and Patent Filing Analysis.* https://www.marketsandmarkets.com/Market-Reports/reality-applications-market-458.html

Online, F. (2020). 20 current augmented reality trends and predictions in 21//22 and beyond. *Finance Online*. https://financesonline.com/augmented-reality-trends/

Ozdemir, M. A. (2021). Virtual Reality (VR) and Augmented Reality (AR) Technologies for Accessibility and Marketing in the Tourism Industry. ICT Tools and Applications for Accessible Tourism, 277-301.

Pirandello. (2021). A Journey into Artworks: Storytelling in Augmented Reality and Mixed Reality. *Cinergie–Il Cinema e le altre Arti*, *19*, 135-145.

Rankohi, S., & Waugh, L. (2014). Review and analysis of augmented reality literature for construction industry. *Visualization in Engineering*, *1*(1), 1–18.

Ribeiro, R., Ramos, J., Safadinho, D., Reis, A., Rabadão, C., Barroso, J., & Pereira, A. (2021). Web AR Solution for UAV Pilot Training and Usability Testing. *Sensors (Basel)*, *21*(4), 1456. doi:10.3390/s21041456 PMID:33669733

Ruan, J., & Xie, D. (2021). Networked VR: State of the Art, Solutions, and Challenges. *Electronics (Basel)*, *10*(2), 166. doi:10.3390/electronics10020166

Santi, G. M., Ceruti, A., Liverani, A., & Osti, F. (2021). Augmented Reality in Industry 4.0 and Future Innovation Programs. *Technologies*, *9*(2), 33. doi:10.3390/technologies9020033

Schuemie, M. J., Van Der Straaten, P., Krijn, M., & Van Der Mast, C. A. (2001). Research on presence in virtual reality: A survey. *Cyberpsychology & Behavior*, *4*(2), 183–201. doi:10.1089/109493101300117884 PMID:11710246

Telecoms. (2018). *A new reality awaits: AR and VR the next big platforms in Telecoms?* https://www.deltapartnersgroup.com/new-reality-awaits-are-ar-and-vr-next-big-platforms

Tone, S. R. J. (2000). Haptic feedback: A brief history from telepresence to virtual reality. In *International Workshop on Haptic Human-Computer Interaction* (pp. 1-16). Springer.

Tosto, C., Hasegawa, T., Mangina, E., Chifari, A., Treacy, R., Merlo, G., & Chiazzese, G. (2021). Exploring the effect of an augmented reality literacy programme for reading and spelling difficulties for children diagnosed with ADHD. *Virtual Reality (Waltham Cross)*, *25*(3), 879–894. doi:10.1007/s10055-020-00485-z

Uppot, R. N., Laguna, B., McCarthy, C. J., De Novi, G., Phelps, A., Siegel, E., & Courtier, J. (2019). Implementing virtual and augmented reality tools for radiology education and training, communication, and clinical care.". *Radiology*, *291*(3), 570–580. doi:10.1148/radiol.2019182210 PMID:30990383

Vergel, R. S., Tena, P. M., Yrurzum, S. C., & Cruz-Neira, C. (2020). A comparative evaluation of a virtual reality table and a HoloLens-based augmented reality system for anatomy training. *IEEE Transactions on Human-Machine Systems*, *50*(4), 337–348. doi:10.1109/THMS.2020.2984746

Westmattelmann, D., Grotenhermen, J. G., Sprenger, M., Rand, W., & Schewe, G. (2021). Apart we ride together: The motivations behind users of mixed-reality sports. *Journal of Business Research*, *134*, 316–328. doi:10.1016/j.jbusres.2021.05.044

Zhang, G. (2021). Bridging the intention–behaviour gap: Effect of altruistic motives on developers' action towards green redevelopment of industrial brownfields. *Sustainability*, *13*(2). Advance online publication. doi:10.3390/su13020977

Chapter 5
Examination of Automation in Human Resource Practices:
A Study of Effective Use of Technology in Employee Induction Programmes in County Clare (Ireland)

Dawid Glowski
Technological University of the Shannon, Ireland

June O'Byrne-Prior
Technological University of the Shannon, Ireland

Noelle O'Connor
Technological University of the Shannon, Ireland

ABSTRACT

This research will study the effective use of technology in employee programmes in County Clare (Ireland). A strong onboarding programme with the assistance of emerging technology can decide a firm's success. This research explores the new technological advancements made in automation and artificial intelligence as well as data analytics and its application to the onboarding experience. The research objectives were established to facilitate the direction of the examination. In order to achieve the objectives, primary and secondary research was conducted. The analysis of the findings interprets data by comparing and contrasting results between participants and current literature to measure synergy between current knowledge and current practitioners' opinions. The research has shown a deep enthusiasm for new efficient technological advancements for the HR department in businesses.

DOI: 10.4018/979-8-3693-1103-5.ch005

INTRODUCTION

The department which holds businesses together, known as HR (Human Resources) has evolved from its traditional roles. This is all thanks to the Smart HR4.0 developments from the new industrial era of Business 4.0. New technological capabilities such as automation tools, AI and analytics are on the rise and are transforming businesses. Specifically looking at the onboarding process, the researchers is curious as to how can this technology be applied ethically and without handing complete control to technology. The choice of the topic is derived from the interest in effective HRM (Human Resource Management), and with emerging technologies, how the department can take its functionality to the next level. The aim of this research will be to examine the importance of human resource management and how it utilizes technological advances to enhance the onboarding experience of new employees. The aim is also to critique the balance of automation to human interaction to ensure the process is effective. The objectives of the research are as follow:

1) Assessing the value of the department of Human Resources in Businesses
2) Measuring the effectivity of current implementation of Automation, AI and Data Analytics in Human Resources during the onboarding process in Ireland
3) Assessing the challenges with implementing automation and AI technology in Human resources
4) Establishing the elements of onboarding which cannot be fully automated / replaced human interaction through AI bots

LITERATURE REVIEW

Induction has a profound influence on an organisations ability to maintain a competitive level of employee retention. It is a vital step in the human resource management process and follows a logical flow in the new recruits first engagement with the company (Salau, Falola, & Akinbode, 2014). Similarly, CIPD (Induction, 2020) defines induction as the process of an employee's adjustment or their acclimatisation to their new role and working environment. According to Antonacopoulou & Güttel (Staff induction practices and organizational socialization: A review and extention of the debate, 2010), staff induction and socialization are key elements to enabling new recruits in becoming functioning members by supporting organizational recreation through sustaining and "renewing aspects of the organization's character". El-Shamy's research suggests that for most new employees, the four firsts are key periods during the induction process (Dynamic Induction: Games, Activities and Ideas to Revitalize your Employee Induction Process, 2003). The four firsts are 1) the first hour 2) the first day 3) the first week and 4) the first month (El-Shamy, 2003). The research suggests that the effectiveness of a company's induction process during these four periods can affect the retention of employees. Onboarding, being a label describing the process of induction, is clarified by Bauer (Onboarding New Employees: Maximizing Success, 2010), to have four distinct levels in the form of four C's;

1. Compliance in teaching policy-related rules and regulations and basic legal policies,
2. Clarification in explaining the new role, tasks and responsibilities and expectations,
3. Culture in introducing recruits to company norms - both formal and informal and
4. Connection referring to interpersonal relationships & networks new hires engage in.

A key purpose that induction serves is explored in the research of Bharthvajan & Kavitha (Impact of Employee Satisfaction towards Induction Training Program, 2019) which clarifies that an organisations achievements rely on the maintenance of a high-quality workforce. Their research explains how training is essential to enhance the workforce's ability to maintain high quality standards and maintain competitivity (Bharthvajan & Kavitha, 2019). A successful induction programme can result in job enrichment and maintain a cheerful outlook amongst employees by embracing culture and practices from day one during the induction process (Salau, Falola, & Akinbode, 2014). Enthusiastic training programmes aid employees in collaboration from an early stage and giving the recruit the tools, they need to achieve company objectives which gives organisations a strong and vibrant strategy (Bharthvajan & Kavitha, 2019). A good induction programme directly correlates to customer satisfaction (Salau, Falola, & Akinbode, 2014). When new recruits are provided with tailored training alongside adequate supports throughout the onboarding period, they will benefit both the company through being able to provide a high level of service, and provides them with job satisfaction (Salau, Falola, & Akinbode, 2014).

Industries are affected by employee retention. According to Ivana & Chiripuci (Human Ressource practices in improving employee retention, 2020), modern organisations are suffering from employees' turnover loss, and in order to stay competitive it is necessary to shine focus retaining skilful employees. Turnover is a major concern for organisations today due to the time and monetary costs to replace employees (Ivana & Chiripuci, 2020). Thus, by reducing employee turnover by taking advantage of strong retention processes through strategic induction practices can hold onto a strong labour force for longer (Bharthvajan & Kavitha,

2019). The findings of the research conducted by Salau et al. (Induction and Staff Attitude towards Retention and Organizational Effectiveness, 2014) agree with these statements as a well packaged induction programme has significant positive influence on employee behaviour and attitude towards retention and effectiveness. During the survey, 72% of the respondents stated that their organisations induction programmes were psychologically incorporated to their work environment, and this exposes new employees to the history and structure of the firm as well as core corporate values and activities of competitors (Salau, Falola, & Akinbode, 2014). The researchers will explain further in the literature review how emerging technology can facilitate the effectiveness of a strong induction model.

Examination of Past, Present, and Potential Trends

The researchers also explored how induction has been conducted in recent times. There have been advancements in human resources due to the fast-paced economic growth of the current century (Amour Al Nooumani & Taqui Syed, 2020). Technological innovations are emerging, driving firms to restructure their departments (Amour Al Nooumani & Taqui Syed, 2020). This is also evident in the research of (Ahmed, 2018) whom explains the automation capabilities HR practitioners can take advantage of such as chatbots and 'AI' (Artificial Intelligence). Recent technological endeavours have resulted in improved performance in HR functions (Amour Al Nooumani & Taqui Syed, 2020). The current 'hype' of AI is making it a trending advancement, but this tool can only be taken to the next level when their algorithms contain accuracy and completeness in order to make it completely user friendly (Ahmed, 2018). The current challenge with it is 'narrow AI,' which relates to the ease of use and providing specific solutions for HR practitioners (Ahmed, 2018). Chatbots are helping employees access information quickly by offering answers to common employee questions thus reducing time spent on tedious tasks (Ahmed, 2018).

In human resource management processes, the utilisation of AI technology creates massive economic benefits as well as improving efficiency in processes like induction (Jia, Guo, Li, Li, & Chen, 2018). Maximising the potential of AI in HRM will increase the value of the department and its productivity (Jia, Guo, Li, Li, & Chen, 2018). A well packaged induction programme that takes advantage of beneficial tools such as AI can influence employee attitude (Salau, Falola, & Akinbode, 2014). Induction programmes have been constantly changing and improving through regular review and this results in employee loyalty and employees having positive attitudes towards work from early-stage employment (Salau, Falola, & Akinbode, 2014). The research of Ahmed (ARTIFICIAL INTELLIGENCE IN HR, 2018) suggests the AI offers opportunities for improvements within human resources such as personalised employee experiences. On their first day, hires undoubtedly have questions and want to meet certain individuals in the organisations as well as acquiring information. In Ahmed's research (ARTIFICIAL INTELLIGENCE IN HR, 2018), he explains how AI could provide training suggestions as well as names the hire should connect with on day one, contact information or locations. This can save time employees and improve their job satisfaction throughout their first days.

Examination of Emerging Advancements

With the emergence of the fourth Industrial Revolution, known as 'Business 4.0,' many highly innovative and powerful technologies were created with immense potential to change businesses on many levels (Deloitte, 2017). Business 4.0 is a framework derived from business behaviours that augments digital advantage to generate customer value (TATA Consultancy Services, 2019). The framework is all about embracing technology and the positive changes it brings (Alam & Khan, 2020). Four business behaviours emerged as a result of business 4.0;

- Creating exponential value: new opportunities of delivering value through AI and big data creating linkages and cross-selling,
- Driving mass personalisation: digital technologies enabling scaled customisation by using analytics and big data tools,
- Leveraging ecosystems: redefining industry boundaries, increasing competition and collaboration,
- Embracing risk: providing agility and flexibility, technology allows businesses to embrace risks (TATA Consultancy Services, 2019).

Furthermore, four technology pillars enable the behaviours as stated by TATA Consultancy Services (Understanding Business 4.0™:The New-Age Transformation Paradigm, 2019) and Alam & Khan (Business 4.0-A New Revolution, 2020);

- Agile: faster response to customers & competitors, innovative approach to making future decisions,
- Automation: through analytics and AI, controlling production, delivery, increasing productivity and value, humans moving away from repetitive tasks,
- Intelligent: data science, natural language and cognitive programmed capabilities enabling machines to act autonomously, taking human capability to next level,
- Cloud: providing pool of IT resources and services through the internet, supporting mobile operations

As a result, human resources departmental value increases as a result of transitioning into business 4.0 and this reconsiders the role of human resources from a service process to undertaking "an active participation in the creative process using digital competencies" (Sergi, Ključnikov, Popkova, Bogoviz, & Lobova, 2022).

The HR domain has been affected by the business 4.0 phenomenon and it has disrupted its traditional roles. Smart HR 4.0 emerged and has changed functions of human resources such as recruitment, onboarding, learning and development, crowd-sourced feedback and social sharing (Sivathanu & Pillai, 2018). Technological advancements from RPA (Robotic Process Automation) and chatbots to AI and machine learning have opened doors in the HR world, leading to the development of "Smart HR" (Deloitte, 2017). Alongside the technological innovations emerging from the industry 4.0, Smart HR has facilitated the customisation of personalised individual onboarding/induction programmes whilst moving away from the traditional universal model (Sivathanu & Pillai, 2018). Thanks to the agile technology pillar, the layers of communication would flatten and allowing for faster decision-making (Sivathanu & Pillai, 2018) (Alam & Khan, 2020) (TATA Consultancy Services, 2019). This re-organisation of management structure can lead to decentralisation of power allowing project teams to work autonomously and adjust quicker to meet project requirements whilst maintaining a constant communication channel between employees and new hires (Sivathanu & Pillai, 2018).

Human resources will embrace automation as an absence of innovation and automation in HR nowadays can endure a crippling impact on a modern workspace (Amour Al Nooumani & Taqui Syed, 2020). Consequently, it is necessary to redefine HR functions in organisations in order to stay competitive and retain success in highly competitive markets (Amour Al Nooumani & Taqui Syed, 2020). This idea is also evident in the research of Alam & Khan (Business 4.0-A New Revolution, 2020), as it highlights the need to embracing change. When innovations appear in the business environment, a firm can either act accordingly and adapt or remain with their old ways which can make or break a firm's competitiveness and cause it to become 'extinct' (Alam & Khan, 2020). It is stated by Ahmed (Artificial Intelligence in HR, 2018), that automation can take over repetitive, low-value tasks for humans to focus on more strategic work such as mentoring and providing continuous feedback which his essential in the onboarding period. A great point made by Sivathanu & Pillai (Smart HR 4.0 – how industry 4.0 is disrupting HR, 2018) is the use of new technology such as Augmented reality (AR) and Virtual Reality (VR) could assist new hires in providing more guidance with processes layout to ensure maximum productivity is derived. Their research states the main benefits of Smart HR 4.0 include the following: developing and retaining new-age talent, quick and efficient HR operations and leaner HR departments.

Ethical Use of Automation

Automation in HR can raise a number of issues in regard to sensitive information gathering and sharing. As HR can be a more complicated part of the business as it processes copious amounts of information (Amour Al Nooumani & Taqui Syed, 2020). AI cannot distinguish the level of sensitivity of employee information without proper programming and regulation (Ahmed, 2018). Establishing what kind of information can be shared as well as who should have access and editing rights to it should be done before the implementation of AI technology in HRM to avoid security and privacy issues (Amour Al Nooumani & Taqui Syed, 2020). HR practitioners should use the European Laws in correlation to their AI usage in order to follow legislation in correct GDPR practices (European Commission, 2018). According to the European Commission (Are there restrictions on the use of automated decision-making?, 2018), "individuals should not be subject to a decision that is based solely on automated processing (such as algorithms) and that is legally binding, or which significantly affects them". The use of automation is only researchers in some cases such as; decision is necessary (no other way to achieve goal), contract purposes, an EU or national law allows the use of algorithms and provides safeguards in order to protect individual rights, legitimate interests and freedoms and when the individual has given clear consent to automated processing (European Commission, 2018).

Edge (The Necessary Evolution of Privacy Program Automation, 2022) provides a two-step framework on safe data automation. Firstly, having a data map of personal data held and processed by an organisation which serves as a foundation for any privacy programme, it can be sourced using an automated data discovery system (Edge, 2022). Then using the Data discovery system to spot gaps in data or discrepancies and standardizing data (Edge, 2022). Finally, the data in other areas of a firm's privacy programme can be tackled (Edge, 2022). It is also vital that organisations establish whether the technology which manages confidential information is built and managed on the inside or given the manage by an outside party (Amour Al Nooumani & Taqui Syed, 2020).

What Should and Should Not Be Automated

The researchers found that AI and Automation have a great benefit in industry. According to Ahmed (Artificial Intelligence in HR, 2018), AI is a tool, and it gives humans a hand in repetitive tasks. Similarly, George & Thomas (Integration of Artificial Intelligence in Human Resource, 2019) describes AI as a support function that can assist humans in administrative and monotonous work whilst HR professionals can concentrate on a strategic level. Gikopoulus (Alongside, not against: balancing man with machine in the HR function, 2019) also points out that

AI has the ability to compliment human employees by providing more insight and eliminating bias. The need for high efficiency means it is time to allow technology to take over monotonous work there are good at so that HR practitioners can focus on what they are good at (George & Thomas, 2019). As mentioned by Gikopoulus (Alongside, not against: balancing man with machine in the HR function, 2019), HR professionals take a lot of time developing an effective onboarding experience to all new hires, and with the use of AI, the burden of onboarding presentation prep amongst other things can be passed on to technology. Having a bot which can guide new employees through orientation and training, answer frequently asked questions, routine questions on setting up printers, password resets or book holidays can be timesaving (Gikopoulus, 2019). Using the AI can help distribute vast amounts of data to hires in less time at a higher rate than people (Ahmed, 2018).

AI can be taken advantage of when accessing well-being and employee engagement by identifying behaviours that can cause poor work performance and spotting patterns in employee work rate (Ahmed, 2018). This way, personalised training plans can be implemented in order to gain competitive benefit and it can be caught early on in the employee's patterns (Ahmed, 2018) (Bharthvajan & Kavitha, 2019). AI is used to gather vast amounts of data as it can be collected at an exponentially higher rate than any HR practitioner (Ahmed, 2018).

Although AI offers much advantages in quality data sorting and sending, problems can arise when it comes to confidentiality of documentation and policies (George & Thomas, 2019) (Ahmed, 2018). Measures have to be taken by HR professionals in conjunction with automation and artificial intelligence to ensure proper use and secure filing is in place (George & Thomas, 2019).

The researchers found that there are advantages to automation and there are various functions in HR which should be automated, but on the other hand, there are things AI cannot replace in human functioning. According to Gikopoulus (Alongside, not against: balancing man with machine in the HR function, 2019), even though automation in HR is an emerging trend, the human touch cannot be fully replaced. Their research highlights that although the integration of AI and automation into HR is occurring in businesses worldwide and technology is taking on more 'human elements' in HR roles, there is a significant difference between man and machine (Gikopoulus, 2019). Technology can negatively affect a business by not being able to make cultural decisions and human can, and pair employees in teams without knowing whether they can physically work together (Gikopoulus, 2019). Ahmed (Artificial Intelligence in HR, 2018) agrees with this as his research states that all company's people management decisions are often culture based, and AI does not have the capability to do such thing. "Human empathy, human interaction, emotion cannot be replicated by machines, first impressions in firms in induction require all three to make the employee feel comfortable and part of the team" (Ahmed, 2018).

According to George & Thomas (Integration of Artificial Intelligence in Human Resource, 2019), HRs should be focusing on dedicating time on employees and business partners and thinking on a more strategic level. AI lacks the quality of empathy and human interaction which HR practitioners have in order to handpick candidates, leave them personal feedback and get to know them on a personal level (Ahmed, 2018). Their valuable time can be used planning, organising, and setting up social HR activities (George & Thomas, 2019). Thus, upon reviewing the research of Ahmed (Artificial Intelligence in HR, 2018), Gikopoulus (Alongside, not against: balancing man with machine in the HR function, 2019) and George & Thomas (Integration of Artificial Intelligence in Human Resource, 2019), using automation can hugely benefit HR practitioners by allowing them to dedicate more time to relationship building, creativity, strategic thinking, problem-solving and emotional intelligence.

METHODOLOGY

The researchers began with a brief discussion of research philosophy and the most appropriate one being chosen. The research approaches the researchers took are outlined through a comparison of quantitative and qualitative research and the clear compatibility of the qualitative data research approach to the study. The design of the research through the use of secondary and primary data will be discussed and their advantages and disadvantages. Setting and participants sampling was discussed in order to establish suitable and achievable study outcomes and the instrument chosen is also discussed in detail followed by limitations met during the research. The researchers is carrying out a primary research study as there is a lack of secondary research on the topic of balanced use of automation and human elements in human resource practices in businesses in County Clare.

Research Philosophy

The definition of philosophy is clearly outlined by Kenaphoom (Introduction to Research Philosophy, 2021) as a study of general and fundamental problems which are concerned with reality, knowledge and values of the world. The essence of philosophy is to investigate answers to questions using a critical and systematic approach with the aid of rational argument (Kenaphoom, 2021). Research is defined as a careful study to discover new knowledge or information through research findings, which are answer research questions based on the core principles of philosophy (Kenaphoom, 2021).

There are four main research philosophies used by researchers (Dudovskiy, 2017). Pragmatism suggests there are multiple ways of interpreting the world and conducting research using a combination of different approaches to provide a broader understanding (Kaushik & Walsh, 2019). Positivism is associated with experimentation and quantitative research as it's considered a deductive and objective research philosophy where a theory's hypo research is tested by a true/false outcome (Ryan, 2018). Realism, direct and critical, relies on independence of reality from the human mind. This philosophy is a scientific approach (Dubovskiy, 2016). Finally, the interpretivism paradigm focuses on individuals' reasoning, motivations and beliefs by using qualitative research methods (Nickerson, 2022).

The researchers used interpretivism to find an answer to the posed research question. Due to the social approach needed for the research questions, interpretivism was the most compatible method. As shown in Fig 3.1, interpretivism was the most compatible research philosophy to choose (Žukauskas, Vveinhardt, & Andriukaitienė, 2018). The method was used to derive qualitative data in primary research in the form of questionnaires containing open-ended questions.

Research Approach

The research approach of this research was focused on a mono-method qualitative data research approach. The researchers decided this was the most effective method as the research question required qualitative data to answer a human resource efficiency problem and the scope of the research was focused on an organisational level through HRM as seen in Fig 3.

Qualitative Research

Qualitative research is accurately defined by Flick (An introduction to qualitative research, 2014) as "...analysing subjective meaning or the social production of issues, events, or practices by collecting non-standardised data and analysing texts and images rather than number and statistics". There are numerous advantages to using qualitative research. Lack of limitations in open-ended questions which yields rich data, greater flexibility in data collection and analysis and qualitative data collection is more targeted (Queirós, Faria, & Almeida, 2017). There are also some disadvantages in using qualitative data research. Sample size of qualitative data research is small, bias can exist during question creation which can lead to inaccurate results, and it can be time-consuming therefore it's difficult to find volunteers (Queirós, Faria, & Almeida, 2017).

Quantitative Research

Quantitative data research is effectively described by DCU Library (HSS Research Methodologies: Quantitative Research, 2022) as collecting and analysing data which is structured and can be represented numerically which make statistical analysis direct and easily measured.

There are advantages to using quantitative research. The method is efficient and fast to get results and analyse them, large data sample size and unbiased statistics (Williams, 2021).

There are also disadvantages to using quantitative research. Data is restricted as there is no deeper meaning or explanation, data measures a specific moment in time and there is little to no flexibility of data during analysis (Rahman, 2016). Upon careful consideration, the researchers chose qualitative research. This method was considered most compatible with the research question as it deals with a social ethics problem which required deeper meaningful data gathered in the form of open-ended questions in a questionnaire.

Research Design

The researchers carried out their secondary research using different sources. Books and journal articles were used and were prioritized during the research process because they yielded the most valuable data. Websites were also sourced due to many respectable researchers publishing their primary research on corporate sites. Some blogs were also used due to the socio-ethical nature of the research. Although secondary research was conducted, the researchers found there was a lack of research in the ethical use of automation in human resource practices, therefore primary research was conducted. This research required primary research to find out what hr practitioners think of the emerging automation and AI technology which affect hr practices and the effective ethical balance of human element and machine learning. The researchers described the way this is done further into the research.

Setting and Participants Sampling

The primary research took place in the region of Clare, in Ireland. This geographic location was chosen as there are many respectable enterprises in this vicinity. The research targeted human resource practitioners as well as managers and studied their view on effective human resource management, implementation of automation and AI technology and ethical considerations with finding the balance between the human element and automation during onboarding. The small sample size was adapted due to the nature of the study being phenomenological.

Instrumentation: Interviews

The researchers firstly decided to brainstorm data collecting instruments. They chose to use the interview. In order to choose the most effective type of the instrument, the researchers looked at the advantages and disadvantages of interviews. The aim of the interviews was to find out the view of Management in Businesses on the importance of HR departments, emerging trends of HR 4.0, automation and artificial intelligence, and the challenges with balanced automation/human interaction in the induction stage of the employee journey.

Types of Interviews

Online Video Interviews were considered by calling potential participants and asking live questions and recording answers. This would have saved time and would prove to be inexpensive if using free video communication applications such as Google Meet or Microsoft Teams. Asking big questions to participants without prior information granted can make them feel uncomfortable or give a poor-quality reply rather than thinking of a more valuable answer. A disadvantage of using online video interviews is the unreliability of stable internet connectivity, this could hinder the results of answers derived and this could lead to a risk of loss of data.

In-house interviews would have involved travelling to meeting points with the participant and questioning each participant face to face. An advantage of this method is that answers would be deeply explained, the topic could be flexibly talked around and additional data could be noted. A disadvantage could be the participants unwilling to meet the researchers at their home or workplace for many reasons and the time cost of the method was a significant factor when considering which method suited the researchers the most. The cost of travel was discouraging as participants weren't located in close proximity.

Telephone interviews were also considered when deciding the interview method. Advantages of telephone interviews include flexibility as they can be conducted at the discretion of the participant, and they don't require any travel. Disadvantages of telephone interviews include no evidence of body language to show the interest of topic by participant, using the sense of hearing only compared to a face-to-face interview is less stimulating and problems can arise due to service issues.

Upon careful consideration, the researchers decided that in-house interviews were the most effective method of collecting data. Otter is a software used for recording and transcribing interviews and conversations. The app allowed a few free exports of audio and transcript from the app onto the computer which kept the cost of conducting field research lower.

The interview questions were created using three main themes which were shared by email alongside the consent form as it made it easier for the participants to think deeply on the topic and allowing them to grasp an idea of topics being discussed the interview. The researchers decreased the risk of the research participation proposal email e-mail being ignored by making a phone call before sending the interview proposal email discussing the details of the study. Originally, the researchers planned to perform online interviews due to their accessibility and travel-free nature, but due to latency issues, in-house interviews were conducted.

Types of Questions for Interviews

The researchers considered three themes when constructing the questions for the interview;

- Value of HRM in Business
- Current Implementation of Automation, AI, Analytics
- Challenges Related to Implementation of Automation, AI & Analytics in HR

Open-ended questions have a different nature to others as they provide unexpected results and allow the respondent to freely talk around the question, yielding original and valuable research data. This poses a problem in analysing the findings obtained. Multiple-choice questions offer a selection of answers for respondents to select which reduces the originality and deeper meaning of the answers.

Two choice questions, having only two options such as yes or no is the easiest form of questionnaire and makes it easier for respondents to answer. The researchers felt the open-ended questions were the most applicable to suit the needs of the researchers' research questions. The open nature of the questions allows participants to add more valuable to each question answered and the researchers would gain more raw data as a result.

Interview Schedule

A total of six interviews were planned over the course of two weeks, with each interview being conducted in-house of the participants, which was in their work offices. Three interviews took place in person and the researchers used the application Otter in order to record and transcribe each entire conversation. Two participants declined the meetings due to emergency meetings with their workplaces, therefore their responses were recorded through email. One participant made no further contact so their interview was discarded and the researchers focused on extracting valuable data from the rest of the participants. The duration of the interview was between twelve and twenty minutes.

The Otter app allowed for instant transcription of live audio recordings, which later had to be adjusted manually due to accents of the researchers and participants as well as error in picking up correct words from the software side.

DATA ANALYSIS

Theme One: Value of HR in Business

Question One: *Do You Think Human Resource Management Is an Essential Department in Business?*

When the researchers compared the participants responses to this question, they found that 100% of participants agreed that HRM is an essential department. Participant one stated that it's an "integral part of the entire operation", and participant two added that HR practitioners play a huge role in maintaining an efficient communication medium. It was also found that 80% of the participants that the department has transcended its traditional role of hiring and getting people in the door, where participant one said that the focus is changed to strategic management of the manpower, and during the covid pandemic, participant three stated that HR expanded to providing supports, work-life balance assistance, wellbeing and mindfulness and emotional support. Salau et al. (Induction and Staff Attitude towards Retention and Organizational Effectiveness, 2014) stated that having the department and its function of welcoming employees along with providing a well-packaged induction programme has a great influence on employee behaviour and wellbeing. According to 100% of participants, businesses cannot function without the element of HR. Participant three stated that today, HR has become invaluable and they wouldn't operate without the department. Participant three also explained that the department is moving away from its traditional role of hiring as confirmed by the research of Sivathanu & Pillai (Smart HR 4.0 – how industry 4.0 is disrupting HR, 2018). The researchers found that their initial thought on the importance of HR was supported by all participants. The development of HR using technological advancement was confirmed by 80% of participants and the research of Sivathanu & Pillai (Smart HR 4.0 – how industry 4.0 is disrupting HR, 2018).

Question Two: What Is Your Opinion on Employee Onboarding Programmes?

According to the interviewed participants, 80% of them agree that onboarding employees is a challenging and complicated process. Traditionally, the onboarding process would have been conducted in person and using paper which involved human error as mentioned by participant one and two. On analysing the question in a collective view, it was found that 80% of participant recognize the movement from physically conducted onboarding programmes to hybrid/technology assisted onboarding. Participant four stated that easily accessible technology-assisted onboarding protocols are necessary, which is backed by participant two who mentioned that softwares assisting the onboarding period allows for easier organisation, focus on data analytics and taking advantage of automated tools is essential for full exploitation of the technology. This agrees with secondary research conducted by the researchers where the delayering of communication pillars and ease of access of information thanks to automation and artificial intelligence would decrease the time of decision-making, decreasing the onboarding programme times and closing the windows of time-wasting (Sivathanu & Pillai, 2018; Alam & Khan, 2020; TATA Consultancy Services, 2019). Participant one stated that innovation is crucial for onboarding, and making the department conducting it effectively and efficiently by exploiting automated solutions is necessary. This reinforces the research of Ahmed (Artificial Intelligence in HR, 2018), where elements of the onboarding programme which are time consuming can be replaced by artificial intelligence. Participant three made an interesting point which recognises the generational change of workforce, and stressed the importance of being able to adapt and innovate is the key to establishing up-to-date modern onboarding programmes. This point is reinforced through online research where it was found that an absence of innovation and automation can cause a crippling effect on workplaces (Amour Al Nooumani & Taqui Syed, 2020). The researchers found that traditional roles of HR have transcended and the onboarding process is challenging and complicated. It was discovered that the movement of physically conducted onboarding programmes are now technologically assisted and the streamlining and delayering of processes has opened up time for better decision-making.

Theme Two: Current Implementation of Automation, AI, and Analytics

Question Three: There Are Countless Software Applications Which Are Used to Facilitate Efficient HR Functions Such as Onboarding. Do You Think That the Use of Automation and AI Bots Is the Future of HRM for Businesses?

The researchers found that 60% of participants fully supported the future of HRM and its exploitation of AI and automation, and 80% of participants identified the time-saving benefits the technology can provide and to reinforce its benefits, participant three describes it as a "streamline" and pressure removal on the department. The researchers found that 60% of participants agree on the way repetitive tasks can be given to AI to handle and this would give time for HR practitioners to focus on a strategy level. George & Thomas (Integration of Artificial Intelligence in Human Resource, 2019) define AI as a supportive assistant that can help people in repetitive tasks, so that HR managers can focus their strategic approaches to innovating and using their soft skills to assist employees. On the other hand, 40% of participants identified that there are both positive and negative aspects to the technology and participant three mentioned that the technological tools and their future in the department have a double-edged sword value. The importance of human interaction and having the element of human involvement is essential when attempting to fuse automation and AI with onboarding programmes as stated by participant one, two and three. Soft skills such as emotional abilities, body language, welcoming attitudes in voice tones and being able to "chat" are essentials which participants one, two and three agree that technology cannot replace.

The researchers found that most participants had full confidence in a technologically led future in HRM. The benefits of passing repetitive tasks to AI and automated tools can help focus on strategic thinking and developing soft skills to assist new team members in settling in on a personal level (George & Thomas, 2019).

Question Four: Do You Think There Are Benefits to This Technology?

When asking this question, the researchers discovered that all participants thought automation and AI save time and free up "manpower". Participants three and four agree that the technology helps to streamline and reduce processes and in turn make the induction process more efficient. Participant one explained how they performed their own primary research in the form of surveys which was distributed to employees and were asked to comment on their onboarding experience with a blended technological approach. Participant one confirmed that satisfaction levels were high and thus reduced staff turnover. This reinforces the need for strategic induction practices to increase employee retention (Bharthvajan & Kavitha, 2019). This question also fortified the idea of automation and AI being able to assist in tedious tasks as stated by participant one,two and three so the department of HR can manage it's valuable resources more effectively. Participants three and four state that this can only be done by designing the software in a user-friendly manner so the practitioners can make the most of the technology, otherwise failure rates may damage it's effectivity. As stated by Ahmed (Ahmed, 2018), the advancements made in AI and it's benefits can only be measured if correct software design is applied to ensure user-friendliness can be seen throughout its features. Participants one and five point out that the technology can help overcome language barriers and assist those who struggle with the workplace language. To ensure its correct use, participants one and three state that correct training of HR managers to master the capabilities of the software is essential and will determine its success or failure in its implementation.

It was found that onboarding experiences can bear the benefits of the technology through blended technological application. It was also found that primary and secondary data agree on high satisfaction levels from the use of technology assisted tools ultimately leading to an increase in retention (Bharthvajan & Kavitha, 2019). It was noted that the participants clearly stated that the benefits can be measured only when the software design is user-friendly to maximise its potential.

Theme Three: Challenges Related to Implementing Automation and AI Technology in HR

Question Five: Are There Any Challenges for Management to Implement This Technology in Ensuring Employees Use It Effectively?

According to 80% of the participants, the biggest challenge for implementation of the technology is the ablitity to adapt to change. Participant one stated that *"I would say like that you would have some people and some managers that might be a little bit afraid of change and afraid of the new technology because they're that bit older and they might not be used to using computers..."*. Lack of knowledge of the technology could hinder the ability to unlock its full potential, and this comes down to cultural challenges as mentioned by participant three, where some people are eager to use technology such as the younger generation, but some not so eager and prefer to learn through physical training. The equal proportion of challenges compared to benefits is highlighted in Fig 2.1. Another challenge detailed by participants two and three is the need for supervision over the technology. Participant two stated that technology can't fully monitor or motivate employees to complete their induction trainings to the best of their ability if they have queries. This is where the technology needs the human soft skills in order to facilitate the shortcomings from that angle and ensure a strong induction support is in place (Bharthvajan & Kavitha, 2019).

Question Six: In Your Opinion, Are There Any Human Elements of Onboarding That Cannot Be Replaced by Automated AI Technology?

As stated by 80% of the participants, the initial face-to-face meeting or the first encounter should be in person and not conducted by AI technology. As mentioned by Participant three when answering question three, "*people like to talk to people*" and this can help the employee put a face to the company as the HR practitioner would be the first point of contact between them and the business. As mentioned by participants two three and five, first impressions are important to put the employee at ease, feel welcome, expressions can be read through body language and the company ethos or culture can be portrayed through the face-to-face human contact. According to participants one two and three, HR managers need proper training to use the technology to deliver high class induction programmes, but they also need training in supporting employees emotionally, and building relationships with new staff. According to participant one and three, this is the reason why the human interactive element cannot be eliminated or mimicked by AI.

CONCLUSIONS AND RECOMMENDATIONS

This research has shown a deep enthusiasm for new efficient technological advancements for the HR department in Businesses, and the primary research has confirmed current research. The researchers identified gap in the current knowledge and made recommendations as per each research objective.

The researchers' aim for this research was to examine current and potential implementation of automation in HRM during the onboarding process and considering the ethical balance of automation to human interaction. In order to achieve this aim, there were four main research objectives derived.

Research Objective One: Assessing the Value of the Department of Human Resources in Businesses

All participants agree that businesses cannot operate without an element of HRM. This corresponds to research derived from the exploration of current research. The participants explain that value of the department has grown due to the changing generation of the workforce, where well-being is becoming the forefront of business focus. The participants have given relevant information which establishes the ever-changing department of HR, and emerging practitioners must redefine HR's current functions and align it with the generational change in society.

Research Objective Two: Measuring the Effectivity of Current Implementation of Automation, AI, and Data Analytics in Human Resources During the Onboarding Process in Ireland

Participants had positive comments on the emerging Automation, AI and Data Analytic examples and have mentioned it has had a positive impact in their own businesses, and they reported the staff were happy with their onboarding experiences which included those technological elements. The research participants mentioned that although the technology is there, careful training is needed in order to effectively implement it. Further research is needed to create a framework to follow for effective implementation specific to different industries.

Research Objective Three: Assessing the Challenges With Implementing Automation and AI Technology in Human Resources

According to the participants of the research, there are many factors which can hinder the effective implementation of the technology in onboarding programmes. They highlighted the user-friendliness of the software will determine the success or failure of its use. Other factors such as age, levels of technological savviness of employees can affect its practicality. More research is needed in accessing risks involved in implementing the technology and a careful guide in the form of a framework is necessary to ensure success rates are high.

Research Objective Four: Establishing the Elements of Onboarding That Cannot Be Fully Automated/ Replace Human Interaction Through AI Bots

Most participants agreed that there are elements of the onboarding experiences which simply cannot be done by automation or AI bots. Soft skills in wellbeing assistance, personal connection-building and welcoming body language expression are among some of the things the participants have said aren't elements which technology can fully master, but it can be done in a hybrid method.

REFERENCES

Ahmed, O. (2018). Artificial intelligence in HR. *International Journal of Research and Analytical Reviews*, *5*(4), 971–978.

Alam, M., & Khan, I. (2020). Business 4.0-A New Revolution. In *Information Technology for Management* (pp. 41–57). KD Publications.

Amour Al Nooumani, R., & Taqui Syed, R. (2020). Human Resource Automation: Benefits and Challenges for Organizations. *People in the center of process automation*, 161-164.

Antonacopoulou, E., & Güttel, W. (2010). Staff induction practices and organizational socialization: A review and extention of the debate. *Society and Business Review*, *5*(1), 22–47. doi:10.1108/17465681011017246

Bauer, T. N. (2010). *Onboarding New Employees: Maximizing Success*. SHRM Foundation.

Bharthvajan, R., & Kavitha, F. (2019). Impact of Employee Satisfaction towards Induction Training Program. *International Journal of Innovative Technology and Exploring Engineering*, *8*(11).

Bhat, A. (2018). *Primary Research: Definition, Examples, Methods and Purpose*. Retrieved January 9, 2023, from https://www.questionpro.com/blog/primary-research/

CIPD. (2020). *Induction*. Retrieved November 13, 2022, from https://www.cipd.ie/news-resources/practical-guidance/factsheets/induction#gref

Deloitte. (2017, January 15). *HR bots: the new super power for the workforce?* Retrieved November 13, 2022, from https://www2.deloitte.com/content/dam/Deloitte/us/Documents/human-capital/us-cons-hr-bots-new-super-power-for-workforce.pdf

Dubovskiy, J. (2016). *Realism Research Philosophy*. Retrieved January 9, 2023, from https://research-methodology.net/research-philosophy/realism/

Dudovskiy, J. (2017). *Research Philosophy*. Retrieved January 9, 2023, from https://research-methodology.net/research-philosophy/

Edge, R. (2022). *The Necessary Evolution of Privacy Program Automation*. Retrieved November 13, 2022, from https://www.onetrust.com/blog/the-necessary-evolution-of-privacy-program-automation/

El-Shamy, S. (2003). *Dynamic Induction: Games, Activities and Ideas to Revitalize your Employee Induction Process*. Routledge.

European Commission. (2018). *Are there restrictions on the use of automated decision-making?* Retrieved November 12, 2022, from https://ec.europa.eu/info/law/law-topic/data-protection/reform/rules-business-and-organisations/dealing-citizens/are-there-restrictions-use-automated-decision-making_en

Flick, U. (2014). *An introduction to qualitative research* (5th ed.). Sage Publications Ltd.

George, G., & Thomas, M. (2019). Integration of Artificial Intelligence in Human Resource. *International Journal of Innovative Technology and Exploring Engineering*, *9*(2), 5069–5072. doi:10.35940/ijitee.L3364.129219

Gikopoulus, J. (2019). Alongside, not against: Balancing man with machine in the HR function. *Strategic HR Review*, *18*(2), 55–61. doi:10.1108/SHR-12-2018-0103

Gupta, A., & Gupta, N. (2022). *Research Methodology*. SBPD Publications.

Ivana, D., & Chiripuci, B. (2020). Human Ressource practices in improving employee retention. *Review of Economic Studies and Research Virgil Madgearu*, *13*(1), 33–43. doi:10.24193/RVM.2020.13.50

Jia, Q., Guo, Y., Li, R., Li, Y., & Chen, Y. (2018). A Conceptual Artificial Intelligence Application Framework in Human Resource Management. *International Conference on Electronic Business*, 106-114.

Kaushik, V., & Walsh, C. (2019). Pragmatism as a Research Paradigm and Its Implications for Social Work Research. *Social Sciences (Basel, Switzerland)*, *8*(9), 255. doi:10.3390/socsci8090255

Kenaphoom, S. (2021). Introduction to Research Philosophy. *Journal of Anthropological And Archaeological Sciences*, *5*(4), 657–661.

Largan, C., & Morris, T. (2019). Qualitative Secondary Research: A Step-By-Step Guide. *Sage (Atlanta, Ga.).*

Library. (2022). *HSS Research Methodologies: Quantitative Research*. DCU Library.

Nickerson, C. (2022). *Simply Sociaology*. Retrieved January 9, 2023, from https://simplysociology.com/interpretivism-paradigm.html

Queirós, A., Faria, D., & Almeida, F. (2017). Strengths and Limitations of Qualitative and Quantitative Research Methods. *European Journal of Education Studies*, *3*(9), 369–383.

Rahman, S. (2016). The Advantages and Disadvantages of Using Qualitative and Quantitative Approaches and Methods in Language "Testing and Assessment" Research: A Literature Review. *Journal of Education and Learning*, *6*(1), 102–108. doi:10.5539/jel.v6n1p102

Ryan, G. (2018). Introduction to positivism, interpretivism and critical theory. *Nurse Researchers, 25*(4), 41-49.

Salau, O. P., Falola, H. O., & Akinbode, J. O. (2014). Induction and Staff Attitude towards Retention and Organizational Effectiveness. *IOSR Journal of Business and Management*, *16*(4), 47–52. doi:10.9790/487X-16464752

Sergi, B. S., Ključnikov, A., Popkova, E. G., Bogoviz, A. V., & Lobova, S. V. (2022). Creative abilities and digital competencies to transitioning to Business 4.0. *Journal of Business Research*, *153*, 401–411. doi:10.1016/j.jbusres.2022.08.026

Sivathanu, B., & Pillai, R. (2018). Smart HR 4.0 – how industry 4.0 is disrupting HR. *Human Resource Management International Digest*, *26*(4), 7–11. doi:10.1108/HRMID-04-2018-0059

SmartSurvey. (2020). *Primary Research Methods Explained.* Retrieved January 9, 2023, from https://www.smartsurvey.co.uk/articles/primary-research-methods

TATA Consultancy Services. (2019, March 28). *Understanding Business 4.0™:The New-Age Transformation Paradigm.* Retrieved November 13, 2022, from https://www.business4.tcs.com/content/dam/tcs_b4/pdf/About%20Business%204.0.pdf

Williams, T. (2021). *Why Is Quantitative Research Important?* Retrieved January 9, 2023, from https://www.gcu.edu/blog/doctoral-journey/why-quantitative-research-important

Žukauskas, P., Vveinhardt, J., & Andriukaitienė, R. (2018). Philosophy and Paradigm of Scientific Research. In *Management Culture and Social Responsibility* (pp. 122–135). IntechOpen.

Chapter 6
Tourism in the Metaverse: What's Next? Building Immersive Experiences

Preeti Mehra
https://orcid.org/0000-0002-8979-9431
Campbell College, Canada

Amit Dutt
Lovely Professional University, India

ABSTRACT

In the travel business, metaverse tourism symbolises a revolutionary paradigm change that reshapes how people discover, interact with, and connect with places. This in-depth chapter examines the revolutionary potential of metaverse tourism and considers how it may affect travel businesses, customer experiences, and the overall exploration environment. The chapter starts out by presenting the idea of the metaverse and highlighting how important it is becoming to modern travel. It moves through the metaverse's history of tourism, stressing the immersive and endless experiences it promises. Key themes influencing metaverse tourism are examined, revealing the growth of NFTs and digital mementos as well as the development of virtual places, personalised adventures, social interactions, and social interactions. The chapter wraps up by recapping the transformational potential of metaverse tourism and issuing an invitation to the travel sector to seize metaverse prospects.

The metaverse has become a ground-breaking idea with the potential to drastically alter many facets of our life in a time when technology is increasingly altering how we view and interact with the world. The metaverse, a dynamic and immersive digital

DOI: 10.4018/979-8-3693-1103-5.ch006

environment that blurs the lines between the physical and digital worlds, is based on the fusion of virtual reality (VR), augmented reality (AR), and networked digital environments (M. Ball, 2020). It is becoming more and more clear that the metaverse is a force that is both palpable and revolutionary, with wide-ranging ramifications, as this digital frontier gains traction. This chapter sets out on a journey through "Emerging Trends of Metaverse Tourism," revealing the significant implications this digital evolution holds for tourism.

METAVERSE AND ITS INCREASING RELEVANCE

The metaverse is a vast digital world that extends our physical reality. It provides areas where users can engage in immersive and interactive interactions with one another and other digital beings. It includes digital settings, augmented reality experiences, and virtual worlds that let people to leave the boundaries of the actual world and go on adventures that were previously constrained by space and time (N. Stephenson, 1992). The increased influence of the metaverse across a variety of industries, including communication, education, entertainment, and business, is a clear indication of its increasing relevance.

The ability of the metaverse to convey a sense of presence and agency sets it apart from conventional digital settings. Users actively shape and manoeuvre these digital environments in accordance with their preferences, making them more than passive viewers. The metaverse is developing into a dynamic environment where creativity, collaboration, and invention merge as technology progresses, altering how we interact with both the digital and physical aspects of our life.

A Synopsis of Traditional Tourism and Its Drawbacks

Traditional tourism has long served as a gateway for people looking to experience different cultures, awe at historical sites, and create priceless memories. The inherent restrictions of this form of research, however, can obstruct accessibility, environmental sustainability, and personalisation. Geographical restrictions, the cost of travel, and the passing of time all prevent people from fully achieving their travel goals. Furthermore, the sustainability of conventional tourist practises is called into question due to the environmental effects of regular physical travel (Gössling, et al., 2021).

The shortcomings of conventional tourism have sparked a search for substitutes that provide equivalent experiences without the environmental consequences and accessibility issues. Metaverse tourism is a concept that uses technology to go around the physical limitations of travel and offer immersive and interesting digital travel experiences as a result of this search.

A Conceptual Introduction to Metaverse Tourism

A fundamental shift in how we think about and interact with travel experiences has been brought about by metaverse tourism. It involves making use of the capabilities of virtual and augmented reality technologies to build virtual excursions to locations outside of physical borders. Metaverse tourism encourages users to enter fully realised virtual worlds, interact with their surroundings, and take part in activities that mimic real-world experiences, rather than just watching from a distance.

Imagine sitting comfortably in your own physical area and travelling through the bustling streets of ancient civilizations, the rich ecosystems of far-off planets, or the depths of the ocean. Travelling via the metaverse expands the definition of exploration by allowing for previously unthinkable journeys spanning time, space, and culture.

The chapters that follow will go into greater detail about the growth of metaverse tourism, looking at the patterns that influence it, the difficulties and possibilities it brings, and its ramifications for the larger travel sector. We want you to think about the possibilities for metaverse tourism to change the way we view the world as we proceed through this investigation.

IDENTIFYING THE METAVERSE

Understanding the metaverse requires embracing a dynamic mix of technology, creativity, and connectivity. The metaverse is a huge digital space that includes a wide variety of augmented reality and virtual reality experiences, frequently spanning connected virtual landscapes and universes. At its core, the metaverse functions as a communal area where people can engage with one another and other digital beings in ways that go beyond the bounds of physical space. This area is not limited to a particular platform or application; rather, it includes a wide range of digital environments and experiences that together comprise its tapestry (M. Ball, 2020).

Definition of the Metaverse and Its Elements

Users can travel across several settings in the metaverse, each with its own interactions, laws, and experiences. These environments can range from fully realised 3D worlds to augmented overlays that enhance the real world with digital data. The metaverse supports a wide range of modes, including social interaction, exploration, and business. It's a place where people may work, play, study, interact with others, socialise, and create while also creating connections and experiences that conflate the physical and digital worlds (J. M. Krum, 2016).

The Merging of Augmented Reality, Virtual Reality, and Online Worlds

The fusion of virtual reality (VR), augmented reality (AR), and virtual worlds is at the core of the metaverse's attraction. Users of virtual reality are completely submerged in digital worlds, giving them a sense of presence and control over manufactured situations. Contrarily, augmented reality augments real-world encounters with digital data and objects by superimposing digital content over the actual world. Users can transition between immersive virtual worlds and enhanced interactions with the real world thanks to the seamless integration of various technologies in the metaverse (S. N. Spencer, 1994).

Within the metaverse, virtual worlds are vast digital settings where users can interact with people, things, and other participants. Users can explore and take part in activities ranging from social gatherings and entertainment to education and commerce in these worlds, which can either be wholly fictional or imitate real-world locations. These technologies and the digital worlds come together to weave a tapestry that encourages exploration, innovation, and creation on a scale never before seen.

How Physical and Digital Realities Are Blurred by the Metaverse

The physical and digital realities are deeply merged in the metaverse, which is more than just a digital simulation. The metaverse produces experiences that appeal to our senses and enhances our interactions with the physical world through VR and AR. Users can walk around physically in virtual environments, interact with virtual items, and even work together in ways that mimic interactions with others in the real world.

How humans interact with content and one another is altered by the metaverse's capacity to connect these realities. It opens up fresh channels for interaction, teamwork, and exploration, allowing people to transcend time and space limitations. The end result is a setting where the lines between the "real" and the "virtual" are blurred, resulting in experiences that contradict conventional ideas of reality (B. J. Wiederhold, 2018).

The chapters that follow will go in-depth on the growth of metaverse tourism, looking at the patterns that influence it, the difficulties and chances it brings, and its ramifications for the larger travel sector. We ask you to reflect on the transformative potential of metaverse tourism and its part in changing how we view the world through this investigation.

AN EXAMINATION OF TOURISM'S METAVERSE ADAPTATION

A revolutionary change from conventional physical travel to digitally immersive experiences that transcend the constraints of space and time can be seen in the metaverse's evolution of tourism. With the use of technology, metaverse tourism presents a fresh method of travel that reimagines how people interact with different places and people.

Examining how the tourism industry is changing to fit the metaverse

The metaverse offers a compelling alternative that reimagines travel through virtual environments as the globe struggles with issues like accessibility and environmental sustainability. By enabling users to visit locations that have been painstakingly replicated in virtual settings, metaverse tourism adapts the essence of travel to the digital sphere. Travellers can see ancient sites up close, stroll through lively markets from bygone eras, and even travel across surreal landscapes that defy the laws of realism. These virtual locations are not only passive simulations; rather, they are immersive, interactive settings that encourage users to interact with their surroundings, with things, and with one other as well as to take part in experiences that are modelled after actual ones (R. Schroeder, 2012). This metaverse adaption encourages exploration that goes beyond the bounds of physical travel in addition to enabling it.

The Possibility of Indulgent and Endless Travel Experiences

The ability of metaverse tourism to offer immersive and unrestricted travel experiences is at the heart of its attractiveness. Users of virtual reality technologies can enter painstakingly recreated digital versions of places, giving them a strong sensation of presence and involvement (J. M. Krum, 2016). Travellers can interact with environments that nearly resemble the actual world, interact with historical artefacts, and even engage in activities that closely like real-life experiences through virtual exploration.

The extraordinary possibility for exploration outside the bounds of the physical world is another feature of the metaverse. Imagine going on a virtual safari across ancient landscapes, exploring the bustling markets of bygone civilizations, or travelling to far-off worlds. By transcending geographical and temporal boundaries, these immersive experiences put the conventional idea of travel to the test. limitations, enabling people to travel in ways that were previously only possible in their imaginations (S. N. Spencer, 1994). The metaverse redefines exploration by giving tourists a singular way to immerse themselves in adventures that push the limits of what is practical.

The Early Metaverse Tourism Projects

Innovative projects that demonstrate the metaverse tourist industry's revolutionary potential are already making their impact in this still-emerging field. In order to provide cultural experiences that transcend geographical limits, virtual museums and art galleries are embracing the metaverse. These online museums allow visitors to interact with artefacts, view exhibitions, and read historical accounts while still in their actual physical locations (A. Proctor, 1997). This blending of physical locations with digital content produces a hybrid experience that transcends the constraints of geography and time.

Travel places from the real world are increasingly extending their offerings into the metaverse. Travel agencies, artists, and engineers are working together to create virtual exhibits that reflect the spirit of real places. Through the perspective of the metaverse, these projects enable users to take virtual city tours, discover architectural wonders, and even take in the grandeur of nature wonders (J. C. Cazes and Freitas, 1999). These locations are expanding their interaction techniques and inviting visitors to experience their charm in fresh and creative ways by embracing metaverse tourism.

As the chapters ahead delve into the complexities of metaverse tourism, we will navigate through the challenges and opportunities that shape this transformative concept. By exploring these trends, we aim to shed light on how metaverse tourism is redefining the very notion of exploration and creating a bridge between the physical and digital realms.

KEY TRENDS SHAPING METAVERSE TOURISM

There are certain key trends that are influencing metaverse tourism such as virtual destinations, personalised experiences, social interactions and digital souvenirs from metaverse travels, as discussed in the following paragraphs.

Virtual Destinations: Creation of Digital Travel Destinations Within Virtual Worlds

The birth of the metaverse has generated a significant trend in the travel and tourist industry: the development of virtual locations inside vast virtual worlds (M. Ball, 2020). Travellers have the exceptional chance to discover places that go beyond physical boundaries thanks to these expertly created digital recreations of real-world and imaginary sites. These digital landscapes, which capture the essence of historical periods, iconic locations, and imaginative worlds, are meticulously constructed.

Due to their realistic and interactive features, these virtual locations set themselves apart from conventional travel encounters (R. Schroeder, 2012). Users are able to interact with their environment, items, and activities that are similar to those in the real world. Imagine exploring a historical city that has been painstakingly recreated, bargaining in lively markets from bygone ages, or standing in awe at architectural wonders that defy the laws of physics. These virtual worlds are more than just exact duplicates; they are vibrant, interesting places that give visitors a fresh opportunity to engage with the known and unknown.

Personalised Experiences: Tailoring Metaverse Adventures to Individual Preferences

A paradigm shift towards personalised trips that take into account each person's tastes and interests is brought about by metaverse tourism. The metaverse gives passengers the opportunity to design their virtual adventures by letting them choose locations, events, and activities that suit their interests. By enabling visitors to interact with destinations in a way that resonates strongly with their particular identities, personalisation revolutionises the idea of exploration.

Imagine going on a virtual culinary adventure, discovering the tastes and scents of many civilizations, or immersing oneself in workshops and pursuits that suit one's interests and goals. By allowing travellers to create memories that are specifically catered to their interests, this level of personalisation gives travel an intimate and genuine aspect (T. D. Ewing, 1997). Thus, the metaverse goes beyond the limitations of conventional exploration by giving users the ability to create experiences that reflect their unique personalities.

Social Interactions: The Metaverse's Need for Shared Experiences and Social Interactions

The ability of the metaverse to enable cross-border social connections and shared experiences is one of its fundamental characteristics (A. Antinori, 2005). Through the creation of shared travel experiences that foster connections between people from various racial and cultural backgrounds, metaverse tourism makes use of this potential. In the metaverse, travelling becomes a shared experience where participants cooperate, interact, and establish connections in live virtual environments.

Imagine reconnecting with friends who live on opposite sides of the world in a virtual café evoking a faraway city, celebrating family milestones in immersive digital environments that cater to shared interests, or having meaningful conversations with fellow travellers while navigating vibrant virtual landscapes. Through encounters that go beyond geographic boundaries and cultural barriers, travel experiences are enriched, resulting in relationships and shared memories (K. Arnold, 2006). The metaverse's significance in promoting social interactions in the travel industry emphasises its potential to promote deep participation in a world of digital connectivity.

Collectibles and Digital Souvenirs From Metaverse Travels: NFTs and Digital Souvenirs

By including non-fungible tokens (NFTs), which are digital mementos and collectible goods that capture the spirit of metaverse journeys, metaverse tourism provides a ground-breaking idea (J. Howells, 2011). NFTs are distinctive digital assets that reflect ownership of things in the metaverse, such as exclusive experiences, virtual real estate, and works of art. By providing users with actual and priceless digital tokens that serve as a memento of their metaverse excursions, this trend alters the idea of souvenirs.

Imagine owning a piece of virtual land inside a bustling city, a limited edition digital artwork that captures the essence of a virtual location, or a virtual artefact from a historical site. These digital tokens are more than simply mementos; they give collectors a physical link to the memories and experiences they create while travelling around the metaverse (A. D. Foster, 2021). Travellers are encouraged to participate with their discoveries on a completely new level thanks to the integration of NFTs and digital keepsakes, which redefines ownership and participation within the digital landscape.

As we examine these tendencies, it becomes clear that metaverse tourism is more than just a new development in technology; it's a paradigm-shifting idea that changes how we perceive and experience travel. The potential for metaverse tourism to fundamentally alter the nature of exploration and participation in the digital age will be revealed when we explore more into the difficulties and opportunities it presents in the next chapters.

OPPORTUNITIES AND CHALLENGES

While there are many opportunities provided by metaverse travel, there are also a number of difficulties that must be carefully considered.

Addressing data privacy and cybersecurity in the metaverse

Data privacy and cybersecurity are two of the main issues (J. W. Goode, 2000). Users' concerns about the security of their data and the possibility of unauthorised access grow as they interact with metaverse platforms and disclose personal information to visit virtual locations.

Personal data can be misused and breached in the digital world, which can result in crimes like identity theft and financial fraud. Users' behaviours and preferences may also be monitored as they interact with others in the metaverse and explore virtual locations, raising questions regarding user surveillance and data profiling (D. Lyon, 2001). Therefore, as metaverse tourism develops, it will be essential to ensure strong data encryption, open data usage policies, and strict cybersecurity measures to protect consumers' privacy.

Promoting Accessibility and Inclusivity via Digital Inclusion in Metaverse Tourism

Only if it is open to all people, regardless of their physical capabilities or technical proficiency, can the attractiveness of metaverse tourism be completely realised (M. Haller, 2019). Ensuring digital inclusion is difficult since not all users may have the tools, know-how, or technical aptitude to explore the metaverse. Additionally, those with disabilities could encounter more obstacles while trying to access and take advantage of immersive virtual experiences.

Metaverse tourism must prioritise design and development techniques that satisfy a range of user needs in order to overcome this obstacle. This entails designing user-friendly interfaces, offering choices for various interaction styles, and including features that cater to users who have disabilities, such as visual impairments or mobility restrictions (J. Lazar, 2006). Metaverse tourism may reach a broader spectrum of people and create a more equal digital travel environment by adopting digital inclusion.

Collaborative Innovation: Collaborations Among Tech Firms, Tourism Organisations, and Creators

Collaboration is necessary between a wide range of stakeholders in order for metaverse tourism to develop (M. A. Cusumano & A. Gawer, 2002). These stakeholders include technology businesses, tourism boards, content developers, and more. These collaborations are necessary to develop seamless experiences that attract users and capture the realism of real-world locations.

Tourism boards provide their knowledge in curating culturally accurate and rich digital experiences, while tech businesses and creators play a crucial role in designing and constructing immersive virtual destinations. The tourism environment in the metaverse is diverse and true to the real-world locations it represents because to collaborative innovation. A delicate balance must be carefully struck between artistic expression and the protection of cultural authenticity, nevertheless (M. J. Druin, 2006).

Digital Tourism in a Sustainable Metaverse: Reducing Environmental Impact

Even in the virtual world, it is crucial to take into account any potential environmental effects of metaverse tourism as it grows popularity (K. Loftus, 2021). To ensure sustainable metaverse tourism, it is important to address issues like the energy required to run virtual worlds, the manufacturing of hardware and data centres, and the carbon footprint of technological infrastructure.

While a low-carbon substitute for actual travel, the metaverse is not fully immune from environmental concerns. To reduce the ecological footprint of metaverse platforms, collaborative efforts must be made to promote eco-friendly behaviours, optimise energy use, and investigate novel solutions (J. Kucklich, 2021). It will be crucial to ensure that technical development and ecological responsibility are balanced.

We discover the nuances of a transformative idea that has the potential to redefine travel experiences as we negotiate the difficulties and opportunities presented by metaverse tourism. The chapters that follow explore the complexities of metaverse tourism in greater detail, including how it affects consumer participation, what it means for the travel business, and how it might even alter what it means to explore.

CASE STUDIES OF METAVERSE TOURISM

By providing users with immersive cultural experiences that go beyond conventional physical boundaries, virtual museums and art galleries are leading the integration of metaverse tourism (S. Schroeder, 1997). Through interactive travels through the past and present, these digital environments connect the worlds of art, history, and technology.

Immersive cultural experiences in the metaverse through virtual museums and art galleries

One of the most well-known cultural organisations in the world, the "Louvre Museum" in Paris, has embraced the metaverse to expand its influence beyond its physical boundaries. The Louvre has collaborated with tech firms to develop virtual galleries that let visitors view its famous works of art and historical artefacts in exquisite detail (J. Hooper-Greenhill, 1994). The museum's halls may be virtually explored by visitors, who can zoom in on individual works of art to learn more about their history and context.

Similar to this, the American "Smithsonian Institution," a network of museums and research institutes, has launched a bold endeavour to digitise its enormous collection. Users can explore the depth of the institution's collections from the comfort of their homes via the institution's virtual platform, "Smithsonian Open

Access," which offers free access to high-resolution photographs of artworks, artefacts, and specimens (www.si.edu/openaccess, 2021). This project demonstrates how metaverse tourism has the ability to democratise access to cultural riches and build an international community of art enthusiasts.

Travel Destination Showcases: Online Promotions by Actual Travel Destinations

Travel destinations in the real world are using the metaverse to build virtual exhibits that capture the essence of their locations and entice viewers to go on immersive adventures. These virtual advertisements not only hold the attention of potential passengers, but also present a special chance to visit the location before making firm trip arrangements.

By collaborating with a virtual reality content producer to create a virtual display of the city-state, 'Visit Singapore', the official tourism board of Singapore, adopted metaverse tourism (www.visitsingapore.com/virtualsingapore/, 2021). Users can explore well-known places, take in panoramic views, and even engage in interactive activities that simulate real-world experiences. Visit Singapore has successfully tapped into the curiosity and wanderlust of potential tourists by developing an engaging digital equivalent to the actual location, providing a tantalising glimpse of what awaits them.

Similar to this, 'Tourism New Zealand' used the metaverse's creative potential to develop a virtual reality experience that immerses viewers in the stunning landscapes of the nation (https://playnz.com, 2021). Users of this programme, known as "PLAY NZ," may digitally kayak along rivers, explore beautiful forests, and even get up close and personal with native species. The ad not only highlights New Zealand's attraction but also arouses amazement and anticipation in potential travellers by immersing them in the breath-taking majesty of the country's natural treasures.

Gaming Crossovers: Adding Metaverse Tourism Elements to Video Games

The incorporation of virtual travel experiences into gaming environments serves as an example of how video games and metaverse tourism connect. The distinction between entertainment and exploration is becoming more hazy as video game creators take advantage of the immersive aspect of games to introduce players to other worlds, civilizations, and landscapes (M. J. P. Wolf, 2002).

The Elder Scrolls Online is a role-playing game that features a vast virtual world with a variety of settings inspired by many real-world civilizations and historical periods (www.elderscrollsonline.com, 2021). Players can travel through grand cities, negotiate challenging alleyways, and discover old ruins that are reminiscent of several civilizations. Players are immersed in virtual locations that mimic real vacation destinations thanks to this hybrid of gaming and metaverse tourism, which encourages them to explore and get involved in the fascinating lore of these digital locations.

Players can enjoy the thrill of flying an aeroplane while exploring beautiful landscapes of actual locations in "Microsoft Flight Simulator" (www.flightsimulator.com, 2021). The game unintentionally encourages metaverse tourism by giving users the chance to virtually fly over famous landmarks, cross continents, and even find hidden treasures that they may want to explore further. This is done by giving players a realistic representation of Earth's surroundings.

These case studies highlight the metaverse's potential to fundamentally alter how people interact with entertainment, travel, and culture. Virtual museums, destination showcases, and gaming crossovers are just a few examples of the many ways that metaverse tourism is changing the exploring landscape and encouraging people to explore new and intriguing digital worlds.

CONSUMER ENGAGEMENT AND EXPERIENCE

The potential impact of metaverse tourism on consumer behaviour and travel decision-making is enormous (S. H. Kim et al. 2015). Users engage with virtual locations, setting off on a trip that transcends the virtual world and influencing how they view and prefer physical travel. Metaverse is instrumental in building consumer engagement.

How Tourism in the Metaverse Improves Consumer Engagement

A new era of consumer interaction that goes beyond the constraints of conventional travel experiences has arrived with the arrival of metaverse tourism (A. Mody, 2016). Travellers now have access to previously unheard-of opportunities to immerse themselves in virtual locations thanks to the convergence of technology, virtual reality (VR), and augmented reality (AR), producing a singular and engrossing form of engagement.

Travel brochure or website browsing becomes an active and interactive experience thanks to metaverse tourism. Travellers can explore virtual landscapes, learn about cultural monuments, and interact with simulations that mirror real-world circumstances using immersive VR settings and interactive AR overlays (R.

Schroeder, 2012). This transition from spectator to participant builds a closer bond between visitors and the places they explore.

Furthermore, gamification features are frequently incorporated into metaverse platforms, making travel an experience that appeals to users' senses of discovery and accomplishment (S. A. DeSmet, 2015). Users are encouraged to actively explore every corner of virtual locations because to the dynamic nature of metaverse experiences, finding treasures and incentives along the way.

Using Metaverse Travel Experiences to Foster Emotional Bonds

The potential of metaverse tourism to elicit sincere emotional ties between users and virtual destinations is one of its most striking features (A. L. Pohlmeyer & M. A. Jones, 2009). Users' emotions are tapped into via immersive settings, sensory stimulation, and storytelling in metaverse experiences, resulting in connections and memories that resemble those made during actual travel.

The ability of the metaverse to mimic real-world experiences and interactions is what allows it to provide emotionally intense experiences. Users can engage in activities that evoke pleasant feelings and recollections while digitally strolling down busy streets, feeling the breeze on their skin, and feeling the breeze on their skin (S. J. Mantovani, 2003). A sense of attachment and personal investment in the virtual experience are facilitated by these emotional responses.

Users can enter historical or cultural contexts through metaverse travel experiences, which enables them to empathise with various viewpoints and engage with various narratives (M. Cantoni & S. Tardini, 2006). A user's view of the location and its significance may be enhanced by this ability to generate empathy and understanding, which has the potential to forge deep emotional connections.

Affects Consumer Behaviour and Travel Decision-Making

First off, metaverse adventures have the potential to be effective promotional tools for real-world travel locations. Travel marketers can pique customers' curiosity and interest and ultimately encourage them to explore more by providing virtual showcases and immersive samples of places (D. Bowen & R. Clarke, 2006). Virtual destination displays act as a sort of anticipatory engagement, encouraging consumers to learn more about and arrange journeys to the real places that have made a good impression online.

Second, metaverse tourism enables visitors to experience places virtually before making a physical trip. Users can evaluate their affinity for a destination's culture, attractions, and activities using this "try before you buy" strategy (A. Mody, 2021).

Travellers are better able to manage their time and resources wisely thanks to metaverse experiences, which leads to more fulfilling and meaningful journeys.

In conclusion, immersive exploration, emotional resonance, and the influencing of travel choices define the consumer experience and involvement in metaverse tourism. Users go on a transformational journey as they develop emotional ties and engage with virtual places, which affects both their activity within the larger travel ecosystem and how they perceive travel.

REPERCUSSIONS FOR THE TRAVEL SECTOR

A disruptive force that has the ability to revolutionise the whole travel industry landscape, metaverse tourism is more than just a new trend (M. Ball, 2020). This transformation goes beyond the confines of conventional travel and provides a new paradigm that questions accepted beliefs while providing unheard-of opportunities for innovation.

How Metaverse Tourism Is Transforming the Travel Industry

The travel sector, which has always catered to physical journeys, is now being forced to change to meet the demands of the digital metaverse. In order to adapt, tourist experiences, interactions with cultures, and memory-making must be rethought. Exploring historical civilizations and taking part in fictitious stories are only a few of the possibilities made possible by the metaverse's capacity to give immersive and personalised experiences that transcend the limitations of physical travel (R. Schroeder, 2012).

Additionally, the metaverse promotes a sense of democratisation because it allows people to access virtual locations and take part in rich cultural experiences even if they do not have the money to travel to expensive real locations (K. E. Haywood, 2020). With this change, travel accessibility may be redefined, ushering in a new era of inclusivity and adventure.

New Business Models: Possibilities for the Travel Industry, Artists, and Tech Pioneers

Innovative business models that address the changing demands and tastes of contemporary tourists are made possible by metaverse tourism (D. Siegel & S. Hall, 2020). Traditional travel agencies can reinvent their services by fusing real-world activities with metaverse counterparts. With the help of these hybrid travel packages, tourists may tailor their vacations to suit their interests by mixing real-world discovery with virtual immersion.

The metaverse additionally offers a platform for content producers, artists, and developers to design immersive experiences that connect with audiences around the world. These producers contribute to the vast ecology of the metaverse, bridging the gap between imagination and technology, from virtual museum curators to digital architects creating virtual locations (J. M. Pearce, 2001).

Technological pioneers are also well-positioned to profit from metaverse tourism. The metaverse tourism experience is improved by the use of augmented reality (AR) and virtual reality (VR) technology, haptic feedback systems, and developments in AI-driven storytelling (S. J. Mantovani, 2003). As these technologies develop further, they provide tech businesses the chance to offer solutions that improve the standard of virtual travel, encouraging greater participation and emotional connections.

Balancing Traditional and Metaverse Travel Offerings in the Hybrid Future

Metaverse tourism adds a supplemental dimension that enhances the whole trip experience rather than indicating that physical travel is becoming obsolete (C. U. Ciborra, 2002). The future of the tourism industry lies in finding a happy medium between conventional and metaverse offers, taking into account a variety of preferences and situations.

Travel agencies can create hybrid itineraries that effortlessly blend real-world exploration with online interaction. For instance, a traveller might discover a historical location during the day and then spend the night-time immersed in a virtual recreation of the same site, deepening their relationship to the place.

Additionally, the metaverse can act as a prologue to actual travel, allowing future travellers to become familiar with locations before starting their actual journeys. This fusing of virtual and real-world events strengthens tourists' emotional ties to their selected locations, resulting in a comprehensive travel narrative that transcends geographical bounds.

In summary, metaverse tourism offers the travel sector a chance to advance, modify, and improve how people see the globe. A more dynamic, inclusive, and inventive travel environment that can accommodate the various needs of contemporary travellers may be produced via the seamless fusion of virtual and physical dimensions.

METAVERSE TOURISM'S PROSPECTS IN THE FUTURE

Numerous opportunities presented by the development of metaverse tourism hold the potential to fundamentally alter how people perceive and interact with travel in the years to come (M. Ball, 2020). Several projections about the future of metaverse tourism are emerging as technology develops and consumer tastes change.

Prognostications for the Future of Metaverse Tourism

First, it is anticipated that the metaverse will grow more immersive and engaging, thus obfuscating the line between reality and virtuality (R. Schroeder, 2012). Users will be able to interact with locations and experiences in ways that closely resemble real-world interactions because to developments in virtual reality (VR) and augmented reality (AR). The emotional connections people develop with virtual places will be strengthened by this improved immersion, making metaverse travel an even more alluring option.

Second, metaverse tourism is likely to become a collaborative endeavor, with users participating in co-created experiences that combine the expertise of travel companies, creators, and technology innovators (D. Siegel, & S. Hall, 2020). This collaborative approach will result in more diverse, engaging, and authentic metaverse travel offerings that cater to a wide range of interests and preferences.

Technological Advancements and Their Influence on Immersive Travel

Technological developments will be crucial in determining how the metaverse tourism industry develops in the future, improving immersive experiences and opening up new opportunities for user involvement (J. A. Regalado, 2017). Users will be able to experience increasingly realistic and detailed virtual settings as virtual reality hardware becomes more affordable and advanced, engaging their senses and strengthening their connection to virtual places.

The use of haptic feedback technologies will improve the sensory appeal of metaverse travel even further (L. Ahn & Y. Kim, 2017). Users may perceive vibrations, temperature changes, and even the textures of virtual surfaces, giving them a stronger sensation of presence in the virtual environment. The development of more realistic and memorable metaverse travel experiences depends on these developments.

According to M. J. P. Wolf (2002), artificial intelligence (AI) will have a big impact on how metaverse tourism develops in the future. AI-driven customization will make it possible to create customised user experiences that fit their tastes and habits. AI will help create a more interesting and immersive metaverse travel environment by doing everything from proposing virtual locations based on past travel to creating dynamic narratives that respond to users' interactions.

The Potential Impact of Metaverse Tourism on the Overall Tourism Industry

The influence of metaverse tourism extends beyond its own domain and has the ability to alter the entire tourism sector (C. U. Ciborra, 2002). The development of metaverse-enhanced marketing efforts by real-world tourism locations, which use the metaverse to display their offerings and engage potential visitors, is one possibility. These advertisements will make use of immersive experiences to encourage users to venture outside of the virtual world by forging a stronger bond between them and the actual location.

Metaverse tourism may also affect how people prepare for and enjoy physical travel (A. Mody, 2021). Before starting their actual journeys, travellers might use metaverse portals to research their destinations, virtually scout out lodging, and partake in cultural experiences. By giving tourists knowledge and connections that augment their physical journeys, anticipatory engagement might improve their overall experiences.

In essence, enhanced immersion, collaborative invention, and technical advancement are all promises of the future of metaverse tourism. The metaverse landscape's development will surely have an impact on how people travel as well as how the larger tourist sector adjusts to the always changing needs of contemporary passengers.

CONCLUSION

Travelling through the metaverse has opened up a world of possibilities that have the potential to change how we perceive and interact with travel. Metaverse tourism has become a driving force behind change in the travel industry, bringing personalised trips, immersive virtual destinations, and shared encounters.

A recap of the Potential for Transformation in Metaverse Tourism

Metaverse tourism, at its core, provides a doorway to discovery free from physical boundaries, enhancing the traveler's story with layers of digital participation. The conventional travel paradigm has been changed into a linked web of virtual and actual interactions as a result of the immersive experiences, emotional resonance, and influence on decision-making offered by the metaverse.

The Wake-Up Call for the Travel Sector to Take Advantage of Metaverse Opportunities

The travel industry is being compelled to accept change and innovation by the metaverse tourism sector's explosive expansion and expanding possibilities (D. Siegel & S. Hall, 2020). It is a strategic requirement to rethink conventional business models, marketing plans, and consumer interactions in order to accommodate the adoption of metaverse platforms and experiences.

Travel agencies will have the chance to enthral audiences with immersive stories that go beyond the bounds of physical travel thanks to metaverse tourism (A. Mody, 2021). Travel agencies may meet the wide range of preferences of contemporary tourists by developing hybrid services that smoothly integrate virtual and real-world experiences, democratising access to exploration.

Concluding Remarks on the Progressing Travel Experiences Landscape in the Digital Age

The development of metaverse tourism serves as evidence of how drastically the travel business has changed in the digital era (S. Richardson, 2016). Travel is no longer limited to a linear sequence of physical departures and arrivals, as the journey across the metaverse demonstrates. Instead, it is a web of experiences that connect the physical and virtual worlds.

It's important to recognise how the digital landscape is always changing and influencing how we interact with the globe as we start this new chapter of travel (L. M. Hiltzik, 2018). In a future where travel is a combination of sensory engagement, emotional resonance, and technology-driven discovery, metaverse tourism is a stepping stone rather than a conclusion.

The travel industry must embrace the metaverse and its disruptive potential, and this is the unambiguous call to action. The industry can reimagine what it means to explore, discover, and connect with locations in the modern day by leveraging the power of immersive experiences, personalised adventures, and collaborative innovation (D. J. Roche, & A. D. Long, 2007).

In the end, metaverse tourism symbolises more than just a novel form of travel; it also denotes a paradigm shift in the way we view and interact with the outside world. A new frontier of exploration has emerged as a result of the merger of technology and human curiosity; it transcends the confines of physical space, blurs the distinction between reality and virtuality, and allows us to set out on exploratory excursions that are as boundless as our imaginations.

REFERENCES

Ahn, L., & Kim, Y. (2017). The Influence of Haptic Feedback on Immersive Virtual Reality Advertising. *Journal of Business Research.*

Antinori, L., & Fiore, A. M. E. (2008). Understanding the Impact of Social Networks on Consumers' Salient Beliefs and Attitudes toward Experiential Marketing. *Journal of Travel Research.*

Arnold, K. (2000). Social Tourism: The Effect of Local Communities on Participating Visitors. *Annals of Tourism Research.*

Bowen, D., & Clarke, R. (2006). Reflections on Tourism and Change. In M. Smith & M. Robinson (Eds.), Tourism and Transition. Academic Press.

Cantoni, M., & Tardini, S. (2006). Designing a Museum Multi-Device and Multi-Location Experience: The Case of Museo della Scienza e della Tecnologia di Milano. *International Journal of Human-Computer Interaction.*

Cazes, J. C., & de Freitas, P. (1999). Virtual Reality in Tourism. *Journal of Travel & Tourism Marketing.*

Ciborra, C. U. (2002). *Teams, Markets, Systems: Business Innovation and Information Technology*. Cambridge University Press.

DeSmet, S. A. (2015). *Gamification in Tourism* [Ph.D. Thesis]. Faculty of Economics and Business, KU Leuven.

Druin, M. J. (2002). The Role of Children in the Design of New Technology. *Behaviour & Information Technology.*

Foster, A. D. (2021). *The NFT Wars Have Begun*. MIT Technology Review.

Goode, J. W. (2000). *Privacy in Cyberspace: Protecting Personal Information in the Online World.* RAND Corporation.

Gössling, S., Scott, D., & Hall, C. M. (2021). Tourism and Water: Dimensions of Tourism (Vol. 1). Channel View Publications.

Haller, M. (2019). Designing for User Engagement in Virtual Reality. *Communications of the ACM.*

Haywood, K. E. (2020). Democratizing Virtual Reality: A Quantitative Exploration of Virtual Reality and Its Implications for Accessibility. *Proceedings of the Human Factors and Ergonomics Society Annual Meeting.*

Hiltzik, L. M. (2018). Digital Travel: How Big Data is Changing the Travel Industry. *Los Angeles Times.*

Hooper-Greenhill, J. (1994). Virtual Reality and the Art Museum. *Curator (New York, N.Y.).*

Howells, J. (2011). *The Dissolving of Private and Public Property: Reconsidering Digital Landscapes.* Research in Art Education.

Kim, S. H., Agrawal, S., & Srivastava, S. (2015). Reciprocity in Online Product Reviews: The Role of Reviewer Identity and Review Valence. *Journal of Marketing.*

Krum, J. M. (2016). *Virtual Reality: Principles and Practice.* Addison-Wesley Professional.

Kucklich, J. (2012). The Consumption of Virtual Worlds: Extraction, Infrastructure, and Labor in MMORPGs. *Journal of Gaming & Virtual Worlds.*

Lazar, J. (2006). *Web Usability: A User-Centered Design Approach.* Pearson.

Loftus, K. (2021). *How Much Energy Does the Internet Use?* BBC News.

Lyon, D. (2001). *Surveillance Society: Monitoring Everyday Life.* Open University Press.

Mody, A. (2016). The Evolution of Tourism and Its Impact on Consumers' Choice. *Journal of Travel Research.*

Mody, A. (2021). *The Future of Tourism in the Post-COVID-19 World.* Tourism Geographies.

Pearce, J. M. (2001). Virtual Reality Pedagogy: A Framework for Designing Educational Experiences. *Australian Journal of Educational Technology.*

Pohlmeyer, A. L., & Jones, M. A. (2009). Engaging Design: Creating Interfaces That Emotionally Connect Users to Brands. *International Journal of Design.*

Proctor, A. (1997). Museum Space and the Exploration of Difference. *Museum & Society.*

Regalado, J. A. (2017). *Virtual Reality's Missing Ingredient: Other People.* MIT Technology Review.

Richardson, S. (2016). The Globalization of Tourism: A Long View. *Journal of Tourism History*.

Roche, D. J., & Long, A. D. (2007). Tourism and Terrorism: A Holistic Approach. *Tourism Geographies*.

Schroeder, R. (2012). *The Social Life of Avatars: Presence and Interaction in Shared Virtual Environments*. Springer Science & Business Media.

Studio, A. (2021). *Microsoft Flight Simulator*. Available: https://www.flightsimulator.com/

KEY TERMS AND DEFINITIONS

Anticipatory Engagement: Building anticipation and intrigue by providing virtual sneak peeks, displays, and interactive experiences of actual locations in order to pique interest and inspire travel decisions.

Collaborative Innovation: Collaborations involving tourism boards, technology companies, creators, and travel agencies to co-create metaverse travel experiences that increase diversity, authenticity, and interest in virtual exploration.

Emotional Resonance: The intense bonds and attachments individuals form to virtual places and events in the metaverse, which are frequently sparked through sensory interaction and storytelling.

Hybrid Future: The coexistence of conventional and metaverse travel options, where real and virtual worlds live peacefully to accommodate various traveller tastes and improve the entire travel ecosystem.

Immersive Experiences: Engaging interactions that immerse people in virtual worlds using virtual reality and augmented reality technologies, activating many senses to enhance a sense of presence and emotional connection.

Metaverse Tourism: A new idea that blends physical and digital exploration by utilising virtual reality, augmented reality, and digital platforms to create immersive and engaging travel experiences inside of virtual locales.

NFTs (Non-Fungible Tokens): Digital collectibles and artwork that serve as proof of ownership or unique item ownership, allowing users to buy and sell virtual trinkets from metaverse travel.

Personalized Adventures: Allowing users to personalise their journeys, conversations, and stories inside virtual places. Tailoring metaverse travel experiences to individual interests.

Chapter 7
Navigating the Metaverse: Opportunities and Challenges in Tourism

Arpita Srivastava
https://orcid.org/0000-0002-9734-8008
G.L. Bajaj Institute of Management and Research, India

Nidhi Srivastava
https://orcid.org/0000-0002-3350-0728
G.L. Bajaj Institute of Management and Research, India

Sunetra Saha
https://orcid.org/0000-0003-0879-774X
Amity Business School, Amity University, Noida, India

ABSTRACT

The metaverse is regarded as the forthcoming advancement in the realm of the internet, representing a collaborative environment wherein physical and digital domains intersect to provide heightened levels of immersion and interactivity for users, frequently encompassing both virtual reality (VR) and augmented reality (AR). The Metaverse is poised to usher in a transformative era for the field of travel and tourism management. It empowers destination awareness, strategic positioning, and brand enhancement while also facilitating efficient coordination through the use of digital twins. Utilizing a systematic review of scholarly literature, media articles, and industry reports, this chapter establishes a comprehensive definition and conceptual framework for the Metaverse ecosystem within the context of tourism and travel. Additionally, this research also underscores the capabilities inherent in the Metaverse and sheds light on the emerging opportunities it presents. Furthermore, it discerns and identifies the challenges that lie ahead for the future development of this domain.

DOI: 10.4018/979-8-3693-1103-5.ch007

1. INTRODUCTION

Information and Communication Technologies (ICTs) have been substantially transforming the foundational elements of competition by instigating significant disruptions within the tourism industry (Werthner & Klein, 1999). Service providers within tourist destinations, tour operators, and other intermediaries are actively developing novel approaches to cater to their customers. They are making investments in innovative sales channels and restructuring their production processes for travel and leisure products. The swift advancement of smartphones and mobile commerce has underscored their capacity to facilitate transformative shifts within the tourism sector (Wang et al., 2016). Smartphones enhance contextual relevance, thereby enabling real-time value co-creation within specific contexts (Buhalis, 2020). Encouraging customers to actively engage in activities within a company's mobile app has been shown to amplify both the frequency and the amount of their purchases (Jang et al., 2021).

This offers unparalleled prospects for the domains of tourism management and marketing, as well as for immersive engagement with various stakeholders. Travelers now have the capability to preview tourism destinations and services prior to making their purchases, and they can also enhance their real experiences at the destination through such digital means (Loureiro et al., 2020; Rauschnabel, 2022).

The Metaverse has gained increasing prominence over the past decade. The release of the Avatar movie in 2009 played a pivotal role in introducing people to virtual technology and significantly raising its public profile. The Metaverse has attracted considerable interest, particularly following Facebook's strategic shift in rebranding itself as Meta and reorienting its business focus toward the Metaverse (Glover, 2022; Pew Research Centre, 2022). The Metaverse represents a novel paradigm for engaging with various facets of reality, encompassing the realms of actuality, augmented reality, virtual reality, and mixed reality. It is an integral component of what is commonly referred to as "Web 3.0," which constitutes a new phase of internet evolution, also characterized by technologies such as artificial intelligence, blockchain, and pioneering developments in the digital and *phygital* spheres. Users gain entry to the Metaverse through 3D viewing interfaces, enabling them to partake in virtual experiences that connect them with lifelike avatars, fellow users, objects, concerts, events, travel, and an array of other offerings (Gent, 2022; Lee,2021 & Ludlow, 2007)

In recent times, the Metaverse has garnered significant attention, capturing the interest of both scholars and industry professionals. This heightened focus has been further accentuated by the constraints imposed by the COVID-19 pandemic, leading to a greater familiarity with virtual tours and an increased willingness to embrace and incorporate the Metaverse into the realm of tourism (El-Said & Aziz, 2022).

As per the analysis by Technavio's experts, the projected market size of the Metaverse within the travel and tourism industry is anticipated to reach a valuation of USD 188.24 billion by the year 2026, demonstrating a steady Compound Annual Growth Rate (CAGR) of 26.01% (refer to figure 1)

According to (Lundmark,2022) by the year 2030, virtually every tangible device capable of digital connectivity will be interconnected. Ultimately, every action executed in the digital realm will exert an impact on the physical world, and conversely, actions in the physical world will influence the digital sphere. Consequently, the concept of the Metaverse transcends mere dependence on virtual reality headsets; instead, it signifies the convergence of complementary technologies, encompassing cloud and edge computing (near data sources), artificial intelligence, blockchain, the Internet of Things, virtual reality, augmented reality, and digital twins.

(Buhalis & Karatay, 2022) emphasize that the Metaverse is poised to bring about a significant transformation within the tourism industry. Nevertheless, the extent to which tourism may undergo change in response to the influence of the Metaverse remains a relatively unexplored area of inquiry.

2. THE EMERGENCE OF METAVERSE

The term "Metaverse" was originally introduced by Neal Stephenson in his 1992 science fiction novel, "Snow Crash." As depicted in the narrative, the Metaverse represents a comprehensive virtual realm that exists in parallel to the physical world. The Metaverse is manifesting as a highly realistic immersive virtual environment where individuals can fluidly navigate for both professional and social purposes. This navigation is facilitated through the use of devices capable of supporting

Figure 1. Projected market size of the Metaverse
Source: https://www.technavio.com/report/Metaverse-market-in-travel-and-tourism-industry-market-industry-analysis

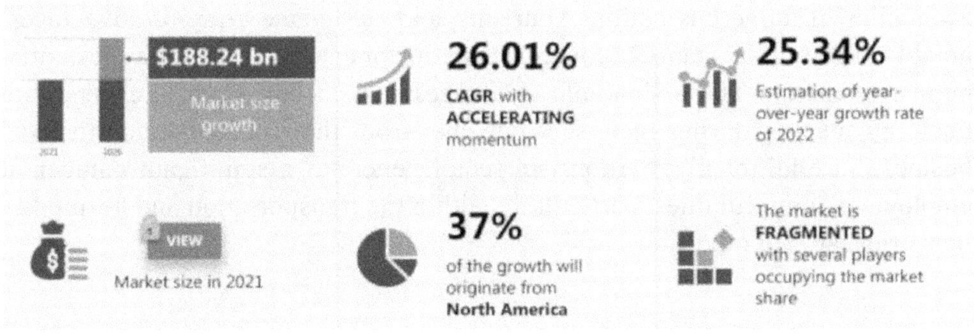

immersive technologies, including Mixed Reality (MR) and Virtual Reality (VR) headsets, as well as smart glasses (Zhang & Ye, 2021). According to (Davis et al. 2009), the term "Metaverse" is delineated as "an immersive three-dimensional virtual world in which individuals engage as avatars, both with each other and with software agents. This interaction employs the metaphor of the physical world but operates without its inherent physical constraints."In the perspective of (Moy & Gadgil, 2022) from J.P. Morgan, the concept of the Metaverse is characterized as "a seamless integration of our physical and digital existence, forging a cohesive virtual community wherein individuals can engage in work, leisure, relaxation, transactions, and social interactions." Oh et al. (2023) define the metaverse as a *"simulated extension of the physical world."*

The advent of the fourth technological revolution, characterized by persistent connectivity, the robust processing capabilities of personal devices, and groundbreaking computing paradigms such as artificial intelligence and blockchain, has catalyzed a transformative shift, enabling the practical realization of the Metaverse. As per insights from the Financial Times, it is projected that interactions within the Metaverse will supplant Smartphone-based communication in the forthcoming decade. Given this trajectory, it is of growing significance to gain a comprehensive understanding of the contemporary Metaverse phenomenon and its potential implications for the tourism industry.

3. THE EMERGENCE OF TOURISM AND TOURISM INDUSTRY

Tourism, as delineated by the United Nations World Tourism Organization (2008), is characterized as a multifaceted social, cultural, and economic occurrence that encompasses the displacement of individuals from their habitual surroundings to foreign countries or locales, driven by personal, business, or professional motives.

The Tourism Industry encompasses all activities associated with the temporary relocation of individuals from their habitual places of residence. This sector ranks among the world's largest industries, playing a significant role in driving the economies of numerous nations.Tourism yields a diverse array of advantages, notably including substantial economic benefits for nations that draw a substantial number of visitors. These economic advantages stem not only from the expenditure made by tourists during their stay but also from their contributions to local businesses. Additionally, the tourism sector generates a significant number of employment opportunities, particularly within the transportation and hospitality industries, among others.

4. HOW METAVERSE IS CHANGING THE TOURISM INDUSTRY

The advent of the Fourth Technological Revolution has ushered in entirely novel forms of tourism and leisure pursuits. Consequently, the concept of virtually traveling back to the Middle Ages has materialized through interactive gaming experiences. This transformative era is eroding the traditional constraints of space and time.In the realms of tourism and hospitality, the conceptualization of Metaverse tourism entails the utilization of Metaverse environments that furnish tourists with immersive spatial or tour-based experiences.

Metaverse tourism transcends conventional technological interfaces, as it integrates technology with ambient intelligence to seamlessly bridge the divide between physical and virtual environments. This holistic approach is poised to deliver a comprehensive tourist experience that encompasses the entire continuum from pre-travel preparations to on-site engagement and post-travel interactions.

The presence of the Metaverse within the hospitality and tourism domain is still in its nascent stages, necessitating deeper engagement from industry practitioners and researchers to elucidate the operational mechanisms that extend beyond existing conceptual frameworks. Within the realm of the hospitality and tourism sector, (Gursoy et al., 2022) have advanced a conceptual framework for Metaverse in the tourism context.

In the context of the definition put forth by Gursoy et al. (2022), the focus lies on highlighting how an innovative virtual environment has the potential to entice tourists to partake in immersive experiences through the utilization of Virtual Reality (VR) headsets, which facilitate a fully immersive ambiance and interactive capabilities. Metaverse Tourism, under this framework, presents an opportunity for tourists to engage with destinations, fostering connections and enjoyment within both the physical and virtual realms.

Tsai (2022) appropriately observes that entering metaverse platforms is a means for travel and tourism customers to establish a profound connection between their cognitive and emotional experiences with the virtual world, simulating the sensation of being genuinely present in environments such as airplanes, hotels, or destinations.

As per Mckinsey Report (2023), As emerging formats gain prominence, novel economic paradigms are beginning to surface. The forthcoming travel landscape is poised to exhibit a departure from exclusive online or offline experiences. Instead, we can anticipate a proliferation of hybrid offerings that amalgamate virtual events, educational entertainment (edutainment), and inspirational content with physical travel destinations.

One effective approach to navigate this multifaceted landscape is to embrace a traveller-centric perspective. By placing themselves in the position of their intended tourists, travel enterprises can discern opportunities to seamlessly incorporate pertinent virtual components into their offerings.

Virtual experiences with significant potential are concentrated on select, distinct phases within the comprehensive traveller journey (refer to figure 2). The critical considerations encompass identifying the touchpoints that are most amenable to effective disruption, those that harbour the greatest prospects for seamless integration, and steps that can be elevated through immersive elements, thereby enabling exhilarating, fantastical, or premium experiences that surpass what the physical world can offer. Among these considerations, three specific touchpoints emerge as particularly promising: travel inspiration, virtual events, and visitor support.

The emergence of the Metaverse presents a substantial $13 billion prospect within the realm of tourism inspiration, primarily propelled by digital travel advertising. Utilizing virtual spaces to exhibit various aspects, such as hotel amenities, airline accommodations, or even entire landmarks, serves to stimulate the inclination for travel. These immersive virtual environments provide a comprehensive depiction of a destination, aid travellers in their decision-making process, showcase a broader array of offerings, and enhance awareness of less-familiar locales.

Certain destinations have been actively investigating the concept of virtual concierge services, aiming to assist travellers throughout every phase of their journey by offering real-time itineraries, information dissemination, troubleshooting assistance, visa-related guidance, and other pertinent support. As an exemplar, Qatar Airways has introduced a MetaHuman cabin crew to facilitate interactive

Figure 2. Distinct phases within the comprehensive traveller journey
Source: https://www.mckinsey.com/industries/travel-logistics-and-infrastructure/our-insights/tourism-in-the-Metaverse-can-travel-go-virtual

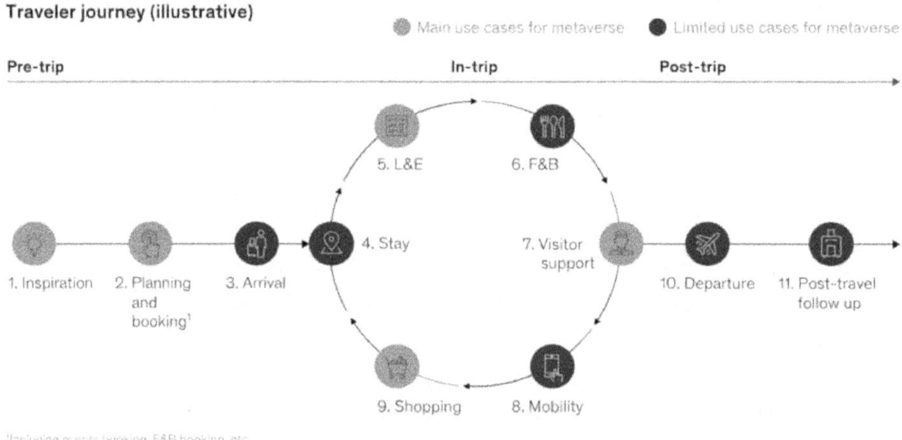

and engaging customer interactions. Notably, immersive applications of this nature already represent more than 1 percent of total investment in chatbot technology, and this figure is poised for further expansion in the foreseeable future.

In response to the travel limitations imposed by the pandemic, ZEPETO World has emerged as a smartphone application enabling users to generate personalized avatars and embark on virtual journeys throughout Korea. One notable feature of this application is its intricately detailed interactive map of Han River Park, which attracts nearly 257,000 visitors daily. In addition to exploring virtual locales, users can engage in interactive communication, indulge in shopping activities, and partake in live performances. As of the present, ZEPETO World boasts an impressive user base of approximately 190 million members.

In the context of Metaverse Tourism, activity components play a pivotal role in augmenting interactions within the virtual environment. The integration of appealing and inventive activities, coupled with gamification elements, serves to enrich the engagement of tourists. Additionally, the Metaverse Tourism framework should offer adaptable activities that align with the demographic profiles and preferences of tourists. Furthermore, it is worth noting that Metaverse Tourism is poised to bolster the growth of the creative economy ecosystem.The emergence of the Metaverse holds the potential to significantly disrupt various sectors within the global economy. Particularly, it presents substantial opportunities for the tourism and travel industries, wherein the possibilities of hybrid and entirely immersive digital destinations loom prominently on the horizon.

At present, opportunities within the Metaverse may be constrained to specific pivotal touchpoints, notably encompassing travel inspiration, events, and educational entertainment (edutainment). The prospect of the Metaverse playing a substantive role in comprehensive end-to-end travel experiences may necessitate an extended timeframe for realization, and it remains uncertain whether this will indeed come to fruition.

4.1 Metaverse Innovations

The advent of the metaverse has the potential to redefine conventional frameworks across various facets of human existence, with marketing being no exception. Certain enterprises are presently offering virtual three-dimensional renditions of genuine physical locales. As an illustration, one can now access the Louvre Museum in Paris through virtual reality (VR). Virtual patrons have the opportunity to peruse exhibits, partake in concerts, or engage in virtual strolls around the museum, even meeting friends in this digital realm.

Qatar Airways has elevated this concept by introducing a fully guided and narrated experience led by a digital cabin crew. A 3D human model will guide users through their virtual encounter, providing detailed explanations of onboard features and delivering an unprecedented level of interaction and immersion, surpassing other virtual reality airline experiences.

Indian enterprises such as Mahindra & Mahindra, Tanishq, and MakeMyTrip have entered the metaverse domain, actively contributing to the shaping of the digital landscape for the future. MakeMyTrip, the prominent travel company, introduced non-fungible tokens (NFTs) portraying virtual vacation experiences centered around India's premier travel destinations. Each NFT was priced at Rs 14,999.

5. METAVERSE MARKET DRIVER IN TRAVEL AND TOURISM INDUSTRY

In this segment we will explore how the Metaverse is going to drive the travel and tourism industry, serving as a catalyst for innovation, enhanced customer engagement, and unprecedented business growth.

5.1 Immersive Destination Previews

Imagine being able to step into your dream travel destination from the comfort of your home. The Metaverse makes this possible by offering immersive destination previews. Travelers can virtually explore their chosen destinations, immersing themselves in lifelike simulations that provide a realistic preview of what to expect. This experience allows travellers to make more informed decisions about their trips, leading to higher levels of customer satisfaction and reducing the chances of disappointment upon arrival. The Metaverse's immersive destination previews have the potential to revolutionize the way travellers plan their trips. Instead of relying solely on static images and reviews, they can step into a virtual representation of the destination, allowing for a more authentic and informed decision-making process.

5.2 Enhanced Booking and Planning

Booking and planning a trip can often be a cumbersome process involving multiple websites and platforms. The Metaverse seeks to streamline this experience by integrating with booking and planning services. Travelers can research, plan, and book their entire trips within the Metaverse, benefiting from seamless transactions and real-time information updates. This integration not only simplifies the traveller's journey but also enhances the overall booking experience. Travelers can access all the information they need in one place, from flights and accommodations to activities and dining options. This convenience saves time and reduces the stress associated with planning a trip, making travel more accessible and enjoyable. According to Buhalis et al. (2023), in the forthcoming era of tourism enriched by the metaverse, individuals will have the capability to explore and choose their accommodations by navigating their avatars within the digital twin space corresponding to the selected venue. Hospitality and tourism entities should strategically leverage the Metaverse to tailor and collaboratively create hybrid experiences that seamlessly integrate both virtual and physical elements.

5.3 Virtual Tours and Activities

One of the exciting possibilities offered by the Metaverse is the ability to host virtual tours and activities that closely mimic real-world experiences. Travelers can explore historical sites, embark on guided tours, or even attend cultural events—all without leaving their homes. This not only broadens the range of experiences available to travellers but also caters to individuals with physical limitations who may otherwise be unable to participate in such activities. For example, a history enthusiast can explore the ancient ruins of Rome through a Metaverse tour, complete with historical context and interactive elements. This level of immersion can significantly enhance the educational and entertainment value of travel experiences.

5.4 Personalized Travel Recommendations

In the era of big data and artificial intelligence, the Metaverse leverages these technologies to provide highly personalized travel recommendations. By analyzing user preferences, past travel behavior, and real-time data, Metaverse platforms can suggest tailored travel itineraries, accommodations, and activities. Imagine receiving travel recommendations that are uniquely crafted to align with your interests, whether you're a foodie, an adventure seeker, or a history buff. This level of personalization not only enhances the traveller's experience but also fosters customer loyalty. Travelers are more likely to return to platforms that consistently provide them with valuable and personalized recommendations.

5.5 Virtual Travel Agencies

Metaverse-based travel agencies are emerging as a novel way to plan and book trips. These virtual agencies operate within the Metaverse, offering expert advice, itinerary planning, and booking services. Travelers can interact with virtual travel agents in real-time, receiving personalized recommendations and guidance. These virtual travel agencies have the potential to revolutionize the travel industry by combining the convenience of online booking with the expertise and personalized service of traditional travel agencies. Travelers can consult with virtual agents to plan complex itineraries, receive destination-specific insights, and access exclusive deals.

5.6 Metaverse-Enhanced Hotels and Accommodations

The Metaverse is not limited to enhancing the planning and booking stages of travel; it can also transform the on-site experience. Hotels and accommodations can leverage Metaverse technology to offer guests unique and customizable experiences. For instance, guests may have the option to customize their room's virtual decor or ambiance, creating a personalized and immersive environment. Whether it's adjusting the lighting, selecting virtual art to adorn the walls, or choosing a virtual view from their room, guests can tailor their accommodations to their preferences. Additionally, hotels can use Metaverse technology to provide virtual concierge services. Guests can interact with virtual concierges to request information, book services, or even explore virtual representations of the hotel's amenities.

5.7 Collaborative Travel Planning

The Metaverse promotes collaborative travel planning, allowing groups of travellers to explore and make decisions together in a shared virtual space. This not only fosters social interaction but also strengthens group dynamics, making the travel experience more enjoyable and memorable. Traveling with friends or family often involves coordinating schedules, preferences, and activities. The Metaverse offers a platform where group members can virtually meet, explore destination options, and collectively plan their trip. This collaborative approach ensures that everyone's interests are considered and accommodated.

5.8 Language and Cultural Preparation

Preparing for international travel often involves learning about the local language and culture. The Metaverse can facilitate this preparation through language learning and cultural immersion programs. Users can interact with native speakers, practice language skills, and familiarize themselves with local customs and traditions. This preparation enhances cross-cultural understanding and communication during travel. Travelers who have engaged in virtual language and cultural immersion are better equipped to navigate foreign destinations, communicate with locals, and appreciate the richness of different cultures.

5.9 Sustainable Travel Initiatives

The Metaverse has the potential to promote sustainable travel practices. By offering virtual experiences that reduce the need for physical travel, it contributes to lowering carbon footprints. Travelers can explore destinations, attend events, and engage in cultural exchanges without the environmental impact associated with traditional travel. Additionally, Metaverse platforms can educate travellers about eco-friendly choices and responsible tourism practices. This awareness can lead to more conscious and sustainable travel decisions, aligning with the growing global interest in environmentally friendly travel.

5.10 Business Opportunities for Local Communities

The Metaverse offers a unique opportunity for local communities to showcase their culture, heritage, and products to a global audience. Small businesses, artisans, and tour guides can establish a presence in the Metaverse, attracting a new customer base and expanding their reach beyond geographical constraints. For example, a local craftsperson can sell handmade goods to a global audience through a Metaverse marketplace. A tour guide can offer virtual tours of their hometown, introducing travellers to hidden gems and local traditions. This not only generates economic opportunities for local communities but also fosters cultural exchange and appreciation

6. KEY METAVERSE MARKET CHALLENGE IN TRAVEL AND TOURISM INDUSTRY

The emergence of the Metaverse in the tourism industry has generated significant excitement due to its potential to create novel experiences and opportunities for tourists and platform owners. However, alongside these prospects, a range of formidable challenges and threats have also come to the fore. These challenges have the potential to not only disrupt established practices but also lead to the co-destruction of value for various stakeholders within the complex tourism ecosystem. In this exploration, we delve into the major challenges posed by the Metaverse in the context of the tourism industry, elucidating each dimension of concern and its potential implications.

6.1 Reality and Illusion Confusion

At the heart of the Metaverse's challenges lies the issue of reality and illusion confusion. The immersive nature of virtual environments within the Metaverse can blur the boundaries between what is real and what is simulated. Analysts and scholars alike have expressed concerns that this blurring of lines may lead to a profound sense of bewilderment among users, making it increasingly challenging to distinguish between reality and illusion. This confusion carries significant consequences. The Metaverse's capacity to obscure reality can diminish critical thinking and imaginative faculties, imperilling users' ability to reflect thoughtfully on their experiences. In essence, the allure of the Metaverse may lead to a decline in users' capacity for introspection and self-awareness, potentially altering their relationship with both the virtual and physical worlds. As users immerse themselves in Metaverse experiences, there is a pressing need for research to understand how this blurring of reality affects their cognitive processes and emotional well-being. Such inquiries can shed light on the psychological impact of the Metaverse, informing strategies to mitigate potential negative effects.

6.2 Technological Challenges

A core challenge in the Metaverse's adoption within the tourism industry is the state of its technological development. Unlike mature technologies, the Metaverse is still predominantly conceptual rather than fully operational. While platforms are gradually evolving, there is a notable absence of established blueprints or best practices to guide its development. This technological uncertainty presents multifaceted challenges. Organizations seeking to establish a virtual presence in the Metaverse must navigate uncharted waters, taking considerable financial and strategic risks. The absence of predefined guidelines exacerbates the complexity of developing platforms and solutions, further heightening the uncertainty imperative (Xu and Buhalis, 2021; Xu et al., 2017, 2016). To navigate this terrain successfully, tourism destinations and organizations must demonstrate a willingness to collaborate with innovators from diverse industries. The cultivation of a virtual presence and digital counterparts, often referred to as "digital twins," necessitates not only financial resources but also creativity and ingenuity. It is akin to embarking on a frontier-land investment, demanding a robust appetite for risk. In this context, the gamification of the tourism ecosystem emerges as a guiding principle. The gaming industry has achieved the highest level of *virtuality* to date and can serve as a compass for tourism organizations seeking to establish themselves in the Metaverse. Consequently, tourism entities must allocate resources not only to platform development but also to the acquisition of users, as attracting individuals to their virtual domains becomes paramount.

6.3 Economic and Consumer Experience Challenges

The economic dimension of Metaverse adoption introduces a host of challenges, particularly for tourism destinations and organizations. Many entities, especially those in peripheral or economically disadvantaged regions, lack the financial and technological resources necessary for Metaverse development. This financial disparity could potentially result in the exclusion of these regions from the Metaverse-driven transformation of the tourism industry. Moreover, the financial hurdles faced by individual users can also pose a significant challenge. The acquisition of necessary equipment, such as VR/MR headsets or sensory attire, can be cost-prohibitive for many. For instance, Meta's recent introduction of the Meta Quest Pro MR headset comes with a hefty price tag, reaching up to USD 1,500. Consequently, individuals and businesses interested in participating in the Metaverse experience must be prepared for a substantial initial investment. This upfront expenditure has the potential to exacerbate economic inequalities in the real world. Marginalized groups, already disadvantaged economically, may find themselves further excluded from the benefits of technological progress due to financial constraints. The exorbitant cost of acquiring equipment may also deepen the digital divide, limiting access to the Metaverse for organizations and potential users alike. It is important to note that the economic challenges extend beyond mere access. The high acquisition costs of equipment may deter users without a compelling desire or clear purpose from venturing into the Metaverse. This raises questions about the role of economic disparities and affordability in determining who can partake in the Metaverse and to what extent. An additional layer of complexity arises from the risk of motion sickness during prolonged immersion in virtual spaces. This physical discomfort, as noted by Pratt (2022), is a valid concern for those who can afford the necessary gadgets. Therefore, addressing the challenges associated with motion sickness is essential for creating a user-friendly Metaverse experience.

6.4 Ethical and Legal Complexities

Ethical and legal challenges abound within virtual environments like the Metaverse, reflecting the multifaceted nature of the medium. These challenges encompass a wide array of concerns, from individual behavior to broader societal implications. Virtual environments may serve as fertile ground for a range of illegal, immoral, or unethical activities. These activities necessitate the establishment of appropriate legislation and vigilant oversight to ensure that virtual spaces do not become lawless domains. This is particularly complex in the context of tourism, where users traverse international borders, rendering the applicability of laws location-dependent. Instances of harassment, aggressive behavior, cyberstalking, threats of violence, and various forms of assault are disturbingly prevalent in virtual environments. Individuals often hide behind virtual personas and engage in behaviours that deviate significantly from their real-world conduct. These instances highlight the potential for ethical and legal transgressions in virtual spaces, necessitating vigilant monitoring and enforcement. Beyond individual behaviour, the Metaverse introduces complex issues related to fraud, cybercrime, money laundering, terrorism, gambling, drug abuse, prostitution, pornography, and child exploitation. These criminal activities represent not only ethical concerns but also significant law enforcement challenges within the Metaverse (Qin et al., 2022). One particularly concerning aspect is the potential for bullying and harassment behaviours in the virtual universe. An illustrative example is the incident in May 2022, where users of Horizon World reported instances of their avatars being raped or sexually harassed (Soon, 2002). Such incidents underscore the gravity of the challenge and the urgent need for mechanisms to combat harassment within the Metaverse. Moreover, the immersive nature of the Metaverse raises concerns about addictive behaviours. In contrast to the traditional Internet experience, the Metaverse blurs the demarcation between the physical and virtual worlds. It offers experiences that users may find challenging to distinguish from reality. As a result, there is an elevated risk of addiction and abuse, particularly when users turn to the Metaverse as an escape.

The potential for addictive behaviours in the Metaverse is a critical concern, as it can lead to excessive participation in digital activities and virtual gaming, potentially resulting in addiction and its associated negative consequences. The World Health Organization acknowledged this concern by adding "gaming disorder" to the 2018 version of its International Classification of Diseases.

6.5 Privacy and Security Concerns

Privacy and security issues loom large in the Metaverse, requiring careful consideration and robust safeguards. Several critical questions and concerns come to the forefront:

a. **Alignment of Virtual Identities with Real Identities**: A fundamental issue in the Metaverse is the alignment of virtual identities with users' real-world identities. This alignment has implications for issues such as accountability, privacy, and user safety.
b. **Management of User Data:** The extensive interactions within the Metaverse generate a massive amount of user data. The storage, management, and usage of this data raise complex privacy and security concerns. Organizations and platforms must navigate the intricate landscape of data protection while providing personalized experiences.

c. **Liability in Multi-Stakeholder Environments:** The Metaverse often involves multiple businesses, organizations, and platforms in a user's experience. Determining liability for privacy and security issues becomes increasingly complex in such multi-stakeholder environments.
d. **Protection of Intellectual Property**: Intellectual property and the infringement of copyrighted content are critical considerations within the Metaverse. Tourism brands and destinations must protect their identities and assets in this digital space.

To address these privacy and security challenges, businesses and platforms must adopt comprehensive precautionary and protective measures. For instance, Meta has introduced a feature called "Personal Boundary" to afford users greater control over their Metaverse experiences. This reflects the proactive approach required to safeguard user privacy and security in virtual environments.

6.6 Leadership in Navigating Challenges

The multifaceted challenges posed by the Metaverse require visionary leadership to steer the course successfully. History has shown that every technological breakthrough, from the advent of the Internet to the proliferation of mobile phones and smart tourism, has disrupted established paradigms and introduced new challenges. However, despite these challenges, the anticipated benefits of the Metaverse propel the next information and communication technology (ICT) revolution. Innovative tourism destinations and organizations must strategically plan for the future to gain a competitive edge (Buhalis, 2020). Effective leadership in this context involves a comprehensive understanding of the potential benefits and risks associated with the Metaverse. It necessitates the formulation of strategies that identify innovative processes and resources required by each organization. With a thorough evaluation of the costs and benefits of Metaverse strategies, leadership teams can make informed decisions regarding the most suitable strategies and tactical approaches for their respective organizations. This might entail embracing a pioneering role or adopting a follower's stance, depending on the organization's goals and capabilities. In conclusion, the introduction of the Metaverse in the tourism industry holds immense promise for value creation, immersive experiences, and novel opportunities. However, these prospects are accompanied by a host of challenges that span technological, economic, ethical, legal, and security dimensions. Addressing these challenges requires a concerted effort, visionary leadership, and interdisciplinary collaboration to ensure that the Metaverse enhances the tourism industry while safeguarding the well-being and rights of all stakeholders involved.

6.7 Value Co-Creation and Co-Destruction

Despite the substantial challenges posed by the Metaverse, it is essential to recognize that this digital frontier has the potential for both value co-creation and co-destruction. While prior research has not extensively explored this phenomenon, scholars in the field of service research must delve into the dynamics of these processes within the context of Metaverse Tourism (Akaka &Vargo, 2014). The Metaverse may herald the development of a novel business model within the ecosystem layer of Metaverse architecture. This could offer tourists a distinct service paradigm and transform their experiences. Future investigations should focus on discerning the most suitable business model for Metaverse Tourism to facilitate the seamless delivery of its services. Moreover, forthcoming research should delve into the management and governance of the creative economy within Metaverse Tourism. Understanding how this ecosystem can thrive through the infusion of innovative capabilities from its network participants is critical. The generative potential of this ecosystem could provide valuable insights for comprehending the mechanisms underpinning future studies of ecosystem platforms in the service-oriented era (Thomas & Tee, 2022).

6.8 Addressing Loneliness

An often-overlooked dimension of the Metaverse's impact is the potential for virtual loneliness. The immersive nature of Extended Reality (XR) can affect interpersonal dynamics among tourists. Feelings of loneliness, paradoxically, can motivate individuals to seek interaction and communication with others. Metaverse Tourism must consider the issue of loneliness and aim to provide a reasonable quantity and quality of social interactions. Consequently, future research should aim to elucidate the impact of Metaverse Tourism on tourist loneliness. It should explore whether interactions and communication in the virtual environment can mitigate the degree of tourist loneliness. Additionally, the potential role of non-player characters (NPCs) in facilitating and enhancing such interactions in the virtual realm warrants investigation.

6.9 Service Failure and Recovery

Service failure and recovery represent another dimension of Metaverse Tourism that requires careful consideration and exploration. The hospitality and tourism industry, characterized as a "people business," demands a profound understanding of the mechanisms underlying service failure and effective recovery strategies (Kim et al., 2010). For instance, tourists may attach significantly greater value to avoiding losses than to accruing gains. Consequently, service failures may trigger heightened negative emotions among tourists. Moreover, the unique virtual environment of

Metaverse Tourism poses distinctive challenges for service recovery, given the absence of direct physical interactions. Research inquiries should delve into the prevalence of service failures in the virtual environment and the emotions elicited in such situations. Additionally, the impact of service failures on other tourists and the optimal modes of interaction and communication to enhance para-social interactions and effectively address failures in the virtual milieu require exploration.

In conclusion, the challenges and opportunities presented by the Metaverse in the tourism industry are multifaceted and interconnected. The successful integration of the Metaverse into tourism practices hinges on a holistic approach that considers technological readiness, economic disparities, ethical and legal concerns, security, leadership, value dynamics, loneliness, and service experiences. As the Metaverse continues to evolve and shape the future of tourism, research and innovation will play a pivotal role in navigating these challenges and unlocking its transformative potential

7. FUTURE OF METAVERSE FOR TOURISM

The advent of a parallel virtual realm, one mirroring the physical world, holds the potential to usher in a multitude of transformative possibilities. Within the Metaverse, the sphere of tourism presents an array of boundless opportunities. The travel and tourism industry, encompassing sectors such as hotels, airlines, cruises, and more, stands poised to reap substantial benefits from the emergence of the Metaverse.

Notably, the Metaverse remains in its nascent stages, eliciting diverse perspectives from various stakeholders. However, the landscape is evolving rapidly, fuelled by the participation of established industry giants like Facebook, Microsoft, Google, and others. These entities are investing across various facets of the Metaverse, spanning gaming, hardware, networking, virtual platforms, financial systems, and social media, among others. This dynamic engagement contributes to the establishment of standardized frameworks and advanced technologies, fostering the maturation and authenticity of the Metaverse. The Metaverse represents a promising avenue for tourists to immerse themselves in enjoyable and pleasurable experiences within a virtual field, replete with various objects and environments. Moreover, Metaverse tourism stands as an alternative approach to promoting cities, locales, and events to a broader audience of tourists and stakeholders. This vision of the Metaverse can be further enriched through synergistic integration with other cutting-edge technologies, including blockchain, artificial intelligence (AI), and digital clothing. Indeed, the advent of the Metaverse signals a pivotal juncture in the evolution of virtual environments, extending beyond mere *virtuality* to encapsulate and extend the boundaries of physical reality. A profound understanding of the Metaverse is integral to crafting a truly comprehensive and digitally immersive experience. Within the realm of tourism, the Metaverse emerges as a viable option for leisure activities, ushering in innovative avenues for the development of Metaverse Tourism. This novel paradigm in tourism will pave the way for inventive approaches to showcase cities, destinations, and events to a diverse audience of tourists and stakeholders.

As interactive devices within the virtual environment continue to evolve, the adaptation of extended reality (XR) technologies becomes increasingly seamless. Moreover, the Metaverse can be synergistically fused with other technologies such as blockchain and digital clothing, amplifying the richness of the tourist experience. With younger generations being inherently tech-savvy and digital natives, their adoption of the Metaverse is anticipated to be swift and comprehensive. Consequently, it appears inevitable that the Metaverse will transition from a speculative concept to a tangible and enduring reality in the not-so-distant future. By comprehending and effectively incorporating the advantages inherent in the Metaverse, which encompass enriched experiences, cost efficiencies, and heightened reliability, managerial personnel can not only meet but surpass customer expectations. This, in turn, culminates in heightened levels of customer satisfaction, loyalty, and advocacy, fostering enduring and mutually beneficial relationships with tourists.

From Metaverse-based travel experiences to expedient virtual reality (VR) tours, the realm of virtual reality has already exerted a substantial influence on the decision-making process related to destination selection, travel bookings, and the discovery of travel inspiration. The increasing ubiquity of VR headsets as a standard consumer accessory is facilitating the rapid integration of VR technology into the everyday lives of a growing number of individuals.

Although its significance is anticipated to grow in the foreseeable future, it remains improbable that Metaverse-based travel experiences will entirely supplant physical travel. Instead, it is more likely that Metaverse technology will augment and complement the conventional travel industry, introducing innovative avenues for engaging with prospective customers.

Furthermore, a prominent practical contribution of this present paper is the illumination of the advantageous features stemming from the foundational technologies that constitute the Metaverse, benefiting both tourists and service providers. This emphasis serves not only as a catalyst for innovation but also furnishes clear guidance to streamline the experiences of tourists and facilitate the operations of tourism professionals. Undoubtedly, as the Metaverse continues to evolve, its potential impact on the tourism sector holds the promise of profound transformation. This evolution is poised to revolutionize the manner in which we perceive, engage with, and partake in the realm of travel, marking a significant milestone in the tourism landscape.

REFERENCES

Akaka, M. A., & Vargo, S. L. (2014). Technology as an operant resource in service (eco)systems. *Information Systems and e-Business Management, 12*(3), 367–384. doi:10.1007/s10257-013-0220-5

Buhalis, D., Lopez, E. P., & Martinez-Gonzalez, J. A. (2020). Influence of young consumers' external and internal variables on their e-loyalty to tourism sites. *Journal of Destination Marketing & Management, 15*, 100409. https://doi.org/. jdmm.2020.100409 doi:10.1016/j

Buhalis, D., & Karatay, N. (2022). Mixed reality for Generation Z in cultural heritage tourism towards Metaverse. In J. L. Stienmetz, B. Ferrer-Rosell, & D. Massimo (Eds.), *Information and communication technologies in tourism 2022* (pp. 16–27). Springer. doi:10.1007/978-3-030-94751-4_2

Buhalis, D., Lin, M., & Leung, D. (2023). Metaverse as a driver for customer experience and value co-creation: Implications for hospitality and tourism management and marketing. *International Journal of Contemporary Hospitality Management, 35*(2), 701–716. doi:10.1108/IJCHM-05-2022-0631

Davis, A., Murphy, J. D., Owens, D., Khazanchi, D., & Zigurs, I. (2009). Avatars, people, and virtual worlds: Foundations for research in Metaverses. *Journal of the Association for Information Systems, 10*(2), 90–117. doi:10.17705/1jais.00183

Dwivedi, Y., Hughes, L., Baabdullah, A., Ribeiro-Navarrete, S., Giannakis, M., Al-Debei, M., Dennehy, D., Metri, B., Buhalis, D., Cheung, C., Conboy, K., Doyle, R., Goyal, D. P., Gustafsson, A., Jebabli, I., Kim, Y.-G., Kim, J., Koos, S., Kreps, D., ... Wamba, F. (2022). Metaverse beyond the hype: Multidisciplinary perspectives on emerging challenges, opportunities, and agenda for research, practice and policy. *International Journal of Information Management, 66*, 102542. doi:10.1016/j. ijinfomgt.2022.102542

Dwivedi, Y., Hughes, L., Wang, Y., Alalwan, A. A., Ahn, S., Balakrishnan, J., Barta, S., Belk, R., Buhalis, D., Dutot, V., Felix, R., & Filieri, R. (n.d.). How Metaverse will change the future of marketing: Implications for Research and Practice. *Psychology and Marketing*. Advance online publication. doi:10.1002/mar.21767

El-Said, O., & Aziz, H. (2022). Virtual tours a means to an end: An analysis of virtual tours' role in tourism recovery post COVID-19. *Journal of Travel Research, 61*(3), 528–548. doi:10.1177/0047287521997567

Gent, E. (2022). Lessons from a Second Life before Meta, Philip Rosedale Created an Online Universe. *IEEE Spectrum, 59*(1), 19. doi:10.1109/MSPEC.2022.9676346

Glover, G. (2022). *Bank of America shares how to invest in the Metaverse and 13 other disruptive technologies that could transform our lives and become a market worth over $6 trillion by 2030.* Retrieved from https://www.businessinsider.com / investing-strategy-tech-6g-Metaverse-flying-cars-ai-moonshots-2021-9

Gursoy, D., Malodia, S., & Dhir, A. (2022). The Metaverse in the hospitality and tourism industry: An overview of current trends and future research directions. *Journal of Hospitality Marketing & Management, 31*(5), 527–534. doi:10.1080/19368623.2022.2072504

Jang, S., Chong, K., & Yoo, C. (2021). The effect of mobile application-driven customer participation on bakery purchase behavior: Evidence from a field experiment. *International Journal of Hospitality Management, 94*, 102865. doi:10.1016/j.ijhm.2021.102865

Kim, J. H., Ritchie, J. R., & Tung, V. W. S. (2010). The effect of memorable experience on behavioral intentions in tourism: A structural equation modeling approach. *Tourism Analysis, 15*(6), 637–648. doi:10.3727/108354210X12904412049776

Lee, L.-H., Braud, T., Zhou, P., Wang, L., Xu, D., Lin, Z., Kumar, A., Bermejo, C., & Hui, P. (2021). All One Needs to Know about Metaverse:A Complete Survey on Technological Singularity, Virtual Ecosystem, and Research Agenda. *J. Latex Cl. Files, 14*, 1–66.

Loureiro, S. M. C., Guerreiro, J., & Ali, F. (2020). 20 years of research on virtual reality and augmented reality in tourism context: A text-mining approach. *Tourism Management, 77*, 104028. doi:10.1016/j.tourman.2019.104028

Ludlow, P., & Wallace, M. (2007). *The Second Life Herald: The Virtual Tabloid that Witnessed the Dawn of the Metaverse*. MIT Press.

Lundmark, P. (2022). *The real future of the Metaverse is not for consumers*. Retrieved from https://www.ft.com/content/af0c9de8-d36e-485b-9db5-5ee1e57716cb

Martončik, M., & Lokša, J. (2016). Do World of Warcraft (MMORPG) players experience less loneliness and social anxiety in online world (virtual environment) than in real world (offline)? *Computers in Human Behavior, 56*, 127–134. doi:10.1016/j.chb.2015.11.035

Moy, C., &Gadgil, A. (2022). *Opportunities in the Metaverse: How businesses can explore the Metaverse and navigate the hype vs reality*. JPMorgan.

Oh, H. J., Kim, J., Chang, H., Jeongheon, J. C., Park, N., & Lee, S. (2023). Social benefits of living in the metaverse: The relationships among social presence, supportive interaction, social self-efcacy, and feelings of loneliness. *Computers in Human Behavior*, *139*, 107498. doi:10.1016/j.chb.2022.107498

Pew Research Center. (2022). *The Metaverse in 2040*. Pew Research Center.

Pratt, M. (2022). *Metaverse pros and cons: Top benefits and challenges*. Retrieved from https://www.techtarget.com/searchcio/tip/Metaverse-pros-and-cons-Top-benefits-and-challenges

Qin, H. X., Wang, Y., & Hui, P. (2022). *Identity, crimes, and law enforcement in the Metaverse*. arXiv preprint arXiv:2210.06134.

Rauschnabel, P. (2022). XR in tourism marketing. In D. Buhalis (Ed.), Encyclopedia of tourism management and marketing. Edward Elgar Publishing. doi:10.4337/9781800377486.xr.in.tourism

Thomas, L. D. W., & Tee, R. (2022). Generativity: A systematic review and conceptual framework. *International Journal of Management Reviews*, *24*(2), 255–278. doi:10.1111/ijmr.12277

Tsai, S. (2022). *Investigating metaverse marketing for travel and tourism*. J Vac Market., doi:10.1177/13567667221145715

Wang, D., Xiang, Z., & Fesenmaier, D. R. (2016). Smartphone use in everyday life and travel. *Journal of Travel Research*, *55*(1), 52–63. doi:10.1177/0047287514535847

Werthner, H., & Klein, S. (1999). *Information technology and tourism: a challenging ralationship*. Springer-Verlag Wien. doi:10.1007/978-3-7091-6363-4

Xu, F., & Buhalis, D. (2021). *Gamification for Tourism. Bristol*. Channel View Publications.

Xu, F., Buhalis, D., & Weber, J. (2017). Serious games and the gamification of tourism. *Tourism Management*, *60*, 244–256. doi:10.1016/j.tourman.2016.11.020

Xu, F., Tian, F., Buhalis, D., Weber, J., & Zhang, H. (2016). Tourists as mobile gamers –gamification for tourism marketing. *Journal of Travel & Tourism Marketing*, *33*(8), 1124–1142. doi:10.1080/10548408.2015.1093999

Zhang, J., & Ye, J. (2021). *Alibaba to test gaming potential of Metaverse as Big Tech firms stampede into virtual world*. Retrieved from https://www.scmp.com/tech/bigtech/article/3159691/alibaba-test-gaming-potential-Metaverse-big-tech-firms-stampede

Chapter 8
Digital Innovation in the Service Sector:
Transforming Customer Experiences

Viana Imad Hassan
https://orcid.org/0000-0002-7372-5059
University of Malta, Malta

Shakeel Basheer
https://orcid.org/0000-0001-7854-8285
Lovely Professional University, India

Faizan Ashraf Mir
https://orcid.org/0009-0008-2983-1584
Central University of Kashmir, India

Simon Georges Abou Fayad
https://orcid.org/0000-0002-8777-9023
Lebanese University, Lebanon

ABSTRACT

This chapter explores digital innovation in the service sector and its impact on customer experiences. It covers the drivers and enablers of digital innovation, emphasizing the role of technologies like AI, data analytics, and mobile apps in transforming interactions. Case studies highlight successful implementations, while challenges such as privacy and change management are discussed. The chapter also explores emerging trends like blockchain, IoT, and VR. A customer-centric approach is emphasized, stressing the importance of understanding and meeting customer needs. Practical recommendations are provided for organizations to embark on their digital innovation journey, including strategic planning, talent acquisition, and fostering an innovative culture. Overall, the chapter offers a roadmap for businesses to leverage digital technologies and revolutionize customer experiences in today's digital era.
DOI: 10.4018/979-8-3693-1103-5.ch008

INTRODUCTION

The process of integrating and utilising digital technology and strategies to revolutionise and improve the delivery of services is known as digital innovation in the service industry (Buhalis et al., 2023). It entails the creation and application of cutting-edge digital solutions that disrupt conventional service models, boost productivity, and provide clients fresh, tailored experiences (Bui, 2023). The adoption of cloud computing, artificial intelligence, data analytics, mobile applications, and online platforms are just a few examples of the many initiatives that make up digital innovation in the service sector (S. M. Park & Kim, 2022). These initiatives are designed to streamline operations, improve service offerings, and generate value for both service providers and customers. Service-oriented businesses can maintain their competitiveness in today's digitally driven market, meet changing customer expectations, and seize new chances for development and distinction by adopting digital innovation. Digital innovation's significance and effects on customer experiences (Akpojaro & Bello, 2019).

1. UNDERSTANDING DIGITAL TRANSFORMATION IN THE SERVICE SECTOR

The process of integrating digital technology and strategies to improve and revolutionise the delivery of services is known as "digital transformation" in the service industry (S. Park & Kim, 2022). It entails utilising recent technological developments to enhance operational effectiveness, customer experience, and overall business success (Jovanović & Milosavljević, 2022). Examples include artificial intelligence, cloud computing, data analytics, and automation. Digital transformation in the service sector has had a substantial impact on a number of sectors, including banking, healthcare, retail, hospitality, and transportation. Organisations are implementing digital platforms and technologies to optimise resource usage, streamline operations, and boost productivity. For instance, users can conduct transactions conveniently through internet banking services at any time, from anywhere, negating the need for physical branches and tedious paperwork (Suh & Ahn, 2022).

In addition, digital transformation enables service providers to tailor and personalise their products to satisfy particular client requirements (Mehraj et al., 2023). Organisations can give personalised suggestions, targeted marketing campaigns, and improved customer assistance with the aid of advanced data analytics and customer relationship management systems. By automating repetitive operations, lowering human error rates, and facilitating quicker service delivery, automation plays a significant role in digital transformation. Virtual assistants and chatbots are being utilised more frequently to answer questions quickly and offer immediate customer service (Higgins-Desbiolles et al., 2022). The service industry benefits from innovation as a result of digital transformation. Companies are utilising new technologies to develop new service offerings, such as ride-sharing platforms in transportation, online marketplaces in retail, and telemedicine in the healthcare sector. These improvements not only increase client comfort and accessibility, but they also open up new commercial prospects (Basheer et al., 2023).

Overall, the delivery, consumption, and experience of services are being transformed through digital transformation in the service industry. It has enormous potential for businesses to increase productivity, boost customer satisfaction, and maintain competitiveness in the ever-changing digital market. To succeed in the quickly evolving business climate of today, service providers must embrace digital transformation.

2. LITERATURE REVIEW

Overview of Digital Transformation in Service Industries

Service industries have seen substantial change as a result of digital transformation, which has completely changed how companies function and engage with their customers (Kamata, 2022). Digital transformation in the service industry entails integrating technology into many business activities, including client engagement, service delivery, back-end operations, and data management (El-Said & Aziz, 2022). With this change, service providers have been able to improve customer satisfaction, increase efficiency, and maintain their competitiveness in a quickly changing digital environment. Service industries have optimised their processes through the use of digital tools and platforms, enabling faster and more precise service delivery (Lu et al., 2022). By eliminating manual processes and utilising artificial intelligence (AI), automation and service providers may concentrate on more value-added operations. Personalised interactions, self-service options, and seamless communication across many touchpoints have all been made possible by digital channels, which have also revolutionised the way organisations connect with their clients (Gursoy et al., 2022). Service sectors now have the ability to make data-driven decisions, streamline operations, and anticipate client needs thanks to data analytics and insights gained from digital technologies. Furthermore, the digital transition has created new business models and revenue streams like subscription-based services and online marketplaces. Overall, the ability to react to shifting consumer expectations, increase operational efficiency, and foster creativity in a technologically advanced society are all made possible by digital transformation for service industries (Kamboj & Joshi, 2021).

3. KEY DRIVERS AND MOTIVATIONS FOR DIGITAL INNOVATION

The quick developments and changes in the current digital era are fueled by a number of important factors and motives for digital innovation (Tiwari et al., 2021). The constantly changing expectations and demands of the client are an important driving. Customers want smooth and tailored interactions across numerous digital platforms as technology becomes more pervasive in our daily lives. To match these expectations, acquire a competitive advantage, and improve consumer happiness, businesses are motivated to innovate digitally. The need for greater production and efficiency is another important motivator (Bolger, 2021). Organisations may automate procedures, streamline operations, and use data analytics for informed decision-making thanks to digital innovation, which eventually results in cost savings and enhanced performance. The search for fresh revenue sources and company ideas is also quite important. Disruptive innovation is made possible by digital technologies, allowing companies to investigate new markets, goods, and services. Additionally, technology's own dynamic and ever-evolving nature acts as a catalyst for digital innovation. Businesses are encouraged to take use of emerging technologies like artificial intelligence (AI), cloud computing, Internet of Things (IoT), and others in order to uncover new opportunities, spur innovation, and stay ahead of the curve. In order to gain a competitive edge and spur organisational growth, fulfilling customer expectations, enhancing efficiency, investigating new business models, and embracing emerging technology are often seen as the major drivers and incentives for digital innovation (Damar, 2021).

3.1 Challenges and Opportunities Associated With Digital Transformation

Opposition to change: Employee, stakeholder, and even customer opposition to change is one of the major issues. People who are used to using traditional methods may find it challenging to switch to new digital tools and workflows.

Talent shortage and skill gaps: Digital change frequently calls for new knowledge and abilities. Finding and keeping employees with the requisite digital skills, such as data analysis, artificial intelligence, cybersecurity, and software development, can be difficult for organisations.

Legacy infrastructure and systems: Many businesses use out-of-date legacy systems that are incompatible with cutting-edge digital technologies. It can be difficult, costly, and time-consuming to integrate new digital solutions with current infrastructure.

Data security and privacy: As a result of greater digitalization, there is a higher danger of data breaches and cyberattacks. To safeguard sensitive information and preserve customer trust, businesses must invest in effective cybersecurity solutions.

Change management: Succinct change management methods are necessary for the implementation of digital transformation initiatives. To facilitate a smooth transition, organisations must explain the advantages, resolve any fears, and offer sufficient training and support to staff.

3.2 Digital Technologies Transforming Service Delivery

Services are being delivered in a variety of businesses in a revolutionary way thanks to digital technologies, which are also improving client experiences (Kye et al., 2021). Service delivery has been more streamlined and effective thanks to the development of digital platforms, cloud computing, artificial intelligence (AI), and the Internet of Things (IoT). The transition to self-service choices is one important component of this revolution (Narin, 2021). Customers no longer need to employ conventional, time-consuming methods to access and administer services because of the advent of user-friendly mobile applications and intuitive user interfaces. Customers are empowered to solve problems, ask questions, and finish transactions on their own thanks to this self-service strategy, which reduces response times and increases customer satisfaction (Kusuma et al., 2021). Digital technologies have also made it possible for service providers to gather enormous volumes of data, giving them important insights into the tastes and behaviour of their clients. Businesses can customise their service offerings by using advanced analytics and AI algorithms to cater to customers' unique demands and preferences (Toubes et al., 2021). In addition to improving the client experience, this personalised strategy enables businesses to offer targeted marketing efforts and cross-sell or upsell pertinent items or services. Furthermore, the delivery of services in industries like healthcare and education has been transformed by digital technologies. With the rise of telemedicine and remote learning, people can now access medical treatments and educational materials at any time, from any location. Greater accessibility and convenience have resulted from this change, especially for people who live in distant locations or have limited mobility. Customers and service providers have both experienced significant cost savings as a result of the usage of digital technologies. Process automation and digitization make it unnecessary for human intervention, which minimises errors, lowers operating costs, and boosts productivity (Cai et al., 2021). Overall, it is clear that digital technologies have a transformative impact on service delivery, revolutionising how customers engage with organisations and creating new opportunities for improved experiences, customisation, accessibility, and efficiency.

4. ROLE OF MOBILE APPLICATIONS AND SMARTPHONES

4.1 Cloud Computing and Its Impact on Service Delivery

Artificial Intelligence (AI) and Machine Learning (ML): By automating processes, enabling personalised experiences, and delivering insightful insights, AI and ML technologies have revolutionised service delivery. Artificial intelligence-powered chatbots and virtual assistants are now widely used in customer care, providing round-the-clock support and answering questions (Cai & McKenna, 2021). These chatbots are capable of handling a variety of consumer encounters, from straightforward questions to challenging problems. In order to find trends and make predictions, machine learning algorithms analyse vast amounts of client data. This allows businesses to anticipate customer requirements and adjust their services accordingly. By automating repetitive operations, reducing errors, and boosting operational efficiency, AI and ML technologies significantly improve service delivery.

4.2 Internet of Things (IoT) and Its Application in the Service Sector

Internet of Things (IoT): The IoT is a network of networked objects equipped with connections, software, and sensors that enable them to gather and share data. By allowing for real-time monitoring, remote management, and predictive maintenance, this technology has completely changed the way services are delivered (Akhtar et al., 2021). IoT devices can track patient vitals, send information to healthcare providers, and send alarms in case of emergencies in sectors like healthcare. Route optimisation, traffic management, and predictive maintenance are made possible in the transportation sector by IoT-enabled sensors in infrastructure and vehicles, resulting in more efficient service delivery. In supply chain management, where real-time tracking and monitoring of items enhance efficiency and cut costs, IoT applications are also widely used.

These are only two instances of how digital technologies are altering the way services are provided. A variety of other technologies, including blockchain, augmented reality, cloud computing, and robotic process automation, are also significantly improving service delivery. The continuous development of digital technologies continues to influence service provision and open up new possibilities for businesses to provide excellent client experiences.

4.3 Artificial Intelligence (AI) and Machine Learning (ML) in Personalized Service

Personalised services have undergone a revolution thanks to artificial intelligence (AI) and machine learning (ML) in many different industries. Businesses may better understand their customers and provide personalised experiences by utilising massive volumes of data and sophisticated algorithms provided by AI and ML. Several applications of AI and ML in personalised services are shown below: Recommendations and Personalised Content: AI-powered recommendation systems provide personalised content, goods, or services based on user preferences, past behaviour, and historical data (Subasinghe et al., 2020). This is demonstrated by how AI algorithms offer movies or songs based on user interests in streaming platforms like Netflix or music streaming services like Spotify. E-commerce Personalization: To offer personalised product recommendations, targeted marketing, and specialised shopping experiences, e-commerce platforms leverage AI and ML algorithms. These systems take into account variables like browsing history, purchasing patterns, and demographic data to provide pertinent recommendations and discounts.

Healthcare Personalization: AI and ML have a huge impact on healthcare personalization. In order to offer individualised treatment plans, disease predictions, and preventive care advice, they can analyse patient data, including medical records, genetic information, and lifestyle data. With AI algorithms assisting doctors and clinicians in making decisions based on unique patient data, personalised medicine is becoming a reality (Papa et al., 2020).

Travel and hospitality: Chatbots and virtual assistants driven by AI improve personalised experiences in these industries. They can help make reservations, offer individualised travel advice, and propose hotels and activities based on customer likes. AI-powered systems can also tailor hotel room settings depending on visitor preferences and improve services to accommodate specific requirements. Overall, by comprehending client preferences, anticipating their wants, and providing customised experiences, AI and ML have the ability to transform personalised services. These innovations help companies increase customer happiness, forge closer bonds with clients, and increase income(González-Rodríguez et al., 2020).

5. PERSONALIZATION AND CUSTOMIZATION OF SERVICES

In today's consumer-driven society, the personalization and customisation of services have gained in importance. Businesses may now adapt their services to the needs and tastes of specific clients thanks to technological improvements and the rise of data analytics (Jeong & Shin, 2020). The term "personalization" describes the practise of providing unique experiences, goods, or services to each individual client based on their unique traits, tendencies, or preferences. It entails gathering and analysing consumer data in order to learn more about their preferences, past purchases, demographics, and other pertinent data. The personalised recommendations, offers, or interactions that result from this data are tailored to each customer's particular needs and interests (Ayuningtyas & Ariwibowo, 2020).

Contrarily, customization takes things a step further by letting clients actively contribute to the design or configuration of the goods or services they choose to buy. Customers have the option to select from a variety of features or alternatives to build a customised solution that satisfies their particular needs (Chang et al., 2020). Colours, sizes, features, and even co-creating products through collaborative platforms can all fall under this category. Both organisations and customers can greatly benefit from customisation and customization. Personalization can promote customer happiness and loyalty, encourage consumer interaction, and eventually result in more sales and revenue from a business standpoint. Businesses may create a more personalised and relevant experience that can set them apart from rivals and foster deeper ties with customers by customising their services to each individual customer.

Personalization and customisation have several benefits for clients. Receiving suggestions or solutions that are especially pertinent to their requirements and preferences can help them save time and effort. Customer satisfaction can also be increased through personalised interactions since it makes clients feel appreciated and understood by the companies they deal with. Customers are given more control over the goods or services they buy thanks to customization, which boosts their sense of satisfaction and makes them feel more emotionally connected to the company.

In general, organisations that want to fulfil the ever-rising expectations of today's consumers must use personalisation and customization. Businesses can build more personalised, engaging experiences that strengthen client relationships and promote corporate growth by utilising data and technology.

1.Real-time data analytics and insights for better decision-making

Real-time data analytics has become a potent tool for businesses to gather insightful information and make wise choices. Businesses can react swiftly to shifting market conditions, spot patterns, and seize opportunities by analysing data as it is generated. Organisations can measure metrics and monitor key performance indicators (KPIs) using real-time data analytics, enabling prompt interventions and strategy modifications (Lapointe, 2020). Organisations are now able to gather and analyse enormous amounts of data from a variety of sources, including consumer interactions, social media, sensors, and transactional data, thanks to the introduction of modern technology and the growing availability of data. Real-time analysis of this data gives decision-makers a complete picture of the business environment, enabling them to spot patterns, spot abnormalities, and get insightful information.

By lessening reliance on past data and gut feelings, real-time data analytics also improves decision-making processes. Organisations can use real-time data to acquire a current and accurate picture of the market and customer behaviour rather than relying exclusively on historical trends. As a result, it is possible to make quick decisions and take advantage of new opportunities or reduce dangers. Real-time data analytics additionally enables proactive decision-making by delivering pertinent alerts and notifications. Businesses can install automated systems that watch data streams and send out warnings when certain thresholds or circumstances are met. This enables decision-makers to respond swiftly to urgent situations, anticipated problems, or developing trends.

In conclusion, real-time data analytics transforms the way decisions are made by delivering the most recent information and enabling proactive responses. Organisations can make educated decisions, adjust to changing conditions, and gain a competitive edge in today's fast-paced business climate by utilising real-time data.

2. Customer self-service alternatives and automation

The way businesses communicate with their clients has been revolutionised by automation and customer self-service choices (Buhalis, 2020). Companies may offer streamlined, effective experiences that enable customers to take charge of their relationships by utilising technological improvements. Customers may access information, conduct transactions, and address concerns at their convenience without requiring human assistance thanks to automated processes and self-service portals. This raises consumer happiness while simultaneously lowering operational expenses for companies. Automation and self-service alternatives, which range from chatbots and self-checkout kiosks to personalised dashboards and online booking systems, provide customers accessibility, speed, and convenience while enabling them to interact with businesses on their terms.

3. Augmented and virtual reality to improve customer interactions

With immersive and engaging experiences like never before, virtual and augmented reality technologies have revolutionised the way businesses interact with their customers. Customers can enter a simulated environment with virtual reality (VR), whereas augmented reality (AR) superimposes virtual components on the actual world. In a variety of businesses, these technologies have improved consumer interactions. Customers can digitally try on garments or accessories in the retail industry, for example, reducing the need for actual fitting rooms and increasing convenience (Kamboj & Joshi, 2021). Customers can, however, use augmented reality (AR) to picture how furniture or other home décor goods would look in their own room before making a purchase. VR and AR have created new opportunities for immersive experiences in the entertainment sector, such as virtual rides at theme parks or interactive games that combine digital and real-world aspects. This increases client involvement while also producing memorable experiences that encourage repeat business.

Additionally, VR and AR have been used in the education and training industries, enabling users to explore virtual worlds, engage with lifelike simulations, and learn new skills in a secure environment. This has shown to be particularly beneficial in industries like healthcare, where experts in the area may train on difficult operations without using actual patients. By providing personalised and engaging experiences that go beyond conventional approaches, virtual and augmented reality have, overall, changed customer relationships. Businesses may fascinate clients, boost decision-making procedures, and ultimately increase customer happiness and loyalty by utilising these technologies.

5. CHALLENGES AND FUTURE TRENDS IN DIGITAL INNOVATION

Cybersecurity Cyber dangers and attacks are more likely as digital technology are incorporated into more areas of our lives. For both businesses and individuals, protecting digital infrastructure, data, and privacy has become a major concern. Data security and morals huge volumes of data are being gathered, stored, and used, which raises privacy and ethical questions. The challenge for innovators is to negotiate intricate legal and regulatory frameworks while upholding morally and ethically correct data practises. Internet Divide There remains a large digital divide despite increased digital connectivity, with some people lacking access to crucial digital tools and services. It is a constant struggle to close this gap and give everyone the same opportunity. Integration and Scalability It can be difficult and expensive to scale up digital technologies to reach wider populations or to integrate them with current systems. It can be difficult to guarantee seamless integration, interoperability, and scalability, particularly in contexts where organisations are complex. Skills and Talent Gap, The availability of qualified professionals frequently lags behind the quick speed of digital innovation. People with knowledge of cutting-edge technologies like blockchain, artificial intelligence, machine learning, and cybersecurity are in greater demand.

6. FUTURE TRENDS

Artificial intelligence (AI) and machine learning (ML) are projected to lead to substantial breakthroughs in a number of industries. These technologies hold the promise of enabling personalised experiences across sectors while automating tasks and enhancing decision-making processes. The Internet of Things (IoT) is a network of networked objects that are equipped with sensors and software to share data. IoT device proliferation will keep growing, creating greater potential for innovation and networked systems. Edge computing: Rather than depending entirely on centralised cloud computing, edge computing involves processing data at the network's edge, nearer the source of data generation. Faster processing, lower latency, and better privacy and security are all made possible by this trend.

Blockchain and Distributed Ledger Technology (DLT): These two technologies offer safe, open-source methods for storing and verifying transactions. Beyond cryptocurrencies, these technologies have uses in decentralised banking, digital identity, and supply chain management. Through the overlaying of digital information or the creation of immersive virtual environments, augmented reality (AR) and virtual reality (VR) technologies improve user experiences. Significant potential exists for these technologies in industries like gaming, education, healthcare, and remote collaboration. Sustainability and green technologies: With heightened awareness of environmental problems, sustainability will likely take centre stage in digital innovation. Future developments will see a rise in the use of green practises, renewable energy, and energy-saving devices. Personalization and Customer Experience: Adapting digital experiences to specific user wants and preferences will remain a major trend. Improved customer experiences will be driven by innovations in personalisation, customer analytics, and user interface design.

It's crucial to keep in mind that these trends and difficulties are dynamic, and as technology advances, new trends and challenges will continue to appear. To manage the constantly shifting environment of digital innovation, innovators need to be flexible, knowledgeable, and nimble.

7. CONCLUSION

The chapter "Digital Innovation in the Service Sector: Transforming Customer Experiences" concludes by examining the substantial influence of digital technologies on the service sector and how they have transformed customer experiences. Service providers now connect with clients in a different way as a result of the rapid development and wide adoption of digital innovation, which has improved efficiency, personalisation, and convenience. We have looked at a variety of facets of digital innovation throughout this chapter, beginning with an overview of its significance in the service industry. We have talked about how old service delivery methods have been transformed into more technologically advanced and customer-focused experiences thanks to digital technologies like artificial intelligence, data analytics, mobile applications, and virtual reality.

One of the main conclusions is that because to digital innovation, service providers can now gather and analyse enormous volumes of client data, giving them a better understanding of their preferences and conduct. Companies may now personalise their goods, customise their services, and develop targeted marketing efforts that appeal to specific customers thanks to this knowledge. Customer loyalty and satisfaction have greatly grown as a result, improving corporate performance. The chapter also emphasises how online marketplaces and digital platforms help with service transactions. These platforms have opened up fresh channels for service providers to connect with a worldwide clientele, extending their market reach and fostering company expansion. Customers gain from the convenience and accessibility provided by digital platforms, which allow them to access a variety of services whenever and wherever they are.

Additionally, the use of cutting-edge technologies, such chatbots and virtual assistants, has transformed customer service by offering round-the-clock assistance and quick answers to questions. As a result, service providers now enjoy higher client satisfaction while paying less for overhead. Recognising the difficulties brought on by digital innovation in the service industry is crucial, though. The digital gap, security and privacy issues, and other key barriers need to be addressed. Organisations also need to understand the complexity of the digital transition and make sure they have the infrastructure, expertise, and strategy in place to make the best use of digital technologies. In conclusion, the transformation of client experiences within the service industry is being driven by digital innovation. Its broad-reaching effects have improved convenience, personalisation, and customer happiness. Service providers are well-positioned to succeed in the digital age if they adopt digital technologies and modify their business models to suit changing client expectations. However, to achieve long-term success in the quickly evolving service market, due thought must be paid to the difficulties and risks involved with digital transformation.

REFERENCES

Akhtar, N., Khan, N., Mahroof Khan, M., Ashraf, S., Hashmi, M. S., Khan, M. M., & Hishan, S. S. (2021). Post-covid 19 tourism: Will digital tourism replace mass tourism? *Sustainability (Basel)*, *13*(10), 5352. Advance online publication. doi:10.3390/su13105352

Akpojaro, J., & Bello, R.-W. (2019). *Smart Healthcare System: A Primer*. https://www.kernelsphere.com/four-internet-things-communications-models/

Ayuningtyas, D., & Ariwibowo, D. A. (2020). The strategic role of information communication technology in succeeding medical tourism. *Enfermeria Clinica, 30*, 170–173. doi:10.1016/j.enfcli.2020.06.039

Basheer, S., Walia, S., Farooq, S., Shah, M. A., & Mir, F. A. (2023). *Exploring the Metaverse*., doi:10.4018/978-1-6684-8898-0.ch012

Bolger, R. K. (2021). Finding wholes in the metaverse: Posthuman mystics as agents of evolutionary contextualization. *Religions*, *12*(9), 768. Advance online publication. doi:10.3390/rel12090768

Buhalis, D. (2020). Technology in tourism-from information communication technologies to eTourism and smart tourism towards ambient intelligence tourism: A perspective article. *Tourism Review*, *75*(1), 267–272. Advance online publication. doi:10.1108/TR-06-2019-0258

Buhalis, D., Leung, D., & Lin, M. (2023). Metaverse as a disruptive technology revolutionising tourism management and marketing. In *Tourism Management* (Vol. 97). Elsevier Ltd. doi:10.1016/j.tourman.2023.104724

Bui, T. X. (2023). *56th Hawaii International Conference on System Sciences (HICCS)*. University of Hawaii at Manoa.

Cai, W., & McKenna, B. (2021). Knowledge Creation in Information Technology and Tourism Research. In Journal of Travel Research (Vol. 60, Issue 4). doi:10.1177/0047287520903142

Cai, W., McKenna, B., Wassler, P., & Williams, N. (2021). Rethinking Knowledge Creation in Information Technology and Tourism. In Journal of Travel Research (Vol. 60, Issue 6). doi:10.1177/0047287520946100

Chang, C. L., McAleer, M., & Ramos, V. (2020). A charter for sustainable tourism after COVID-19. *Sustainability (Basel)*, *12*(9), 3671. Advance online publication. doi:10.3390/su12093671

Damar, M. (2021). *Metaverse Shape of Your Life for Future: A bibliometric snapshot*. Academic Press.

El-Said, O., & Aziz, H. (2022). Virtual Tours a Means to an End: An Analysis of Virtual Tours' Role in Tourism Recovery Post COVID-19. *Journal of Travel Research*, *61*(3), 528–548. Advance online publication. doi:10.1177/0047287521997567

González-Rodríguez, M. R., Díaz-Fernández, M. C., & Pino-Mejías, M. Á. (2020). The impact of virtual reality technology on tourists' experience: A textual data analysis. *Soft Computing*, *24*(18), 13879–13892. doi:10.1007/s00500-020-04883-y

Gursoy, D., Malodia, S., & Dhir, A. (2022). The metaverse in the hospitality and tourism industry: An overview of current trends and future research directions. *Journal of Hospitality Marketing & Management*, *31*(5), 527–534. doi:10.1080/19368623.2022.2072504

Higgins-Desbiolles, F., Bigby, B. C., & Doering, A. (2022). Socialising tourism after COVID-19: Reclaiming tourism as a social force? *Journal of Tourism Futures*, *8*(2), 208–219. Advance online publication. doi:10.1108/JTF-03-2021-0058

Jeong, M., & Shin, H. H. (2020). Tourists' Experiences with Smart Tourism Technology at Smart Destinations and Their Behavior Intentions. *Journal of Travel Research*, *59*(8), 1464–1477. doi:10.1177/0047287519883034

Jovanović, A., & Milosavljević, A. (2022). VoRtex Metaverse Platform for Gamified Collaborative Learning. *Electronics (Basel)*, *11*(3), 317. Advance online publication. doi:10.3390/electronics11030317

Kamata, H. (2022). Tourist destination residents' attitudes towards tourism during and after the COVID-19 pandemic. *Current Issues in Tourism*, *25*(1), 134–149. Advance online publication. doi:10.1080/13683500.2021.1881452

Kamboj, S., & Joshi, R. (2021). Examining the factors influencing smartphone apps use at tourism destinations: A UTAUT model perspective. *International Journal of Tourism Cities*, *7*(1), 135–157. doi:10.1108/IJTC-05-2020-0094

Kusuma, P. A., Mutiarin, D., & Damanik, J. (2021). Strategi pemulihan dampak wabah covid pada sektor pariwisata di daerah istimewa yogyakarta. *Journal of Tourism and Economic*, *4*(1), 47–59. Advance online publication. doi:10.36594/jtec.v4i1.110

Kye, B., Han, N., Kim, E., Park, Y., & Jo, S. (2021). Educational applications of metaverse: Possibilities and limitations. In Journal of Educational Evaluation for Health Professions (Vol. 18). doi:10.3352/jeehp.2021.18.32

Lapointe, D. (2020). Reconnecting tourism after COVID-19: The paradox of alterity in tourism areas. *Tourism Geographies*, *22*(3), 633–638. Advance online publication. doi:10.1080/14616688.2020.1762115

Lu, J., Xiao, X., Xu, Z., Wang, C., Zhang, M., & Zhou, Y. (2022). The potential of virtual tourism in the recovery of tourism industry during the COVID-19 pandemic. *Current Issues in Tourism*, *25*(3), 441–457. Advance online publication. doi:10.1080/13683500.2021.1959526

Mehraj, D., Qureshi, I. H., Singh, G., Nazir, N. A., basheer, S., & Nissa, V. (2023, December). Green marketing practices and green consumer behavior: Demographic differences among young consumers. *Business Strategy & Development*, *6*(4), 571–585. Advance online publication. doi:10.1002/bsd2.263

Narin, N. G. (2021). A Content Analysis of the Metaverse Articles. *Journal of Metaverse*, *1*(1).

Papa, A., Mital, M., Pisano, P., & Del Giudice, M. (2020). E-health and wellbeing monitoring using smart healthcare devices: An empirical investigation. *Technological Forecasting and Social Change*, *153*, 119226. Advance online publication. doi:10.1016/j.techfore.2018.02.018

Park, S., & Kim, S. (2022). Identifying World Types to Deliver Gameful Experiences for Sustainable Learning in the Metaverse. *Sustainability (Basel)*, *14*(3), 1361. Advance online publication. doi:10.3390/su14031361

Park, S. M., & Kim, Y. G. (2022). A Metaverse: Taxonomy, Components, Applications, and Open Challenges. *IEEE Access : Practical Innovations, Open Solutions*, *10*, 4209–4251. Advance online publication. doi:10.1109/ACCESS.2021.3140175

Subasinghe, M., Magalage, D., Amadoru, N., Amarathunga, L., Bhanupriya, N., & Wijekoon, J. L. (2020). Effectiveness of artificial intelligence, decentralized and distributed systems for prediction and secure channelling for Medical Tourism. *11th Annual IEEE Information Technology, Electronics and Mobile Communication Conference, IEMCON 2020*, 314–319. 10.1109/IEMCON51383.2020.9284898

Suh, W., & Ahn, S. (2022). Utilizing the Metaverse for Learner-Centered Constructivist Education in the Post-Pandemic Era: An Analysis of Elementary School Students. *Journal of Intelligence*, *10*(1), 17. Advance online publication. doi:10.3390/jintelligence10010017 PMID:35324573

Tiwari, A., Dhiman, V., Iesa, M. A. M., Alsarhan, H., Mehbodniya, A., & Shabaz, M. (2021). Patient Behavioral Analysis with Smart Healthcare and IoT. *Behavioural Neurology*, *2021*, 1–9. Advance online publication. doi:10.1155/2021/4028761 PMID:34900023

Toubes, D. R., Vila, N. A., & Fraiz Brea, J. A. (2021). Changes in consumption patterns and tourist promotion after the covid-19 pandemic. *Journal of Theoretical and Applied Electronic Commerce Research*, *16*(5), 1332–1352. Advance online publication. doi:10.3390/jtaer16050075

Chapter 9
Tourism in the Metaverse: Opportunities and Challenges

Albérico Travassos Rosário
https://orcid.org/0000-0003-4793-4110
GOVCOPP, IADE, Universidade Europeia, Portugal

Joana Carmo Dias
https://orcid.org/0000-0001-5900-2121
COMEGI, Universidade Lusíada, Portugal

ABSTRACT

Metaverse tourism is an emerging concept that refers to the practice of exploring and experiencing virtual worlds and digital environments. It offers a wide range of immersive experiences, social interactions, and exploration opportunities. In the metaverse, tourists can visit and interact with various virtual destinations, which can be designed to replicate real-world locations, historical periods, fantasy realms, or entirely new and imaginative landscapes. Tourists can embark on virtual adventures, solve puzzles, or participate in multiplayer games with people worldwide. It is important to note that the metaverse concept is still evolving, and the extent of its development and adoption may vary over time. However, as technology advances and virtual experiences become more immersive, metaverse tourism will likely become an increasingly popular and accessible form of travel and exploration. Based on the above, the authors intend to systematically review the bibliometric literature on tourism in the metaverse using the Scopus database with the analysis of 75 academic and/or scientific documents

INTRODUCTION

The tourism sector is currently undergoing significant transformations due to disruptive technological innovations in the digital domain, notably the emergence of

DOI: 10.4018/979-8-3693-1103-5.ch009

the metaverse. Buhalis et al. (2023) have defined the metaverse as the convergence of physical and digital realms, enabling users to seamlessly navigate between them for various purposes, including work, education, health, exploration of interests, and social interaction. This groundbreaking innovation is made possible by the advancement of the Internet of Things, facilitating three-dimensional (3D) simulation and supporting immersive technologies like virtual reality (VR), augmented reality (AR), and mixed reality (MR) (Monaco & Sacchi, 2023). As these technologies continue to evolve, the tourism industry is integrating them to enhance service delivery, customer experiences, and operational efficiency. For instance, the metaverse creates a parallel digital environment where travelers can virtually explore destinations, interact with fellow tourists, and engage in activities that were once confined by physical limitations (Koo et al., 2022). Consequently, the metaverse-driven transformation holds the potential to make travel more accessible, customizable, and environmentally sustainable. Therefore, the implementation of the metaverse in the tourism sector has generated unprecedented growth prospects.

Metaverse innovations enable individuals to engage in hyper-realistic virtual interactions, transactions, and experiences. Gursoy et al. (2022) elaborate that this immersion in the metaverse enables people to naturally interact within both digital and physical settings. Within metaverse-based tourism, these immersive innovations and opportunities are of paramount importance as they enhance customer engagement and experiences. For instance, a tourist can utilize virtual resources and digital environments to pre-visit a specific destination (Go & Kang, 2023). This capability enables them to assess the desirability and suitability of the destination before the actual visit, providing valuable insights for better preparation.

Furthermore, the metaverse has the potential to facilitate cultural exchange and foster inclusivity on an unprecedented scale. In this context, virtual communities can connect individuals from various parts of the world, promoting cross-cultural understanding and dialogue (Suanpang et al., 2022). Additionally, tourists can leverage the metaverse to gain insights into a destination's local customs, languages, and traditions by participating in virtual cultural exchanges. This enriches the traveler's experience while promoting global understanding and empathy. Despite these opportunities, the increasing adoption of metaverse tourism brings forth several challenges, including issues related to privacy, authenticity, and its impact on physical tourism destinations (Monaco & Sacchi, 2023).

Therefore, our study intends to comprehend the intersection of the metaverse and the tourism sector, specifically focusing on how the tourism industry can harness the potential of the metaverse while mitigating its associated negative consequences. This study highlights the transformative impact of disruptive technological innovations, such as the metaverse, on the tourism sector. It discusses the benefits and opportunities brought about by the integration of immersive technologies in travel, such as enhanced customer experiences, accessibility, customization, and environmental sustainability. In sum, this systematic literature review with bibliometric analysis (SLRBA) synthesizes findings from 75 sources to offer insights into how the tourism sector can strategically adopt and benefit from metaverse innovations while managing potential drawbacks.

The paper is structured as follows. First, we explain the methodological process that was conducted to gather all the documents related with metaverse and the tourism sector. This section elucidates the rigorous process we employed to gather a diverse and representative collection of literature, which forms the foundation of our study. Then, we present some data resulted from the bibliometric analyses. Next, we describe the theoretical perspectives resulting from the analysis carried out. Finally, we distill the essential takeaways from our research and discuss their implications for practitioners and scholars alike. Additionally, we outline avenues for future research, pinpointing unexplored areas and potential research directions that can further advance our understanding of data-driven marketing.

METHODOLOGICAL APPROACH

The research employed the systematic literature review with bibliometric analysis (SLRBA) methodology to discern relevant sources and synthesize their findings. SLRBA is a robust methodology that offers a comprehensive overview of existing research within a specific field, facilitating the identification of literature gaps and trends. Through the systematic collection and analysis of data encompassing citation patterns, publication trends, and author collaborations, this approach provides valuable insights into knowledge evolution and key contributors in the domain. This methodology also enhances review process rigor by ensuring objective and transparent study selection, crucial for producing reliable and evidence-based research outcomes (Donthu et al., 2021).

In contrast to traditional literature reviews, SLRBA adheres to a repeatable, scientific, and transparent methodology that minimizes bias. It accomplishes this through a comprehensive examination of both published and unpublished literature relevant to the research topic, as emphasized by Rosário and Dias (2023), Rosário et al. (2023), and Raimundo and Rosario (2022). Furthermore, researchers provide an audit trail to enable readers to assess the quality of the research, as well as the procedures and conclusions presented in the study.

Therefore, SLRBA involves the thorough examination and selection of information sources to ensure data validity and accuracy—a process delineated into three stages and six steps, as detailed by Rosário and Dias (2023), Rosário et al. (2023), and Raimundo and Sario (2022) (refer to Table 1).

This research approach facilitates a meticulous and structured examination of existing scholarship in the field of metaverse tourism. As elucidated by Linnenluecke et al. (2019), SLRBA enables the systematic identification and aggregation of a diverse range of scholarly publications, fostering diverse perspectives and research outcomes. Given the growing popularity of the metaverse concept and the dynamic evolution of the tourism sector, there has been a proliferation of recent research studies in these domains.

In this study, researchers used the Scopus database to identify and locate reputable sources within the realms of science and academia. However, it is important to acknowledge a limitation of this research, which is its exclusive reliance on the Scopus database while excluding other scientific and academic databases. The choice of the Scopus database over others is justified due to its comprehensive coverage across multiple disciplines, stringent quality criteria for indexed content, and robust citation analysis tools. Scopus's multidisciplinary approach allows researchers to access a diverse range of scholarly literature, ensuring a holistic understanding of the subject matter, while its global reach facilitates international research collaboration.

The literature search encompassed peer-reviewed scientific and scholarly publications published up to September 2023, and Scopus data were utilized to review relevant studies. The initiation of the literature search involved selecting the Scopus database as the primary source. Subsequently, an initial literature search was conducted using the keyword "tourism," resulting in a corpus of 147,169 documents. These outcomes underwent a screening process based on keywords, titles, and abstracts to assess their alignment with the eligibility criteria. Following this, the keyword "metaverse" was introduced to refine the search results to the most relevant sources. This filtration process ultimately led to the compilation of 75 references from the literature review.

Figure 1 shows the data collection and analysis process following the four phases of the PRISMA protocol (identification, screening, eligibility, and inclusion)

Table 1. Process of systematic SLRBA.

Fase	Step	Description
Exploration	Step 1	formulating the research problem
	Step 2	searching for appropriate literature
	Step 3	critical appraisal of the selected studies
	Step 4	data synthesis from individual sources
Interpretation	Step 5	reporting findings and recommendations
Communication	Step 6	Presentation of the LRSB report

Source: adapted *Rosário and Dias (2023), Rosário, et al. (2023), Raimundo and Rosário (2022).*

Figure 1. PRISMA flow diagram for systematic review
Adapted from Pacheco-Velázquez et al.

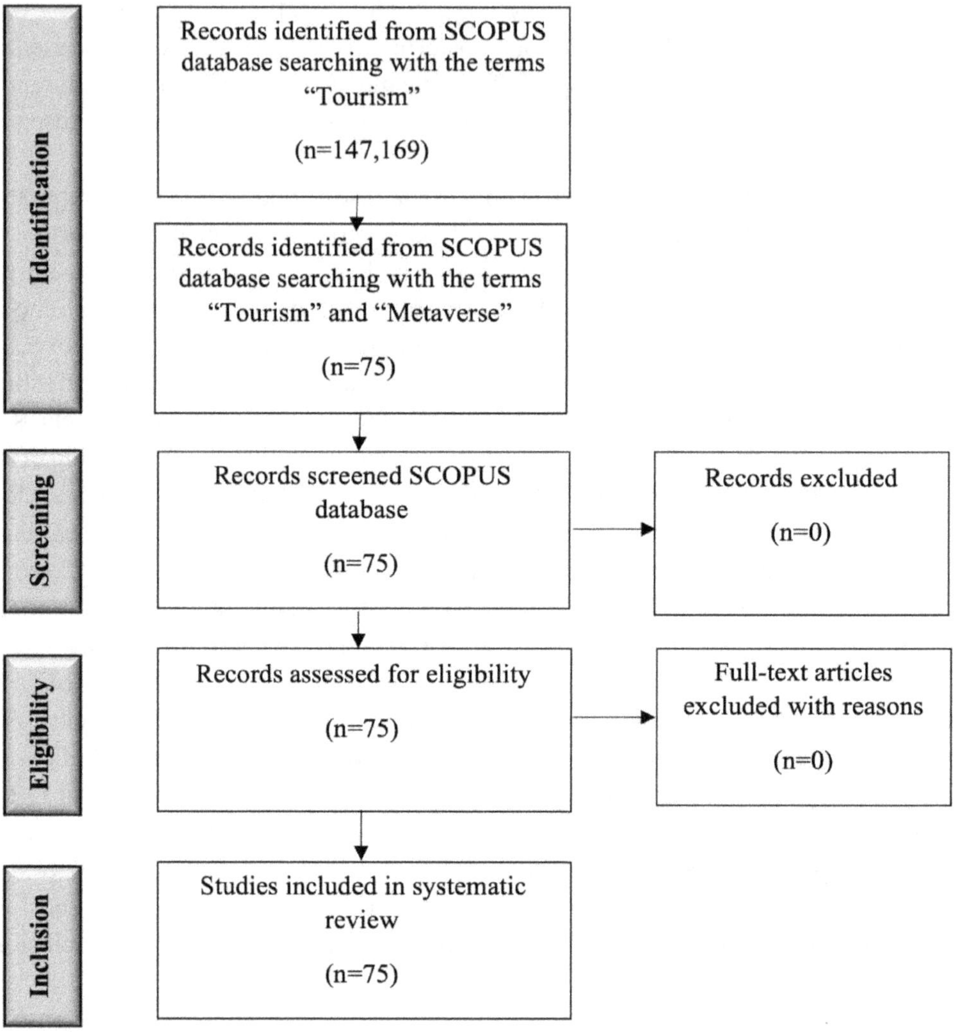

(Pernencar et al., 2022). In the identification phase, we present the results of the search for descriptors. In the next phase, screening, all duplicate documents were removed. In the eligibility stage, publications that met the inclusion criteria were considered. In the last stage, the inclusion stage, the articles were considered after carrying out a qualitative analysis of each one of them according to the research question.

This research process includes inclusion criteria for selecting studies, such as (i) peer-reviewed journal articles or conference papers, (ii) studies in English language,

(iii) directly addressing or closely related to the research problem or question defined for the systematic review, (iv) clearly explain the research methods used to collect and analyze data, and (v) provide sufficient data and analysis to support their findings and conclusions.

To systematically analyze and present the diverse set of documents, we employed content and thematic analysis methodologies, following the established approaches outlined by Rosário and Dias (2023), Rosário et al. (2023), and Raimundo and Rosario (2022). Among the 48 selected documents, 12 were sourced from Conference Proceedings, 8 were part of Book Series, and 7 were classified as monographs.

PUBLICATION DISTRIBUTION

Peer-reviewed scholarly articles pertaining to tourism within the metaverse domain were examined up to September 2023. Notably, the year 2023 witnessed the highest volume of such peer-reviewed publications, totaling 422. Figure 2 provides a comprehensive summary of the peer-reviewed literature encompassing this subject matter, extending up to September 2023.

Figure 3 depicts an analysis of countries demonstrating robust scientific output within specific research domains, with particular emphasis on China and India, both of which exhibit the highest number of research publications.

Figure 2. Documents by year
Source: own elaboration

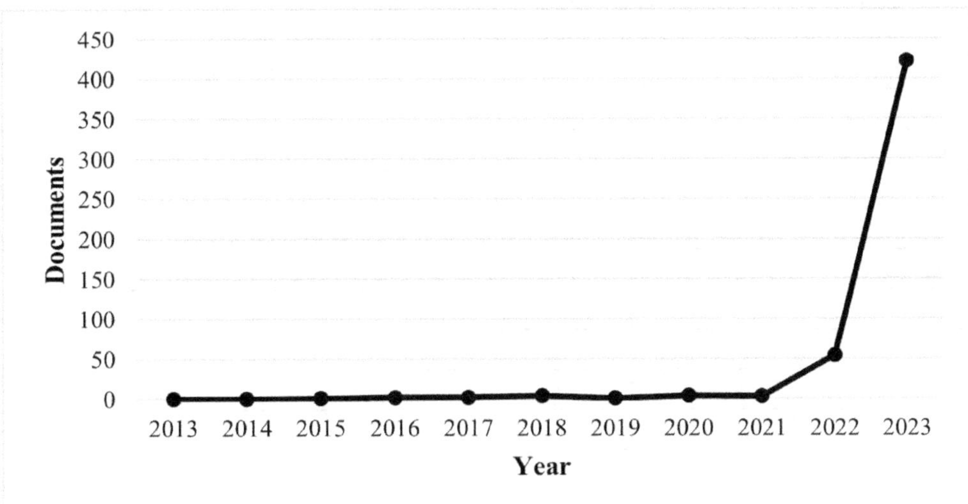

Figure 3. Scientific production by country

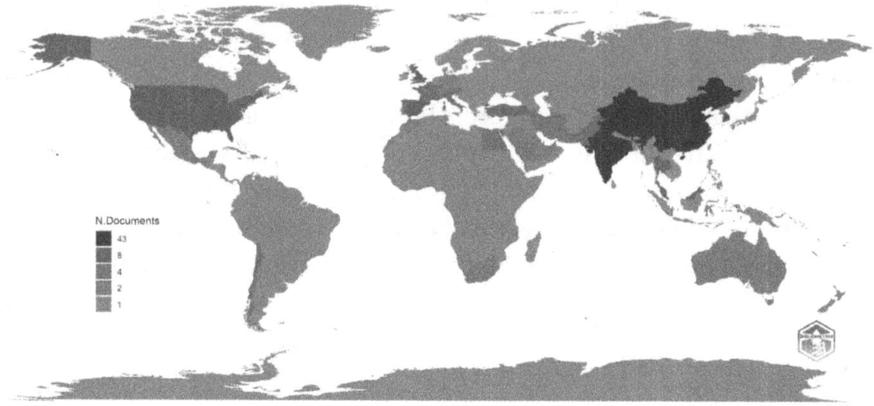

In conjunction with Figure 5, Table 2 presents an overview of the top 10 countries exhibiting the highest scientific performance across the investigated terms. It is important to note that the purpose of this analysis is not solely to emphasize countries' research productivity, but rather to ascertain the extent of their engagement in research pertaining to tourism within the virtual realm.

The publications were categorized as follows: "Information Technology and Tourism" (10 publications), "Sustainability Switzerland" (6 publications), "Springer Proceedings in Business and Economics" (4 publications), "Lecture Notes in Computer Science including subseries Lecture Notes in Artificial Intelligence and

Table 2. Top 10 countries by number of publications

Country	Number of Publications
China	43
India	35
South Korea	14
UK	11
Singapore	10
Spain	10
USA	9
Malaysia	8
Thailand	8
France	6

Source: own elaboration

Lecture Notes in Bioinformatics" (3 publications), and 2 publications for each of the following: "Tourism Review," "Journal of Hospitality and Tourism Insights," "International Journal of Contemporary Hospitality Management," "Influencer Marketing Applications Within the Metaverse," and "Current Issues in Tourism." The remaining publications had a single document each.

Table 3 presents an analysis of the Scimago Journal & Country Rank (SJR), best quartile, and the H index. Notably, "Tourism Management" emerges as the most frequently cited publication with an SJR score of 3,560, a Q1 ranking, and an H index of 236. Within the quartile breakdown, there are 22 publications in Q1, 5 in Q2, 3 in Q3, and 4 in Q4. Q1 publications account for 44% of the 75 titles, while Q2 represents 10%, Q3 represents 6%, and Q4 comprises 8% of the total titles. Furthermore, 16 publications lack indexing data, constituting 32% of the total publications. It's evident from Table 4 that the majority of publications fall within the Q1 category.

Table 3. Scimago Journal and country rank impact factor

Title	SJR	Best Quartile	H index
Tourism Management	3,560	Q1	236
Journal Of Hospitality Marketing And Management	2,520	Q1	67
International Journal Of Contemporary Hospitality Management	2,500	Q1	113
Journal Of Travel And Tourism Marketing	2,130	Q1	95
Current Issues In Tourism	2,060	Q1	94
Tourism Review	1,880	Q1	48
Journal Of Hospitality And Tourism Research	1,360	Q1	84
Information Technology And Tourism	1,340	Q1	30
International Journal Of Tourism Research	1,300	Q1	75
Interactive Learning Environments	1,170	Q1	57
Journal Of Vacation Marketing	1,114	Q1	72
Tourism Economics	1,090	Q1	69
Virtual Reality	1,080	Q1	57
Tourism Recreation Research	1,070	Q1	57
Frontiers In Psychology	0,890	Q2	157
Journal Of Tourism Futures	0,760	Q1	27
International Journal Of Geoheritage And Parks	0,710	Q1	13
Journal Of Computer Information Systems	0,690	Q1	71
Sustainability Switzerlan	0,660	Q1	136

continued on following page

Table 3. Continued

Title	SJR	Best Quartile	H index
Information Switzerland	0,660	Q2	46
Journal Of Hospitality And Tourism Insights	0,640	Q2	17
Museum Management And Curatorship	0,630	Q1	37
Electronics Switzerland	0,630	Q2	62
Heliyon	0,610	Q1	69
Heritage Science	0,550	Q1	29
Procedia Computer Science	0,510	-*	109
Applied Sciences Switzerland	0,490	Q2	101
Lecture Notes In Computer Science Including Subseries Lecture Notes In Artificial Intelligence And Lecture Notes In Bioinformatics	0,320	Q3	446
Tropical Geography	0,220	Q3	10
E3s Web Of Conferences	0,180	-*	33
Lecture Notes Of The Institute For Computer Sciences Social Informatics And Telecommunications Engineering Lnicst	0,160	Q4	50
Studies In Big Data	0,150	Q4	30
Risti Revista Iberica De Sistemas E Tecnologias De Informacao	0,150	Q4	16
Lecture Notes In Networks And Systems	0,150	Q4	27
Lecture Notes On Data Engineering And Communications Technologies	0,130	Q3	23
Proceedings Of The Annual Hawaii International Conference On System Sciences	0	-*	95
Proceedings IEEE Consumer Communications And Networking Conference Ccnc	0	-*	16
Springer Proceedings In Business And Economics	-*	-*	-*
Influencer Marketing Applications Within The Metaverse	-*	-*	-*
Tourism Hospitality And Event Management	-*	-*	-*
Routledge Handbook Of Trends And Issues In Global Tourism Supply And Demand	-*	-*	-*
Promoting Consumer Engagement Through Emotional Branding And Sensory Marketing	-*	-*	-*
Proceedings Of The 17th Indiacom 2023 10th International Conference On Computing For Sustainable Global Development Indiacom 2023	-*	-*	-*
Proceedings 2022 International Conference On Culture Oriented Science And Technology Cost 2022	-*	-*	-*
Proceedings 2022 IEEE Acis 7th International Conference On Big Data Cloud Computing And Data Science Bcd 2022	-*	-*	-*
Marketing And Managing Tourism Destinations Third Edition	-*	-*	-*
Journal Of Metaverse	-*	-*	-*

continued on following page

Table 3. Continued

Title	SJR	Best Quartile	H index
Iranian Journal Of Public Health	-*	-*	-*
Cultural Marketing And Metaverse For Consumer Engagement	-*	-*	-*
Creative Business Education Exploring The Contours Of Pedagogical Praxis	-*	-*	-*
9th International Conference On ICT For Smart Society Recover Together Recover Stronger And Smarter Smartization Governance And Collaboration Iciss 2022 Proceeding	-*	-*	-*

Note: *data not available.
Source: own elaboration

The 75 scientific and academic documents encompassed various subject areas, with the following distribution: Business, Management, and Accounting (40); Computer Science (37); Social Sciences (26); Environmental Science (12); Economics, Econometrics, and Finance (12); Engineering (8); Energy (8); Mathematics (3); Earth and Planetary Sciences (3); Materials Science (2); Decision Sciences (2); Arts and Humanities (2); Psychology (1); Physics and Astronomy (1); Multidisciplinary (1); Medicine (1); Chemistry (1); and Chemical Engineering (1).

The most highly cited article, "Role of artificial intelligence in operations environment: a review and bibliometric analysis" by Dogan et al. (2022), accumulated 100 citations and was published in the Journal of Hospitality Marketing and Management with an SJR score of 2,520. It is categorized in the best quartile (Q1) and holds an H index of 67. This article delves into the metaverse concept within the context of hospitality and tourism, presenting a conceptual framework for crafting metaverse experiences, identifying research gaps, and proposing agenda items that can significantly benefit stakeholders in the hospitality and tourism sectors.

Figure 4 provides an analysis of citation trends for documents published up to September 2023. During the period spanning ≤2013-2023, there is a discernible positive net growth in citations, characterized by an R2 of 31%, ultimately culminating in 422 citations in 2023.

The h-index serves as a metric for assessing the productivity and impact of published works by determining the maximum number of included articles that have been cited at least the same number of times. Among the documents considered for the h-index calculation, 13 were cited at least 13 times. The total number of citations for all scientific and academic documents, spanning the period from ≤2013 to April 2023, amounted to 493 citations. Of the 75 documents analyzed, 40 received no citations. Additionally, self-citations of documents during the period spanning ≤2013 to September 2023 amounted to 459 occurrences. Utilizing primary keywords, this bibliometric study investigated and identified indicators pertaining

Figure 4. Evolution of citations between 2013 and 2023
Source: own elaboration

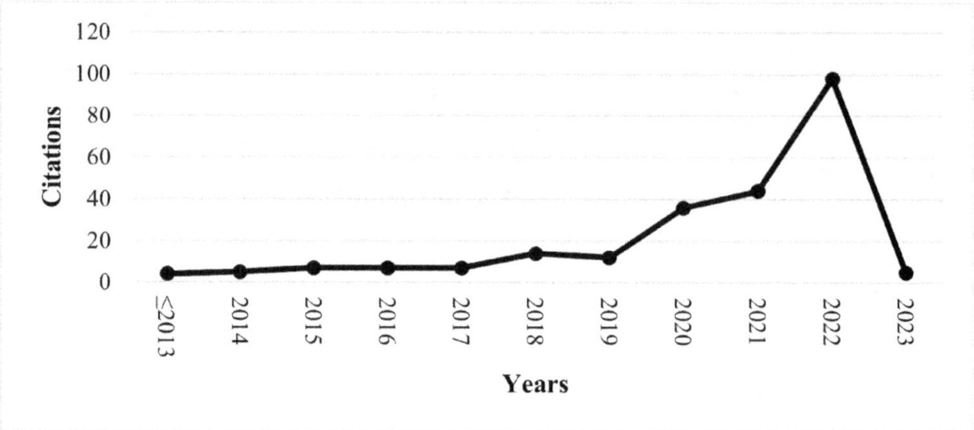

to the dynamics and evolution of scientific and academic information within the documents (as depicted in Figure 4). The results were extracted using the scientific software VOSviewer, with a specific focus on identifying the primary search keywords related to "Tourism in the metaverse."

This study is founded on a corpus of scientific and academic documents pertaining to the subject of "Tourism in the metaverse." Figure 6 presents an in-depth exploration of the associated keywords, enabling us to unveil the intricate network of keywords interconnected within each scientific article. This network analysis aids in the identification of prevalent research themes and provides insights into potential future research trends. Furthermore, Figure 7 illustrates numerous instances of co-citations and units of analysis related to cited references, offering a comprehensive view of the scholarly landscape within this field.

THEORETICAL PERSPECTIVES

In recent years, the tourism sector has undergone a profound and far-reaching transformation driven by disruptive technologies, with the metaverse being a notable catalyst for change. This technological innovation is fundamentally reshaping the way travellers perceive and engage with destinations, primarily through the integration of virtual reality, augmented reality, and interconnected digital spaces, as expounded upon by Zhang and Wang (2023). At the heart of the metaverse lie a constellation of cutting-edge technologies, including artificial intelligence (AI), machine learning, augmented reality (AR), virtual reality (VR), blockchain, and spatial

Figure 5. Network of all keywords

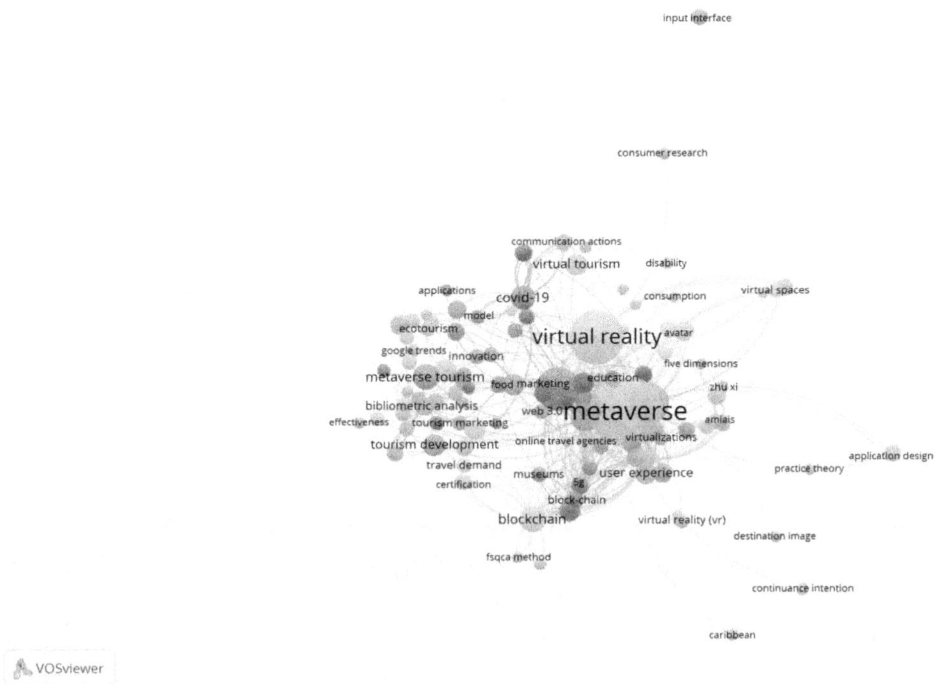

Figure 6. Network of linked keywords

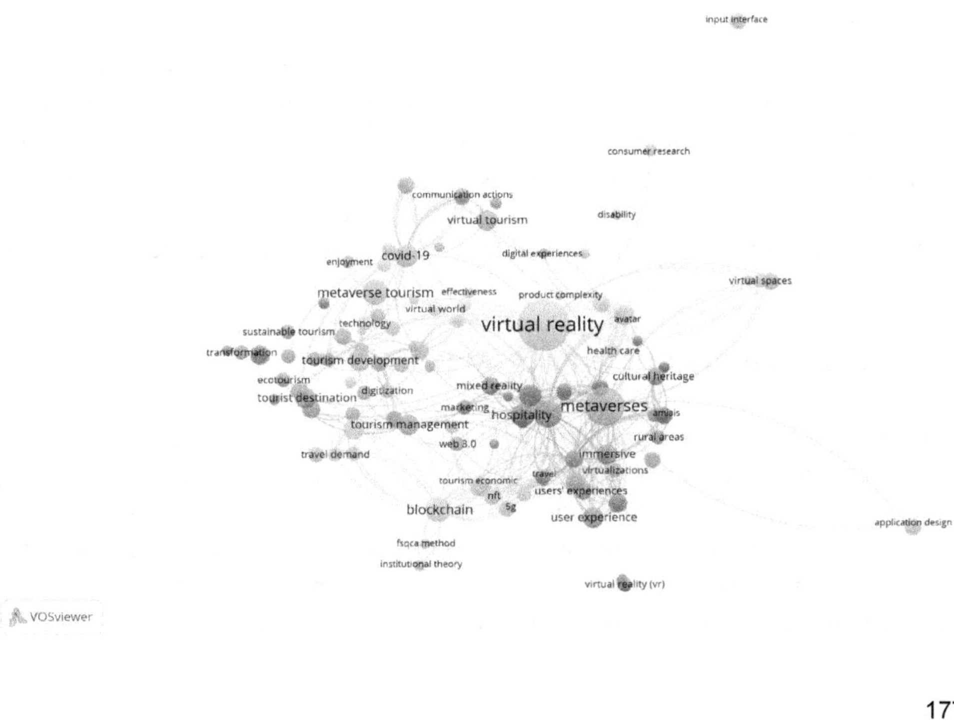

Figure 7. Network of co-citation

computing. These technological enablers empower tourists within the virtual realm to replicate real-world experiences and craft fully immersive, personalized journeys, as elucidated by Gursoy et al. (2023). Furthermore, these technologies are ushering in a new era of travel that is characterized by heightened accessibility, inclusivity, and customization. This is achieved through hyper-realistic virtual tours of historical sites and the provision of personalized travel planning facilitated by AI-driven virtual agents, as posited by Baggio and Ruggieri (2023) and Faulkner (2022). However, it is imperative to acknowledge that alongside the myriad opportunities presented by the metaverse, significant concerns loom on the horizon. These concerns encompass issues related to privacy in the virtual realm and the potential ramifications for physical tourism destinations. These challenges necessitate careful consideration and proactive measures on the part of industry leaders to harness the full spectrum of opportunities. Therefore, this literature review section delves into the conceptual framework of the metaverse and its practical applications in the realm of tourism, with a specific focus on the identification of opportunities and challenges inherent to this transformative phenomenon.

Metaverse: Definitions and Origins

The metaverse, as characterized by Ampountolas et al. (2023), constitutes a virtual realm wherein users engage socially while employing digital avatars to collaboratively generate value and co-craft experiences. It is further delineated by its virtual and interconnected nature, encompassing a tapestry of digital spaces, environments, and experiential domains, in accordance with the definition by Ampountolas et al. (2023). Inder (2022) offers insight by describing the metaverse as a three-dimensional

(3D) virtual environment with a pronounced emphasis on fostering interpersonal relationships. By capitalizing on Mixed Reality (MR) technology, the metaverse adeptly bridges the divide between the digital and physical domains, permitting users to amalgamate resources and partake in holistic experiences. Unlike traditional virtual worlds or video games, the metaverse transcends the boundaries of individual platforms or applications. It proffers a seamless, immersive, and enduring digital ecosystem wherein users navigate, interact, and actively contribute, as detailed by Baker et al. (2023). Furthermore, these immersive 3D encounters, which pivot around social interactions, foreshadow a paradigm shift toward integrated living. With the advent of Information and Communication Technology (ICT), consumers and developers are now equipped to seamlessly integrate virtual and digital realities into their daily routines.

The origins of the metaverse concept trace back to Neal Stephenson's 1992 science fiction novel "Snow Crash". In this literary work, the metaverse denoted a virtual reality-based successor to the internet—an expansive digital domain wherein users engaged with each other and digital environments in multifarious ways, as chronicled by Basheer et al. (2023) and Gursoy et al. (2022). Stephenson's imaginative portrayal of the metaverse wielded substantial influence and laid the theoretical groundwork for the evolution of virtual worlds and online communities. Nonetheless, substantive discussions concerning the metaverse burgeoned in the 21st century, as outlined by Chen et al. (2023). This resurgence in interest was galvanized by pivotal technological strides in Virtual Reality (VR) and Augmented Reality (AR) technologies, heightened online connectivity, and the emergence of platforms such as Second Life, followed by the ascent of social media platforms, per Huang et al. (2023) and Hui et al. (2023). Furthermore, the substantial investments made by companies like Facebook (now Meta Platforms, Inc.) in the development of immersive digital environments and technologies have played an instrumental role in catapulting the concept of the metaverse into mainstream awareness. Consequently, businesses across diverse sectors, including the tourism industry, have increasingly embraced metaverse innovations, harnessing their manifold opportunities for advancement.

The Metaverse and the Tourism Industry

The integration of the metaverse within the domain of the tourism industry heralds a profound transformation in the way travelers engage with and perceive their journeys, spanning the entire spectrum from initial planning to post-travel reminiscences. This paradigm shift exerts its influence across diverse facets of tourism services, encompassing destination exploration, cultural immersion, entertainment offerings, and the intricacies of travel planning, as expounded by Jafar and Ahmad (2023). Moreover, the metaverse stands as an unprecedented catalyst that obfuscates the demarcations separating the physical and virtual realms, thereby presenting extraordinary opportunities to all stakeholders embedded within the tourism ecosystem, in consonance with the insights provided by Liew et al. (2023).

For instance, metaverse-driven innovations are driving a dynamic metamorphosis within the tourism landscape, compelling a fundamental reimagining of established business processes, operational methodologies, and strategic management paradigms, as attested by the work of Jo (2023) and Kim & Kim (2023). This transformative influence is discernible through a spectrum of metaverse applications, which notably encompass the enhancement of travelers' decision-making capabilities concerning destination selection, active participation in virtual tours, the facilitation of bookings, and even the engagement in virtual travel experiences, such as the virtual attendance of concerts. The extensive array of these metaverse applications prompted the investigation conducted by Gursoy et al. (2022), which scrutinized the underlying motives (hedonic vs. functional) and the degree of interactivity (low vs. high) shaping the creation of metaverse experiences, thereby providing valuable insights tailored to the tourism sector, as visualized in Figure 8.

It is pertinent to acknowledge that, while metaverse-based tourism endeavors may not wholly replicate the tangible and authentic experiences associated with physical travel, notable advancements in technology, particularly concerning the quality and immersive capabilities offered by Virtual Reality (VR) headsets, are steadily rendering metaverse tourism applications increasingly captivating and engrossing.

Figure 8. Metaverse travel and tourism experiences (Gursoy et al., 2022).

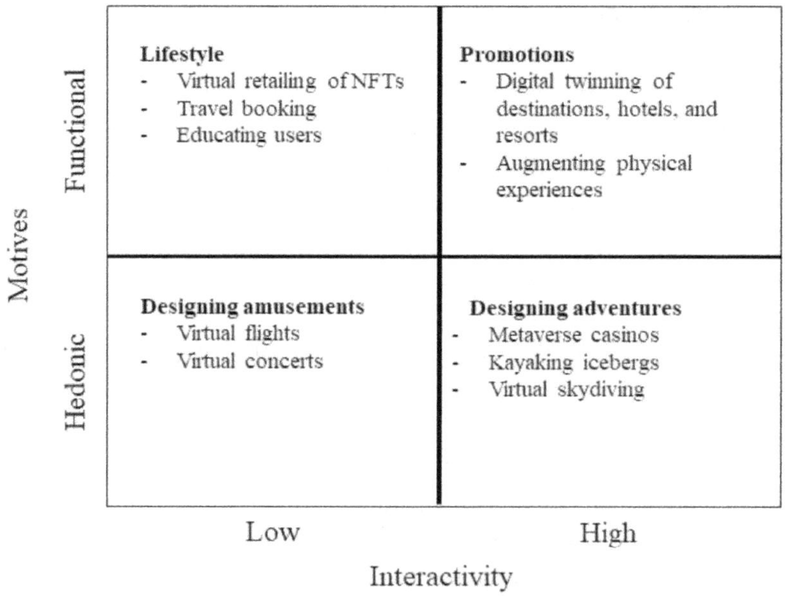

Characteristics of the Metaverse Tourism

Metaverse tourism is distinguished by several exceptional features that set it apart from traditional travel experiences. These characteristics collectively forge a distinctive and immersive environment for tourists, allowing them to explore and interact with destinations in unparalleled ways. Furthermore, they provide a dynamic and personalized journey, elevating customer experiences and overall satisfaction.

Avatars and Profiles

In the metaverse, the concept of avatars or profiles plays a pivotal role in shaping the tourist experience. Avatars, as defined by Koo et al. (2022), are digital representations of users within the virtual environment. Conversely, profiles encompass information concerning tourists' preferences, history, and interactions. These avatars and profiles act as the conduit between the physical and digital realms, enabling tourists to navigate and personalize their metaverse experiences, as elucidated by Monaco & Sacchi (2023). For example, tourists possess the ability to tailor their avatars to mirror their identity, preferences, and even physical appearance. This customization augments the sense of agency and self-expression, empowering them to assume any persona they desire within the metaverse, as noted by Nijjer et al. (2023) and Poonkuzhali et al. (2023). Furthermore, avatars facilitate social interactions, enabling tourists to engage with other users through their digital personas. These interactions can closely mirror real-world social dynamics, fostering connections and relationships that transcend geographical boundaries.

Metaverse profiles play a crucial role in storing valuable data pertaining to tourists' interactions and preferences. This information can be harnessed to enhance the personalization of metaverse tourism experiences, as observed in the works of Rameshwar & King (2023) and Shaygani et al. (2022). For instance, an AI-driven virtual travel agent can utilize this data to offer recommendations for destinations, activities, and experiences tailored to the tourist's preferences, as highlighted by Ud Din & Almogren (2023). Consequently, metaverse profiles empower businesses within the tourism sector to cater to individual needs and preferences by crafting a dynamic and immersive virtual space for users to explore and interact, in accordance with Tsai (2022). However, it is imperative to acknowledge that the collection and utilization of personal data within the metaverse also give rise to significant privacy and security considerations that must be diligently addressed to ensure a safe and responsible tourism environment.

Immersive Experiences

Immersive experiences are a defining hallmark of metaverse tourism. Within the metaverse, tourists can step into virtual worlds that provide a level of immersion unparalleled by traditional travel mediums, as highlighted by Zhu et al. (2023). This immersive quality is attained through advanced technologies such as Virtual Reality (VR) and Augmented Reality (AR), which transport travelers into immersive digital environments. These environments are meticulously crafted to engage all the senses, allowing tourists to not only see and hear but also interact with the virtual surroundings, as noted by Fan et al. (2022) and Çolakoğlu et al. (2023). For instance, tourists can embark on explorations of ancient civilizations, traverse virtual cityscapes, or plunge into underwater wonders, all from the comfort of their own homes. It is the profound sense of presence and interactivity inherent in these immersive metaverse experiences that distinguishes them from other forms of digital tourism, such as smart tourism.

Furthermore, metaverse tourism actively encourages tourists to engage within the virtual environment, transitioning them from passive observers to active participants. In this context, tourists have the capacity to interact with objects, characters, and fellow users, rendering each visit a unique and interactive endeavor, as expounded by Morales et al. (2023). This characteristic opens up possibilities for gamified tourism experiences, educational journeys, and even social interactions within the virtual realm, in alignment with the insights of Morrison (2023). The immersive nature of metaverse tourism augments its entertainment value and offers a safe and accessible means for individuals to explore destinations and cultures that they may not have the opportunity to visit physically, as underscored by Prodinger & Neuhofer (2023) and Özdemir Uçgun & Şahin (2023). Consequently, metaverse innovations are instrumental in making tourism more accessible and inclusive.

Tangibilizing Services

Metaverse tourism introduces a distinctive twist to the concept of tangible services. While tourism conventionally involves physical experiences like accommodation, dining, and sightseeing, the metaverse introduces a novel dimension to tangibility, as discussed by Martí-Testón et al. (2023). In this context, tangible services encompass the transformation of physical services and experiences into virtual counterparts that can be perceived and interacted with in the digital realm, in accordance with Koo et al. (2022). For instance, tourists can virtually dine at digital renditions of renowned restaurants, relishing dishes crafted by celebrity chefs. They can also "stay" at virtual hotels featuring meticulously designed digital rooms that faithfully replicate real-world accommodations, as evidenced by the work of Lee (2022) and

Martins et al. (2022). Furthermore, metaverse tourism facilitates activities such as attending virtual concerts, cultural events, or exploring natural wonders. These virtual experiences strive to recreate the sensory elements of the physical world, including taste, touch, and sound, in order to offer a multisensory encounter.

Additionally, tangible services within the metaverse not only offer an exciting alternative to physical tourism but also create opportunities for novel revenue streams and collaborations. In this scenario, tourism businesses can expand their offerings into the metaverse, accessing a global audience without the limitations imposed by physical infrastructure, in alignment with the insights of Lin et al. (2023) and Rejeb et al. (2023). For instance, hotels and restaurants can virtually replicate their signature dishes and provide intricately crafted virtual accommodations, conjuring the illusion of a luxurious suite experience, as demonstrated by Montoya Esquer & Lara López (2023). Moreover, cultural institutions, travel agencies, and event organizers can collaborate on virtual experiences to broaden their reach to a global audience. Therefore, the metaverse's capacity to offer tangible services fosters entrepreneurial innovation and cross-industry partnerships, further reshaping the landscape of tourism and entertainment.

Building Blocks for Metaverse Tourism

The development of metaverse tourism brings about innovations for all stakeholders. These innovations, serving as the primary building blocks, encompass processes, platforms, and offerings that empower all stakeholders to collaboratively create value. As outlined by Buhalis et al. (2023), four key building blocks for metaverse tourism were identified (Figure 9), and these will be analyzed in the following section.

Network Infrastructure

Network infrastructure stands as one of the foundational building blocks for the advancement of metaverse tourism. It encompasses the digital backbone that facilitates seamless connectivity and the swift transfer of data within the metaverse. High-speed internet connections, minimal latency, and robust data networks constitute indispensable components of this infrastructure, as noted by Buhalis et al. (2023). Furthermore, the metaverse heavily relies on real-time interactions, high-definition content streaming, and the exchange of vast volumes of data, all of which necessitate a sturdy and dependable network infrastructure, in accordance with the insights of Liew et al. (2023) and Rejeb et al. (2023).

Hence, the availability of 5G technology and forthcoming generations of wireless connectivity assumes paramount importance in unleashing the full potential of the metaverse, as highlighted by Suanpang et al. (2022). These technologies offer

Figure 9. Metaverse tourism building blocks (Buhalis et al., 2023)

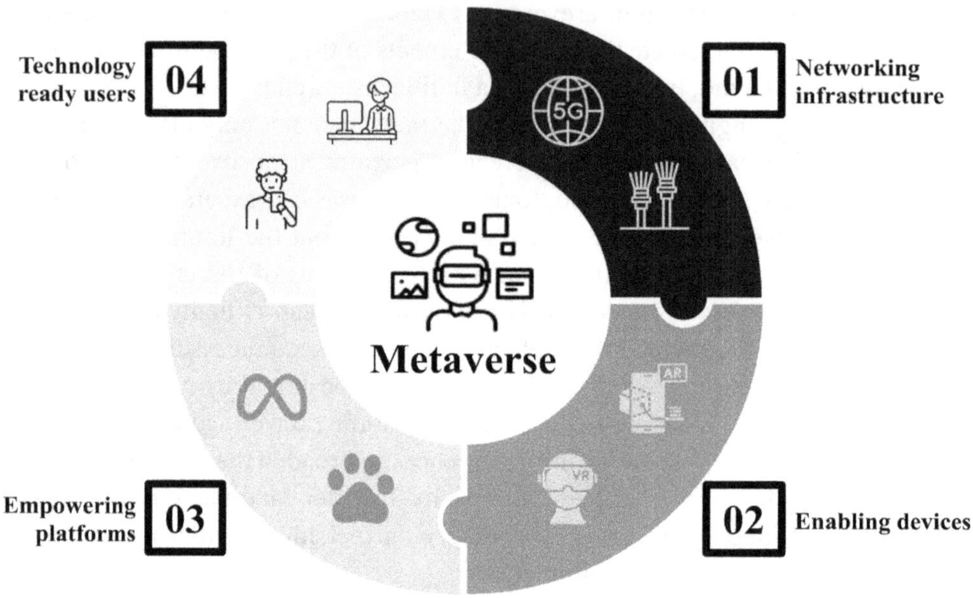

swifter data speeds, diminished latency, and enhanced capacity, thereby enabling more immersive and responsive metaverse experiences. Additionally, the evolution of edge computing, which brings computational power closer to the user, further augments the efficiency of metaverse applications, in line with Buhalis et al. (2023). As metaverse tourism continues its evolution, network infrastructure will play a pivotal role in ensuring that users can seamlessly explore virtual destinations, engage with others, and access content from any corner of the globe.

Enabling Devices

Enabling devices are the hardware components that serve as gateways for users to access and engage with the metaverse. These devices encompass VR headsets, AR glasses, haptic feedback controllers, and other peripherals designed to enhance the sensory experience, as outlined by Buhalis et al. (2023). These gadgets play a pivotal role in bridging the divide between the physical and digital realms, enabling users to fully immerse themselves in metaverse tourism experiences. For instance, VR headsets transport users into virtual environments, delivering a visual and auditory experience that closely mirrors real-world settings, as elucidated by Arafat (2023) and Yoon et al. (2022). AR glasses overlay digital information onto the physical world, enriching real-world experiences with digital elements. Meanwhile, haptic controllers replicate touch and tactile sensations, further enhancing the immersive experience, as observed by Yang & Wang (2023). As technology continues to advance and these devices become more accessible and affordable, they empower users to explore virtual destinations, partake in interactive experiences, and engage with the metaverse in increasingly intuitive and realistic ways, in line with the insights of Zaman et al. (2022) and Wei (2023). The diverse range of enabling devices caters to various preferences and needs, ensuring that metaverse tourism remains inclusive and accessible to a broad spectrum of users, regardless of their technological proficiency or physical abilities. These devices play a pivotal role in making metaverse tourism an engaging and personalized venture.

Empowering Platforms

Empowering platforms constitute the digital environments and ecosystems where metaverse tourism experiences are crafted, shared, and accessed. These platforms serve as the canvas upon which developers, content creators, and businesses construct virtual worlds, experiences, and services, as elaborated by Buhalis et al. (2023). They provide the essential tools, frameworks, and infrastructure needed to fashion the digital landscapes of the metaverse. Metaverse platforms encompass a wide spectrum in terms of scope and purpose, ranging from user-generated content platforms like Second Life to extensive virtual reality ecosystems such as Oculus, as noted by Wei (2022) and Wang et al. (2022). Additionally, social media platforms like Facebook (Meta Inc.) are transitioning into prominent players in the metaverse domain, as observed by Qadir & Fatah (2023). These platforms empower content creators and businesses to design immersive destinations, cultural experiences, and virtual events for connecting and engaging with their audiences, as highlighted by Undale et al. (2023). Therefore, empowering platforms play a central role in the growth of metaverse tourism, providing the means to create engaging and diverse experiences, foster social connections, and drive economic activities within the metaverse ecosystem.

Technology-Ready Users

Technology-ready users are individuals equipped with the digital literacy, skills, and access required to effectively engage with the metaverse. They possess the knowledge and familiarity necessary to navigate virtual environments, utilize enabling devices, and interact with empowering platforms, as outlined by Buhalis et al. (2023). Technology readiness stands as a crucial building block for the success of metaverse tourism since it ensures that users can fully harness the metaverse's potential. To attain technology readiness, users may require training, exposure to virtual environments, and access to enabling devices, as suggested by Volchek

& Brysch (2023) and Chan et al. (2023). Tourism businesses may need to offer education and user support to enhance user readiness, particularly as the metaverse evolves and introduces new technologies and interfaces. The commitment to provide these additional services should be grounded in the understanding that technology-ready users contribute to the growth of the metaverse ecosystem, as emphasized by Corne et al. (2023). These users generate content, engage in social interactions, and drive economic activities within virtual environments, thereby enriching the overall metaverse tourism experience for themselves and others. Therefore, empowering users with the skills and knowledge to navigate this digital frontier is fundamental to the long-term success of the metaverse as it continues to evolve.

Opportunities of the Metaverse in the Tourism Industry

The integration of the metaverse into tourism offers numerous opportunities for businesses to enhance their growth and improve customer experiences. For example, the capacity for metaverse users to explore a destination before their actual visit enhances trip planning, ultimately contributing to their overall satisfaction and experience, as demonstrated by David & Chalon (2023). Additionally, metaverse tourism empowers businesses to reach a global audience, potentially leading to increased revenues. This section of the literature review delves into the various opportunities presented by metaverse tourism.

Improved Tourism Management and Marketing

The metaverse presents a significant opportunity for tourism management and marketing. For instance, it provides a wealth of data and analytics capabilities, allowing destination managers and marketers to gain deeper insights into traveler behavior, preferences, and trends, as indicated by Morrison (2023) and Erdem & Barakazı (2023). This data-driven approach enables more targeted and effective marketing strategies, helping destinations tailor their promotional efforts to specific customer segments. Moreover, metaverse platforms can serve as virtual showcases for destinations, offering immersive previews of attractions, accommodations, and experiences, as highlighted by Garrido-Iñigo & Rodríguez-Moreno (2015). This virtual marketing can influence travel decisions and provide potential visitors with a more comprehensive understanding of a destination's offerings, as suggested by He et al. (2023). Additionally, metaverse-based simulations and predictive analytics can assist in managing tourist flows, optimizing resource allocation, and mitigating overcrowding at popular tourist sites, thereby contributing to better overall tourism management.

Improved Customer Experience

The metaverse reimagines the customer experience in tourism by offering travelers highly personalized and immersive journeys. For example, the utilization of avatars, profiles, and AI-driven recommendations in the metaverse enables tourists to create and navigate virtual environments that cater to their interests and preferences, as outlined by Koohang et al. (2023). This level of personalization enhances the overall customer experience, ensuring that travelers have more enjoyable and meaningful interactions within the metaverse, as highlighted by Rather (2023). For instance, virtual assistants can guide tourists through virtual destinations, providing real-time assistance and recommendations, enabling them to make the most of their virtual travels, as demonstrated by Kumar et al. (2023) and Buhalis et al. (2023). This personalized approach fosters customer loyalty, positive reviews, and repeat business, all of which are valuable to the tourism industry. Moreover, metaverse tourism has transformed how tourists plan, explore, and engage with destinations, as exemplified by Morales et al. (2023) and Su et al. (2023). For instance, users can virtually preview and interact with destinations and accommodations before making decisions, reducing uncertainty and enhancing the booking process, as indicated by Filimonau et al. (2022). Since metaverse tourism transcends geographical constraints and time zones, travelers from different parts of the world can embark on adventures at their convenience. This opportunity makes metaverse tourism more inclusive, ultimately improving customer satisfaction and experiences.

Opportunity for Value Co-Creation

The metaverse introduces the concept of value co-creation in tourism, where tourists actively participate in designing their travel experiences. Through metaverse platforms, users can collaborate with creators, designers, and fellow tourists to shape virtual destinations, events, and activities, as elucidated by Buhalis et al. (2023). This participatory approach empowers tourists to contribute their ideas, preferences, and creativity to the development of the metaverse, fostering a sense of ownership and community. For example, users can co-create virtual events, design virtual attractions, or even contribute to the development of virtual cultural exhibits, as demonstrated by Cheng et al. (2023) and El-Din et al. (2023). This co-creation enriches the quality and diversity of metaverse tourism experiences and establishes a sense of shared responsibility and engagement, strengthening the connection between tourists and the destinations they explore. Additionally, businesses can utilize customer insights gained through co-creation activities to improve their offerings, as highlighted by Kumar et al. (2023). This approach can help enhance business performance while also ensuring that the services and products provided throughout the user journey are tailored to their interests and needs.

Customized Travel Experiences

Metaverse tourism excels in providing customized travel experiences tailored to individual preferences. For instance, metaverse platforms can curate travel itineraries, activities, and content that align with each traveler's interests and desires through AI algorithms and user profiles, as demonstrated by Li et al. (2023). Integrating recommendation systems into a metaverse platform can help recommend virtual tours of historical sites for history enthusiasts, culinary experiences for food lovers, or adventure simulations for thrill-seekers, as evidenced by Sánchez-Amboage et al. (2023) and Zarrouk & El Aidouni (2023). This customization ensures that tourists have more relevant and enjoyable experiences, reducing the likelihood of dissatisfaction or disappointment. Consequently, the metaverse's ability to deliver highly personalized travel journeys contributes to higher customer satisfaction and fosters a sense of empowerment among travelers, thereby enhancing their overall experiences.

Talent Management

The metaverse also offers opportunities for talent management within the tourism industry. Virtual tour guides, event hosts, and experience creators play essential roles in the metaverse tourism ecosystem, as highlighted by Dutta et al. (2023). As demand for metaverse tourism experiences grows, there is an increasing need for skilled individuals who can craft and deliver these experiences. This trend creates new career paths and entrepreneurial opportunities for individuals with expertise in virtual experience design, content creation, and immersive storytelling, as exemplified by Inder (2022) and Martí-Testón et al. (2023). Tourism professionals can transition their skills to the metaverse, providing an avenue for career growth and diversification within the industry, as discussed by Lin et al. (2023). Additionally, virtual tourism also attracts talent from diverse fields, such as 3D modeling, animation, and virtual event production, contributing to a vibrant and dynamic metaverse tourism talent pool.

Virtual Cultural Exchange

Virtual cultural exchange within the metaverse fosters cross-cultural understanding and global connectivity, thus creating a transformative opportunity for the tourism industry. In this digital realm, tourists can engage in immersive cultural experiences that transcend geographical boundaries, as highlighted by Fan et al. (2022). They can participate in virtual festivals, explore historical reenactments, and attend virtual cultural exhibitions, all while interacting with people from diverse backgrounds, as discussed by Martins et al. (2022) and Kumar et al. (2023). For instance, a tourist in New York can virtually join a traditional Japanese tea ceremony, learn about the customs and rituals, and even converse with hosts and participants from Japan. This level of cultural immersion not only enriches the traveler's perspective but also forges connections and friendships that span the globe, transcending language and cultural barriers, as noted by Zhang et al. (2022). Tourists can immerse themselves in foreign cultures, explore historical epochs, and engage in cross-cultural dialogues without traveling to foreign countries. This fosters cultural understanding, empathy, and appreciation, promoting global awareness and tolerance.

Moreover, cultural institutions, museums, and heritage sites can leverage the metaverse to showcase their artifacts, art collections, and historical sites to a global audience. Users can explore ancient ruins, visit world-renowned museums, and virtually step into historical periods, all with a level of detail and interactivity that enriches their understanding of different cultures, as emphasized by Martí-Testón et al. (2023). This not only supports the preservation of cultural heritage but also democratizes access to these treasures, making them available to individuals who might never have the opportunity to visit them physically, as highlighted by Fan et al. (2022). Therefore, virtual cultural exchange in the metaverse is a powerful tool for promoting cross-cultural dialogue, preserving cultural heritage, and enriching global human experiences.

Sustainable Tourism Development

The metaverse has the potential to advance sustainable tourism development by reducing the environmental impact of travel. Offering virtual alternatives to physical tourism can help alleviate issues related to over-tourism, carbon emissions, and strain on natural resources, as discussed by Go & Kang (2023). For instance, virtual tourism experiences can divert some demand away from crowded tourist destinations, easing the burden on delicate ecosystems and heritage sites. This promotes responsible tourism practices and supports the conservation of natural and cultural treasures, in line with the findings of Hui et al. (2023). Additionally, the metaverse can serve as a platform for raising awareness about sustainability issues and inspiring travelers to make eco-conscious choices when they embark on physical journeys, as noted by Lee (2022). Ultimately, metaverse tourism contributes to a more sustainable and balanced approach to tourism development.

Beyond environmental considerations, the metaverse contributes to sustainable tourism by addressing various socio-cultural and economic issues. For instance, virtual tourism experiences can empower local communities to share their cultures and traditions with a global audience, as highlighted by Monaco & Sacchi (2023). This practice can enable them to derive economic benefits from the metaverse tourism industry. Additionally, metaverse-based tourism can contribute to economic diversification in regions that may not have traditional tourism infrastructure, as observed by Pellegrino et al. (2023) and Su et al. (2023). This innovation provides opportunities for small businesses and entrepreneurs to offer virtual products and services, creating new revenue streams and promoting inclusive economic growth, as emphasized by Inder (2022). Therefore, the metaverse plays a pivotal role in building resilient and sustainable tourism destinations that benefit both the environment and the communities by encouraging the active participation of local communities and fostering a deeper understanding of cultural heritage.

Challenges of Implementing the Metaverse in the Tourism Industry

While metaverse tourism presents multiple opportunities, it is also associated with numerous challenges. For instance, the metaverse integrates numerous data technologies that facilitate massive user data collection and analysis. This raises concerns over user data protection and usage, as highlighted by Koohang et al. (2023). Other challenges, such as the costs of acquiring the technologies and inadequate digital literacy, are slowing down the adoption of metaverse tourism. This section provides an in-depth analysis of these challenges to enable business leaders and entrepreneurs to make informed decisions and implement relevant solutions.

Technology Barriers

Technological barriers are one of the primary challenges in implementing the metaverse in the tourism industry. Metaverse experiences often rely on advanced hardware such as VR headsets, AR glasses, and powerful computing devices, as noted by Monaco & Sacchi (2023). These technologies can be expensive, making them unaffordable for some tourists. Moreover, technology in the metaverse is continually evolving, requiring users to keep pace with the latest hardware and software updates, as highlighted by Buhalis et al. (2023). This poses an ongoing challenge for both consumers and industry stakeholders. Therefore, the pursuit of affordability, accessibility, and compatibility across diverse devices and platforms remains a central concern on the journey to realize the full potential of metaverse tourism.

Privacy and Security Concerns

The metaverse involves extensive user interactions, potentially including the sharing of personal information, financial transactions, and sensitive data. The use of data technologies to collect, analyze, and manage this massive user data increases the metaverse ecosystem's vulnerability to privacy and security issues, as highlighted by Buhalis et al. (2023). Therefore, ensuring the robust protection of user data from breaches and unauthorized access is paramount to maintaining trust in metaverse tourism, as noted by Chen et al. (2022). Moreover, the metaverse raises concerns about surveillance within virtual spaces, with prevalent questions about illegal monitoring and data ownership. Balancing between safeguarding user privacy and delivering personalized and engaging experiences is also an intricate challenge, as discussed by Yang & Wang (2023) and Sun et al. (2022). Thus, implementing effective cybersecurity measures, transparent privacy policies, and user education initiatives is essential to protect user information and uphold their digital rights. Additionally, as metaverse tourism grows, regulatory frameworks must evolve to address these concerns comprehensively, as recommended by Buhalis et al. (2023). They should define guidelines for data ownership, user consent, and security standards to ensure a safe and secure metaverse experience for all participants.

Barriers Digital Divide

The digital divide refers to disparities in access to technology and the internet among different groups of people. In metaverse tourism, the digital divide encompasses inequalities in access to technology, internet connectivity, and digital literacy, significantly impacting individuals' ability to engage with metaverse tourism, as discussed by Kouroupi & Metaxas (2023) and Poonkuzhali et al. (2023). For instance, access to high-end hardware such as VR headsets and computing devices remains limited for many, posing economic and social barriers to participation. Furthermore, unreliable or the lack of high-speed internet connectivity in rural and underserved areas hinders individuals' ability to access and enjoy metaverse experiences, as noted by Koohsari et al. (2023). Bridging this gap necessitates infrastructure development and affordable internet services to make access universal. Other potential solutions to this problem include providing digital literacy programs to empower users, particularly older adults and those less technologically savvy, to navigate the metaverse effectively, as proposed by Buhalis et al. (2023). In addition, inclusivity and representation within the metaverse environment can help ensure that content and experiences accommodate diverse demographics and cultural backgrounds, preventing further exclusion. Addressing the digital divide challenge through collaborative efforts can create an inclusive and accessible metaverse tourism landscape for all.

User Behavior and Addiction

The immersive nature of the metaverse can raise concerns about user behavior and the potential for addiction. The highly stimulating and captivating metaverse environments, designed to offer engaging and rewarding experiences, may lead to addictive behaviors, as highlighted by Buhalis et al. (2023). Users may struggle to disengage from the metaverse, resulting in excessive screen time and a preoccupation with virtual interactions and activities, as observed by Monaco & Sacchi (2023). This can have adverse effects on users' mental and physical health, including issues such as eye strain, sedentary lifestyles, and sleep disturbances. Businesses also face the challenge of finding a balance between encouraging engagement and promoting responsible usage, as noted by Yaqoob et al. (2023). Nevertheless, it is essential to monitor and address issues related to excessive screen time, social isolation, and disconnection from the physical world. Therefore, tourism businesses should provide educational initiatives and user guidelines to promote healthy metaverse usage while mitigating potential negative consequences.

CONCLUSION

The integration of the metaverse into the tourism industry represents a transformative shift, redefining the travel experience from planning to post-travel reflections. This transformation is driven by advanced technologies, including Artificial Intelligence (AI), Augmented Reality (AR), Virtual Reality (VR), Mixed Reality (MR), and blockchain, converging to bridge the gap between physical and digital realms. Tourism businesses are adapting their strategies to embrace these changes.

Metaverse tourism is pioneering customer-centric strategies that empower travelers to actively partake in value creation processes. For instance, tourists can leverage virtual environments to navigate their chosen destinations and engage in meaningful dialogues with travel agencies, effectively articulating their expectations and preferences. This symbiotic interaction facilitates the customization of services to align with individual customer needs, thereby augmenting overall satisfaction and elevating the quality of travel experiences.

The metaverse tourism ecosystem is underpinned by a robust foundation comprising network infrastructure, enabling devices, potent platforms, and a community of tech-savvy users. This amalgamation of technology and personalization holds the potential to revolutionize how tourists conceptualize, explore, and engage with destinations, thereby unfurling novel horizons for the industry.

Metaverse tourism also equips stakeholders with tools for talent management, facilitates virtual cultural exchange, and promotes sustainable tourism development.

Nevertheless, it is crucial to recognize that metaverse tourism is not without its challenges. Concerns surrounding massive data collection, ambiguous data ownership policies, and resultant privacy and protection issues are paramount. Furthermore, limited access to requisite technologies, digital literacy deficits, and inadequate internet connectivity have exacerbated the challenges of the digital divide. Research also highlights the potential connection between metaverse engagement and addictive behavior, with hyper-reality increasing the risk of user disorientation and confusion over time. Therefore, tourism businesses keen on harnessing the full potential of the metaverse must institute robust measures to address these multifaceted challenges.

Tourism in the metaverse is a concept that has materialized with the advancement of technology and the integration of virtual and augmented reality into our daily lives. Although the metaverse is still in its infancy and continues to evolve, it possesses the potential to significantly impact both the tourism industry and society. Here are several key dimensions of its potential impact:

- Accessibility: The metaverse makes travel accessible to those with physical limitations. Virtual tourism allows exploration for individuals who cannot travel physically.
- Cost-Efficiency: Virtual travel reduces costs associated with physical travel, making tourism more affordable and accessible.
- Environmental Impact: Reduced physical travel lowers carbon emissions, promoting sustainable tourism.
- Global Reach: Metaverse tourism attracts a global audience by enabling virtual visits to destinations worldwide.
- Personalization: Virtual reality and augmented reality provide highly personalized travel experiences, aligning with individual preferences.
- Cultural Exchange: The metaverse facilitates cultural immersion, promoting understanding and appreciation of diverse cultures.
- Economic Opportunities: It creates economic prospects for businesses and individuals, fostering entrepreneurship.
- Data Utilization: Tourism in the metaverse generates valuable data for refining offerings and enhancing marketing.

In conclusion, future research should aim to address the challenges of data, accessibility, digital literacy, and addiction while harnessing the opportunities for talent management, cultural exchange, sustainable tourism, and economic growth presented by metaverse tourism. By advancing our understanding in these areas, we can ensure the responsible and sustainable growth of this transformative sector.

ACKNOWLEDGMENT

We would like to express our gratitude to the Editor and the Reviewers. They offered valuable suggestions or improvements. The authors were supported by the GOVCOPP Research Center of the University of Aveiro and COMEGI—Centro de Investigação em Organizações, Mercados e Gestão Industrial da Universidade Lusíada.

REFERENCES

Ampountolas, A., Menconi, G., & Shaw, G. (2023). Metaverse research propositions: Online intermediaries. *Tourism Economics*. Advance online publication. doi:10.1177/13548166231159520

Arafat, S. (2023). SoK: Can NFTs solve the economic problems of countries with ancient heritage? egypt as a case study. *Lecture Notes of the Institute for Computer Sciences, Social-Informatics and Telecommunications Engineering, LNICST.* doi:10.1007/s40558-023-00269-6

Baker, J., Nam, K., & Dutt, C. S. (2023). A user experience perspective on heritage tourism in the metaverse: Empirical evidence and design dilemmas for VR. *Information Technology & Tourism, 25*(3), 265–306. Advance online publication. doi:10.1007/s40558-023-00256-x

Basheer, S., Walia, S., Farooq, S., Shah, M. A., & Mir, F. A. (2023). Exploring the metaverse: The future of tourism through AI and virtual reality. In Influencer Marketing Applications Within the Metaverse (pp. 195-204). doi:10.4018/978-1-6684-8898-0.ch012

Buhalis, D., Leung, D., & Lin, M. (2023). Metaverse as a disruptive technology revolutionising tourism management and marketing. *Tourism Management, 97*, 104724. doi:10.1016/j.tourman.2023.104724

Buhalis, D., Lin, M. S., & Leung, D. (2023). Metaverse as a driver for customer experience and value co-creation: Implications for hospitality and tourism management and marketing. *International Journal of Contemporary Hospitality Management, 35*(2), 701–716. doi:10.1108/IJCHM-05-2022-0631

Buhalis, D., O'Connor, P., & Leung, R. (2023). Smart hospitality: From smart cities and smart tourism towards agile business ecosystems in networked destinations. *International Journal of Contemporary Hospitality Management, 35*(1), 369–393. doi:10.1108/IJCHM-04-2022-0497

Chan, C. H., Wong, K. Y., & Lui, T. W. (2023). *Marketing tourism products in virtual reality: moderating effect of product complexity*. Springer Proceedings in Business and Economics.

Chen, S., Chan, I. C. C., Xu, S., Law, R., & Zhang, M. (2023). Metaverse in tourism: Drivers and hindrances from stakeholders' perspective. *Journal of Travel & Tourism Marketing*, *40*(2), 169–184. doi:10.1080/10548408.2023.2227872

Chen, Z., Wu, J., Gan, W., & Qi, Z. (2022, December). Metaverse security and privacy: An overview. In *2022 IEEE International Conference on Big Data (Big Data)* (pp. 2950-2959). IEEE. 10.1109/BigData55660.2022.10021112

Cheng, X., Zhang, S., Liu, W., & Mou, J. (2023). Understanding visitors' metaverse and in-person tour intentions during the COVID-19 pandemic: A coping perspective. *Proceedings of the Annual Hawaii International Conference on System Sciences*. 10.1108/JHTI-09-2022-0426

Corne, A., Massot, V., & Merasli, S. (2023). The determinants of the adoption of blockchain technology in the tourism sector and metaverse perspectives. *Information Technology & Tourism*, *25*(4), 605–633. Advance online publication. doi:10.1007/s40558-023-00263-y

David, B., & Chalon, R. (2023). Digitalization and virtual assistive systems in tourist mobility: evolution, an experience (with observed mistakes), appropriate orientations and recommendations. Lecture Notes in Computer Science (including subseries Lecture Notes in Artificial Intelligence and Lecture Notes in Bioinformatics).

Donthu, N., Kumar, S., Mukherjee, D., Pandey, N., & Lim, W. M. (2021). How to conduct a bibliometric analysis: An overview and guidelines. *Journal of Business Research*, *133*, 285–296. doi:10.1016/j.jbusres.2021.04.070

Dutta, D., Srivastava, Y., & Singh, E. (2023). Metaverse in the tourism sector for talent management: A technology in practice lens. *Information Technology & Tourism*, *25*(3), 331–365. Advance online publication. doi:10.1007/s40558-023-00258-9

El-Din, D. M., Hassanein, A. E., & Darwish, A. (2023). Multimodal data challenge in metaverse technology. In Studies in Big Data (Vol. 123, pp. 185-210). doi:10.1007/978-3-031-29132-6_11

Erdem, A., & Barakazı, M. (2023). Innovative technology applications in hotel businesses. In Tourism, Hospitality and Event Management (Vol. Part F275, pp. 17-36). doi:10.1007/978-3-031-31682-1_2

Fan, Z., Chen, C., & Huang, H. (2022). Immersive cultural heritage digital documentation and information service for historical figure metaverse: A case of Zhu Xi, Song Dynasty, China. *Heritage Science*, *10*(1), 148. Advance online publication. doi:10.1186/s40494-022-00749-8 PMID:36185636

Faulkner, D. (2022). Hyper-reality: a dangerous modern phenomenon. In Creative Business Education: Exploring the Contours of Pedagogical Praxis (pp. 185-198). doi:10.1007/978-3-031-10928-7_11

Filimonau, V., Ashton, M., & Stankov, U. (2022). Virtual spaces as the future of consumption in tourism, hospitality and events. *Journal of Tourism Futures*. doi:10.1108/JTF-07-2022-0174

Garrido-Iñigo, P., & Rodríguez-Moreno, F. (2015). The reality of virtual worlds: Pros and cons of their application to foreign language teaching. *Interactive Learning Environments*, *23*(4), 453–470. doi:10.1080/10494820.2013.788034

Go, H., & Kang, M. (2023). Metaverse tourism for sustainable tourism development: Tourism Agenda 2030. *Tourism Review*, *78*(2), 381–394. doi:10.1108/TR-02-2022-0102

Gursoy, D., Malodia, S., & Dhir, A. (2022). The metaverse in the hospitality and tourism industry: An overview of current trends and future research directions. *Journal of Hospitality Marketing & Management*, *31*(5), 527–534. doi:10.1080/19368623.2022.2072504

Gursoy, I. T., Aktas, E., Tecim, V., & Kurgun, O. A. (2023). Beta tourist world: A conceptual framework for organizing an event in the metaverse. *Information Technology & Tourism*, *25*(4), 529–548. Advance online publication. doi:10.1007/s40558-023-00266-9

He, J., Wang, M., Xi, G., Zhu, H., Dai, J., & Zhang, X. (2023). Research progress and prospects of Chinese cybergeography against the background of the digital transition. *Tropical Geography*, *43*(4), 567–580. doi:10.13284/j.cnki.rddl.003667

Huang, X. T., Wang, J., Wang, Z., Wang, L., & Cheng, C. (2023). Experimental study on the influence of virtual tourism spatial situation on the tourists' temperature comfort in the context of metaverse. *Frontiers in Psychology*, *13*, 1062876. Advance online publication. doi:10.3389/fpsyg.2022.1062876 PMID:36687952

Hui, X., Raza, S. H., Khan, S. W., Zaman, U., & Ogadimma, E. C. (2023). Exploring regenerative tourism using media richness theory: Emerging role of immersive journalism, metaverse-based promotion, eco-literacy, and pro-environmental behavior. *Sustainability (Basel)*, *15*(6), 5046. Advance online publication. doi:10.3390/su15065046

Inder, S. (2022). Entrepreneurial opportunities in metaverse. In Promoting Consumer Engagement Through Emotional Branding and Sensory Marketing (pp. 52-62). doi:10.4018/978-1-6684-5897-6.ch006

Jafar, R. M. S., & Ahmad, W. (2023). Tourist loyalty in the metaverse: The role of immersive tourism experience and cognitive perceptions. *Tourism Review*. Advance online publication. doi:10.1108/TR-11-2022-0552

Jo, H. (2023). Tourism in the digital frontier: A study on user continuance intention in the metaverse. *Information Technology & Tourism*, *25*(3), 307–330. Advance online publication. doi:10.1007/s40558-023-00257-w

Kim, M. J., & Kim, D. Y. (2023). The metaverse as a new travel marketing platform. In Routledge Handbook of Trends and Issues in Global Tourism Supply and Demand (pp. 209-220). doi:10.4324/9781003260790-22

Koo, C., Kwon, J., Chung, N., & Kim, J. (2022). Metaverse tourism: Conceptual framework and research propositions. *Current Issues in Tourism*, 1–7. doi:10.1080/13683500.2022.2122781

Koohang, A., Nord, J. H., Ooi, K. B., Tan, G. W. H., Al-Emran, M., Aw, E. C. X., Baabdullah, A. M., Buhalis, D., Cham, T.-H., Dennis, C., Dutot, V., Dwivedi, Y. K., Hughes, L., Mogaji, E., Pandey, N., Phau, I., Raman, R., Sharma, A., Sigala, M., ... Wong, L. W. (2023). Shaping the metaverse into reality: A holistic multidisciplinary understanding of opportunities, challenges, and avenues for future investigation. *Journal of Computer Information Systems*, *63*(3), 735–765. doi:10.1080/08874417.2023.2165197

Koohsari, M. J., McCormack, G. R., Nakaya, T., Yasunaga, A., Fuller, D., Nagai, Y., & Oka, K. (2023). The metaverse, the built environment, and public health: Opportunities and uncertainties. *Journal of Medical Internet Research*, *25*, e43549. doi:10.2196/43549 PMID:36780208

Kouroupi, N., & Metaxas, T. (2023). Can the Metaverse and Its Associated Digital Tools and Technologies Provide an Opportunity for Destinations to Address the Vulnerability of Overtourism? *Tourism and Hospitality*, *4*(2), 355–373. doi:10.3390/tourhosp4020022

Kumar, S., Dhiraj, A., & Hassan, S. C. C. (2023). Metaverse and cultural marketing in hospitality and tourism. In Cultural Marketing and Metaverse for Consumer Engagement (pp. 224-233). doi:10.4018/978-1-6684-8312-1.ch016

Kumar, S., Dhiraj, A., Shah, M. A., & Rani, D. (2023). Application of metaverse in the hospitality industry. In Influencer Marketing Applications Within the Metaverse (pp. 178-194). doi:10.4018/978-1-6684-8898-0.ch011

Lee, U. K. (2022). Tourism using virtual reality: Media richness and information system successes. *Sustainability (Basel)*, *14*(7), 3975. Advance online publication. doi:10.3390/su14073975

Li, J., Hu, P., Cui, W., Huang, T., & Cheng, S. (2023). Deepsea: A meta-ocean prototype for undersea exploration. *Information Technology & Tourism*, *25*(3), 391–409. Advance online publication. doi:10.1007/s40558-023-00260-1

Liew, Z. Q., Du, H., Bryan Lim, W. Y., Xiong, Z., Niyato, D., & Yu, H. (2023). *Economics of semantic communication in metaverse: an auction approach. In Proceedings - IEEE Consumer Communications and Networking Conference*. CCNC.

Lin, K. J., Ye, H., & Law, R. (2023). Understanding the development of blockchain-empowered metaverse tourism: An institutional perspective. *Information Technology & Tourism*, *25*(4), 585–603. Advance online publication. doi:10.1007/s40558-023-00262-z

Linnenluecke, M. K., Marrone, M., & Singh, A. K. (2019). Conducting systematic literature reviews and bibliometric analyses. *Australian Journal of Management*, *45*(2), 175–194. doi:10.1177/0312896219877678

Martí-Testón, A., Muñoz, A., Gracia, L., & Solanes, J. E. (2023). Using WebXR metaverse platforms to create touristic services and cultural promotion. *Applied Sciences (Basel, Switzerland)*, *13*(14), 8544. Advance online publication. doi:10.3390/app13148544

Martins, D., Oliveira, L., & Amaro, A. C. (2022). From co-design to the construction of a metaverse for the promotion of cultural heritage and tourism: The case of Amiais. *Procedia Computer Science*. doi:10.3390/su15043348

Monaco, S., & Sacchi, G. (2023). Travelling the metaverse: Potential benefits and main challenges for tourism sectors and research applications. *Sustainability (Basel)*, *15*(4), 3348. doi:10.3390/su15043348

Montoya Esquer, J. E., & Lara López, G. (2023). Wordsphere: Virtual reality text input interface. *Virtual Reality (Waltham Cross)*, *27*(3), 2769–2785. doi:10.1007/s10055-023-00842-8

Morales, J., Cornide-Reyes, H., Rossel, P. O., Sáez, P., & Silva-Aravena, F. (2023). Virtual reality, augmented reality and metaverse: customer experience approach and user experience evaluation methods. literature review. Lecture Notes in Computer Science (including subseries Lecture Notes in Artificial Intelligence and Lecture Notes in Bioinformatics).

Morrison, A. M. (2023). *Marketing and Managing Tourism Destinations* (3rd ed.). doi:10.4324/9781003343356

Nijjer, S., Singh, J., Sharma, P., Malhotra, M., & Verma, R. (2023). *Unraveling a new age of travel in blockchain based metaverse*. Lecture Notes in Networks and Systems. doi:10.1007/978-981-19-7982-8_47

Özdemir Uçgun, G., & Şahin, S. Z. (2023). How does Metaverse affect the tourism industry? Current practices and future forecasts. *Current Issues in Tourism*, 1–15. Advance online publication. doi:10.1080/13683500.2023.2238111

Pacheco-Velázquez, E. A., Vázquez-Parra, J. C., Cruz-Sandoval, M., Salinas-Navarro, D. E., & Carlos-Arroyo, M. (2023). Business Decision-Making and Complex Thinking: A Bibliometric Study. *Administrative Sciences, 13*(3), 80. doi:10.3390/admsci13030080

Pellegrino, A., Wang, R., & Stasi, A. (2023). Exploring the intersection of sustainable consumption and the Metaverse: A review of current literature and future research directions. *Heliyon, 9*(9), e19190. Advance online publication. doi:10.1016/j.heliyon.2023.e19190 PMID:37681133

Pernencar, C., Saboia, I., & Dias, J. C. (2022). How Far Can Conversational Agents Contribute to IBD Patient Health Care—A Review of the Literature. *Frontiers in Public Health, 10*, 862432. doi:10.3389/fpubh.2022.862432 PMID:35844879

Poonkuzhali, S., Archana, J. S., & Anand, T. P. P. (2023). Metaverse 3C: concept, components, and challenges in travel and tourism sector. In Lecture Notes on Data Engineering and Communications Technologies (Vol. 171, pp. 699-713). doi:10.1007/978-981-99-1767-9_51

Prodinger, B., & Neuhofer, B. (2023). *Never-ending tourism: tourism experience scenarios for 2030*. Springer Proceedings in Business and Economics.

Qadir, A. M. A., & Fatah, A. O. (2023). Platformization and the Metaverse: Opportunities and Challenges for Urban Sustainability and Economic Development. *EAI Endorsed Transactions on Energy Web, 10*(1).

Raimundo, R., & Rosário, A. T. (2022). Cybersecurity in the Internet of Things in Industrial Management. *Applied Sciences (Basel, Switzerland)*, *12*(3), 1598. doi:10.3390/app12031598

Rameshwar, J. R., & King, G. S. (2023). Analysis of Caribbean XR Survey Creates an XR Development Strategy as a Path to the Regional Metaverse Evolution. *Journal of Metaverse*, *3*(1), 43–65. doi:10.57019/jmv.1179104

Rather, R. A. (2023). Metaverse marketing and consumer research: Theoretical framework and future research agenda in tourism and hospitality industry. *Tourism Recreation Research*, 1–9. Advance online publication. doi:10.1080/02508281.2023.2216525

Rejeb, A., Rejeb, K., & Treiblmaier, H. (2023). Mapping metaverse research: Identifying future research areas based on bibliometric and topic modeling techniques. *Information (Basel)*, *14*(7), 356. Advance online publication. doi:10.3390/info14070356

Rosário, A. T., & Dias, J. C. (2023). How Industry 4.0 and Sensors Can Leverage Product Design: Opportunities and Challenges. *Sensors (Basel)*, *23*(3), 1165. doi:10.3390/s23031165 PMID:36772206

Rosário, A. T., Lopes, P. R., & Rosário, F. S. (2023). Metaverse in Marketing: Challenges and Opportunities. In A. Khang, V. Shah, & S. Rani (Eds.), *Handbook of Research on AI-Based Technologies and Applications in the Era of the Metaverse* (pp. 204–227). IGI Global. doi:10.4018/978-1-6684-8851-5.ch010

Sánchez-Amboage, E., Enrique Membiela-Pollán, M., Martínez-Fernández, V. A., & Molinillo, S. (2023). Tourism marketing in a metaverse context: The new reality of European museums on meta. *Museum Management and Curatorship*, *38*(4), 468–489. doi:10.1080/09647775.2023.2209841

Shaygani, F., Marzaleh, M. A., & Peyravi, M. (2022). Metaverse: A Modern Approach to Medical Tourism Industry. *Iranian Journal of Public Health*, *51*(12), 2844–2845. doi:10.18502/ijph.v51i12.11480 PMID:36742228

Su, P. Y., Hsiao, P. W., & Fan, K. K. (2023). Investigating the relationship between users' behavioral intentions and learning effects of VR system for sustainable tourism development. *Sustainability (Basel)*, *15*(9), 7277. Advance online publication. doi:10.3390/su15097277

Suanpang, P., Niamsorn, C., Pothipassa, P., Chunhapataragul, T., Netwong, T., & Jermsittiparsert, K. (2022). Extensible metaverse implication for a smart tourism city. *Sustainability (Basel)*, *14*(21), 14027. doi:10.3390/su142114027

Sun, J., Gan, W., Chao, H. C., & Yu, P. S. (2022). *Metaverse: Survey, applications, security, and opportunities.* https://doi.org//arXiv.2210.07990 doi:10.48550

Tsai, S. P. (2022). Investigating metaverse marketing for travel and tourism. *Journal of Vacation Marketing*. Advance online publication. doi:10.1177/13567667221145715

Ud Din, I., & Almogren, A. (2023). Exploring the psychological effects of Metaverse on mental health and well-being. *Information Technology & Tourism*, *25*(3), 367–389. Advance online publication. doi:10.1007/s40558-023-00259-8

Undale, S., Kulkarni, A., Mude, G., Patil, H., Raut, N., Banswal, D., & Undale, G. (2023). A bibliometric analysis of citations and publications on metaverse. *Proceedings of the 17th INDIACom; 2023 10th International Conference on Computing for Sustainable Global Development, INDIACom 2023.*

Volchek, K., & Brysch, A. (2023). *Metaverse and tourism: from a new niche to a transformation*. Springer Proceedings in Business and Economics.

Wang, X., Shi, T., Bai, W., Peng, K., Li, J., & Shi, Y. (2022). The research of metaverse application in intelligent railway passenger station. Lecture Notes in Computer Science (including subseries Lecture Notes in Artificial Intelligence and Lecture Notes in Bioinformatics). doi:10.1007/978-3-031-23518-4_10

Wei, D. (2022). Gemiverse: The blockchain-based professional certification and tourism platform with its own ecosystem in the metaverse. *International Journal of Geoheritage and Parks*, *10*(2), 322–336. doi:10.1016/j.ijgeop.2022.05.004

Wei, W. (2023). A buzzword, a phase or the next chapter for the Internet? The status and possibilities of the metaverse for tourism. *Journal of Hospitality and Tourism Insights*. doi:10.1108/JHTI-11-2022-0568

Yang, F. X., & Wang, Y. (2023). Rethinking metaverse tourism: A taxonomy and an agenda for future research. *Journal of Hospitality & Tourism Research (Washington, D.C.)*. Advance online publication. doi:10.1177/10963480231163509

Yang, F. X., & Wang, Y. (2023). Rethinking Metaverse Tourism: A Taxonomy and an Agenda for Future Research. *Journal of Hospitality & Tourism Research (Washington, D.C.)*. Advance online publication. doi:10.1177/10963480231163509

Yaqoob, I., Salah, K., Jayaraman, R., & Omar, M. (2023). Metaverse applications in smart cities: Enabling technologies, opportunities, challenges, and future directions. *Internet of Things : Engineering Cyber Physical Human Systems*, *23*, 100884. doi:10.1016/j.iot.2023.100884

Yoon, T. H., Do, J. K., & Jeong, S. C. (2022). Developing Songjeong metaverse surfing village: development of metaverse-based platform specialized for marine tourism. *Proceedings - 2022 IEEE/ACIS 7th International Conference on Big Data, Cloud Computing, and Data Science, BCD 2022*. 10.1109/BCD54882.2022.9900793

Zaman, U., Koo, I., Abbasi, S., Raza, S. H., & Qureshi, M. G. (2022). Meet your digital twin in space? profiling international expat's readiness for metaverse space travel, tech-savviness, covid-19 travel anxiety, and travel fear of missing out. *Sustainability (Basel)*, *14*(11), 6441. Advance online publication. doi:10.3390/su14116441

Zarrouk, I., & El Aidouni, A. (2023). The digital marketing practiced by the Moroccan tourism sector: national-scale communication actions and environmental management. *E3S Web of Conferences*.

Zhang, W., & Wang, Y. (2023). An empirical study of the impact of metaverse storytelling on intentions to visit. *Information Technology & Tourism*, *25*(3), 411–432. Advance online publication. doi:10.1007/s40558-023-00261-0

Zhang, X., Yang, D., Yow, C. H., Huang, L., Wu, X., Huang, X., Guo, J., Zhou, S., & Cai, Y. (2022). Metaverse for cultural heritages. *Electronics (Basel)*, *11*(22), 3730. Advance online publication. doi:10.3390/electronics11223730

Zhu, C., Wu, D. C. W., Hall, C. M., Fong, L. H. N., Koupaei, S. N., & Lin, F. (2023). Exploring non-immersive virtual reality experiences in tourism: Empirical evidence from a world heritage site. *International Journal of Tourism Research*, *25*(3), 372–383. doi:10.1002/jtr.2574

ADDITIONAL READING

Chu, C. H. (2023). Deep resource allocation for a massively multiplayer online finance of tourism gamification in metaverse. *Information Technology & Tourism*. doi:10.1007/s40558-023-00267-8

Colakoglu, U., Anis, E., Esen, O., & Tuncay, C. S. (2023). The evaluation of tourists' virtual reality experiences in the transition process to Metaverse. *Journal of Hospitality and Tourism Insights*. doi:10.1108/JHTI-09-2022-0426

Din, I. U., & Almogren, A. (2023). Exploring the psychological effects of Metaverse on mental health and well-being. *Information Technology & Tourism, 25*(3), 367-389. doi:10.1007/s40558-023-00259-8

Dwivedi, Y. K., Hughes, L., Wang, Y. C., Alalwan, A. A., Ahn, S. J., Balakrishnan, J., . . . Wirtz, J. (2023). Metaverse marketing: How the metaverse will shape the future of consumer research and practice. *Psychology & Marketing, 40*(4), 750-776. doi:10.1002/mar.21767

Mladenovic, D., Ismagilova, E., Filieri, R., & Dwivedi, Y. K. (2023). MetaWOM - toward a sensory word-of-mouth (WOM) in the metaverse. *International Journal of Contemporary Hospitality Management.* https://doi.org/ doi:10.1108/IJCHM-04-20230474

Sanchez-Amboage, E., Membiela-Pollan, M. E., Martinez-Fernandez, V. A., & Molinillo, S. (2023). Tourism marketing in a metaverse context: The new reality of European museums on meta. *Museum Management and Curatorship, 38*(4), 468-489. doi:10.1080/09647775.2023.2209841

Tejedor, S., Martinez, J., & Tusa, F. (2023). Analysis of the websites of cathedrals in Europe: Structure, content and communication strategies in the era. *Transinformação, 35*, C7–e236868. doi:10.1590/2318-0889202335e236868

Ucgun, G. O., & Sahin, S. Z. (2023). How does Metaverse affect the tourism industry? Current practices and future forecasts. *Current Issues in Tourism.* doi:10.1080/13683500.2023.2238111

KEY TERMS AND DEFINITIONS

Artificial Intelligence: Is a multidisciplinary field of study that covers several areas of knowledge, a system's ability to correctly interpret external data, learn from this data and use this learning to achieve specific objectives and tasks through flexible adaptation.

Augmented Reality: The integration of virtual elements or information into real-world views through a camera and with the use of motion sensors such as a gyroscope and accelerometer.

Blockchain: It is associated with a ledger, which records transactions and asset tracking on a network. It is shared and immutable, thus facilitating the process of recording these transactions.

Co-Creation: Is the product or service design process in which consumer information plays a central role from start to finish.

Machine Learning: Is a subfield of engineering and computer science that evolved from the study of pattern recognition and the theory of computational learning in artificial intelligence, which gives computers the ability to learn without being explicitly programmed.

Mixed Reality: It is the technology that combines characteristics of virtual reality with augmented reality.

Virtual Reality: Is an interface technology between a user and an operating system through 3D graphic resources or 360º images whose objective is to create the sensation of presence in an environment created by computational techniques different from the real one.

Chapter 10
Service Innovation Through Blockchain Technology in the Tourism and Hospitality Industry:
Applications, Trends, and Benefits

Amrik Singh
https://orcid.org/0000-0003-3598-8787
Lovely Professional University, India

Shuaibu Chiroma Hassan
https://orcid.org/0000-0002-8779-9462
Isa Kaita College of Education, Nigeria

ABSTRACT

Blockchain technology is an emerging technology useful to provide innovative solutions in various sectors. The real world uses cases of blockchain technology such as faster cross-border payments, identity management, crypto currencies, smart contracts, and supply chain-blockchain technology are here to stay and have become the next innovation just like internet. There have been attempts to formulate and introduce digital money, but they have not been successful due to security and trust issues. Blockchain has moved past crypto currency and discovered implementations in other real-life applications; this is where we can expect blockchain technology to be simplified and not remain a complex concept. Blockchain technology's desirable characteristics are decentralization, integrity, immutability, verification, fault tolerance, anonymity, audibility, and transparency. The present chapter aims to investigate the applications, trends, and benefits in a real-world environment. This chapter presents a detailed review of blockchain technology, the benefits, and its applications in different fields.

DOI: 10.4018/979-8-3693-1103-5.ch010

INTRODUCTION

Application of IT is now an essential requirement of new forms of tourism emerging across the globe (Caddes and Pinna (2021). *Blockchain*, therefore, is an emerging technology disrupting innovations (Barkel,Kurgun and Groen, 2021), including in the hospitality and tourism industry. The technology is expected to occupy 10% of the global GDP by the year 2025, with 2016 being the age of its prototypes, with 2017 witnessing a mass scale of implementation of the technology in all government and industrial sectors across the developed economies like the banks (India Blockchain Alliance, nd). Charted Accountants Australia and New Zealand (2017), highlight that the total capital investments in the Bitcon and the Blockchain start-ups had exceeded $1.1 billion U.S. dollar globally. It possess the potentials of revolutionising many aspects of businesses, technology, governance, etc (Dogru and Leonardi, 2018). One of the key differentiator of the Blockchain is its dis-intermediation of the ledger – i.e., its ability to transact without any need of third or trusted party (Charted Accountants Australia and New Zealand, 2017). In addition, its tamper-evident, trust-free, as well as its cryptographic security structure enables its*fiat*currencies, and the development of centralized autonomous organisations, creating smart contracts, etc, (Dogru and Leonardi, 2018).Similarly, it eliminates the cost of the third party and other frictions in the processes (Charted Accountants Australia and New Zealand, 2017). These are among the justifications for adopting the technology into hospitality and tourism industry.

Though the technology is in its infancy stage, hospitality (hotel and restaurants), and tourism (transport and travel agents, Airlines, DMOs) can apply it for their guests' experience (satisfactions), service quality, as well as profitability by integrating the technology into the business. As a result, all the stakeholders in the hospitality and tourism businesses will benefit from its application (Dogru and Mody, 2018). As a result, it will enhance the competitiveness of the firms, attract more customers, and make the business operations cost-effective.

The Purpose of the Study: The purpose of this research is two-fold; to explore and identify the benefits of Blockchain technology; and to identify the areas the Technology could be applied to in the tourism and hospitality industry to reap the benefits associated with it. To enhance trust between business parties and stakeholders, to avoid some costs, by providing transparency in the business.

Academic and Industrial Justification of the Study: Hospitality and Tourism industry is a customer-oriented, with volumes of customer-industry interactions. The organisations need reliable trusts between clients and the industry as well as need for cost-cutting strategies to reduce overheads. Blockchain, as a technology, has huge potentials to achieve these and other benefits from both the customer to the tourism and hospitality organisations. This research, therefore, is exploring the ways Blockchain could be applied in the industry as well as increasing the frontier of knowledge in the area, which tourism experts, scholars and students could make use of in the field of studies.

Research Gap and Novelty: The study identifies the potentials of Blockchain, and how the technology could help in fostering trust in the industry. This reveals how a new technological tool 'Naplozz' could be used, as a cutting edge, to leverage technology for convenience in hospitality businesses. Furthermore, it presents the future trends of the technology in the industry. The technology, will therefore be used continuously for convenience and security. The study presents the potentials of adopting the Blockchain technology that previous researches did not reveal in the past.

LITERATURE REVIEW

Blockchain, is a sort of distributed Ledger technology that is made up of digitally recorded data in packages- called 'blocks' that linked together in a chronological order(Lovells, 2023). Dogru and Mody (2018) describe it as an online platform that records data of transactions chronologically as well as transacts assets through its distributed ledger. Meanwhile, a distributed ledger is a shared, replicated, and synchronized digital data structure spread across a network, with participants, or 'node', of which can be in multiple sites, institutions, and or countries (Lovells, 2023); smart contracts, distributed ledgers, P2P (Barkel, Kurgun and Groen, 2021). These transactions in a network could include, but not limited to receiving and sending money, services and products payments, hotel bookings and reservations, contract agreements entries, etc (Dogru and Mody, 2018). As a result, the most effective and efficient way for using the technology is in the complex markets with a multiple of ways that interact with each other (Charted Accountants Australia and New Zealand, 2017). This has made it huge prospects and potential in the future for developed and emerging economies, as well as tourism and hospitality organisations.

Barkel, Kurgun and Groen (2021) assert that it is a system for the storage of information, and that there is no single user controlling the information alone but all the entire parties involved. That means there is no manipulation by organisatios or individuals, Barkel et al, further revealed. Blockchain, as an emerging technological phenomenon, could be employed to harness the creation of trust and forging it in the tourism and hospitality industry – through a trusting and transparent relationships between the firms and the customers (Rejeb and Rejeb, 2019).Trust in the hospitality industry is an essential ingredient for success, however, it is being a challenge by various factors such as supply-chains disruptions, consumer expectations, stringent regulatory requirements, and frauds, particularly in food aspects (Zuhal, 2023). In addition, it also enables the tracking of ownerships of assets along with the right to use in a situation where by the asset is leased to third party (Dogru, Mody and Leonardi, 2018). Therefore, to build and maintain a trust in the sector, it istherefore vital to ensure traceability and transparency in all aspects of activities, like transactions (Zuhal, 2023). This provides the business of the firm with validity, reliability, and certainty, thereby creating trust between the clients and the organisations in the tourism industry. As is the main ingredient that sustain businesses.

Zuhal (2023) identify 'Naplozz' as a solution to trust challenges in hospitality industry. One of the main challenges of application of modern technology is lack of public trust or public confidence; therefore, Blockchain technology has now been a solution to that (Caddes and Pinna, 2021). It is a ground-breaking Platform which combine the power of Blockchain technology with comprehensive suite of features that are designed for various industries – aiming to revolutionise various sectors by offering transparent, secure and efficient solutions for supply management, quality assurance, food safety assurance and compliance. All economies rely on ultimately on the creation of trust in their systems (Charted Accountants Australia and New Zealand, 2017). This App will boost transparency in the businesses which will improve the trust between the employees and the employer on one hand, and customers and the employer on the other. With its telecom technology policy, the Federal Government of Nigeria is going big in accepting the Blockchain (Singh & Singh, 2024; Bhall et.al, 2024). On the 3rd of May, 2023, the Federal Ministry of Communications and Digital Economy (FMCDE) announces the acceptance and approval of a national Blockchain policy – the government is supporting the emerging technology that will facilitate the country's digital economy (Nnamani and Omoniyi, 2023; Singh & Singh, 2024; Bhall et.al, 2024). This has shown the demand for the technology by institutions and governments across the globe, which will shape the future trends of the businesses and industries.

Areas of Blockchain Technology Application in Hospitality and Tourism Industry

Blockchain is currently applied in transport and hospitality sectors and in hotel bookings (Charted Accountants Australia and New Zealand, 2017).Dogru and Mody (2018) include sending and receiving of money, payments, bookings and reservations in hospitality businesses, among others.

i) **Identity, Credential Management and Privacy** – For enhancing the safety and protecting the privacy of the travelers in the tourism sector, digital traveler identity concept is made for personal identifications. This will therefore solve the problem of identity theft that tourists often encounter (Caddes and Pinna, 2021), as well as mismanagement and delays (Rejeb and Rejeb, 2019). This often result to money and time being lost for both the Airline and the passenger, Rejeb and Rejeb further highlight.

ii) **Ticketing and Reservations** – The technology of Blockchain can be employed to make hotel reservations, and issuingof tickets, and as well to contrast the Black market – by creating certain standards protocols that will allow customers to use their e-wallets for proof of their ownerships. For instance, WICKET (7) App launched by an Italian start-up for ticketing (Caddes and Pinna, 2021; Singh & Singh, 2024; Bhall et.al, 2024).

iii) **Reliable Online Travel Reviews** – this will enable a reliable online reviews for the tourism and hospitality firms. Previous researches show that online reviews are the most impacting factors that affect hotel online bookings. Many online reviews are manipulated by the organisations, or people that had no prior experience of the hotel and tourism services could post reviews to damage the reputations of the organisation. Blockchain can offer solutions tothisby ensuring that only served customers could write and post a review (Rejeb and Rejeb, 2019; Singh & Singh, 2024; Bhall et.al, 2024).

iv) **Naplozz Platform** – through leveraging the unique multifaceted Blockchain capabilities, the

v) **Traceability of Food Products** – in this way, the technology is served aas a tool to trace the food supply chains of products in food tourism in terms of local supplies, organic or sustainable food products. In spite of this, it can also serve as a system to trace the data on the origin or sources of food products. In practical application, this could be attained through scanning of OR Code, or directly scanning the bar codes of the product through devices that are registered in the Blockchain (Caddes and Pinna, 2021).

vi) Platform empowers many businesses to overcome challenges they face in trust-building, as well as fostering a customer loyalty that leads to improved performance, and long term growths(Zuhal, 2023; Singh & Singh, 2024; Bhall et.al, 2024). In order to understand how the hospitality sector will benefit from a Blockchain-based solutions like the 'Naplozz', the idea will focus on two fundamental points; quality control and regulatory compliance. The Platform will help the hospitality businesses to implement and navigate compliance, quality control issues to help maintain high standards of product/service quality. Additionally, the *$NAP Token*is at the core of the Naplozz ecosystem as a utility token. The Token will enable businesses and their entities to incentivise staff members, access features which enable better work quality, and also generate high revenues by actively benefitting from the platform, while refining their services. It as well facilitates organisation's transactions –ensuring a seamless operations, and adherence to regulatory norms and quality standards. Similarly, the NAP chain's innovative solutions such as the NAP Certification system, quality-related data tracking, compliance, all help to enhance the platform's capabilities (Zuhal, 2023; Singh & Singh, 2024; Bhall et.al, 2024).

vii) The technology of Blockchain enables the **tracking of asset** ownerships along with the 'Right-to-use' in the event of assets licensed to third party. Therefore, anything of significant value may be tracked, recorded or exchanged or leased on Blockchain platform, and therefore duplicate records of the transactions are shared simultaneously with the participating agents in the 'network'. Meanwhile, these records are further protected with mathematically configured, or cryptographic keys to ensure for their security (Dogru and Mody, 2018; Singh & Singh, 2024; Bhall et.al, 2024).

viii) Another area where the Blockchain technology could be applied in hospitality sector is in the **inventory management** – inventory system refers to a number of rooms available in the hotel, or the number of seats in an airplane. Specifically, this will provide accurate and unaltered information on coverage and availability rate, by sharing the information with various stakeholders involved, thereby replacing other Property Management Systems (PMS), or CRS, with a consequential removal of third party intermediaries, and other expenses (Caddes and Pinna, 2021).

ix) Luggage/Baggage Tracking – the technology of Blockchain can be a solution problems arising from baggage and luggage lost, where it can be used to track the passengers' luggage through monitoring at various points through the automatic data entries in the public register. This will speed up check-ins, and reduce the waiting times of the passengers. Moreover, it will make tracking sequences protected, and as well generate the security of data of all the parties /stakeholders involved (Caddes and Pinna, 2021).

The diagramme below shows, in summary, the main benefits of applying the Blockchain technology for the tourism and hospitality organisations which the study identifies.

Blockchain technology is very reliable and trustworthy way of incorporating in a business. For instance, in Germany, *ALDI,* a UK food chain company, misled the public on its product as "Halal", which was not – contained pig blood. This led to a controversy in the country (Moftah, 2015; Singh & Singh, 2024; Bhall et.al, 2024).With the Blockchain technology adopted, this problem will be eliminated. Similarly, the technology prevent fraud by making an exact copy of ledger or any business transactions made that could not be manipulated by any of the parties involved. It also provides transparency in the business operations and transactions between the clients and the organisations as well as other stakeholders. Eventually, this will empower the organisations and as well reduce the costs in the operations. To harness these benefits, hospitality and

Figure 1. Benefits of applying blockchain technology in hospitality and tourism industry
Sources: Author Elaborations

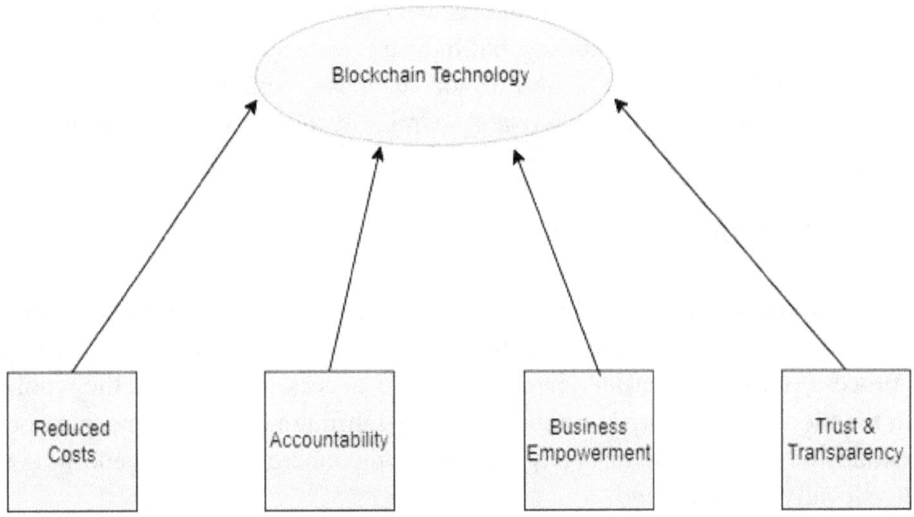

tourism organisations should, therefore, employ the best talents in the field, or train their current employees to master the area for reaping the full potentials of the technology. This is not without costs, and other change and transformation implications, which must be borne with.

Ways the Blockchain Can Be Used Within the Travel Industry

Although the potential uses for the blockchain within the travel industry are almost limitless, some applications have emerged and have a transformative effect, while others are just around the corner. Three of the most important ways the blockchain can be used are explained in more depth below:

Secure Payments

The most obvious practical application of blockchain in the hotel industry will be secure payments. Whether it is the acceptance of cryptocurrency like Bitcoin or Ethereum, or simply providing a transparent, safe, global ledger, bank payments can be streamlined, and associated hotel costs can be reduced.

ID and Security

One of the most exciting potential uses for the blockchain within the hospitality industry is related to identification and security services. Passengers must provide ID at various stages of their journey, but industry-wide adoption of the blockchain could potentially allow for a shared digital database, with passengers providing, for example, a fingerprint to quickly and seamlessly verify who they are, reducing waiting times.

Loyalty Programs

Loyalty reward schemes are an important part of generating return customs. Blockchain technology can enhance the quality of loyalty programs by simplifying the process, making it easier for customers to access and redeem their points. With the blockchain, rewards can be distributed through digital tokens that could, potentially be used anywhere, at any time, while the inherent security benefits could reduce loyalty scheme fraud.

Baggage Tracking

Finally, the uses of the blockchain within the travel industry extend to things like luggage tracking. Typically, a traveler's luggage changes hands many times throughout a journey, which can result in logistical issues. The centralized nature of the blockchain can allow different companies to share easily and access related data.

Airlines Use of Blockchain to Distribute Frequent Flier Miles

Both Lufthansa and Swiss Air announced integrating blockchain technology into their frequent flier programs. This means that airlines can distribute miles based on how much money a customer has spent with an airline. This might seem pretty straightforward, but the current system is, in fact, quite complicated—so complicated, in fact, that many airlines are losing millions of dollars per year.

The current system for distributing miles was first developed in the 1980s by American Airlines. Since then, it has grown to include dozens of global partners, each with its rules and regulations regarding how miles are distributed. The system is so complex that many airlines have resorted to giving up on it altogether. So what can blockchain do? Blockchain-based systems are transparent, automated, and secure—three qualities that are ideal for keeping track of miles earned by frequent fliers. Blockchain also reduces the possibility of fraud. Because there is no central authority governing the blockchain network, consumers can see exactly where their data is headed at all times (and even view the transaction history).

CONCLUSION AND FUTURE IMPLICATIONS

Blockchain technology hospitality trends and uses outlined, blockchain is also a concept that is closely associated with the metaverse. This refers to a network of 3D metaverse virtual words, where users are able to interact socially, and a growing number of hospitality businesses are waking up to its full potential. In conclusion, the adoption of blockchain technology has the potential to revolutionize the hotel and tourism industry in Asian countries by improving the efficiency, transparency, and security of the industry. However, there are several challenges that need to be addressed before its widespread adoption, such as the lack of standardization and interoperability and the high cost of implementation. Future research could focus on developing standardized protocols and frameworks for interoperability and exploring the potential of blockchain in other areas of the tourism industry. This research chapter is limited in scope and only provides a brief overview of the current and potential use of blockchain in the hotel and tourism industry in Asian countries. Additionally, the research is based on secondary sources, and primary data collection could provide more in-depth insights into the topic. While there has been some research on the use of blockchain in the hotel and tourism industry, there is still a need for more comprehensive studies on the potential benefits and challenges of its adoption in Asian countries. Future research could focus on developing standardized protocols and frameworks for interoperability between different blockchain platforms, as well as exploring the potential of blockchain for improving other areas of the tourism industry, such as destination management and marketing.

REFERENCES

Barkel, C., Kurgun, H., & Groen, B. (2021). Blochchain in the Hospitality and Tourism Industry. In C. Cobanoglu, S. Dogan, K. Berezina, & G. Collins (Eds.), *Hospitality and Tourism Information Technology*. University of South Florida.

Bhalla, A., Singh, P., & Singh, A. (2023). Technological Advancement and Mechanization of the Hotel Industry. In R. Tailor (Ed.), *Application and Adoption of Robotic Process Automation for Smart Cities* (pp. 57–76). IGI Global. doi:10.4018/978-1-6684-7193-7.ch004

Caddes, F., & Pinna, A. (2021). *Opportunities and Challenges of Blockchain-Oriented Systems in the Tourism Industry*. arXiv:2107.06732v1[<s.CY]11mar 2021

Charted Accountants Australia and New Zealand. (2017). *The Future of Blockchain: Application and Implications of Distributed Ledger Technology. Deloitte and Future (inc)*. Perspectives on Prosperity. chartedaccountantsanz.com/futureinc

Dogru, T., Mody, C., & Leonard, C. (2018). Blockchain Technology & its Implications for the Hospitality Industry. *Boston Hospitality Review*. www.bu.edu/bhr

Habib, G., Sharma, S., Ibrahim, S., Ahmad, I., Qureshi, S., & Ishfaq, M. (2022). Blockchain Technology: Benefits, Challenges, Applications, and Integration of Blockchain Technology with Cloud Computing. *Future Internet*, *14*(11), 341. doi:10.3390/fi14110341

India Blockchain Alliance. (n.d.). *AI in Blockchain Technology – The Possibilities of Integrating AI with Blockchain*. White Paper.

Lovells, H. (2023). *Digital Assets and Blockchain Hub – Blockchain Overview*. Engage Premium. https://engagepremium.hoganlovells.com/resources/bolckchain/overview

Moftah, L. (2015). Halal Pork? Aldi Supermarket Apologises to Muslims After Selling 'Halal-Certified' Black Pudding With Pig Blood. *IBT – World.*

Nnamani, C., & Omoniyi, F. (2023) Nigeria's New Blockchan Policy Leaves Crypto in the Cold. *10 Techcabal, May 13.*

Rejeb, A., & Rejeb, K. (2019) Blockchain Technology in Tourism: Applications and Possibilities. *World Scientific News–An International Scientific Journal, 137*, 119-144. ww.worldscientificnews.com

Singh, V., & Singh, A. (2024). Digital Health Revolution: Enhancing Well-Being Through Technology. In V. Nadda, P. Tyagi, R. Moniz Vieira, & P. Tyagi (Eds.), *Implementing Sustainable Development Goals in the Service Sector* (pp. 213–219). IGI Global. doi:10.4018/979-8-3693-2065-5.ch016

Zuhal, E. (2023). Naplozz Revolutionises the Hospitality Industry with Blockchain Technology. *The Crypto Basic*. https://thecryptobasic.com/2023/04/12/naplozz-revolutionizes-the-hospitality-industry

Chapter 11
Exploring Enlarged Perceptions of Value: The Utilization of Virtual Reality in Indian Tourism

Ankit Garg
Ajay Kumar Garg Institute of Management, India

Himanshu Sharma
Ajay Kumar Garg Institute of Management, India

TR Pandey
Ajay Kumar Garg Institute of Management, India

Anubhav Kumar Singh
Ajay Kumar Garg Institute of Management, India

Ritesh Kumar Singhal
https://orcid.org/0000-0002-3690-0401
Ajay Kumar Garg Institute of Management, India

ABSTRACT

This chapter explores how virtual reality (VR) technology has been used in Indian tourism with a focus on how users view it as valuable. In order to do this, the chapter introduces a thorough framework that takes into account a variety of elements, including perceived advantages (such as utility, novelty, social image, telepresence, and enjoyment), sacrifices (comprising complexity, health risk, physical risk, and cost), and the overall perceived value. This research is used in the chapter to examine Indian travelers. The chapter's findings will point to a number of important patterns. First, it helps prove that people's judgements of VR's value are significantly influenced by their perceived telepresence—the sensation of being there in a virtual environment—and its perceived usefulness. Contrarily, the main trade-offs that influence how much people value VR usage are the perceived health risk and physical risk. It's interesting to note the perceived expense of using VR to be a significant factor in determining perceived value or not.

DOI: 10.4018/979-8-3693-1103-5.ch011

INTRODUCTION

Data has always been crucial to human existence on all fronts. It is widely accessible and readily available. Whether new data is created or already existing data is used, the amount of data is increasing exponentially. According to the survey, data generation of 74 zeta bytes is anticipated to continue until the end of 2022 and double in 2024 (Needham, 2020). The word "data" refers to a large collection of datasets that have an exponential growth tendency throughout time. Three types of data exist that is, a semi-organized, unorganized, and organized state. Data is defined as information that has been parsed by a digital system and can be read, evaluated, and communicated in a knowledge-based manner. The benefits that data digitization offers to end users in the form of knowledge, facilities, and decision-making make it essential in the twenty-first century. The process of producing decisions in the form of conclusions is known as data analytics.

The fierce rivalry between various supermarkets and shopping centers has intensified due to the swift advancement of globalization and electronic commerce. Supermarkets like Big Bazar, D-Mart, Jio-Mart Reliance Fresh, and Big Mart, to name a few, strive to attract potential customers by providing simple, rapid, and customized transactions in an effort to handle the dynamic nature of business. This calls for efficient tracking and estimating of every product in an effort to keep an eye on supply and demand, logistics, shipping, and stock management. Accordingly, these supermarkets' inventory management systems lean toward the application of sophisticated and enhanced methods, allowing the group of products to be categorized using data analytics and visualized using augmented reality and virtual reality. This encourages the use of ML-based data analysis techniques in conjunction with enhanced visual analytics. Furthermore, the COVID-19 pandemic has had a significant impact on meetings, gatherings, and even teaching and learning. It has eliminated the opportunity for online instruction. To simulate face-to-face communication in this scenario, interactive visualization is required. This serves as even more motivation to change the way people communicate online, especially in the context of education in schools, where augmented reality is desperately needed.

Problem Description

In a number of industries, including science and technology, finance, and education, data visualization is essential. Making information easily readable can benefit decision-makers, clients, and other stakeholders. Data density and choosing the right visual metaphor are two aspects of data visualization that still need to be addressed (Alalwan et al., 2018). In the fields of data analytics and education, augmented reality is not well recognized. For data analytics and the education sector, "Marker-based visualization using mobile device" and "data visualization using HoloLens's" are suggested. The outcomes will be compared with the current models to demonstrate the efficacy.

Chapter Objectives

The following is a list of the aims in accordance with the problem definition and motivation mentioned above:

- To gather, examine, and display the Bigmart dataset through mobile device augmentation of information (marker-based augmented reality).
- To create a three-dimensional data visualization and analyze it.
- To employ swarm-based classifier optimization for Bigmart dataset robustness study.
- To verify the Bigmart dataset's classification using marker-based methods.

Chapter Details and Discussion

Amidst the advent of AR and VR, data visualization has become increasingly significant. Data visualization is a skill that may be developed through practice to show data in a variety of ways. The literature on data visualization, augmented reality, various tools available for AR and their comparison, use of mobile devices for AR, etc., has been conducted and presented in accordance with the motivation of marker-based augmented reality techniques for visualization data analytics.

Analysis of Data

Data analysis is an investigative procedure that is frequently started with certain inquiries. Finding and analysing the solutions typically calls for well-developed analytical abilities. It frequently entails a thorough investigation and analysis of the user data in order to make insightful judgments regarding a certain parameter or group of parameters. Data cleansing, validation, and estimation procedures are all included in data analysis, in addition to visualization. The fields of statistics, mathematics, programming, problem-solving, creative data capture, and the process of organizing, arranging, and aligning data are all included in data analytics (Ameen et al., 2018). Both organized and unstructured data are dealt with in data analytics. Numerous application domains, including digital advertisements, online research, recommender systems, picture and speech recognition, etc., use data analytics.

The added-value contribution varies with complexity, as seen in Figure. Among the several types of data analytics are descriptive, diagnostic, prescriptive, and

Figure 1. The relationship between complexity and added-value contribution variation (Bekker, 2017)

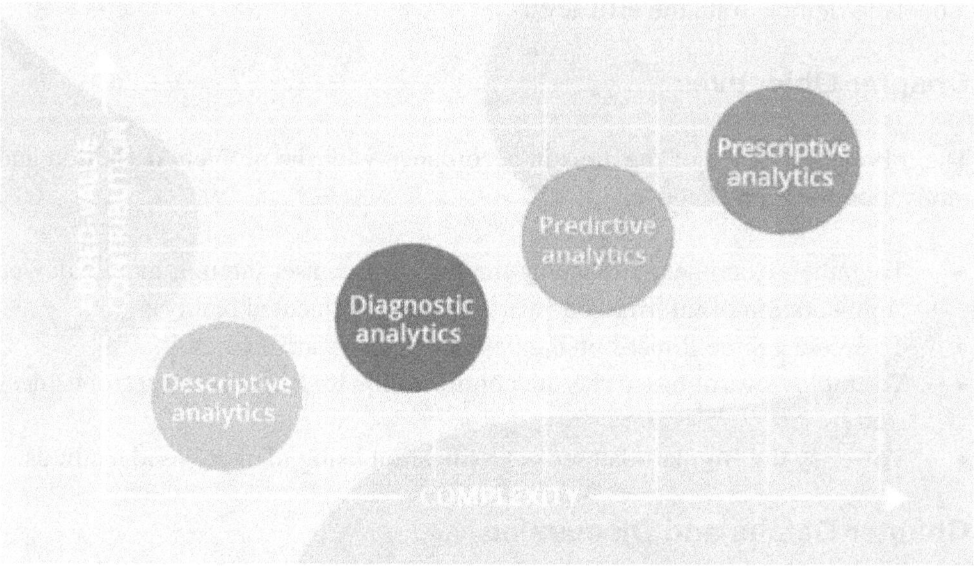

predictive analytics. Numerous industries, including gaming, tourism, energy management, and healthcare, use data analytics. R, Tableau Public, Apache Spark, and other languages are among the data analysis tools and languages utilized. These days, everyone creates data every minute, whether they are global enterprises or consumers. Therefore, the field of data analytics is worth billions of dollars. The process of extracting significant information from massive amounts of data, including odd shapes, undiscovered relationships, industry dynamics, and client requirements, is known as data analytics.

Data Filtering Types

Selecting a tiny portion of a dataset, or a subset of information, and using it for viewing or analysis is known as data filtering (Bagozzi & Yi, 1988). One method of filtering is to do calculations on a subset of data. To choose which circumstances to include in the analysis, filtering requires the development of a rule or logic. Filtering is sometimes referred to as "sub-setting" or "drill-down" data. Data filtering is mostly done to make it simpler to focus on particular information within a large dataset or table of data. The different types of data filters can be used to modify reports, query results, or other information result formats. Removing observations that might contain errors or are unsuitable for an analysis is a key justification for data filtering (Bonthu & Bindu, 2018b).

Data filtering can also lead to important results for the implementation of quantifiable computations and models. The basic idea behind data filtering is to divide the example into at least two groups, apply the inquiry to each group separately, and then examine the results. This kind of filtering would select situations at random rather than using a standard that is dependent on the input. This is commonly referred to as planning, testing, and approving and guarantees the validity of the examination. Among the many uses for which filtering is commonly employed are the following:

- Analyze the outcomes for a specific time frame.
- Compute the results for the different interest groups.
- Erroneous or "bad" observations should be excluded from any analysis or study.
- Validate and train statistical models.
- Data resemblance metrics

A metric for determining how comparable two information things are is the similarity measure. A similarity measure in an information mining or artificial intelligence (AI) scenario is a distance that takes into account the highlights of an object (Bem, 1981). The provisions exhibit a substantial degree of resemblance at the point where the distance between the elements is negligible. Conversely, a low degree of similarity exists between traits when there is a considerable distance between them. The scale used to measure similarity is 0 to 1 [0,1]. In the field of machine learning, the score that falls between 0 and 1 is referred to as the similarity score (Shirkhorshidi, 2015). Thus, the following are two crucial factors to consider while evaluating a similarity:

Assume there are two objects, P and Q.

Upon P = Q, similarity is equal to 1.

Similarity = 0 is the case where P/ = Q.

The following are the data similarity measures:

- Eclesiastical distance
- Manhattan's separation
- Minkowski spacing
- Comparing the cosine
- Jaccard resemblance
- Regression and classification algorithms
- Unknown Forest

A method of supervised learning is employed by the random forest algorithm. It can be applied to machine learning tasks including both regression and classification. It solves a complicated issue and enhances the performance of the model by combining several classifiers. Rather than depending on a single decision tree, the random forest forecasts the outcome based on the majority vote of predictions made from each tree (Alam et al., 2022).

Naïve Bayes and Bayes Net

A group of classification algorithms based on Bayes' Theorem are known as naive Bayes classifiers. It is actually a family of algorithms rather than a single method, and they are all based on the same principle—that is, each pair of features being classified stands alone. Because of its ease of use and capacity to handle both categorical and numerical data, Naive Bayes has found widespread application. Its performance is however constrained by the absence of feature correlation modeling. Furthermore, the real-world dataset's noise and outliers significantly impair the classification performance (Wang et al., 2022).

Meta-heuristic optimization algorithms

Optimizing Elephant Herding (EHO)

Elephant herding behavior served as the model for the EHO approach. In the wild, matriarchs rule over groups of elephants that are distinct from one another, and as the males mature, they separate from their families. The two operators that result from these two behaviors are the clan updating operator and the separation operator. Through the clan updating operator, each clan's matriarch and current rank are updated for each elephant in EHO (Bilandzic & Busselle, 2011). Subsequently, the separation operator is implemented to potentially improve population variety during the subsequent search phase. In order to showcase EHO's efficacy, fifteen test cases are used to compare it with BBO, DE, and GA. The findings demonstrate that EHO outperforms those three metaheuristic algorithms in finding superior values on the majority of benchmark issues (Wang et al., 2015).

Optimization of Monarch Butterflies (MBO)

The research (Wang et al., 2019) proposes a novel type of nature-inspired metaheuristic algorithm dubbed monarch butterfly optimization (MBO), which simplifies and optimizes the migration of monarch butterflies. This is the first of its kind. Every single monarch butterfly in MBO is located in two different countries, i.e. Mexico (Land 2), southern Canada, and the northern United States (Land 1).

As a result, there are two ways to update the locations of the monarch butterflies. First, the migration operator generates the offspring (position updating), which is modifiable by the migration ratio. Using a butterfly adjusting operator, the positions for more butterflies are then adjusted. To maintain population stability and reduce fitness assessments, the total of the freshly created butterflies by these two methods stays the same as the initial population. To show that the MBO algorithm performs better than five other metaheuristic algorithms, a comparison study using thirty-eight benchmark problems are completed. The findings unequivocally demonstrate the MBO method's capacity to identify increased function values on the majority of benchmark issues in comparison to the other five algorithms (Wang et al., 2019).

Optimization of Harris Hawk (HHO)

The primary source of inspiration for HHO is the surprise pounce, or cooperative, chasing manner of Harris' hawks in the wild. Several hawks work together to startle their target by simultaneously pounced on it from various directions. This is an intelligent tactic. Based on the dynamic nature of the situations and the prey's escape techniques, Harris hawks can exhibit a range of pursuit patterns. In order to create an optimization method, this work mathematically mimics such dynamic patterns and behaviors. The suggested HHO optimizer's efficacy is evaluated by comparing it to other nature-inspired methods on 29 benchmark issues as well as a number of engineering difficulties from the real world. According to Heidari et al. (2019), statistical findings and comparisons demonstrate that the HHO algorithm offers extremely promising and occasionally competitive outcomes when compared to well-established metaheuristic methodologies.

Algorithm for Slime Mold (SMA)

With its innovative mathematical model that employs adaptive weights to mimic the process of generating positive and negative feedback of the slime mold propagation wave based on a bio-oscillator to form the ideal path for connecting food with exceptional exploratory ability and exploitative propensity, SMA boasts a number of new features (Business Line, 2018). To confirm its effectiveness, the suggested SMA is measured against the most recent metaheuristics using a large collection of benchmarks. Additionally, the algorithm's effectiveness in optimizing constrained issues is estimated using four classical engineering problems. The findings show that the suggested SMA performs competitively and frequently very well on various search landscapes (Li et al., 2020).

Eclesiastical Distance

The Euclidean distance between two points is the length of the path that connects them. Finding the Euclidean distance is the most often used method of measuring distance. In cases where the data is dense or continuous, this is the most accurate proximity measure. One can determine the distance between two data points using Pythagoras' theorem.

The Pythagorean Theorem is used to calculate the two-dimensional Euclidean distance in Figure 2.

The Euclidean distance can be computed in the following ways if q and vectors are present: For a single dimension.

Manhattan's Separation

The distance between two vectors that is not equal to the Euclidean distance is called the Manhattan distance, or "city block" distance. Other names for the Manhattan distance include Manhattan length, rectilinear distance, Murkowski's L1 distance, city block distance, L1 standard, taxi metric, and city block distance. Think about points A and B. To find the Manhattan distance between them, all that was required was to sum up the absolute differences in the x- and y-axes. This means that it must determine how these two points, A and B, differ from the X- and Y-axes. In more formal terms, the Manhattan distance is the separation between two points measured along axes at right angles. Examine a plane at (x1, y1) and (x2, y2), respectively, p1 and p2. Algebraically,

Manhattan distance is equal to lx1 - x2l + ly1 - y2l~ (2.5).

Figure 2. Euclidean distance in two dimensions using the Pythagorean theorem (Fgnievinski, 2022).

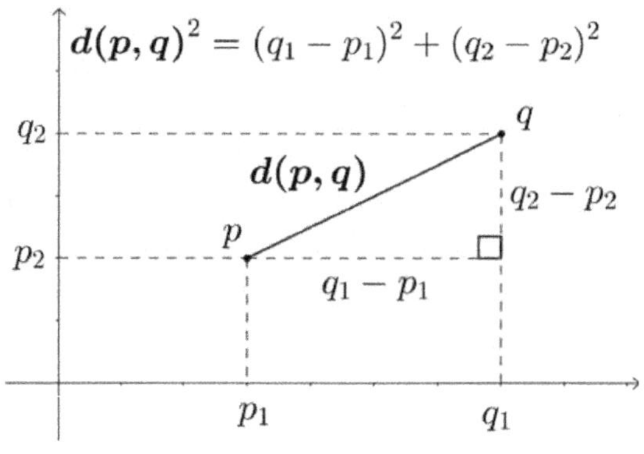

Minkowski Spacing

A Minkowski distance is a generalized metric form of the Manhattan and Euclidean distances. Algebraically,

Where k is the variable file, n is the total number of components y, and λ is the request for the Minkowski metric. MKD (i,j) is the Minkowski distance between the information record i and j. The formula mentioned above is defined for $\lambda > 0$, which occasionally uses values other than 1,2.

- It is a Manhattan distance when $\lambda = 1$.
- It is an Euclidean distance when $\lambda = 2$.
- It is the Chebyshev distance for $\lambda = \infty$. L-max Norm and Chessboard distance reference are equivalent terms.

Cosine Comparability

Cosine similarity is the normalized dot product of two vectors. Determining the cosine similarity of two items makes finding their cosine angle simple. Angle 00 (Cosine 0) has a cosine of 1, while all other angles have a cosine of less than 1. As a result, cosine similarity is a direction rather than greatness judgment. When two vectors have the same direction, their cosine similarity is 1. Cosine similarity is specifically used in some spaces, where the result is perfectly confined in [0,1]. One rationale is that cosine similarity is preferred because it is incredibly efficient to evaluate, particularly for sparse vectors.

A cosine similarity can be used to classify an orange from an apple. As demonstrated in Fig., the normalized dot product of two distinct vectors can be computed. The cosine similarity of 2 is utilized in categorization.

Jaccard Resemblance

Another name for the Jaccard similarity is an intersection over union, or Jaccardindex.

The conditional Jaccard similarity formulation J(A, B) specifies that A union of B is meant by "U," and that the separation of the intersection of A and B is the mean of the arch shape (Chawla & Joshi, 2018). The mathematical expression for Jaccard similarity is represented by 2.7. The formula calculates the exact amount of overlap between A and B.

After a discussion of all the similarity metrics, the Euclidean distance was selected as the suitable metric with the following rationale:

In summary, when attributes are similar, the Euclidean distance is utilized to determine the separation between two data points. Manhattan distance is the preferred distance for the higher dimensions. Minkowski distance is applied to category features (Chen et al., 2006). When vector direction rather than magnitude is a concern, cosine similarity is employed. Since it is necessary to determine the distance between two data points, Euclidean distance is employed in this study.

Data Presentation

Data visualization is just the distribution of data displayed in a unique graphic. The graphic convention creates lists, charts, graphs, and maps, among other things. The graphical display makes it easier for end users to understand every aspect of the data distribution. It's included in data analysis. This field of study and work is known by many names, including advanced analytics, data analytics, data science, and a few less common ones (Childers et al., 2001). It involves understanding the issues facing one's organization, business, or agency, gathering data to help solve those issues, cleaning and analysing data, developing and testing hypotheses, drawing conclusions, and presenting the findings. The noteworthy uses of data visualization are emphasized in Figure 2.

People may quickly understand complex information and determine the pertinent characteristics of that information set thanks to data visualization. On the other hand, there are two methods for doing data analysis: prescriptive and descriptive. While prescriptive analysis enables firms to foresee pertinent opportunities for improved prospects, descriptive analysis concentrates on what has actually happened (Davis, 1989). Information analysis and sharing work best when done through visualization. A picture is helpful in a matter of seconds, transfer data to the human brain and discover connections among various datasets. Visual interpretations facilitate the visualization of data from various perspectives.

Outlining issues and comprehending current patterns are helpful. Data can be categorized according to the following standards:

- The creation technique involves gathering data through surveys, experiments, interviews, and other means, and then putting it into a graphical format.
- Quantity of data visualization: The amount of data that is displayed is the focus of this criterion. Google location maps and company expense sheets are two examples.
- Degree of creativity used: This criterion is applied to data that is graphically generated, colorfully made, or that uses black and white to show vital data.

Organize Data From a Given Dataset Visually

The field of advances has rapidly expanded because to the influence of visualization. Information visualization and scientific visualization might be arranged in the exhibition. Data visualization is used for visual analysis of public and private stores, such as corporate datasets, understudy datasets, and clinical datasets, at the point where information is not directly processed and transmitted as data (Mellon, 2020). People who use social media sites, such as YouTube, Facebook, and Google, share their followers through online media and let other exam-takers follow them using online media databases. The investigation of geo-tested web-based media content, in addition to the development designs and visual analytics of examined directions, was cited by the former researchers.

Linear, planar, volumetric, multidimensional, network, temporal, hierarchical, and other types of data visualization and presentation can be identified. According to Gokhale and Mahajan (2020), a few of the well-liked tools are Google Charts, Many Eyes, Tableau, AutoQ3D, AC3D, Time-flow, Google Fusion Tables, Tableau Public, D3, and Sigma.js. By enhancing the data and presenting it on augmented reality (AR) applications or devices, data visualization has been investigated. Data analytics and the creation of augmented reality applications were used in the design of this project (Disztinger et al., 2017). A variety of tools for data visualization and representation are displayed.

Data visualization deals with strong and definitive opinions regarding datasets, regardless of how big or complicated they are. Correlation values, proportions, anomalies, trajectories, and patterns may all be clearly seen and agreed upon once it is visualized. For instance, it would be extremely difficult to identify any irregularities in 1,000 data points that were gathered and analyzed from various sources; these could include a minor decrease in sales over the previous month or a significant drop in customer feedback regarding a new offering. In any case, it's critical to recognize these irregularities so that you can choose how best to address them moving forward. In a different case, if monthly revenues are continuously increasing throughout a certain marketing campaign, those success drivers can be recognized and reproduced to keep the business moving forward. While it was once difficult, there are now a lot of tools available to help in data visualization. A visual analytics tool like Tableau Desktop, for instance, can convert vast amounts of data into interactive visual representations like graphs and charts (Tableau, 2020). It assists users.

With ease, spot trends, anomalies, or behaviors, and create projections for upcoming tasks. Whatever the source of the data, Tableau provides a multitude of ways to interact with it in order to extract and provide the information that customers require (Dobrowolski et al., 2014). On the other hand, Python Jupyter, i.e. Anacondas´ Jupyter uses numerous Python scripts, including Numpy, Scipy, and Matplotlib, to help construct open-source tools, open standards, and services for collaborative computing. Additionally, Google Chart is a robust, user-friendly, interactive data visualization tool that works with both mobile and browser-based platforms. It features an extensive chart gallery that may be customized to meet specific needs. Chart rendering is based on HTML5/SVG technologies.

Techniques and Tools for Visualization

Based on their features, support, qualities, and offices offered, the visualization tools were assessed and given a rating. Each of these devices was evaluated with a few datasets of different density; since Google Charts and Apache Zeppelin were able to evade the inspection test, they were considered necessary. As said in the writing review, Tableau is a visualization tool utilized in many corporate activities and building areas (Tableau, 2020). Its primary function is to generate maps, pie charts, and outlines for graphical analysis (Fotakis & Economides, 2008). In terms of price, a single client can get Tableau for $200 per year. Combination Charts XL, a new JavaScript e-outlines for the web and portable by Info soft Global Private Constrainer, provide a remarkable degree of resemblance for web programmers (Mozilla Firefox, Google Chrome, and Safari). In addition, techniques like outlines, line charts, pie diagrams, and others can be made using the meticulously mapped code. Numerous social media giants, including Facebook, Twitter, and others, use data wapper devices for reporting and analytics. It is easy to use, requires practically no code, and has a user-friendly interface. One of Google's most user-friendly APIs for data visualization is Google Charts. tries their hand at every cutting-edge program and is adept at sorting through data from HDFS for big data, MySQL, and an excel spreadsheet. The primary drawback of Google graphs is that in order to display the visual material, a system connection is required (Fox et al., 2009). The API is compatible with an integrated programming environment (IDE, such as Eclipse), making this representation style perfect for use in the suggested notion. The SQL data can be imported into Eclipse by using modules and container records availability approaches.

No matter the quantity or volume of data, a company can find all of its needs in one place with a data platform. A data platform is entering the high-performance computing space because to its capacity for quick deployment, support for several data formats, real-time data analysis, and report generating. Two data computing platforms with a lot of adjustable characteristics are Hadoop and Spark. An optimal arrangement of the settings can greatly increase performance, but a poor design might sometimes have unanticipated consequences. It is really time-consuming to manually configure the parameters. To find the optimal plan for automatically adjusting the

Hadoop and Spark parameters, a range of techniques were examined and analyzed, including machine learning, neural networks, creating various frameworks, etc. The word was only created in the last ten years, specifically in the second half. Data includes all of the currently available huge volumes of data as well as the entire processing, organizing, and evaluating process. The fact that data platforms are being used to improve the world is the most significant. Data platforms like Cloudera, VMware, Apache Hadoop and Spark, Oracle, Tableau, etc. are evolving at a really good rate these days.

Visual tools such as maps, graphs, and charts facilitate the perception and recognition of patterns, outliers, and trends within a data distribution. Visualization facilitates information absorption for humans. In layman's terms, data visualization is a graphical representation of data that is obtained in order to quickly make a decision. Transmitting actionable insights is the goal of data visualization, which goes beyond simply producing visually appealing graphics. An effective use of graphics in data visualization should enable the clear and concise description of a data collection. The most effective infographics simplify data understanding at a glance. It simplifies complex information so that the intended audience may easily comprehend it and use it as a foundation for judgment (Chen et al., 2009). Try to visualize an increasing number of datasets in different ways. Analyze user feedback from different categories to determine the most effective model. The bright side is: How can insight from data be explained to a child? It takes planning ahead, asking the correct questions, and taking the design into consideration to create a fantastic data visualization. If sufficient effort is spent comprehending the motivations behind data visualization procedures and the intended audience, significant benefits will be realized. According to Nguyen et al. (2013), there are five typical forms of data visualization: 2D area, temporal, multi-dimensional, hierarchical, and network categories.

Geospatial data, or the relative position of objects on the earth's surface, can be displayed using 2D area kinds of data visualization. Dot distribution maps, cartograms, and choropleths are a few types of 2D area maps.

The start and finish times of temporal visualizations may overlap in value. Polar area diagrams, time series, linked scatter plots, and many other types of graphs are among the examples.

Data is shown in multi-dimensional visualizations like scatter plots, pie charts, and histograms.

Finally, two examples of hierarchical data sets are ring charts and dendrograms.

Large data sets can be easily represented with a variety of layouts, designs, frameworks, and other elements provided by data visualization (Gardiner et al., 2013). A designer's job is made easier by data that can have hundreds or thousands of points that automatically generate a representation. Dashboards, investor presentation decks, yearly reports, marketing and sales materials, and almost anyplace else where data needs to be instantly understood can all benefit from the use of data visualization. The following are a few of the main advantages of data visualization.

Saving Decision-Makers Time

It is simple to extract insights in order to make quick, data-driven decisions that will benefit the company. Reviewing rows of data on an Excel sheet can be time-consuming for decision-makers, who typically have limited resources. Rather than reading through 200 evaluated data points, consider spending two seconds seeing a scatter plot (Marques et al., 2019).

Visually appealing displays, such as colors, patterns, and drawings, instantly captivate humans. As a result, it is much simpler to draw in and keep audiences' attention while they listen to and comprehend the material that is being provided when data visualization is used. This is especially helpful when trying to persuade a room full of C-suite executives to support a plan or project that you want to put into action. A colored pie chart or bar graph would undoubtedly defeat a sheet of statistics in the game of persuasion because, in the end, aesthetics do matter (Ali et al., 2016).

Simple to Comprehend

Decisive and understandable insights into complex and large datasets are provided by data visualization. When patterns and trajectories are represented, it is simpler to recognize and comprehend them (Kumar & Goyal, 2016).

Graphical Analytics

The goal of visual analytics is to skew more toward analytical reasoning and computation. In order to automatically choose how to present supplied information, the study area integrates data mining approaches. It is employed to examine intricate correlations between variables.

- Regression analysis: From independent variables, it predicts continuous dependent variables. This is an attempt to determine the impact of one variable on another. For instance, when prices drop, sales rise.
- When there is a relationship between the dependent and independent variables and the dependent variable is continuous, ordinary least squares regression is employed.

- When there are just two possible outcomes for the dependent variable, logistic regression is employed.
- When data is nested, hierarchical linear modelling is utilized.
- Duration models: They're used to calculate how long a process will take.
- Grouping methods: Grouping is the process of classifying observations into meaningful chunks.
- Multiple equation models are used to examine the relationships between independent and dependent variables.
- Tools for visual analytics are helpful for data extraction. With the aid of these technologies, users produce insights from information sources. Modern technology makes mining possible knowledge.

Businesses benefit from the interactive, graphic, and visual nature of the tools. The main patterns are identified by the software. This facilitates the extraction of useful business insights. As a result, the data is applied in several fields (Gautam, 2012). Interfaces are where it is most effectively used. The goal of the visualization, the target audience, the degree to which deep learning of data visualization is required, and the desired software budget will all influence the tool selection. In recent years, Excel and Numbers have produced some excellent visualization tools. If they are a little light on analysis, Power-Point or Keynote will work well to display them in presentation style (use Word or Pages for documents). You can perform analysis and visualize your findings using OpenOffice or LibreOffice's counterparts, such as Google Sheets, Google Charts, OpenOffice, and others. Dedicated visualization solutions like as Tableau, SAS, PowerBI, Qlik Sense, and Tibco represent the next step. In this domain, Tableau is the pioneer. These are corporate market-focused visualization tools that are strong but pricey. A few open-source substitutes for Tableau, etc., are Plotly, Apache Superset, and RAW Graphs. helpful if you have a tight budget but still want to create complex images.

Enhanced Reality

AR, seen broadly, is nothing more than the technological enhancement of the human biological apparatus through the mediation of sensory input or output to the central nervous system. The current focus is primarily on superimposing actual imagery on top of digital images, either through transparent displays or by using a camera to provide a video feed that is then processed by software to change the video stream before it is transferred to a normal display. More broadly, it can be any real-world information from any sensory device combined with any extra digital data and processed in any way imaginable before being shown via a sensory input mediating device (Molina-Solana et al., 2017).

In the broadest sense, it would be more correct to characterize augmented reality as the fusion of technology and the central nervous system for enhancement, taking into account future direct brain interfaces and implants (Global Travel Intention, 2018). Similar applications in medicine are utilized to replace or restore broken functionality. Artificial limbs and similar medical devices with brain connectivity fall under this category. The fact that both uses aim to make up for disability is a significant distinction. An alternative philosophical stance on augmentation is that default or normal can be made better. According to Peña et al. (2017), the history of technology can be defined as augmentation, with a steady shift in focus from altering the world to altering ourselves. In other words, the history of technology is the history of augmentation.

Changing our surroundings to better meet our wants is the essence of augmenting nature. (But with ever-more severe trade-offs.) Augmenting tools are expanding our physical capabilities.

Changing and extending cognitive reality (experience) is the process of augmenting reality. It expands our potential and experience to the boundaries of technology and makes ambient computing possible. It integrates social sharing and connectivity into all modalities of experience. The trend is in the direction of virtual reality (Haider et al., 2018). It enables the software to gradually eliminate reliance on physical reality by replacing the majority of tangible tools and materials. Many of the limitations of physical reality are removed, including the need for physical existence as a precondition for experiencing an object or location, as well as physical laws and resource availability. Though augmented reality may not yet have fully developed into a recognized technology, given its explosive rise in popularity across nations, there is little doubt that AR will eventually be developed to the point where it surpasses its competing technologies. It is impossible to state precisely, though, because new technology frequently replaces older ones, rendering the former useless gadgets (Janssen et al., 2017).

AR magic is captured by devices like Wikitude, Layar, Alive app, Areal app (Adstuck), i-Tag action figure, etc. Additionally, the technology typically requires accessories like GPS, accelerometers, GPRS, gesture recognition, and object identifying technologies when utilized with smartphones. Keep in mind that, depending on the method used, they are a component of the AR function. With Wikitude, for example, users may use their physical surroundings to get information about hotels, restaurants, schools, play games, train stations, and other establishments using an augmented reality browser. The Wikitude software will take a picture and then provide an output of relevant inputs, therefore they will need to train their camera on their surroundings (Hair et al., 2010). Data and visuals are superimposed over what is visible to the naked eye in the real world to create augmented reality. Smartphones are already being used for this, allowing users to hold their devices up to display nearby directions and local information. The military is also testing it to help with situational awareness. Our vision will be enhanced by technologies like Microsoft Hololens and comparable products from other companies. Indeed, it will be linked to the Internet in order to monitor its whereabouts and actions.

There are four main types of AR. Marker-less is the first, marker-based is the second, projection-based is the third, and superimposition-based is the fourth. The present study uses augmented reality based on markers.

- Marker-based AR: In order to specify the location and orientation of AR objects, a predetermined picture or object (referred to as the marker) is needed. The AR program detects the marker when the user points their device's camera at it, and then displays an item or animation. Keep in mind that for these augmented reality applications to function, the marker must always be visible to the camera. Almost any device with a camera may run these kinds of augmented reality apps (Pei et al., 2019).
- Marker-less AR: These types of AR experiences produce a virtual 3D mesh of the surrounding environment by using SLAM (Simultaneous Localization and Mapping) to establish the location of the AR device in the world and the fundamental structural definition of the items around the user. To determine where objects are in the world, it locates feature points—points in the environment that it recognizes—and monitors changes to their position in relation to the movement of the AR device. AR objects can be placed in an environment that recognizes both horizontal and vertical surfaces and can even interact with it using this spatial knowledge. Accelerometers and gyroscopes are the exact motion sensors required by the device in order to use marker-less AR experiences. These sensors are present in newer, higher-end gadgets, but they are absent from earlier, less expensive models. Both Google and Apple offer SDKs (ARKit and AR- Core) for creating these kinds of apps. The Microsoft HoloLens and Magic Leap operate using the same idea. In summary, Marker-less AR is connected to the physical environment surrounding the device, whereas Marker-based AR is always linked to a physical image pattern marker (Macedo et al., 2014).
- Projection-based AR: Makes use of a combination of projectors and vision sensors to display interactive, step-by-step pictures onto any work space. Compared to tablet-based and wearable AR, projected AR is more precise and practical for manufacturing applications. Projected AR bridges the divide between production that is focused on humans and automation. By combining the best of human intelligence and technology, it maximizes the benefits of Industry 4.0 by empowering and retaining employees while improving productivity, throughput, and training efficacy. It is feasible to use

augmented reality techniques based on projection to make manufacturing floors safer, smarter, and more productive. Employee productivity increases significantly and training time is significantly decreased as a result of workers being instructed to "follow the lights" via projected augmented reality.

- Superimposition-based augmented reality: This type of AR makes use of object detection. The original image is replaced, either fully or partially, with the augmented image. In the tourism industry, this kind of AR is frequently utilized to add interest to a trip itinerary. Superimposition: Today, augmented reality is used in a number of sectors, such as those that train soldiers and provide entertainment.

Images superimposed on the actual world include graphics, alpha numerics, photos, films, and more. This is known as augmented reality. The truth is what we typically see in stereoscopic three-dimensional (3D) without the use of any special viewing equipment. Virtual reality (VR) is the state in which an individual can only perceive the artificially generated pictures as a simulation of reality (a "virtual world"), and not the actual world (e.g., through opaque headsets). Augmented reality is when a user puts on transparent AR goggles or AR glasses that let them see the real environment through them while superimposing additional images—which could possibly be in stereoscopic 3D. The program first scans the image from the phone camera, processes it using the HOG algorithm, and finds points that are comparable to both the marker photos and the camera images. Following a successful discovery, the application evaluates the image's rotation and position and immediately modifies the animation to account for these points (Kumar et al., 2017). The overlaying of digital information in real-time inside the user's surroundings is known as augmented reality (Interrante et al., 2018).

Since VR and AR have been a part of the same hype cycle, there is sometimes a great deal of confusion between the two. To put it simply, AR adds artificial components to the environment whereas VR immerses the user in an artificial environment.

-VR (virtual reality) is similar to dreaming. AR is similar to a hallucination in that fake objects appear everywhere. In contrast to AR, where nearly everyone carries a portable device such as their phone's camera, VR requires a type of headset in order to fully immerse the viewer. The application is now being shown out through animated effects or stickers on Facebook, Instagram, and Snapchat. One other well-known AR example is Pokemon Go.

when users are in the camera view and the augmented reality character is superimposed on the scene. Not only phones can access the AR. Augmented reality is used in most, if not all, sports broadcasts on television. See the first down line graphic in a football game, AR, which flawlessly resembles a line on the field. Real-world vision and graphic elements are combined in wearables and glasses like the Magic Leap and HoloLens. These kinds of wearables are the AR of the future (Bueno et al., 2020).

Augmented reality has several useful applications outside of entertainment, such as assisting in the selection of the ideal furniture for a home by superimposing it in real-time into the scene. There are countless uses for graphic displays, such as wayfinding in crowded airports, medical and industrial training, and car windshields that assist drivers in maintaining their focus on the road. The Earth is a vast canvas that will soon be covered in data. With the introduction of the Fall Creator Update for Windows 10, Microsoft added a few tools to enable Mixed Reality headsets. A computer's camera can be used by a software called the Mixed Reality Viewer to show a real-time view of a living area. 3D objects can be imported, scaled, rotated, and positioned against the background of the actual display. AR technology have being used by the online gaming business more and more. However, now, AR is also being used in more recent and developing fields. We talk about a few of these here. The first is Audi, a major player in the automobile sector, which incorporates AR features in its app. Simply pointing a smartphone at any component of the car will allow the app to display all of the facts. Retail and e-commerce apps like as Lenscart offer virtual try-ons and trailers. With AR, the medical field is able to treat patients' fears of heights, water, and other things without putting them in real-world scenarios. Using virtual dwellings, the real estate sector uses augmented reality to pitch potential customers (Kumra, 2008). Therefore, it is safe to say that technology like augmented reality are here to stay. It will even completely change how our markets function, how anyone can access our entertainment, and how the service sector runs. It's only a matter of time and requirement to fully explore AR's advantages (Muñoz-Saavedra et al., 2020).

To put it simply, augmented reality is the overlaying of digital or virtual information over the physical world. It has had a significant effect on numerous other industries.

- Real estate and interior design: Have you ever considered the effect of a vase next to a brown couch against a green wall in a corner? Fortunately, AR now makes all of this visible. Google "Asian Paints Augmented Reality" or "Ikea Place App" (Alaseeri, 2021; Park et al., 2017).
- Healthcare: During intravenous injections, the Accuvien scanner pinpoints and projects the precise position of veins and valves. as a diversionary activity where patients who are afraid of injections can successfully converse with virtual characters while their IVs are being registered (Li et al., 2017).

- Industrial: AR and IoT sensors are merged as part of industry 4.0 to enable communication between many components of a single value chain and the user. The user can communicate using lenses, a head-mounted display (HMD), a head-up display (HUD), or a mobile phone. One of the most famous instances of this is when, in Iron Man 2, Tony Stark uses hand gestures to communicate with JARVIS while creating a new element for the Arc Reactor to replace Palladium (Cranmer et al., 2020).
- Print Media and Advertising: Leading global publishing organizations are creating applications to leverage augmented reality technology to give their users dynamic digital material. Similar to this, advertising agencies worldwide are experimenting with new and inventive forms of advertising and looking to technology to improve the way their clients engage with their brands (Flavián et al., 2019).
- Text and language interpretation: Apps that use augmented reality to interpret text and language can aid individuals in understanding written or spoken foreign languages more effectively (Lampropoulos et al., 2020).
- Event industry: The event and brand marketing industries have undoubtedly profited the most from augmented reality applications. Wearable technology, AR-capable apps, and interactive solutions such as green screen photo booths have all become more popular (Danielsson, 2020).

Game programming, data analytics, machine learning, and artificial intelligence (AI) are some of the different technology kinds that combine to create augmented reality. With computer-generated technology, augmented reality enhances the real-world aspects around us, making it more interactive, useful, and informative. By superimposing digital visual and auditory signals over real-world scenes, augmented reality elevates the overall experience to a whole new level.

What Separates AR From VR

Through the use of augmented reality (AR), users can encounter a real environment that has been somewhat enhanced digitally. Conversely, virtual reality (VR) assists in removing the user from that particular real-world experience and substituting it with a fully simulated environment. Virtual reality (VR) technologies completely block out the outside world since their use demands total immersion. While they are transparent, the smart glasses' lenses provide augmented reality functionality. Understanding these distinctions is essential to figuring out which use cases are ideal for each. While VR enables us to create a completely immersive virtual experience, AR may be utilized to enhance a scene in the real world (Lee et al., 2015). In contrast to virtual reality, which is 75% virtual and 25% real, augmented reality (AR) is 25%

virtual and 75% real. With augmented reality, a headset is typically not needed. When using AR, end users of the product interact with virtual objects around them while staying linked to the real world; in contrast, when using VR, the user is completely submerged in a virtual environment. AR makes use of depth monitoring, mapping, and computer vision to help display appropriate content to the user.

The user's physical environment is substantially enhanced in near real-time or in real-time through augmented reality with pertinent content. Augmented reality can also be explored using a smartphone. The main goal of virtual reality is to simulate vision. The VR headgear must be positioned in front of the user's eyes to prevent interaction with the real world. When a user is using virtual reality, two lenses are positioned in between the screens. Based on his eye motions and placement, the user would have to adjust his eyes. An HDMI cable is used to render the images when the user's smartphone or personal computer is connected to it. Goggles, speakers, and portable wearable technology are all used in virtual reality to provide users a realistic experience. Users in virtual reality can use tactile, visual, and audio stimuli, which adds to the immersive nature of the created environment.

Augmented Reality With Markers

In marker-based augmented reality, a camera and a visual marker—such as a QR or 2D code—are utilized to display a result only in response to a reader detecting the marker. For a marker-based augmented reality experience, a static image—also called a trigger photo—that the user can scan with their mobile device is necessary. Pre-produced content (video, animation, 3D, or other) will overlay the pre-produced marking when the smartphone is scanned. Both marker databases and recognition can happen on the device since marker recognition can be either local or cloud-based. Databases can be kept in the cloud, and servers can handle recognition tasks by receiving point clouds from phones. In contrast, device-based recognition can occur instantaneously; nevertheless, when cloud recognition is utilized.

It would probably take longer for the content to download from the server. Usually, the user doesn't notice anything for a few seconds. Since the trigger image needs to be unique, stock photos should be avoided at all costs as they might have already been used in other apps or projects. It's usually better to capture unique material or create a custom design in order to avoid issues such as these. If the marker picture was made appropriately, marker-based augmented reality material would provide high-quality experiences and the tracking would be very stable, so the AR content wouldn't sway. Anyone using it for the first time doesn't need detailed instructions because it is so easy to use. When the mobile camera or image capture device is moved away from the marker, the augmented reality experience disappears and the trigger photo needs to be scanned once more. It is also possible to use a more comprehensive tracking system (Ma et al., 2018). Scanning will not work if the markers reflect light. Markers with a high black-to-white contrast will help to stabilize tracking. If not, the recognition process will be challenging due to the gradual color shift (Figure 2). The idea of numerous data sources and different device targets in augmented reality is demonstrated.

Marker-based augmented reality is not going away; instead, any image or place can be used as a marker instead of simply certain patterns like bar codes or QR codes. Marker-based technology assists in inserting virtual things only when the visual pattern is recognized, but marker less technology permits placing virtual objects wherever in the actual environment. AR with markers works similarly to a trigger to display the virtual object. A few years ago, AR was only possible with marker-based systems due to a lack of sensor hardware-software integration and an algorithm and hardware in mobile phones that were not yet capable of handling computation. However, it is now able to construct a 3D model of the surrounding environment and insert virtual items thanks to sophisticated sensors and algorithms like ARKit and ARCore (Minisry of Tourism, 2018). HelloStar serves as a bridge between the general public and the influencers of their dreams. Augmented reality enhances human experience, while virtual reality takes the place of it. Enhanced replay Real-time computer-generated enhancements are superimposed on top of reality through the utilization of physical things and the current reality in ality. It's virtual reality when individuals view their favourite star on a television or internet device. An augmented reality is created when a star tags a fan or sends a personalized message. Considering the enthusiasm that Indians have for celebrities and influencers, the HelloStar team feels that there is a greater unexplored potential for the shoutout procedure in India. HelloStar was founded with the primary goal of providing influencers in any industry with a safe haven. Every celebrity or influencer on the HelloStar platform will receive a favourable rating. The customer can pay by clicking on their preferred celebrity (Moorehouse et al., 2018). In the next seven days, he or she gets a shootout. Any Bollywood star who is accustomed to having personal relationships with and showing concern for their fans is welcome to participate. Influencers can simply generate more revenue by using the platform that their fans have created. In the rural areas of India, there are a lot of content developers. A good number of them also obtained the golden play button from YouTube. Millions of Indian subscribers provide them with food. The fact that teenagers and younger viewers don't miss any of their videos is the most intriguing aspect. Virtual reality is highly popular among young, educated people. Most of them wait for their favorite show to return with new content and in a different format.

Visual computer content is added to the human field of vision through augmented reality. To put it simply, augmented reality (AR) has far more effects than just holographic games and selfie overlays. While trying to educate computers to see the world like humans do, mostly through vision, the practice of educating humans to connect with computers visually is evident. This is an essential step in fully utilizing AI's potential. A step in the right direction was the development of cameras for computers, which will enable them to observe the outside world and potentially lead to the evolution of a symbiotic relationship between humans and computers. Furthermore, there's a chance that advancement will happen faster than people can handle. The augmented reality business card functions by means of a QR scanning code, which initiates user engagement when the user points the marker using the camera on their device (phone, tablet, etc.). Therefore, a mobile device with a webcam—basically, a scanner webcam app—and the marker, which is a business card, are both necessary. The idea of having the business card itself be in augmented reality is very unique. Since this is currently a limitation in augmented reality, AR cards can either incorporate an AR marker directly into the card or modify the logo to have a solid black border for use as a marker. This marker can then be used as the trigger to present information to the user. Augmented reality has a plethora of applications, ranging from interactive maps that automatically display addresses to links that allow users to write emails or make phone calls immediately, as well as interactive portfolios. There are countless options. The imagination is the only limit. Using the extra information a computer generates within real-world data to improve our experience of our natural surroundings is the essence of augmented reality. Among the cutting-edge AR technologies are computer vision and integrated AR cameras.

Apps for smartphones and object recognition are making the real world more dynamic and digitally altered. The fields of education, communications, medical, and entertainment have all made extensive use of augmented reality. By allowing students to visualize the materials and 3D models provided by augmented reality technology, teachers may more clearly impart abstract concepts that can be difficult to understand. By looking at the objects from different perspectives and angles, it would be much easier for the kids to understand the concepts and help them retain them for a longer period of time. AR almost turns into a living textbook that teaches students knowledge and abilities.

An Augmented Reality Without Markers

Unlike marker-based augmented reality, marker less augmented reality retrieves content by merely scanning the surrounding environment; a trigger photo is not required.

Augmented Reality Based on Superimposition

With superimposition-based augmented reality, an object's original view can be partially or fully replaced with a newly enhanced view of the same thing. Superimposition-based augmented reality uses object recognition. This type of augmented reality is commonly employed in the medical field to overlay an X-ray onto a patient's body (Okcu et al., 2019). It can be applied to augmented reality to show, for example, how a structure or statue looked years ago, how it has aged, and so on. In superimposition-based augmented reality, item recognition is essential because without it, the programmer cannot replace the original view with an improved one. Contrarily, object recognition lies behind all of AR's capabilities and might be similar to projection-based AR. For example, outlining AR can identify and highlight the limits of the road for the user when he parks his car in the dark. In architecture and engineering, this AR method can also be used to outline structures and the pillars that support them. Figure. 2.14 illustrates how augmented reality superimposition is used in historical excursions.

The business sector now has new opportunities that were not possible in the past thanks to data analytics and augmented reality. Nonetheless, because of recently developed technologies and connectivity issues, there have been many seismic shifts in the modern era. Due to the restricted amount of data instances and datasets available, many augmented reality applications are experiencing issues with limitations and restrictions. In industries like manufacturing, advertising, tourism, telcom, education, health care, defense, energy, UI science, entertainment, and financial services, the impact of data and augmented reality is especially evident. Technology known as "augmented reality" blends virtual reality and the physical world through the use of computer-generated graphics to digitally enhance live video imagery.

Difficulties With Augmented Reality

Even though implementing and using applications with augmented reality technology can be entertaining, there are challenges in making things work in real-world scenarios. Many difficulties have been noted when using augmented reality in the technology industry (Ashtari et al., 2020). Let's review the main issues in the following points:

- Cost of implementation: There are several approaches to putting augmented reality apps into practice, and each has a different price tag. The cost of creating an app from scratch for a business would be in the range of six figures.
- Technology and talent gap: Businesses that offer augmented reality solutions have the opportunity to win over customers by providing education and

demonstrations up front, making it simple for executives to understand how augmented reality could improve their bottom line.

The human brain translates any image in 2D form captured into 3D image space within some computational time, and that is saved by directly giving a 3D input to the brain. Because of the above reasons, augmented reality is a great weapon for visualizing data. This research work aimed at displaying knowledge or representing knowledge by the medium of mixed reality devices, such as Microsoft HoloLens II. This is a simple knowledge-representing technique that takes the dataset as input to the AR application, which is developed in Unity AR Studio/engine. Figure. 2.15 shows the application of Microsoft HoloLens in a mechanical field where the user interact with a device using AR technique for better understanding.

Mechanism of HoloLens

The augmented content is projected using see-through optics and two light engines in the HoloLens. It boasts a 'holographic resolution' of 2.3 total light points and a 'holographic density of more than 2.5 light points per radian, and it automatically calibrates pupillary distance. In addition to the depth camera and the two photo/ video cameras, it uses four dedicated cameras to scan the environment. It also has a head movement tracking inertial measurement unit (IMU), an ambient light sensor, a spatial sound system, and four microphones (Ooi & Tan, 2016). Microsoft designed a unique CPU, the Holographic Processing Unit, to process sensor data and camera feeds (HPU). There is more information on the device. HPU creates a three-dimensional model of the environment. This model can then be utilized in Apps to place holograms without compromising the Atom processor's capacity to handle sensor input. HoloLens can run most 32-bit processor-compatible Windows universal platform apps like a Windows 10 device. Non-holographic programmers appear as floating virtual screens in the environment. The procedure for building an application to be deployed on the Microsoft HoloLens is very specific. Standard game platforms are targeted for simple compilation in the Unity editor, but while building an application for HoloLens, one needs to introduce an additional step wherein the Unity engine creates an intermediary visual studio solution. The compilation of this solution then takes place in the visual studio platform. Thus, for de- veloping this application, two different compilers were used. The application designed helps to observe the Augmented Reality environment and allows students to actively interact with the synthetically designed 3D holographic objects, and also allows the 3D.

Augmented Reality Using Mobile Devices

Nowadays, all Android phones support Augmented Reality as a feature, among which devices that support ARCore have plane detection capability which is useful for face detection. Only Android phones with ARCore support plane detection feature. For the smooth working of AR applications, smartphone cameras and sensors play an important role. If the smartphone is equipped with a good camera and the latest version of Android OS, then it also supports Augmented Reality. Marker-based are supported by all Android devices, whereas for Marker less-based AR, the phone need to support ARCore Library, which was supported by a few phone earlier, now the count is increasing very rapidly (Guven et al., 2009).

Study Deficit

Two-dimensional data visualization has been studied and is easily accessible for statistically demonstrating and elucidating data. For web-based 2D visualization, Free Open Source Software (FOSS) tools like Google Charts and Tableau are available. When it comes to end users' needs in the smart era of AR and VR today, 3D visualization with interactive capability is essential for making informed decisions. The research claims that there are significant gaps in data visualization, including those related to position accuracy, rotational rotation, zoom-in and out capabilities, and 3D user interaction. The curiosity and motivation behind the current research activity reported here have been piqued by this necessity (Padilla-Melendez et al., 2013). The statistics of 3D visualizations can be understood and communicated to individuals with the use of augmented reality. The business and technology industries make decisions more quickly thanks to the 3D augmented reality representation of data analytics. However, our most individualized and often utilized gadgets are still our smartphone applications. The number of mobile devices in use today has increased to over 2 billion. Things are a little more developed here, and although corporations are drawn to AR and VR technologies, and mobile AR and VR receive significantly more funding and development. In order to enable interaction, measurement, scaling, rotation, and movement of real things, mobile phones must be integrated with AR and VR.

VISUALIZATION BASED ON MARKERS USING MOBILE DEVICES

Readying of the Model

The model is composed of a predictive classification algorithm that produces predictions in the categories of health, unhealthy, and both target variables using the pre-processed Bigmart dataset as the input. In the last stage, data transformation techniques such data generalization, aggregation, and data smoothing were used to the dataset. The dataset has 15 attributes, one of which is the class label. Selected attributes are computed to make the dataset suitable for supervised learning. Our machine learning algorithms received the final cleaned and imputed dataset and used it for categorization. The 'Bigmart' dataset has been taken into consideration and fed into the Python code to carry out the machine learning-based classification according to item kind, outlet size, and health status. This is the BigMart dataset's dimension (Dataset, 2020). There are 8524 samples in all. There are 1,44,891 features total. There are seventeen qualities. Outlet size, item type, and health status were the goal labels. Afterwards, analytics were acquired in the form of categorization visualizations. The unity engine receives the analytics in order to integrate them with the augmented reality application. Without the need for additional reading materials or instructions, users of the program can install it from the cloud and access the data analytics. Tuning the hyperparameters has helped to explore how those factors affect predictive classification. Next, the comparative group's top predictive classifier is suggested. For this goal, nine different classifiers have been constructed, including the J48 decision tree, Hoeffding tree, Random forest, Random tree, REPTree, Bayes net, Naïve Bayes, OneR, and Decision table. The augmented reality application uses the classification that is derived from the predictive classification to enhance the visualizations and provide users three-dimensional views.

Pre-Processing of the Dataset

The development of augmented reality applications and data analysis comprise the two sections of the system implementation depicted above. The following is an in-depth explanation of each of the tiers.

Taking Out the Features

Feature extraction in machine learning, pattern recognition, and image processing begins with an initial set of measured data. It creates derived values, or features, with the intention of being non-redundant and informative (Rouibah et al., 2016).

This helps with the following stages of learning and generalization and, in some situations, results in improved interpretations by humans. Dimensionality reduction is associated with feature extraction. An algorithm's input data can be reduced to a smaller set of features (also known as a feature vector) when it is deemed redundant or too big to handle (such as the same measurement in feet and meters or the repetition of images displayed as pixels). Feature selection is the process of choosing a portion of the initial features. It is anticipated that the features that have been chosen will include pertinent information from the input data. Rather than utilizing all of the original data, this simplified representation could be used to accomplish the intended purpose. Range, summation, minimum, standard error, maximum, count, mean, mode, median, and standard deviation were extracted using a statistical method in this study.

- Root node: As the name suggests, this is the primary node from which other nodes branch out.
- Decision node: A node that is bifurcating to produce new branches is referred to as a decision node since it must decide how to classify a data piece.
- Pruning is the process of removing a branch or portion of a tree. The main purpose of this is to stop the model from overfitting the training set.

Arbitrary Forest

A method of supervised learning is employed by the random forest algorithm. It can be applied to machine learning tasks including both regression and classification. It solves a complicated issue and enhances the functionality of the model by combining several classifiers. Rather than depending just on a single decision tree, the random forest predicts the outcome by using the forecasts from each tree and calculating the majority vote of those predictions. Figure. 4.4 illustrates how simple trees and random forests function.

Arbitrary Tree

A computer program that creates (builds) a decision tree from a given dataset is known as a random tree algorithm. The attributes (sometimes called features or characteristics) and the class attribute will make up the dataset. Target and outcome are other words for class attributes. We will make further predictions about this property. A decision tree model is constructed via the decision tree algorithm. A root node, branches, and leaf nodes make up the model (Schmidt et al., 2013). As a recursive algorithm, the decision tree algorithm analyzes the data and calls itself repeatedly until the halting conditions are satisfied. When the data runs out or if every example in the subset is in the same class—that is, each example has the same attribute value for the class attribute—then this criterion is often applied. Information gain is computed by the ID3 algorithm for every attribute in the dataset, not only the class attributes. For the root node, the property with the highest value is selected. After that, the data is divided based on the value of that property, and each attribute in the subsets that are produced after partitioning is then calculated. This keeps going till the halting requirement is satisfied. The entropy equation is extended to include information gain. The gain Ratio is used by C4.5 to identify the ideal characteristic. This is a further development of knowledge acquisition. The links above provide all the pertinent information regarding these algorithms. A classification problem is a particular kind of problem where categorical data is the answer or the final product. For example, if the user is asked to indicate whether or not a person is afflicted with a sickness, the response will undoubtedly be either yes or no. Since the decision tree algorithm most closely resembles the functioning of the human brain, it is chosen over other algorithms. An if-else series of assertions, with each subsequent statement depending on the outcome of the preceding one, is how a decision tree algorithm works.

Naive Bayes and Bayes Net

Classification algorithms known as "Bayes Classifiers" employ the Bayes theorem in situations when there is a high degree of independence among the data's attributes. The probabilistic classifier family is composed of these classifiers. A Bayesian classifier establishes correlations between the features to create a probabilistic model. It is significantly simpler to create the model if these relationships are understood in advance. Next, the generated model is applied to forecast the class of a freshly fed example. A subset of this family is the Naive Bayes Classifier, in which each data instance is conditionally independent and has no hidden characteristics that could influence its categorization. Furthermore, the characteristics are distinct factors. Determining the likelihood that an instance belongs to a specific class is the fundamental concept underlying the model. The Bayes theorem is used to calculate this probability. When dealing with multiple class difficulties, the instance is assigned the class with the highest likelihood.

Creation of QR Codes

The QR code that is needed to enhance the virtual data on top of the fundamental physical layer is described in 4.16. The primary focus of Vuforia, an augmented reality SDK, is mobile applications. The SDK allows for enhanced artificial intelligence by combining machine learning and computer vision. Both 2D and 3D targets, including marker-based picture targets, are supported by Vuforia. Through the target manager online, the engine itself augments the image that is presented in the Vuforia database. As seen in Fig., the 3D picture etched on the smartphone device and the QR code enhanced in the vuforia engine are in line. 4.16. The surface view of the items with low, medium, and high fats, proteins, and carbs is the increased information (Business Standard, 2014). The surface view provides a more accurate representation of both healthful and unhealthy food goods by generating analytics through query processing of the data. On the user interface, 2D visualization can be shown as pie charts, bar graphs, and maps. With the aid of the vuforia plugin in the Unity IDE, an application package file compatible with smart devices was generated. The targets were upgraded for AR marker-based photos. Figure. "Target features" for our marker-based AR image are displayed.

Type of Item

Regarding item kind, the first classification has been carried out. Items such as dairy, soft drinks, meat, fruits, and vegetables, household goods, baked goods, snack foods, frozen foods, breakfast, health and hygiene, canned foods, starchy foods, breads, seafood, and others were divided into 16 classes (labels). Table 4.3 displays the categorization of sixteen different item categories that were created with nine classifiers taking training set and k-fold cross-validation into account. A test set was used to assess the developed model that was built using a training set. The Bigmart training datasets had 8524 samples in total. Just 70% of the entire Bigmart dataset was utilized for classification using the Training set, while the remaining 30% was used for classification using the Test set.

Confusion Matrix and Detailed Evaluation of Performance of Classifiers for Classification of Health Status

Here confusion matrix and detailed evaluation of the performance of classifiers for classification of health status are presented. There were three classes (labels) in item type such as healthy, unhealthy and both (healthy and unhealthy). The table shows the classification of 3 item types designed using nine classifiers considering k-fold cross- validation and training set. A test set was used to assess the developed model that was built using a training set. The confusion matrix for the classifier, which exhibits the highest accuracy for a particular classification model, is presented to understand classification and misclassification. Figure. 4.34 depicts the confusion matrix for classification using the REPTree classifier considering ten-fold cross-validation. Figure. 4.35 shows detailed performance for classification using the REPTree classifier considering ten-fold cross-validation.

Clan Updating Operator

An elephant must be in peak physical condition to be considered a matriarch. The formula for updating the elephants in the clan, aside from the matriarch, is as follows:

$X(new, ci, j) = X(ci, j) + \alpha \times (X(best, ci) - X(ci, j)) \times r$ (4.2)

where X(new, ci, j) and X(ci, j) are the newly updated and old positions for ele- phant j in clan ci.

Clan Separating Operator

When male elephants reach the age of puberty, they will leave their family group and live on their own for the first time. Consider the elephants with the lowest fitness values and run the separation operator at each generation, as shown in the diagram below:

$$X(worst, ci) = X(min) + (X(max) - X(min) + 1) \times rand \quad (4.3)$$

where Xmax and Xmin are respectively upper and lower bound. In this case, the upper and lower bounds of the location of the elephant individual, which are derived from the initialized parameters, are accordingly.

Optimization of Monarch Butterflies (MBO)

Butterfly belong to the type of Lepidoptera and over and above 18,000 species are found all over the realm. Up to now, the three most significant optimizer approaches related to butterflies were anticipated, excluding monarch butterfly optimization. Through im- dating search mechanism for earning food and breeding conduct of butterflies, butterfly optimizer was proposed first that was engaged for solving globe optimization and problems from the engineering domain. Motivated through a breed-discovery style of a few butterfly classes, an artificial butterfly optimizer was presented that offers a novel operative computation outline for resolving optimization difficulties. Likewise, motivated through the breeding conduct of butterfly classes in the environment, a butterfly mating optimizer was proposed that was divided into 4 stages to deploy a hunting course (Yoon et al., 2015). Among these, the monarch butterfly optimizer turns out to be the greatest. The classic MBO seems to be modest and easier to deploy. In monarch butterfly optimizer, there exist 2identical-size sub-populations, called as sub-population_1 and sub-population_2. Consequently, 2plans are created in arch butterfly optimizers such as relocation operative and butterfly altering operative. At the end of the iteration, the globe optimum info is preserved, and two sub-populations are restructured into a populace once more.

Afterwards, the complete populace is divided into two sub-populations as stated by the fresh fitness rate.

Suggestions

A thorough summary of virtual reality's application in the travel and hospitality sectors is given in this chapter's content. The chapter covers the distinctions between augmented and virtual reality, the range of uses for augmented reality, and the difficulties and constraints associated with integrating virtual reality in the travel industry. The application of virtual reality in inventory management systems and the significance of data analytics in decision-making are also highlighted in this chapter.

Overall, the chapter does a good job of illuminating the concerns, difficulties, and patterns associated with the book's suggested theme. It could be better, though, if more detailed case studies and examples of virtual reality's application in the travel and hospitality sectors were provided. The chapter might also benefit from a deeper examination of how virtual reality can affect the travel and tourism sector, particularly how technology might change how tourists book and enjoy their vacations.

Furthermore, even though the material on technology is extensive, it might be better described in relation to the travel and tourism industry (Yung & Khoo-Lattimore, 2017). More detailed examples of virtual reality's application in the tourism sector, such as virtual tours of popular tourist spots, might be included in this chapter, along with how it improves travellers' overall trip experiences.

Further researchers might think about adding more case studies and real-world examples of virtual reality applications in the travel and hospitality sector. They should also give a more thorough explanation of the possible effects of virtual reality on the industry.

The chapter would also benefit from a deeper examination of the difficulties and restrictions associated with the use of virtual reality in the travel and hospitality sectors, including the expense of putting this technology into practice and the possibility that it will lessen the authenticity of the travel experience.

Summary

In this chapter, a detailed design, analysis, and visualization of the Bigmart dataset using marker-based augmented reality and mobile devices is presented. The 'Bigmart' dataset was considered and provided as an input and classification with respect to item type, outlet size, and health status using machine learning is presented using different classifiers such as J48 decision tree, Hoeffding tree, Random forest, Random Tree,

REPTree, Bayes net, Naïve Bayes, OneR, and Decision Table. The methodology clearly classifies and visualizes the data appropriately in 3D form. The confusion matrix in 3D form is clear, easy to understand classification and misclassification. The four meta-heuristic optimizers were employed to improve the classification accuracy that systemically assists hyperparameter tuning. Later, the visualizations of classification were obtained in the form of a confusion matrix and forwarded to the Unity engine for embedding it with the AR application for augmenting the visualizations and displaying 3D views to the end-users. The OneR classifier and Monarch butterfly optimization are recommended for the classification of item type and outlet size Bigmart data.

The concerns, challenges, and trends surrounding the application of virtual reality in the travel and hospitality sectors are skilfully covered in this chapter. Nonetheless, there exist prospects to augment the comprehensive treatment of the subject matter by placing greater attention on specific facets.

1. Emphasising Current Trends: A more thorough examination of the use of virtual reality in the travel and hospitality sectors would be beneficial for this chapter. This could include new developments in the field of virtual reality technology, creative applications, and developing trends that will influence the direction the industry takes with virtual reality. The chapter can provide readers a more current grasp of the subject by highlighting current trends.
2. Case Studies and Examples: Highlighting the useful uses and advantages of this technology can be accomplished by providing particular case studies and illustrations of effective virtual reality installations in the travel and hospitality sector. The chapter can successfully highlight the effects of virtual reality on improving the travel experience and industrial operating efficiency by presenting real-world examples.
3. Handling Possible Obstacles: Although the chapter mentions the difficulties and constraints of using virtual reality in the travel industry, there is a chance to emphasise this point more. The chapter can present a more impartial analysis of the subject by going into greater detail on the potential drawbacks, such as financial ramifications, technological obstacles, and issues with authenticity.
4. Impact on Consumer Experience: The chapter should go into more detail about how virtual reality might affect how customers interact with the travel and hospitality sectors. Examining how virtual reality is changing how tourists book and enjoy their vacations, as well as how technology affects customer expectations and behaviour, can provide important insights into how the travel business is changing.

This can enhance the overall coverage of the issues, problems, and trends related to virtual reality in the context of the tourism and hospitality industry by incorporating these recommendations and putting more emphasis on current trends, practical applications, potential challenges, and the impact on the consumer experience.

FUTURE DIRECTIONS

Overall, the chapter provides a balanced and comprehensive overview of the issues, problems, and trends related to the utilization of virtual reality in the tourism and hospitality industry. However, there are some areas where the chapter may have over-emphasized or under-emphasized certain aspects.

One area where the chapter may have under-emphasized is the potential impact of virtual reality on the consumer experience in the tourism and hospitality industry. While the chapter briefly touches on this aspect, there is an opportunity to provide a more in-depth discussion of how virtual reality is transforming the way travellers plan and experience their trips. By exploring the potential impact of virtual reality on consumer behavior and expectations, the chapter can provide valuable insights into the evolving landscape of the industry.

On the other hand, the chapter may have over-emphasized the importance of data analytics in decision-making. While data analytics is undoubtedly an essential aspect of the tourism and hospitality industry, the chapter could benefit from a more balanced discussion of the role of virtual reality in enhancing operational efficiency and improving the overall travel experience for consumers. By providing more specific examples of how virtual reality is being used in the industry, the chapter can effectively illustrate the practical applications and benefits of this technology.

To improve the chapter's coverage in these areas, the author(s) could consider incorporating more case studies and examples of virtual reality usage in the tourism and hospitality industry to emphasize the practical applications and benefits of this technology. Additionally, the author(s) could provide a more in-depth discussion of the potential impact of virtual reality on the consumer experience in the industry. By doing so, the chapter's contents will be more comprehensive and provide a deeper understanding of the utilization of virtual reality in the context of tourism and hospitality.

REFERENCES

Alalwan, A. A., Baabdullah, A. M., Rana, N. P., Tamilmani, K., & Dwivedi, Y. K. (2018). Examining the adoption of mobile internet in Saudi Arabia: Extending TAM with perceived enjoyment, innovativeness and trust. *Technology in Society*, *55*, 100–110. Advance online publication. doi:10.1016/j.techsoc.2018.06.007

Ameen, N., Willis, R., & Shah, M. H. (2018). An examination of the gender gap in smartphone adoption and use in Arab countries: A cross-national study. *Computers in Human Behavior*, *89*(December), 148–162. doi:10.1016/j.chb.2018.07.045

Bagri, S. C., & Kala, D. (2015). Tourists' satisfaction at Trijuginarayan: An emerging spiritual and adventure tourist destination in Garhwal Himalaya India. Turizam, 19(4), 165– 182. Bagozzi, R. P., & Yi, Y. (1988). On the evaluation of structural equation models. *Journal of the Academy of Marketing Science*, *16*(1), 74–94.

Bem, S. L. (1981). Gender schema theory: A cognitive account of sex typing. *Psychological Review*, *88*(4), 354–364. doi:10.1037/0033-295X.88.4.354

Berger, H., Dittenbach, M., Merkl, D., Bogdanovych, A., Simoff, S., & Sierra, C. (2007). Opening new dimensions for e-tourism. *Virtual Reality (Waltham Cross)*, *11*(2-3), 75–87. doi:10.1007/s10055-006-0057-z

Bilandzic, H., & Busselle, R. W. (2011). Enjoyment of films as a function of narrative experience, perceived realism and transportability. *Communication Theory*, *18*(2), 255–280.

Bloomberg. (2018). Tourism in India is booming. But why is everyone so worried? - The Economic Times. Retrieved March 3, 2019, from https://economictimes.indiatimes.com/ industry/services/travel/tourism-in-india-is-booming-butwhy-is-everyone-so worried/articleshow/64890122.cms? from=mdr

Business line. (2018). It's real: AR/VR market to grow 76% over 5 years - The Hindu Business Line. Retrieved from https://www. thehindubusinessline.com/info-tech/its-real-arvr-market-togrow-76-over-5-years/article10010306.ece

Business Standard. (2014, July 23). Travel agent arrested for cheating people. Retrieved from https://www.businessstandard.com/article/pti-stories/travel-agent-arrested-forcheating-people114072301737_1.html Tussyadiah, I. P., Wang, D., Jung, T. H., & tom Dieck, M. C. (2018).

Chadda, R. K., & Deb, K. S. (2013). Indian family systems, collectivistic society and psychotherapy. Indian Journal of Psychiatry, 55 (suppl 2), S299–S309. doi: Chaudhary, M. (2000). India's image as a tourist destination—a perspective of foreign tourists. Tourism Management, 21(3), 293–297. doi:10.4103/00195545.105555

Chawla, D., & Joshi, H. (2018). The moderating effect of demographic variables on mobile Banking adoption: An empirical Investigation. *Global Business Review*, *19*(3_suppl), S90–S113. doi:10.1177/0972150918757883

Chen, V. H. H., Duh, H. B. L., Phuah, P. S. K., & Lam, D. Z. Y. (2006). Enjoyment or engagement? Role of social interaction in playing massively mulitplayer online role-playing games (MMORPGS). In Proceedings of International Conference on Entertainment Computing (pp. 262-267). Springer, Berlin, Heidelberg.

Childers, T. L., Carr, C. L., Peck, J., & Carson, S. (2001). Hedonic and utilitarian motivations for online retail shopping behavior. *Journal of Retailing*, *77*(4), 511–535. doi:10.1016/S0022-4359(01)00056-2

Cho, Y. H., Wang, Y., & Fesenmaier, D. R. (2002). Searching for experiences: The web-based virtual tour in tourism marketing. *Journal of Travel & Tourism Marketing*, *12*(4), 1–17. doi:10.1300/J073v12n04_01

Csikzentmihalyi, M. (1977). *Beyond Boredom and Anxiety*. Jossey-Bass.

Davis, F. D. (1989). Perceived usefulness, perceived ease of use, and user acceptance of information technology. *Management Information Systems Quarterly*, *13*(3), 319–340. doi:10.2307/249008

Davis, F. D., Bagozzi, R. P., & Warshaw, P. R. (1992). Extrinsic and intrinsic motivation to use computers in the workplace. *Journal of Applied Social Psychology*, *22*(14), 1111–1132. doi:10.1111/j.1559-1816.1992.tb00945.x

Disztinger, P., Schlögl, S., & Groth, A. (2017). Technology acceptance of virtual reality for travel planning. In R. Schegg & B. Stangl (Eds.), *Information and communication technologies in tourism 2017* (pp. 255–268). Springer. doi:10.1007/978-3-319-51168-9_19

Dobrowolski, P., Pochwatko, G., Skorko, M., & Bielecki, M. (2014). The effects of virtual experience on attitudes toward real brands. Cyberpsychology, Behavior, and Social Networking, 17(2), 125–128. Economic Times. (2017). India to have 530mn smartphone users in 2018: Study. Retrieved from: https://telecom.economictimes.indiatimes.com/news/india-to-have-530mnsmartphone-users-in-2018-study/61097817

Fotakis, T., & Economides, A. A. (2008). Art, science/technology and history museums on the web. *International Journal of Digital Culture and Electronic Tourism*, *1*(1), 37–63. doi:10.1504/IJDCET.2008.020134

Fox, J., Arena, D., & Bailenson, J. N. (2009). Virtual reality: A survival guide for the social scientist. *Journal of Media Psychology*, *21*(3), 95–113. doi:10.1027/1864-1105.21.3.95

Gaines, J., & Lee, C. V. (2019). Medical tourism. Travel Medicine, 371–375. Gardiner, S., King, B., & Wilkins, H. (2013). The travel behaviours of international students: Nationality-based constraints and opportunities. *Journal of Vacation Marketing*, *19*(4), 287–299.

Gautam, V. (2012). An empirical investigation of consumers' preferences about tourism services in Indian context with special reference to state of Himachal Pradesh. *Tourism Management*, *33*(6), 1591–1592. doi:10.1016/j.tourman.2011.12.014

Haider, M. J., Changchun, G., Akram, T., & Hussain, S. T. (2018). Does gender differences play any role in intention to adopt Islamic mobile banking? An empirical study. *Journal of Islamic Marketing*, *9*(2), 439–460. doi:10.1108/JIMA-11-2016-0082

Hair, J. F., Black, W. C., Babin, B. J., & Anderson, R. E. (2010). *Multivariate data analysis* (7th ed.). Prentice-Hall.

Haugstvedt, A. C., & Krogstie, J. (2012). Mobile augmented reality for cultural heritage: A technology acceptance study. In *Proceedings of International Symposium on Mixed and Augmented Reality (ISMAR)*, (pp. 247–255). IEEE. 10.1109/ISMAR.2012.6402563

In, T. Jung, & M. C. tom Dieck (eds.), Augmented reality and virtual reality (pp. 93–107). Cham: Springer. Global Travel Intention (GTI). (2018). Indian travelers take longer trips, more frequently, and spend 40% more than their regional counterparts - Visa Study | Press Release | Visa. Retrieved from https://www.visa.co.in/about-visa/newsroom/press-releases/indian-travelers-take-longer-tripsmore-frequently-and-spend-40-percent-more-than-theirregional-counterparts-visa-study.html

Kumar, R., Mukherjee, A., & Singh, V. P. (2017). Traffic noise mapping of Indian roads through smartphone user community participation. *Environmental Monitoring and Assessment*, *189*(1), 17. doi:10.1007/s10661-016-5741-1 PMID:27975332

Kumra, R. (2008, May). Service quality in rural tourism: A prescriptive approach. In *Proceedings of conference on tourism in India-Challenges ahead*, 15–17 May 2008 (pp. 424–431), IIMK.

Lee, H., Chung, N., & Jung, T. (2015). Examining the cultural differences in acceptance of mobile augmented reality: Comparison of South Korea and Ireland. In I. Tussyadiah & A. Inversini (Eds.), *Information and communication technologies in tourism 2015* (pp. 477–491). Springer. doi:10.1007/978-3-319-14343-9_35

Ma, E., Hsiao, A., & Gao, J. (2018). Destination attractiveness and travel intention: The case of Chinese and Indian students in Queensland, Australia. *Asia Pacific Journal of Tourism Research*, *23*(2), 200–215. doi:10.1080/10941665.2017.1411964

McCarthy, N. (2019). The Cost of Mobile Internet Around the World I Statista. Retrieved from https://www.statista.com/chart/ 17247/the-average-cost-of-mobile-data-in-selected-countries/. Ministry of Tourism. (2018). Tourism Ministry launches 360° Virtual Reality (VR) video on Incredible India. Retrieved from http://pib.nic.in/newsite/PrintRelease.aspx?relid=178945

Moorhouse, N., tom Dieck, M. C., & Jung, T. (2018). Technological Innovations Transforming the consumer Retail experience: A Review of literature. In T. Jung & M. C. tom Dieck (Eds.), *Augmented reality and virtual reality* (pp. 133–143). Springer., doi:10.1007/978-3-319-64027-3_10

Okcu, S., Hancerliogullari Koksalmis, G., Basak, E., & Calisir, F. (2019). Factors Affecting Intention to Use Big Data Tools: An Extended Technology Acceptance Model. In F. Calisir, E. Cevikcan, & H. C. Akdag (Eds.), *Industrial Engineering in the Big Data Era* (pp. 401–416). Springer. doi:10.1007/978-3-030-03317-0_33

Ooi, K.-B., & Tan, G. W.-H. (2016). Mobile technology acceptance model: An investigation using mobile users to explore smartphone credit card. *Expert Systems with Applications*, *59*, 33–46. doi:10.1016/j.eswa.2016.04.015

P. VISHWAKARMA ET AL.

Padilla-MeléNdez, A., Del Aguila-Obra, A. R., & Garrido-Moreno, A. (2013). Perceived playfulness, gender differences and technology acceptance model in a blended learning scenario. *Computers & Education*, *63*(1), 306–317. doi:10.1016/j.compedu.2012.12.014

Rouibah, K., Lowry, P. B., & Hwang, Y. (2016). The effects of perceived enjoyment and perceived risks on trust formation and intentions to use online payment systems: New perspectives from an Arab country. *Electronic Commerce Research and Applications*, *19*, 33–43. doi:10.1016/j.elerap.2016.07.001

Schmidt, M., Kafka, J. X., Kothgassner, O. D., Hlavacs, H., Beutl, L., & Felnhofer, A. (2013). Why Does It Always Rain on Me? Influence of Gender and Environmental Factors on Usability, Technology Related Anxiety and Immersion in Virtual Environments. In D. Reidsma, H. Katayose, & A. Nijholt (Eds.), *Advances in Computer Entertainment* (pp. 392–402). Springer. doi:10.1007/978-3-319-03161-3_29

Virtual reality, presence, and attitude change: Empirical evidence from tourism. Tourism Management, 66, 140–154. doi:10.1016/j.tourman.2017.12.003

Yoon, S. Y., Choi, Y. J., & Oh, H. (2015). User attributes in processing 3D VR-enabled showroom: Gender, visual cognitive styles, and the sense of presence. *International Journal of Human-Computer Studies*, *82*, 1–10. doi:10.1016/j.ijhcs.2015.04.002

Yung, R., & Khoo-Lattimore, C. (2017). New realities: A systematic literature review on virtual reality and augmented reality in tourism research. *Current Issues in Tourism*, •••, 1–26.

Compilation of References

Abass, M., & Zohry, M. (2022). Mixed Reality Drama Towards Metaverse Technology in Smart Hotels: An Exploratory Study on Egyptian Hotels Evidence from Guests' Perspectives. *Journal of Association of Arab Universities for Tourism and Hospitality*, *23*(2), 130–154. Advance online publication. doi:10.21608/jaauth.2022.177500.1411

Ahmad, M. (2023). Exploring the Role of OpenStreetMap in Mapping Religious Tourism in Pakistan for Sustainable Development. In V. João Pereira Domingues Martinho (Ed.), *Experiences, Advantages, and Economic Dimensions of Pilgrimage Routes*. IGI Global. doi:10.4018/978-1-6684-9923-8.ch002

Ahmad, M., & Ali, A. (2023). Integrated Geospatial Information Management in the World of Metaverse. In P. Lekhi & G. Kaur (Eds.), *Concepts, Technologies, Challenges, and the Future of Web 3* (pp. 248–270). IGI Global. doi:10.4018/978-1-6684-9919-1.ch013

Ahmad, N. M., Sohail, R., & Ahmad, M. M. (2022). Impact of Religious Tourism on the Development of Smokeless Industry in Pakistan. *Global Social Sciences Review*, *7*(2), 77–89. Advance online publication. doi:10.31703/gssr.2022(VII-II).08

Ahmed, O. (2018). Artificial intelligence in HR. *International Journal of Research and Analytical Reviews*, *5*(4), 971–978.

Ahn, L., & Kim, Y. (2017). The Influence of Haptic Feedback on Immersive Virtual Reality Advertising. *Journal of Business Research*.

Akaka, M. A., & Vargo, S. L. (2014). Technology as an operant resource in service (eco)systems. *Information Systems and e-Business Management*, *12*(3), 367–384. doi:10.1007/s10257-013-0220-5

Akhtar, N., Khan, N., Mahroof Khan, M., Ashraf, S., Hashmi, M. S., Khan, M. M., & Hishan, S. S. (2021). Post-covid 19 tourism: Will digital tourism replace mass tourism? *Sustainability (Basel)*, *13*(10), 5352. Advance online publication. doi:10.3390/su13105352

Akpojaro, J., & Bello, R.-W. (2019). *Smart Healthcare System: A Primer*. https://www.kernelsphere.com/four-internet-things-communications-models/

Alalwan, A. A., Baabdullah, A. M., Rana, N. P., Tamilmani, K., & Dwivedi, Y. K. (2018). Examining the adoption of mobile internet in Saudi Arabia: Extending TAM with perceived enjoyment, innovativeness and trust. *Technology in Society*, *55*, 100–110. Advance online publication. doi:10.1016/j.techsoc.2018.06.007

Alam, M., & Khan, I. (2020). Business 4.0-A New Revolution. In *Information Technology for Management* (pp. 41–57). KD Publications.

Al-Ghaili, A. M., Kasim, H., Al-Hada, N. M., Hassan, Z. Bin, Othman, M., Tharik, J. H., Kasmani, R. M., & Shayea, I. (2022). A Review of Metaverse's Definitions, Architecture, Applications, Challenges, Issues, Solutions, and Future Trends. In IEEE Access (Vol. 10). doi:10.1109/ACCESS.2022.3225638

Alizadehsalehi, S., Hadavi, A., & Huang, J. C. (2021). Assessment of AEC Students' Performance Using BIM-into-VR. *Applied Sciences (Basel, Switzerland)*, *11*(7), 3225. doi:10.3390/app11073225

Almarzouqi, A., Aburayya, A., & Salloum, S. A. (2022). Prediction of User's Intention to Use Metaverse System in Medical Education: A Hybrid SEM-ML Learning Approach. *IEEE Access : Practical Innovations, Open Solutions*, *10*, 43421–43434. Advance online publication. doi:10.1109/ACCESS.2022.3169285

Almuhrzi, H. (2020). Islamic tourism: Management of travel destinations. *Journal of Heritage Tourism*, *15*(4), 480–482. Advance online publication. doi:10.1080/1743873X.2019.1658351

Altinay, L., Var, T., Hines, S., & Hussain, K. (2007). Barriers to sustainable tourism development in Jamaica. *Tourism Analysis*, *12*(1–2), 1–13. doi:10.3727/108354207780956690

Ameen, N., Willis, R., & Shah, M. H. (2018). An examination of the gender gap in smartphone adoption and use in Arab countries: A cross-national study. *Computers in Human Behavior*, *89*(December), 148–162. doi:10.1016/j.chb.2018.07.045

Amour Al Nooumani, R., & Taqui Syed, R. (2020). Human Resource Automation: Benefits and Challenges for Organizations. *People in the center of process automation*, 161-164.

Ampountolas, A., Menconi, G., & Shaw, G. (2023). Metaverse research propositions: Online intermediaries. *Tourism Economics*. Advance online publication. doi:10.1177/13548166231159520

Anshari, M., Syafrudin, M., Fitriyani, N. L., & Razzaq, A. (2022). Ethical Responsibility and Sustainability (ERS) Development in a Metaverse Business Model. *Sustainability (Basel)*, *14*(23), 15805. Advance online publication. doi:10.3390/su142315805

Antinori, L., & Fiore, A. M. E. (2008). Understanding the Impact of Social Networks on Consumers' Salient Beliefs and Attitudes toward Experiential Marketing. *Journal of Travel Research*.

Antonacopoulou, E., & Güttel, W. (2010). Staff induction practices and organizational socialization: A review and extention of the debate. *Society and Business Review*, *5*(1), 22–47. doi:10.1108/17465681011017246

Arafat, S. (2023). SoK: Can NFTs solve the economic problems of countries with ancient heritage? egypt as a case study. *Lecture Notes of the Institute for Computer Sciences, Social-Informatics and Telecommunications Engineering, LNICST.* doi:10.1007/s40558-023-00269-6

Arnold, K. (2000). Social Tourism: The Effect of Local Communities on Participating Visitors. *Annals of Tourism Research.*

Ayorekire, J., Obua, J., Mugizi, F., & Byaruhanga, B. M. (2020). Opportunities and challenges of religious tourism development in Uganda: Policy, planning and institutional perspectives. In International Journal of Religious Tourism and Pilgrimage (Vol. 8, Issue 3).

Ayoub & Pulijala. (2019). The application of virtual reality and augmented reality in Oral & Maxillofacial Surgery. *BMC Oral Health*, *19*(1), 1-8.

Ayuningtyas, D., & Ariwibowo, D. A. (2020). The strategic role of information communication technology in succeeding medical tourism. *Enfermeria Clinica*, *30*, 170–173. doi:10.1016/j.enfcli.2020.06.039

Bagri, S. C., & Kala, D. (2015). Tourists' satisfaction at Trijuginarayan: An emerging spiritual and adventure tourist destination in Garhwal Himalaya India. Turizam, 19(4), 165– 182. Bagozzi, R. P., & Yi, Y. (1988). On the evaluation of structural equation models. *Journal of the Academy of Marketing Science*, *16*(1), 74–94.

Baker, J., Nam, K., & Dutt, C. S. (2023). A user experience perspective on heritage tourism in the metaverse: Empirical evidence and design dilemmas for VR. *Information Technology & Tourism*, *25*(3), 265–306. Advance online publication. doi:10.1007/s40558-023-00256-x

Bale, A. S., Ghorpade, N., Hashim, M. F., Vaishnav, J., & Almaspoor, Z. (2022). A Comprehensive Study on Metaverse and Its Impacts on Humans. In *Advances in Human-Computer Interaction* (Vol. 2022). Hindawi Limited. doi:10.1155/2022/3247060

Barkel, C., Kurgun, H., & Groen, B. (2021). Blochchain in the Hospitality and Tourism Industry. In C. Cobanoglu, S. Dogan, K. Berezina, & G. Collins (Eds.), *Hospitality and Tourism Information Technology*. University of South Florida.

Basheer, S., Walia, S., Farooq, S., Shah, M. A., & Mir, F. A. (2023). *Exploring the Metaverse.*, doi:10.4018/978-1-6684-8898-0.ch012

Bauer, T. N. (2010). *Onboarding New Employees: Maximizing Success.* SHRM Foundation.

BBC News. (2022, January 23). *What is greenwashing?* BBC News [Video]. YouTube. https://www.youtube.com/watch?v=0XGAMJsm6Tg

Bem, S. L. (1981). Gender schema theory: A cognitive account of sex typing. *Psychological Review*, *88*(4), 354–364. doi:10.1037/0033-295X.88.4.354

Berger, H., Dittenbach, M., Merkl, D., Bogdanovych, A., Simoff, S., & Sierra, C. (2007). Opening new dimensions for e-tourism. *Virtual Reality (Waltham Cross)*, *11*(2-3), 75–87. doi:10.1007/s10055-006-0057-z

Bhalla, A., Singh, P., & Singh, A. (2023). Technological Advancement and Mechanization of the Hotel Industry. In R. Tailor (Ed.), *Application and Adoption of Robotic Process Automation for Smart Cities* (pp. 57–76). IGI Global. doi:10.4018/978-1-6684-7193-7.ch004

Bharthvajan, R., & Kavitha, F. (2019). Impact of Employee Satisfaction towards Induction Training Program. *International Journal of Innovative Technology and Exploring Engineering*, *8*(11).

Bhat, A. (2018). *Primary Research: Definition, Examples, Methods and Purpose*. Retrieved January 9, 2023, from https://www.questionpro.com/blog/primary-research/

Bhattacharya, P., Saraswat, D., Savaliya, D., Sanghavi, S., Verma, A., Sakariya, V., Tanwar, S., Sharma, R., Raboaca, M. S., & Manea, D. L. (2023). Towards Future Internet: The Metaverse Perspective for Diverse Industrial Applications. *Mathematics*, *11*(4), 941. Advance online publication. doi:10.3390/math11040941

Bilandzic, H., & Busselle, R. W. (2011). Enjoyment of films as a function of narrative experience, perceived realism and transportability. *Communication Theory*, *18*(2), 255–280.

Birt, J., & Vasilevski, N. (2021). Comparison of single and multiuser immersive mobile virtual reality usability in construction education. *Journal of Educational Technology & Society*, *24*(2), 93–106.

Bloomberg. (2018). Tourism in India is booming. But why is everyone so worried? - The Economic Times. Retrieved March 3, 2019, from https://economictimes.indiatimes.com/ industry/services/travel/tourism-in-india-is-booming-butwhy-is-everyone-so worried/articleshow/64890122.cms?from=mdr

Bocken, N. M. P., Rana, P., & Short, S. W. (2015). Value mapping for sustainable business thinking. *Journal of Industrial and Production Engineering*, *32*(1), 67–81. doi:10.1080/21681015.2014.1000399

Bolger, R. K. (2021). Finding wholes in the metaverse: Posthuman mystics as agents of evolutionary contextualization. *Religions*, *12*(9), 768. Advance online publication. doi:10.3390/rel12090768

Boon, P. I., Burridge, T. R., & Fluker, M. (2002). A case for supply-led nature-based tourism within the marine and coastal temperate systems of south-eastern Australia. *Journal of Ecotourism*, *1*(2-3), 93–103. doi:10.1080/14724040208668117

Bowen, D., & Clarke, R. (2006). Reflections on Tourism and Change. In M. Smith & M. Robinson (Eds.), Tourism and Transition. Academic Press.

Buhalis, D., Lopez, E. P., & Martinez-Gonzalez, J. A. (2020). Influence of young consumers' external and internal variables on their e-loyalty to tourism sites. *Journal of Destination Marketing & Management, 15*, 100409. https://doi.org/. jdmm.2020.100409 doi:10.1016/j

Buhalis, D. (2020). Technology in tourism-from information communication technologies to eTourism and smart tourism towards ambient intelligence tourism: A perspective article. *Tourism Review*, *75*(1), 267–272. Advance online publication. doi:10.1108/TR-06-2019-0258

Buhalis, D., & Karatay, N. (2022). Mixed reality for Generation Z in cultural heritage tourism towards Metaverse. In J. L. Stienmetz, B. Ferrer-Rosell, & D. Massimo (Eds.), *Information and communication technologies in tourism 2022* (pp. 16–27). Springer. doi:10.1007/978-3-030-94751-4_2

Buhalis, D., Leung, D., & Lin, M. (2023). Metaverse as a disruptive technology revolutionising tourism management and marketing. In *Tourism Management* (Vol. 97). Elsevier Ltd. doi:10.1016/j.tourman.2023.104724

Buhalis, D., Lin, M. S., & Leung, D. (2023). Metaverse as a driver for customer experience and value co-creation: Implications for hospitality and tourism management and marketing. *International Journal of Contemporary Hospitality Management, 35*(2), 701–716. Advance online publication. doi:10.1108/IJCHM-05-2022-0631

Buhalis, D., O'Connor, P., & Leung, R. (2023). Smart hospitality: From smart cities and smart tourism towards agile business ecosystems in networked destinations. *International Journal of Contemporary Hospitality Management, 35*(1), 369–393. doi:10.1108/IJCHM-04-2022-0497

Bui, T. X. (2023). *56th Hawaii International Conference on System Sciences (HICCS)*. University of Hawaii at Manoa.

Business line. (2018). It's real: AR/VR market to grow 76% over 5 years - The Hindu Business Line. Retrieved from https://www. thehindubusinessline.com/info-tech/its-real-arvr-market-togrow-76-over-5-years/article10010306.ece

Business Standard. (2014, July 23). Travel agent arrested for cheating people. Retrieved from https://www.businessstandard.com/article/pti-stories/travel-agent-arrested-forcheating-people114072301737_1.html Tussyadiah, I. P., Wang, D., Jung, T. H., & tom Dieck, M. C. (2018).

Butler, R. (2020). Risk and safety challenges for religious tourism and events. *Current Issues in Tourism, 23*(3), 388–390. Advance online publication. doi:10.1080/13683500.2018.1502860

Caddes, F., & Pinna, A. (2021). *Opportunities and Challenges of Blockchain-Oriented Systems in the Tourism Industry*. arXiv:2107.06732v1[<s.CY]11mar 2021

Cai, W., & McKenna, B. (2021). Knowledge Creation in Information Technology and Tourism Research. In Journal of Travel Research (Vol. 60, Issue 4). doi:10.1177/0047287520903142

Cai, W., McKenna, B., Wassler, P., & Williams, N. (2021). Rethinking Knowledge Creation in Information Technology and Tourism. In Journal of Travel Research (Vol. 60, Issue 6). doi:10.1177/0047287520946100

Cantoni, M., & Tardini, S. (2006). Designing a Museum Multi-Device and Multi-Location Experience: The Case of Museo della Scienza e della Tecnologia di Milano. *International Journal of Human-Computer Interaction*.

Carbone, M., Domeneghetti, D., Cutolo, F., D'Amato, R., Cigna, E., Parchi, P. D., Gesi, M., Morelli, L., Ferrari, M., & Ferrari, V. (2021). Can Liquid Lenses Increase Depth of Field in Head Mounted Video See-Through Devices? *Journal of Imaging*, *7*(8), 138. doi:10.3390/jimaging7080138 PMID:34460773

Cárdenas, R. M., & Puente, O. T. (2017). The perception of security of the tourists in a site of religious tourism. *International Journal of Scientific Management and Tourism*, *3*, 255–274.

Cazes, J. C., & de Freitas, P. (1999). Virtual Reality in Tourism. *Journal of Travel & Tourism Marketing*.

Chadda, R. K., & Deb, K. S. (2013). Indian family systems, collectivistic society and psychotherapy. Indian Journal of Psychiatry, 55 (suppl 2), S299–S309. doi: Chaudhary, M. (2000). India's image as a tourist destination—a perspective of foreign tourists. Tourism Management, 21(3), 293–297. doi:10.4103/00195545.105555

Chan, C. H., Wong, K. Y., & Lui, T. W. (2023). *Marketing tourism products in virtual reality: moderating effect of product complexity*. Springer Proceedings in Business and Economics.

Chang, C. L., McAleer, M., & Ramos, V. (2020). A charter for sustainable tourism after COVID-19. *Sustainability (Basel)*, *12*(9), 3671. Advance online publication. doi:10.3390/su12093671

Charted Accountants Australia and New Zealand. (2017). *The Future of Blockchain: Application and Implications of Distributed Ledger Technology. Deloitte and Future (inc)*. Perspectives on Prosperity. chartedaccountantsanz.com/futureinc

Chawla, D., & Joshi, H. (2018). The moderating effect of demographic variables on mobile Banking adoption: An empirical Investigation. *Global Business Review*, *19*(3_suppl), S90–S113. doi:10.1177/0972150918757883

Chen, V. H. H., Duh, H. B. L., Phuah, P. S. K., & Lam, D. Z. Y. (2006). Enjoyment or engagement? Role of social interaction in playing massively mulitplayer online role-playing games (MMORPGS). In Proceedings of International Conference on Entertainment Computing (pp. 262-267). Springer, Berlin, Heidelberg.

Chen, Z., Wu, J., Gan, W., & Qi, Z. (2022, December). Metaverse security and privacy: An overview. In *2022 IEEE International Conference on Big Data (Big Data)* (pp. 2950-2959). IEEE. 10.1109/BigData55660.2022.10021112

Cheng, X., Zhang, S., Liu, W., & Mou, J. (2023). Understanding visitors' metaverse and in-person tour intentions during the COVID-19 pandemic: A coping perspective. *Proceedings of the Annual Hawaii International Conference on System Sciences*. 10.1108/JHTI-09-2022-0426

Chengoden, R., Victor, N., Huynh-The, T., Yenduri, G., Jhaveri, R. H., Alazab, M., Bhattacharya, S., Hegde, P., Maddikunta, P. K. R., & Gadekallu, T. R. (2023). Metaverse for Healthcare: A Survey on Potential Applications, Challenges and Future Directions. *IEEE Access : Practical Innovations, Open Solutions*, *11*, 12765–12795. Advance online publication. doi:10.1109/ACCESS.2023.3241628

Cheng, R., Wu, N., Chen, S., & Han, B. (2022). Will Metaverse Be NextG Internet? Vision, Hype, and Reality. *IEEE Network*, *36*(5), 197–204. Advance online publication. doi:10.1109/MNET.117.2200055

Chen, S., Chan, I. C. C., Xu, S., Law, R., & Zhang, M. (2023). Metaverse in tourism: Drivers and hindrances from stakeholders' perspective. *Journal of Travel & Tourism Marketing*, *40*(2), 169–184. doi:10.1080/10548408.2023.2227872

Chen, W. (2023). Developing a Sustainable Business Model of Ecotourism in Ethnic-Minority Regions Guided by the Green Economy Concept. *Sustainability (Basel)*, *15*(2), 1400. doi:10.3390/su15021400

Chen, Y. (2020). An overview of augmented reality technology. *Journal of Physics: Conference Series* (Vol. 1237, No. 2, p. 022082). doi:10.1088/1742-6596/1575/1/012027

Childers, T. L., Carr, C. L., Peck, J., & Carson, S. (2001). Hedonic and utilitarian motivations for online retail shopping behavior. *Journal of Retailing*, *77*(4), 511–535. doi:10.1016/S0022-4359(01)00056-2

Cho, Y. H., Wang, Y., & Fesenmaier, D. R. (2002, October 1). Searching for Experiences. *Journal of Travel & Tourism Marketing*, *12*(4), 1–17. Advance online publication. doi:10.1300/J073v12n04_01

Ciborra, C. U. (2002). *Teams, Markets, Systems: Business Innovation and Information Technology*. Cambridge University Press.

CIPD. (2020). *Induction*. Retrieved November 13, 2022, from https://www.cipd.ie/news-resources/practical-guidance/factsheets/induction#gref

Cipresso, P., & Giglioli, I. A. C. (2018). The Past, Present, and Future of Virtual. *Frontiers in Psychology*.

Colley, A., Suoheimo, M., & Häkkilä, J. (2020). Exploring VR and AR Tools for Service Design. *19th International Conference on Mobile and Ubiquitous Multimedia*, 309-311. 10.1145/3428361.3432074

Colors, C. I. (2023, October 18). *In Bali, "sea-sun-sand" tourists threaten ancient rainforest*. Eco-Business. https://www.eco-business.com/news/in-bali-sea-sun-sand-tourists-threaten-ancient-rainforest

Corne, A., Massot, V., & Merasli, S. (2023). The determinants of the adoption of blockchain technology in the tourism sector and metaverse perspectives. *Information Technology & Tourism*, *25*(4), 605–633. Advance online publication. doi:10.1007/s40558-023-00263-y

Cruz-Lara, S., Cabello, J. M., Osswald, T., Collado, A., Franco, J. M., & Barrera, S. (2011). Tourism in virtual worlds: Means, goals and needs. In Handbook of Research on Practices and Outcomes in Virtual Worlds and Environments (Vol. 1). doi:10.4018/978-1-60960-762-3.ch009

Csikzentmihalyi, M. (1977). *Beyond Boredom and Anxiety*. Jossey-Bass.

Cugini, A. (2021). Religious tourism and Sustainability: From Devotion to Spiritual Experience. In Tourism in the Mediterranean Sea. doi:10.1108/978-1-80043-900-920211006

Cunha, L. (2003). *Introdução ao Turismo*. Editorial Verbo.

Damar, M. (2021). *Metaverse Shape of Your Life for Future: A bibliometric snapshot*. Academic Press.

Daricha, D. N. (2019). Religious Tourism Development in Ethiopia: Challenges and Opportunities at Adyame Yordanos Wonkshet St. Gabriel Monastery. *Journal of Tourism, Hospitality and Sports*. doi:10.7176/JTHS/40-02

David, B., & Chalon, R. (2023). Digitalization and virtual assistive systems in tourist mobility: evolution, an experience (with observed mistakes), appropriate orientations and recommendations. Lecture Notes in Computer Science (including subseries Lecture Notes in Artificial Intelligence and Lecture Notes in Bioinformatics).

Davis, A., Murphy, J. D., Owens, D., Khazanchi, D., & Zigurs, I. (2009). Avatars, people, and virtual worlds: Foundations for research in Metaverses. *Journal of the Association for Information Systems*, *10*(2), 90–117. doi:10.17705/1jais.00183

Davis, F. D. (1989). Perceived usefulness, perceived ease of use, and user acceptance of information technology. *Management Information Systems Quarterly*, *13*(3), 319–340. doi:10.2307/249008

Davis, F. D., Bagozzi, R. P., & Warshaw, P. R. (1992). Extrinsic and intrinsic motivation to use computers in the workplace. *Journal of Applied Social Psychology*, *22*(14), 1111–1132. doi:10.1111/j.1559-1816.1992.tb00945.x

De Ponti, R., Marazzato, J., Maresca, A. M., Rovera, F., Carcano, G., & Ferrario, M. M. (2020). Pre-graduation medical training including virtual reality during COVID-19 pandemic: A report on students' perception. *BMC Medical Education*, *20*(1), 1–7. doi:10.1186/s12909-020-02245-8 PMID:32977781

de Reget, A. (2020). The Virtual Reality Chain. *Business Horizons*, *63*(6), 737–748. doi:10.1016/j.bushor.2020.08.002

Deloitte. (2017, January 15). *HR bots: the new superpower for the workforce?* Retrieved November 13, 2022, from https://www2.deloitte.com/content/dam/Deloitte/us/Documents/human-capital/us-cons-hr-bots-new-super-power-for-workforce.pdf

Demircioğlu, A. (2020). Introducing the cities of Ghazali in the context of religious tourism. In Global Development of Religious Tourism. doi:10.4018/978-1-7998-5792-1.ch003

DeSmet, S. A. (2015). *Gamification in Tourism* [Ph.D. Thesis]. Faculty of Economics and Business, KU Leuven.

Di Giovine Michael, A., & Elsner, J. (2016). Pilgrimage tourism. In H. Jafari Jafar and Xiao (Ed.), Encyclopedia of Tourism (pp. 722–724). Springer International Publishing. doi:10.1007/978-3-319-01384-8_146

Di Milano Milano Italy, M. C. P. (n.d.). *Emotion Tracking in Virtual Reality Fashion Shows | Extended Reality*. Guide Proceedings. https://dl.acm.org/doi/abs/10.1007/978-3-031-43401-3_31

Diekfuss, J. A., Bonnette, S., Hogg, J. A., Riehm, C., Grooms, D. R., Singh, H., Anand, M., Slutsky-Ganesh, A. B., Wilkerson, G. B., & Myer, G. D. (2021). Practical training strategies to apply neuro-mechanistic motor learning principles to facilitate adaptations towards injury-resistant movement in youth. *Journal of Science in Sport and Exercise*, *3*(1), 3–16. doi:10.1007/s42978-020-00083-0

Disztinger, P., Schlögl, S., & Groth, A. (2017, January 1). *Technology Acceptance of Virtual Reality for Travel Planning*. Springer eBooks. doi:10.1007/978-3-319-51168-9_19

Dobrowolski, P., Pochwatko, G., Skorko, M., & Bielecki, M. (2014). The effects of virtual experience on attitudes toward real brands. Cyberpsychology, Behavior, and Social Networking, 17(2), 125–128. Economic Times. (2017). India to have 530mn smartphone users in 2018: Study. Retrieved from: https://telecom. economictimes.indiatimes.com/news/india-to-have-530mnsmartphone-users-in-2018-study/61097817

Dogru, T., Mody, C., & Leonard, C. (2018). Blockchain Technology & its Implications for the Hospitality Industry. *Boston Hospitality Review*. www.bu.edu/bhr

Donthu, N., Kumar, S., Mukherjee, D., Pandey, N., & Lim, W. M. (2021). How to conduct a bibliometric analysis: An overview and guidelines. *Journal of Business Research*, *133*, 285–296. doi:10.1016/j.jbusres.2021.04.070

Druin, M. J. (2002). The Role of Children in the Design of New Technology. *Behaviour & Information Technology*.

Drumm, A., Moore, A., & Conservancy, N. (2002, January 1). *Ecotourism Development: The business of ecotourism development and management*. Academic Press.

Dubé-Rioux, L. (1990). *The Power of Affective Reports in Predicting Satisfaction Judgments*. https://www.semanticscholar.org/paper/The-Power-of-Affective-Reports-in-Predicting-Dub%C3%A9-Rioux/be71ecf2e6e96da73faeab2c78775a10fb484998

Dubovskiy, J. (2016). *Realism Research Philosophy*. Retrieved January 9, 2023, from https://research-methodology.net/research-philosophy/realism/

Dudovskiy, J. (2017). *Research Philosophy*. Retrieved January 9, 2023, from https://research-methodology.net/research-philosophy/

Dutta, D., Srivastava, Y., & Singh, E. (2023). Metaverse in the tourism sector for talent management: A technology in practice lens. *Information Technology & Tourism*, *25*(3), 331–365. Advance online publication. doi:10.1007/s40558-023-00258-9

Dwivedi, Y., Hughes, L., Baabdullah, A., Ribeiro-Navarrete, S., Giannakis, M., Al-Debei, M., Dennehy, D., Metri, B., Buhalis, D., Cheung, C., Conboy, K., Doyle, R., Goyal, D. P., Gustafsson, A., Jebabli, I., Kim, Y.-G., Kim, J., Koos, S., Kreps, D., ... Wamba, F. (2022). Metaverse beyond the hype: Multidisciplinary perspectives on emerging challenges, opportunities, and agenda for research, practice and policy. *International Journal of Information Management*, *66*, 102542. doi:10.1016/j.ijinfomgt.2022.102542

Dwivedi, Y., Hughes, L., Wang, Y., Alalwan, A. A., Ahn, S., Balakrishnan, J., Barta, S., Belk, R., Buhalis, D., Dutot, V., Felix, R., & Filieri, R. (n.d.). How Metaverse will change the future of marketing: Implications for Research and Practice. *Psychology and Marketing*. Advance online publication. doi:10.1002/mar.21767

Ecotourism World. (2021b, April 19). *What is Ecotourism? The Evolution of Ecotourism in Recent Years.* https://ecotourism-world.com/what-is-ecotourism-the-evolution-of-ecotourism-in-recent-years/

Edge, R. (2022). *The Necessary Evolution of Privacy Program Automation.* Retrieved November 13, 2022, from https://www.onetrust.com/blog/the-necessary-evolution-of-privacy-program-automation/

El-Din, D. M., Hassanein, A. E., & Darwish, A. (2023). Multimodal data challenge in metaverse technology. In Studies in Big Data (Vol. 123, pp. 185-210). doi:10.1007/978-3-031-29132-6_11

El-Said, O., & Aziz, H. (2022). Virtual tours a means to an end: An analysis of virtual tours' role in tourism recovery post COVID-19. *Journal of Travel Research*, *61*(3), 528–548. doi:10.1177/0047287521997567

El-Shamy, S. (2003). *Dynamic Induction: Games, Activities and Ideas to Revitalize your Employee Induction Process.* Routledge.

Erdem, A., & Barakazı, M. (2023). Innovative technology applications in hotel businesses. In Tourism, Hospitality and Event Management (Vol. Part F275, pp. 17-36). doi:10.1007/978-3-031-31682-1_2

European Commission. (2018). *Are there restrictions on the use of automated decision-making?* Retrieved November 12, 2022, from https://ec.europa.eu/info/law/law-topic/data-protection/reform/rules-business-and-organisations/dealing-citizens/are-there-restrictions-use-automated-decision-making_en

Evans, J. R., & Lindsay, W. M. (2013). *Managing for quality and performance excellence.* Cengage Learning.

Ezenagu, N., Okpoko, P. U., & Okpoko, C. (2021). Faith-based activities and religious tourism in southwestern Nigeria: Challenging factors. *Ikenga*, *22*(3), 1–25. Advance online publication. doi:10.53836/ijia/2021/22/3/006

Falk, R.F., & Miller, N.B. (1992). *A Primer for Soft Modeling.* University of Akron Press. https://www.scirp.org/reference/ReferencesPapers?ReferenceID=1323343

Fan, Z., Chen, C., & Huang, H. (2022). Immersive cultural heritage digital documentation and information service for historical figure metaverse: A case of Zhu Xi, Song Dynasty, China. *Heritage Science*, *10*(1), 148. Advance online publication. doi:10.1186/s40494-022-00749-8 PMID:36185636

Farshid, M., Paschen, J., Eriksson, T., & Kietzmann, J. (2018). Go boldly! Explore augmented reality (AR), virtual reality (VR), and mixed reality (MR) for business. *Business Horizons*, *61*(5), 657–663. doi:10.1016/j.bushor.2018.05.009

Faulkner, D. (2022). Hyper-reality: a dangerous modern phenomenon. In Creative Business Education: Exploring the Contours of Pedagogical Praxis (pp. 185-198). doi:10.1007/978-3-031-10928-7_11

Fennell, D. A. (2003). *Ecotourism: An Introduction* (2nd ed.). Routledge.

Fernandes, F., & Werner, C. (2022). *Accessibility in the Metaverse: Are We Prepared?* doi:10.5753/waihcws.2022.226618

Fernández-Álvarez, Ó., González-González, M., & Ouali-Fernández, S. (2022). Religious Heritage: Reconciliation between Spirituality and Cultural Concerns. *Rupkatha Journal on Interdisciplinary Studies in Humanities*, *14*(4). Advance online publication. doi:10.21659/rupkatha.v14n4.29

Filimonau, V., Ashton, M., & Stankov, U. (2022). Virtual spaces as the future of consumption in tourism, hospitality and events. *Journal of Tourism Futures*. doi:10.1108/JTF-07-2022-0174

Flick, U. (2014). *An introduction to qualitative research* (5th ed.). Sage Publications Ltd.

Folgieri, R., Gricar, S., & Baldigara, T. (2023). NFTs: What opportunities and challenges in tourism? *Tourism & Hospitality Industry 2022, Congress Proceedings*. 10.20867/thi.26.3

Fornell, C., & Larcker, D.F. (1981). Evaluating Structural Equation Models with Unobservable Variables and Measurement Error. *Journal of Marketing Research, 18,* 39-50. https://www.scirp.org/reference/ReferencesPapers?ReferenceID=1927929

Foster, A. D. (2021). *The NFT Wars Have Begun*. MIT Technology Review.

Fotakis, T., & Economides, A. A. (2008). Art, science/technology and history museums on the web. *International Journal of Digital Culture and Electronic Tourism*, *1*(1), 37–63. doi:10.1504/IJDCET.2008.020134

Fox, J., Arena, D., & Bailenson, J. N. (2009). Virtual reality: A survival guide for the social scientist. *Journal of Media Psychology*, *21*(3), 95–113. doi:10.1027/1864-1105.21.3.95

Gaafar, A. A. (2021). Metaverse In Architectural Heritage Documentation & Education. *Advances in Ecological and Environmental Research, 6*.

Gaines, J., & Lee, C. V. (2019). Medical tourism. Travel Medicine, 371–375. Gardiner, S., King, B., & Wilkins, H. (2013). The travel behaviours of international students: Nationality-based constraints and opportunities. *Journal of Vacation Marketing*, *19*(4), 287–299.

Garrido-Iñigo, P., & Rodríguez-Moreno, F. (2015). The reality of virtual worlds: Pros and cons of their application to foreign language teaching. *Interactive Learning Environments*, *23*(4), 453–470. doi:10.1080/10494820.2013.788034

Gartner. (2015). *Gartner says the Internet of things installed base will grow to 26 billion units by 2020.* Retrieved May 30, 2019, from https://www.mcit.gov.sa/en/media-center/news/91424

Gautam, V. (2012). *An empirical investigation of consumers' preferences about tourism services in indian context with special reference to state of Himachal Pradesh.* https://ideas.repec.org/a/eee/touman/v33y2012i6p1591-1592.html

Gautam, V. (2012). An empirical investigation of consumers' preferences about tourism services in Indian context with special reference to state of Himachal Pradesh. *Tourism Management*, *33*(6), 1591–1592. doi:10.1016/j.tourman.2011.12.014

Gefen, D., & Straub, D. W. (1997, December 1). Gender Differences in the Perception and Use of E-Mail: An Extension to the Technology Acceptance Model. *Management Information Systems Quarterly*, *21*(4), 389. Advance online publication. doi:10.2307/249720

Gent, E. (2022). Lessons from a Second Life before Meta, Philip Rosedale Created an Online Universe. *IEEE Spectrum*, *59*(1), 19. doi:10.1109/MSPEC.2022.9676346

George, G., & Thomas, M. (2019). Integration of Artificial Intelligence in Human Resource. *International Journal of Innovative Technology and Exploring Engineering*, *9*(2), 5069–5072. doi:10.35940/ijitee.L3364.129219

Gettecla. (2018). *Augmented Reality and Accessibility.* https://gettecla.com/blogs/news/augmented-reality-and-accessibility

Gikopoulus, J. (2019). Alongside, not against: Balancing man with machine in the HR function. *Strategic HR Review*, *18*(2), 55–61. doi:10.1108/SHR-12-2018-0103

Global Tourism Investors Summit 2023 | Tourism Investors Meet Delhi, India. (n.d.). https://www.gtistourism.in/

Glover, G. (2022). *Bank of America shares how to invest in the Metaverse and 13 other disruptive technologies that could transform our lives and become a market worth over $6 trillion by 2030.* Retrieved from https://www.businessinsider.com /investing-strategy-tech-6g-Metaverse-flying-cars-ai-moonshots-2021-9

Go, H., & Kang, M. (2023). Metaverse tourism for sustainable tourism development: Tourism Agenda 2030. *Tourism Review*, *78*(2), 381–394. Advance online publication. doi:10.1108/TR-02-2022-0102

Goni, F. A., Gholamzadeh Chofreh, A., Estaki Orakani, Z., Klemeš, J. J., Davoudi, M., & Mardani, A. (2021). Sustainable business model: A review and framework development. *Clean Technologies and Environmental Policy*, *23*(3), 889–897. doi:10.1007/s10098-020-01886-z

González-Rodríguez, M. R., Díaz-Fernández, M. C., & Pino-Mejías, M. Á. (2020). The impact of virtual reality technology on tourists' experience: A textual data analysis. *Soft Computing*, *24*(18), 13879–13892. Advance online publication. doi:10.1007/s00500-020-04883-y

Goode, J. W. (2000). *Privacy in Cyberspace: Protecting Personal Information in the Online World*. RAND Corporation.

Gössling, S., Scott, D., & Hall, C. M. (2021). Tourism and Water: Dimensions of Tourism (Vol. 1). Channel View Publications.

Grandviewresearch. (2020). *Augmented Reality Market Size, Share & Trends Analysis Report By Component, By Display (HMD & Smart Glass, HUD, Handheld Devices), By Application, By Region, And Segment Forecasts, 2021 – 2028*. https://www.grandviewresearch.com/industry-analysis/augmented-reality-market

Grundmann, G., Klein, F., & Josten, F. (2022, December 21). Sustainability in business: Staying ahead of the curve. *Deloitte Insights*. https://www2.deloitte.com/xe/en/insights/topics/strategy/sustainability-in-business-staying-ahead-of-the-curve.html

Guan, J., Irizawa, J., & Morris, A. (2022). Extended Reality and Internet of Things for Hyper-Connected Metaverse Environments. *Proceedings - 2022 IEEE Conference on Virtual Reality and 3D User Interfaces Abstracts and Workshops, VRW 2022*. 10.1109/VRW55335.2022.00043

Gupta, S., & Kim, H.W. (2010). Value-Driven Internet Shopping The Mental Accounting Theory Perspective. *Psychology and Marketing, 27*, 13-35. https://www.scirp.org/reference/references papers?referenceid=2503340

Gupta, A., & Gupta, N. (2022). *Research Methodology*. SBPD Publications.

Gursoy, D., Malodia, S., & Dhir, A. (2022). The metaverse in the hospitality and tourism industry: An overview of current trends and future research directions. *Journal of Hospitality Marketing & Management*, *31*(5), 527–534. Advance online publication. doi:10.1080/19368623.2022.2072504

Gursoy, I. T., Aktas, E., Tecim, V., & Kurgun, O. A. (2023). Beta tourist world: A conceptual framework for organizing an event in the metaverse. *Information Technology & Tourism*, *25*(4), 529–548. Advance online publication. doi:10.1007/s40558-023-00266-9

Guttentag, D. A. (2010). *Virtual reality: Applications and implications for tourism*. https://econpapers.repec.org/article/eeetouman/v_3a31_3ay_3a2010_3ai_3a5_3ap_3a637-651.htm

Habib, G., Sharma, S., Ibrahim, S., Ahmad, I., Qureshi, S., & Ishfaq, M. (2022). Blockchain Technology: Benefits, Challenges, Applications, and Integration of Blockchain Technology with Cloud Computing. *Future Internet*, *14*(11), 341. doi:10.3390/fi14110341

Haider, M. J., Changchun, G., Akram, T., & Hussain, S. T. (2018). Does gender differences play any role in intention to adopt Islamic mobile banking? An empirical study. *Journal of Islamic Marketing*, *9*(2), 439–460. doi:10.1108/JIMA-11-2016-0082

Hair, J. F., Anderson, R. E., Tatham, R. L., & Black, W. C. (1995). *Multivariate data analysis.* Prentice-Hall. https://www.scirp.org/reference/referencespapers?referenceid=435421

Hair, J.F., Black, W.C., Babin, B.J., & Anderson, R.E. (2010). *Multivariate Data Analysis.* Pearson. https://www.scirp.org/reference/ReferencesPapers?ReferenceID=1841396

Hair, J. F., Black, W. C., Babin, B. J., & Anderson, R. E. (2010). *Multivariate data analysis* (7th ed.). Prentice-Hall.

Haller, M. (2019). Designing for User Engagement in Virtual Reality. *Communications of the ACM.*

Hanafizadeh, P., Behboudi, M., Koshksaray, A. A., & Tabar, M. J. S. (2014). Mobile-Banking Adoption by Iranian Bank Clients. *Telematics and Informatics, 31*, 62-78. https://www.scirp.org/reference/referencespapers?referenceid=2915106

Haq, F. (2013). Islamic spiritual tourism: An innovative marketing framework. *International Journal of Social Entrepreneurship and Innovation*, *2*(5), 438. Advance online publication. doi:10.1504/IJSEI.2013.059320

Harrisson, T. (2020, August 27). *Tourism responsible for 8% of global greenhouse gas emissions, study finds*. Carbon Brief. https://www.carbonbrief.org/tourism-responsible-for-8-of-global-greenhouse-gas-emissions-study-finds /-

Haugstvedt, A. C., & Krogstie, J. (2012). Mobile augmented reality for cultural heritage: A technology acceptance study. In *Proceedings of International Symposium on Mixed and Augmented Reality (ISMAR)*, (pp. 247–255). IEEE. 10.1109/ISMAR.2012.6402563

Havard, V., Jeanne, B., Lacomblez, M., & Baudry, D. (2019). Digital twin and virtual reality: A co-simulation environment for design and assessment of industrial workstations. *Production & Manufacturing Research*, *7*(1), 472–489. doi:10.1080/21693277.2019.1660283

Haywood, K. E. (2020). Democratizing Virtual Reality: A Quantitative Exploration of Virtual Reality and Its Implications for Accessibility. *Proceedings of the Human Factors and Ergonomics Society Annual Meeting.*

He, J., Wang, M., Xi, G., Zhu, H., Dai, J., & Zhang, X. (2023). Research progress and prospects of Chinese cybergeography against the background of the digital transition. *Tropical Geography*, *43*(4), 567–580. doi:10.13284/j.cnki.rddl.003667

Henderson, J. C. (2011). Religious tourism and its management: The hajj in Saudi Arabia. *International Journal of Tourism Research*, *13*(6), 541–552. Advance online publication. doi:10.1002/jtr.825

Hendricks, D. (2023, March 1). *How to Create a Sustainable Business Model.* business.com. https://www.business.com/articles/how-to-create-a-sustainable-business-model

Higgins-Desbiolles, F., Bigby, B. C., & Doering, A. (2022). Socialising tourism after COVID-19: Reclaiming tourism as a social force? *Journal of Tourism Futures*, *8*(2), 208–219. Advance online publication. doi:10.1108/JTF-03-2021-0058

Higham, J. (2007). Ecotourism: Competing and conflicting schools of thought. *Critical issues in ecotourism: Understanding a complex tourism phenomenon*, 1-19.

Hillmann, C. (2019, January 1). *The VR Ecosystem and What to Expect in the Years to Come*. Apress eBooks. doi:10.1007/978-1-4842-4360-2_1

Hiltzik, L. M. (2018). Digital Travel: How Big Data is Changing the Travel Industry. *Los Angeles Times*.

Hirunyawipada, T. (n.d.). *Consumer Innovativeness and Perceived Risk: Implications for High Technology Product Adoption*. eCommons. https://ecommons.udayton.edu/mgt_fac_pub/66/

Hollensen, S., Kotler, P., & Opresnik, M. O. (2022). Metaverse – the new marketing universe. *The Journal of Business Strategy*. Advance online publication. doi:10.1108/JBS-01-2022-0014

Hooper-Greenhill, J. (1994). Virtual Reality and the Art Museum. *Curator (New York, N.Y.)*.

Howells, J. (2011). *The Dissolving of Private and Public Property: Reconsidering Digital Landscapes*. Research in Art Education.

Huang, X. (2021). The technological essence and philosophical significance of the Metaverse. *Metaverse*, *2*(2), 10. Advance online publication. doi:10.54517/met.v2i2.1786

Huang, X. T., Wang, J., Wang, Z., Wang, L., & Cheng, C. (2023). Experimental study on the influence of virtual tourism spatial situation on the tourists' temperature comfort in the context of metaverse. *Frontiers in Psychology*, *13*, 1062876. Advance online publication. doi:10.3389/fpsyg.2022.1062876 PMID:36687952

Huang, Y. C., Backman, K. F., Backman, S. J., & Chang, L. L. (2016). Exploring the implications of virtual reality technology in tourism marketing: An integrated research framework. *International Journal of Tourism Research*, *18*(2), 116–128. doi:10.1002/jtr.2038

Huang, Y., Li, Y. J., & Cai, Z. (2023). Security and Privacy in Metaverse: A Comprehensive Survey. *Big Data Mining and Analytics*, *6*(2), 234–247. Advance online publication. doi:10.26599/BDMA.2022.9020047

Hui, X., Raza, S. H., Khan, S. W., Zaman, U., & Ogadimma, E. C. (2023). Exploring regenerative tourism using media richness theory: Emerging role of immersive journalism, metaverse-based promotion, eco-literacy, and pro-environmental behavior. *Sustainability (Basel)*, *15*(6), 5046. Advance online publication. doi:10.3390/su15065046

Hutson, J., & Hutson, P. (2023). Museums and the Metaverse – Emerging Technologies to Promote Inclusivity and Engagement. In *Application of Modern Trends in Museums*. IntechOpen. doi:10.5772/intechopen.110044

Hwang, K., tom Dieck, M. C., Jung, T., & Kwon, O. (2023). The influence of virtual reality on the experience of religious cultural heritage content. *Internet Research*. Advance online publication. doi:10.1108/INTR-08-2022-0669

Idris, J. (2019). Spiritual motivation for religious tourism destinations. In Spiritual and religious tourism : motivations and management. doi:10.1079/9781786394163.0059

Imoize, A. L., Adedeji, O., Tandiya, N., & Shetty, S. (2021). 6G Enabled Smart Infrastructure for Sustainable Society: Opportunities, Challenges, and Research Roadmap. *Sensors (Basel), 21*(5), 1709. doi:10.3390/s21051709 PMID:33801302

In, T. Jung, & M. C. tom Dieck (eds.), Augmented reality and virtual reality (pp. 93–107). Cham: Springer. Global Travel Intention (GTI). (2018). Indian travelers take longer trips, more frequently, and spend 40% more than their regional counterparts - Visa Study | Press Release | Visa. Retrieved from https://www.visa.co.in/about-visa/ newsroom/press-releases/indian-travelers-take-longer-tripsmore-frequently-and-spend-40-percent-more-than-theirregional-counterparts-visa-study.html

Inder, S. (2022). Entrepreneurial opportunities in metaverse. In Promoting Consumer Engagement Through Emotional Branding and Sensory Marketing (pp. 52-62). doi:10.4018/978-1-6684-5897-6.ch006

India Blockchain Alliance. (n.d.). *AI in Blockchain Technology – The Possibilities of Integrating AI with Blockchain*. White Paper.

Internet and social media users in the world 2023. (n.d.). Statista. Retrieved November 29, 2023, from https://www.statista.com/statistics/617136/digital-population-worldwide /

Irfan, E., & Ali, Y. (2020). Religious tourism in Pakistan: Scope, obstacles & strategies. *Journal of Convention & Event Tourism, 22*(2), 134–154. Advance online publication. doi:10.1080/15470148.2020.1852990

Ivana, D., & Chiripuci, B. (2020). Human Ressource practices in improving employee retention. *Review of Economic Studies and Research Virgil Madgearu, 13*(1), 33–43. doi:10.24193/RVM.2020.13.50

Jackson, C. M., Chow, S., & Leitch, R. A. (1997). Toward an understanding of the behavioral intention to use an information system. *Decision Sciences, 28*(2), 357–389. doi:10.1111/j.1540-5915.1997.tb01315.x

Jafar, R. M. S., & Ahmad, W. (2023). Tourist loyalty in the metaverse: The role of immersive tourism experience and cognitive perceptions. *Tourism Review*. Advance online publication. doi:10.1108/TR-11-2022-0552

Jang, S., Chong, K., & Yoo, C. (2021). The effect of mobile application-driven customer participation on bakery purchase behavior: Evidence from a field experiment. *International Journal of Hospitality Management, 94*, 102865. doi:10.1016/j.ijhm.2021.102865

Jennett, C., Cox, A. L., Cairns, P., Dhoparee, S., Epps, A., Tijs, T., & Walton, A. (2008). Measuring and defining the experience of immersion in games. *International Journal of Human-Computer Studies, 66*(9), 641–661. doi:10.1016/j.ijhcs.2008.04.004

Jeong, M., & Shin, H. H. (2020). Tourists' Experiences with Smart Tourism Technology at Smart Destinations and Their Behavior Intentions. *Journal of Travel Research*, *59*(8), 1464–1477. doi:10.1177/0047287519883034

Jepkorir, C., Mose, T., & Mwalili, T. (2022, October 14). Factors affecting adoption of internet of things in selected greenhouse farms in Kenya. *International Journal of Technology and Systems*. doi:10.47604/ijts.1668

Jiang, J. (2022). Metaverse: Homogenization experience and cultural illusion. *Metaverse*, *3*(1), 8. Advance online publication. doi:10.54517/met.v3i1.1811

Jiang, S. (2016). Purchase intention for electric vehicles in China from a customer-value perspective. *Social Behavior and Personality*, *44*(4), 641–656. doi:10.2224/sbp.2016.44.4.641

Jia, Q., Guo, Y., Li, R., Li, Y., & Chen, Y. (2018). A Conceptual Artificial Intelligence Application Framework in Human Resource Management. *International Conference on Electronic Business*, 106-114.

Ji, Q., Deng, H., Zhang, H., Jiang, W., Zhong, F., & Rao, F. (2021). Optical See-through 2D/3D Compatible Display Using Variable-Focus Lens and Multiplexed Holographic Optical Elements. *Photonics*, *8*(8), 297. doi:10.3390/photonics8080297

Jo, H. (2023). Tourism in the digital frontier: A study on user continuance intention in the metaverse. *Information Technology & Tourism*, *25*(3), 307–330. Advance online publication. doi:10.1007/s40558-023-00257-w

Jones, P. R., Somoskeöy, T., Chow-Wing-Bom, H., & Crabb, D. P. (2020). Seeing other perspectives: Evaluating the use of virtual and augmented reality to simulate visual impairments (OpenVisSim). *NPJ Digital Medicine*, *3*(1), 1–9. doi:10.1038/s41746-020-0242-6 PMID:32195367

Jovanović, A., & Milosavljević, A. (2022). VoRtex Metaverse Platform for Gamified Collaborative Learning. *Electronics (Basel)*, *11*(3), 317. Advance online publication. doi:10.3390/electronics11030317

Jung, T. H., Lee, H., Chung, N., & Tom Dieck, M. C. (2018). Cross-cultural differences in adopting mobile augmented reality at cultural heritage tourism sites. *International Journal of Contemporary Hospitality Management*, *30*(3), 1621–1645. doi:10.1108/IJCHM-02-2017-0084

Jun, J., Cho, I., & Park, H. (2018). Factors influencing continued use of mobile easy payment service: An empirical investigation. *Total Quality Management & Business Excellence*, *29*(9–10), 1043–1057. doi:10.1080/14783363.2018.1486550

Kaddoura, S., & Al Husseiny, F. (2023). The rising trend of Metaverse in education: Challenges, opportunities, and ethical considerations. *PeerJ. Computer Science*, *9*, e1252. Advance online publication. doi:10.7717/peerj-cs.1252 PMID:37346578

Kamata, H. (2022). Tourist destination residents' attitudes towards tourism during and after the COVID-19 pandemic. *Current Issues in Tourism*, *25*(1), 134–149. Advance online publication. doi:10.1080/13683500.2021.1881452

Kamboj, S., & Joshi, R. (2021). Examining the factors influencing smartphone apps use at tourism destinations: A UTAUT model perspective. *International Journal of Tourism Cities*, *7*(1), 135–157. doi:10.1108/IJTC-05-2020-0094

Kaushik, V., & Walsh, C. (2019). Pragmatism as a Research Paradigm and Its Implications for Social Work Research. *Social Sciences (Basel, Switzerland)*, *8*(9), 255. doi:10.3390/socsci8090255

Kenaphoom, S. (2021). Introduction to Research Philosophy. *Journal of Anthropological And Archaeological Sciences*, *5*(4), 657–661.

Kersten, T. P., & Edler, D. (2020). *Special issue "methods and applications of virtual and augmented reality in geo-information sciences". Deutsche Gesellschaft für Photogrammetrie, Fernerkundung und Geoinformation*. DGPF.

Khandelwal, K., & Upadhyay, A. K. (2021). Virtual reality interventions in developing and managing human resources. *Human Resource Development International*, *24*(2), 219–233. doi:10.1080/13678868.2019.1569920

Kim, J. (2021). Advertising in the Metaverse: Research Agenda. In Journal of Interactive Advertising (Vol. 21, Issue 3). doi:10.1080/15252019.2021.2001273

Kim, M. J., & Kim, D. Y. (2023). The metaverse as a new travel marketing platform. In Routledge Handbook of Trends and Issues in Global Tourism Supply and Demand (pp. 209-220). doi:10.4324/9781003260790-22

Kim, B., Kim, S., & King, B. (2020). Religious tourism studies: Evolution, progress, and future prospects. *Tourism Recreation Research*, *45*(2), 185–203. Advance online publication. doi:10.1080/02508281.2019.1664084

Kim, J. H., Ritchie, J. R., & Tung, V. W. S. (2010). The effect of memorable experience on behavioral intentions in tourism: A structural equation modeling approach. *Tourism Analysis*, *15*(6), 637–648. doi:10.3727/108354210X12904412049776

Kim, J., & Fesenmaier, D. R. (2015). Measuring emotions in real time: Implications for tourism experience design. *Journal of Travel Research*, *54*(4), 419–429. doi:10.1177/0047287514550100

Kim, S. H., Agrawal, S., & Srivastava, S. (2015). Reciprocity in Online Product Reviews: The Role of Reviewer Identity and Review Valence. *Journal of Marketing*.

Klungseth, N. J., & Danivska, V. (2021). Service management – focus on customer experience. In Routledge eBooks (pp. 205–219). doi:10.1201/9781003128786-18

Koo, C., Kwon, J., Chung, N., & Kim, J. (2023). Metaverse tourism: conceptual framework and research propositions. In Current Issues in Tourism (Vol. 26, Issue 20). doi:10.1080/13683500.2022.2122781

Koohang, A., Nord, J. H., Ooi, K. B., Tan, G. W. H., Al-Emran, M., Aw, E. C. X., Baabdullah, A. M., Buhalis, D., Cham, T.-H., Dennis, C., Dutot, V., Dwivedi, Y. K., Hughes, L., Mogaji, E., Pandey, N., Phau, I., Raman, R., Sharma, A., Sigala, M., ... Wong, L. W. (2023). Shaping the metaverse into reality: A holistic multidisciplinary understanding of opportunities, challenges, and avenues for future investigation. *Journal of Computer Information Systems*, *63*(3), 735–765. doi:10.1080/08874417.2023.2165197

Koohsari, M. J., McCormack, G. R., Nakaya, T., Yasunaga, A., Fuller, D., Nagai, Y., & Oka, K. (2023). The metaverse, the built environment, and public health: Opportunities and uncertainties. *Journal of Medical Internet Research*, *25*, e43549. doi:10.2196/43549 PMID:36780208

Kouroupi, N., & Metaxas, T. (2023). Can the Metaverse and Its Associated Digital Tools and Technologies Provide an Opportunity for Destinations to Address the Vulnerability of Overtourism? *Tourism and Hospitality*, *4*(2), 355–373. doi:10.3390/tourhosp4020022

Krum, J. M. (2016). *Virtual Reality: Principles and Practice*. Addison-Wesley Professional.

Kshetri, N., Rojas-Torres, D., & Grambo, M. (2022). The Metaverse and Higher Education Institutions. *IT Professional*, *24*(6), 69–73. Advance online publication. doi:10.1109/MITP.2022.3222711

Kucklich, J. (2012). The Consumption of Virtual Worlds: Extraction, Infrastructure, and Labor in MMORPGs. *Journal of Gaming & Virtual Worlds*.

Küçük, S., Kapakin, S., & Göktaş, Y. (2016). Learning anatomy via mobile augmented reality: Effects on achievement and cognitive load. *Anatomical Sciences Education*, *9*(5), 411–421. doi:10.1002/ase.1603 PMID:26950521

Kumar, S., Dhiraj, A., & Hassan, S. C. C. (2023). Metaverse and cultural marketing in hospitality and tourism. In Cultural Marketing and Metaverse for Consumer Engagement (pp. 224-233). doi:10.4018/978-1-6684-8312-1.ch016

Kumar, S., Dhiraj, A., Shah, M. A., & Rani, D. (2023). Application of metaverse in the hospitality industry. In Influencer Marketing Applications Within the Metaverse (pp. 178-194). doi:10.4018/978-1-6684-8898-0.ch011

Kumar, A. M., & Dutta, R. (2021). Development of an augmented reality-based scaffold to improve the learning experience of engineering students in embedded system course. *Computer Applications in Engineering Education*, *29*(1), 244–257. doi:10.1002/cae.22245

Kumar, R., Mukherjee, A., & Singh, V. P. (2017). Traffic noise mapping of Indian roads through smartphone user community participation. *Environmental Monitoring and Assessment*, *189*(1), 17. doi:10.1007/s10661-016-5741-1 PMID:27975332

Kumra, R. (2008, May). Service quality in rural tourism: A prescriptive approach. In *Proceedings of conference on tourism in India-Challenges ahead*, 15–17 May 2008 (pp. 424–431), IIMK.

Kusuma, P. A., Mutiarin, D., & Damanik, J. (2021). Strategi pemulihan dampak wabah covid pada sektor pariwisata di daerah istimewa yogyakarta. *Journal of Tourism and Economic*, *4*(1), 47–59. Advance online publication. doi:10.36594/jtec.v4i1.110

Kye, B., Han, N., Kim, E., Park, Y., & Jo, S. (2021). Educational applications of metaverse: Possibilities and limitations. In Journal of Educational Evaluation for Health Professions (Vol. 18). doi:10.3352/jeehp.2021.18.32

Lapointe, D. (2020). Reconnecting tourism after COVID-19: The paradox of alterity in tourism areas. *Tourism Geographies*, *22*(3), 633–638. Advance online publication. doi:10.1080/14616688.2020.1762115

Largan, C., & Morris, T. (2019). Qualitative Secondary Research: A Step-By-Step Guide. *Sage (Atlanta, Ga.)*.

Lazar, J. (2006). *Web Usability: A User-Centered Design Approach*. Pearson.

Lee, H., Chung, N., & Jung, T. (2015). Examining the cultural differences in acceptance of mobile augmented reality: Comparison of South Korea and Ireland. In I. Tussyadiah & A. Inversini (Eds.), *Information and communication technologies in tourism 2015* (pp. 477–491). Springer. doi:10.1007/978-3-319-14343-9_35

Lee, K.-S. (2017). A study of the impacts of virtual reality guided tours' affordances on user experiences. *International Journal of Tourism and Hospitality Research*, *31*(3), 105–118. Advance online publication. doi:10.21298/IJTHR.2017.03.31.3.105

Lee, L.-H., Braud, T., Zhou, P., Wang, L., Xu, D., Lin, Z., Kumar, A., Bermejo, C., & Hui, P. (2021). All One Needs to Know about Metaverse: A Complete Survey on Technological Singularity, Virtual Ecosystem, and Research Agenda. *J. Latex Cl. Files*, *14*, 1–66.

Lee, U. K. (2022). Tourism using virtual reality: Media richness and information system successes. *Sustainability (Basel)*, *14*(7), 3975. Advance online publication. doi:10.3390/su14073975

Lemmi, E. (2020). Heritage and new communication technologies: development perspectives on the basis of the Via Francigena experience. *Hthic*, 43–62. https://www.academia.edu/42977285/Heritage_and_new_communication_technologies_development_perspectives_on_the_basis_of_the_Via_Francigena_experience

Library. (2022). *HSS Research Methodologies: Quantitative Research*. DCU Library.

Liew, Z. Q., Du, H., Bryan Lim, W. Y., Xiong, Z., Niyato, D., & Yu, H. (2023). *Economics of semantic communication in metaverse: an auction approach. In Proceedings - IEEE Consumer Communications and Networking Conference*. CCNC.

Li, J., Hu, P., Cui, W., Huang, T., & Cheng, S. (2023). Deepsea: A meta-ocean prototype for undersea exploration. *Information Technology & Tourism*, *25*(3), 391–409. Advance online publication. doi:10.1007/s40558-023-00260-1

Lin, K. J., Ye, H., & Law, R. (2023). Understanding the development of blockchain-empowered metaverse tourism: An institutional perspective. *Information Technology & Tourism*, *25*(4), 585–603. Advance online publication. doi:10.1007/s40558-023-00262-z

Linnenluecke, M. K., Marrone, M., & Singh, A. K. (2019). Conducting systematic literature reviews and bibliometric analyses. *Australian Journal of Management*, *45*(2), 175–194. doi:10.1177/0312896219877678

Liu, Z., Gong, S., Tan, Z., & Demian, P. (2023). Immersive Technologies-Driven Building Information Modeling (BIM) in the Context of Metaverse. *Buildings*, *13*(6), 1559. Advance online publication. doi:10.3390/buildings13061559

Loftus, K. (2021). *How Much Energy Does the Internet Use?* BBC News.

Loureiro, S. M. C., Guerreiro, J., & Ali, F. (2020). *20 years of research on virtual reality and augmented reality in tourism context: A text-mining approach* (Vol. 77). Tourism Management.

Loureiro, S. M. C., Guerreiro, J., & Ali, F. (2020). 20 years of research on virtual reality and augmented reality in tourism context: A text-mining approach. *Tourism Management*, *77*, 104028. doi:10.1016/j.tourman.2019.104028

Lovells, H. (2023). *Digital Assets and Blockchain Hub – Blockchain Overview*. Engage Premium. https://engagepremium.hoganlovells.com/resources/bolckchain/overview

Ludlow, P., & Wallace, M. (2007). *The Second Life Herald: The Virtual Tabloid that Witnessed the Dawn of the Metaverse*. MIT Press.

Lu, J., Xiao, X., Xu, Z., Wang, C., Zhang, M., & Zhou, Y. (2022). The potential of virtual tourism in the recovery of tourism industry during the COVID-19 pandemic. *Current Issues in Tourism*, *25*(3), 441–457. Advance online publication. doi:10.1080/13683500.2021.1959526

Lundmark, P. (2022). *The real future of the Metaverse is not for consumers*. Retrieved from https://www.ft.com/content/af0c9de8-d36e-485b-9db5-5ee1e57716cb

Luz, N. (2020). Pilgrimage and religious tourism in Islam. *Annals of Tourism Research*, *82*, 102915. Advance online publication. doi:10.1016/j.annals.2020.102915

Lyon, D. (2001). *Surveillance Society: Monitoring Everyday Life*. Open University Press.

Ma, E., Hsiao, A., & Gao, J. (2018). Destination attractiveness and travel intention: The case of Chinese and Indian students in Queensland, Australia. *Asia Pacific Journal of Tourism Research*, *23*(2), 200–215. doi:10.1080/10941665.2017.1411964

Mafudi, M., Sugiarto, S., & Praptapa, A. (2021). Emerging Opportunities for Halal Tourism in Rural Areas: Insights from Indonesia. *Fokus Bisnis : Media Pengkajian Manajemen Dan Akuntansi*, *20*(1), 16–26. Advance online publication. doi:10.32639/fokusbisnis.v10i1.726

Mahmoud, H. H. H., Amer, A. A., & Ismail, T. (2021). 6G: A comprehensive survey on technologies, applications, challenges, and research problems. *Transactions on Emerging Telecommunications Technologies*, *32*(4), e4233. doi:10.1002/ett.4233

Markets and Market. (2020a). *Virtual market reality. Online Document.* https://www.marketsandmarkets.com/Market-Reports/reality-applications-market-458.html

Markets and Market. (2020b). *Augmented Reality and Virtual Reality – M&A Private Equity Investment, and Patent Filing Analysis.* https://www.marketsandmarkets.com/Market-Reports/reality-applications-market-458.html

Martí-Testón, A., Muñoz, A., Gracia, L., & Solanes, J. E. (2023). Using WebXR metaverse platforms to create touristic services and cultural promotion. *Applied Sciences (Basel, Switzerland)*, *13*(14), 8544. Advance online publication. doi:10.3390/app13148544

Martončik, M., & Lokša, J. (2016). Do World of Warcraft (MMORPG) players experience less loneliness and social anxiety in online world (virtual environment) than in real world (offline)? *Computers in Human Behavior*, *56*, 127–134. doi:10.1016/j.chb.2015.11.035

McCarthy, N. (2019). The Cost of Mobile Internet Around the World | Statista. Retrieved from https://www.statista.com/chart/ 17247/the-average-cost-of-mobile-data-in-selected-countries/. Ministry of Tourism. (2018). Tourism Ministry launches 360° Virtual Reality (VR) video on Incredible India. Retrieved from http://pib.nic.in/newsite/PrintRelease.aspx?relid=178945

Mehraj, D., Qureshi, I. H., Singh, G., Nazir, N. A., basheer, S., & Nissa, V. (2023, December). Green marketing practices and green consumer behavior: Demographic differences among young consumers. *Business Strategy & Development*, *6*(4), 571–585. Advance online publication. doi:10.1002/bsd2.263

Mercadal, T. (2017). Religious Tourism. In L. L. Lowry (Ed.), *The SAGE International Encyclopedia of Travel and Tourism*. SAGE Publications, Inc. https://doi.org/https://doi.org/10.4135/9781483368924

Merkx, C., & Nawijn, J. (2021). Virtual reality tourism experiences: Addiction and isolation. *Tourism Management*, *87*, 104394. Advance online publication. doi:10.1016/j.tourman.2021.104394

Mody, A. (2021). *The Future of Tourism in the Post-COVID-19 World.* Tourism Geographies.

Mody, A. (2016). The Evolution of Tourism and Its Impact on Consumers' Choice. *Journal of Travel Research.*

Moftah, L. (2015). Halal Pork? Aldi Supermarket Apologises to Muslims After Selling 'Halal-Certified' Black Pudding With Pig Blood. *IBT – World.*

Momtaz, P. P. (2022). Some Very Simple Economics of Web3 and the Metaverse. SSRN *Electronic Journal.* doi:10.2139/ssrn.4085937

Monaco, S., & Sacchi, G. (2023). Travelling the Metaverse: Potential Benefits and Main Challenges for Tourism Sectors and Research Applications. *Sustainability (Basel), 15*(4), 3348. Advance online publication. doi:10.3390/su15043348

Montoya Esquer, J. E., & Lara López, G. (2023). Wordsphere: Virtual reality text input interface. *Virtual Reality (Waltham Cross), 27*(3), 2769–2785. doi:10.1007/s10055-023-00842-8

Moorhouse, N., tom Dieck, M. C., & Jung, T. (2018). Technological Innovations Transforming the consumer Retail experience: A Review of literature. In T. Jung & M. C. tom Dieck (Eds.), *Augmented reality and virtual reality* (pp. 133–143). Springer., doi:10.1007/978-3-319-64027-3_10

Morales, J., Cornide-Reyes, H., Rossel, P. O., Sáez, P., & Silva-Aravena, F. (2023). Virtual reality, augmented reality and metaverse: customer experience approach and user experience evaluation methods. literature review. Lecture Notes in Computer Science (including subseries Lecture Notes in Artificial Intelligence and Lecture Notes in Bioinformatics).

Morrison, A. M. (2023). *Marketing and Managing Tourism Destinations* (3rd ed.). doi:10.4324/9781003343356

Moy, C., &Gadgil, A. (2022). *Opportunities in the Metaverse: How businesses can explore the Metaverse and navigate the hype vs reality*. JPMorgan.

Mustafa, B. (2022). Analyzing education based on metaverse technology. *Technium Social Sciences Journal, 32*, 278–295. Advance online publication. doi:10.47577/tssj.v32i1.6742

Muthukumar, T. I. D. P. (2023). *Role of ecotourism in sustainable development: An overview*. www.pnrjournal.com

Muwandeniya, W. A. K. C. B., & Eranda, B. A. N. (2022). Virtual Reality for Enhancing Customer Value in Sri Lankan Hospitality and Tourism Industry: Perspective of Industry Experts. *Sri Lanka Journal of Marketing, 8*(2), 64–83. Advance online publication. doi:10.4038/sljmuok.v8i2.102

Narin, N. G. (2021). A Content Analysis of the Metaverse Articles. *Journal of Metaverse, 1*(1).

Nickerson, C. (2022). *Simply Sociaology*. Retrieved January 9, 2023, from https://simplysociology.com/interpretivism-paradigm.html

Nijjer, S., Singh, J., Sharma, P., Malhotra, M., & Verma, R. (2023). *Unraveling a new age of travel in blockchain based metaverse*. Lecture Notes in Networks and Systems. doi:10.1007/978-981-19-7982-8_47

Nnamani, C., & Omoniyi, F. (2023) Nigeria's New Blockchan Policy Leaves Crypto in the Cold. *10 Techcabal, May 13.*

Nyst, A. (2023, July 17). 134 Social Media Statistics You Need To Know For 2023. *Search Engine Journal*. https://www.searchenginejournal.com/social-media-statistics/480507 /

Oh, H. J., Kim, J., Chang, H., Jeongheon, J. C., Park, N., & Lee, S. (2023). Social benefts of living in the metaverse: The relationships among social presence, supportive interaction, social self-efcacy, and feelings of loneliness. *Computers in Human Behavior*, *139*, 107498. doi:10.1016/j.chb.2022.107498

Okcu, S., Hancerliogullari Koksalmis, G., Basak, E., & Calisir, F. (2019). Factors Affecting Intention to Use Big Data Tools: An Extended Technology Acceptance Model. In F. Calisir, E. Cevikcan, & H. C. Akdag (Eds.), *Industrial Engineering in the Big Data Era* (pp. 401–416). Springer. doi:10.1007/978-3-030-03317-0_33

Online, F. (2020). 20 current augmented reality trends and predictions in 21//22 and beyond. *Finance Online*. https://financesonline.com/augmented-reality-trends/

Ooi, K.-B., & Tan, G. W.-H. (2016). Mobile technology acceptance model: An investigation using mobile users to explore smartphone credit card. *Expert Systems with Applications*, *59*, 33–46. doi:10.1016/j.eswa.2016.04.015

Ouerghemmi, C., Ertz, M., Bouslama, N., & Tandon, U. (2023). The Impact of Virtual Reality (VR) Tour Experience on Tourists' Intention to Visit. *Information (Basel)*, *14*(10), 546. Advance online publication. doi:10.3390/info14100546

Özdemir Uçgun, G., & Şahin, S. Z. (2023). How does Metaverse affect the tourism industry? Current practices and future forecasts. *Current Issues in Tourism*, 1–15. Advance online publication. doi:10.1080/13683500.2023.2238111

Ozdemir, M. A. (2021). Virtual Reality (VR) and Augmented Reality (AR) Technologies for Accessibility and Marketing in the Tourism Industry. ICT Tools and Applications for Accessible Tourism, 277-301.

Pacheco-Velázquez, E. A., Vázquez-Parra, J. C., Cruz-Sandoval, M., Salinas-Navarro, D. E., & Carlos-Arroyo, M. (2023). Business Decision-Making and Complex Thinking: A Bibliometric Study. *Administrative Sciences*, *13*(3), 80. doi:10.3390/admsci13030080

Padilla-MeléNdez, A., Del Aguila-Obra, A. R., & Garrido-Moreno, A. (2013). Perceived playfulness, gender differences and technology acceptance model in a blended learning scenario. *Computers & Education*, *63*(1), 306–317. doi:10.1016/j.compedu.2012.12.014

Page, S. J., & Dowling, R. K. (2002). *Ecotourism*. Pearson Education.

Papa, A., Mital, M., Pisano, P., & Del Giudice, M. (2020). E-health and wellbeing monitoring using smart healthcare devices: An empirical investigation. *Technological Forecasting and Social Change*, *153*, 119226. Advance online publication. doi:10.1016/j.techfore.2018.02.018

Park, S. M., & Kim, Y. G. (2022). A Metaverse: Taxonomy, Components, Applications, and Open Challenges. *IEEE Access : Practical Innovations, Open Solutions*, *10*, 4209–4251. Advance online publication. doi:10.1109/ACCESS.2021.3140175

Park, S., & Kim, S. (2022). Identifying World Types to Deliver Gameful Experiences for Sustainable Learning in the Metaverse. *Sustainability (Basel), 14*(3), 1361. Advance online publication. doi:10.3390/su14031361

Pearce, J. M. (2001). Virtual Reality Pedagogy: A Framework for Designing Educational Experiences. *Australian Journal of Educational Technology.*

Pellegrino, A., Wang, R., & Stasi, A. (2023). Exploring the intersection of sustainable consumption and the Metaverse: A review of current literature and future research directions. *Heliyon, 9*(9), e19190. Advance online publication. doi:10.1016/j.heliyon.2023.e19190 PMID:37681133

Pernencar, C., Saboia, I., & Dias, J. C. (2022). How Far Can Conversational Agents Contribute to IBD Patient Health Care—A Review of the Literature. *Frontiers in Public Health, 10*, 862432. doi:10.3389/fpubh.2022.862432 PMID:35844879

Pew Research Center. (2022). *The Metaverse in 2040.* Pew Research Center.

Pipia, S., & Pipia, S. (2020). Challenges of religious tourism in the conflict region: An example of Jerusalem. Global Development of Religious Tourism. doi:10.4018/978-1-7998-5792-1.ch009

Pirandello. (2021). A Journey into Artworks: Storytelling in Augmented Reality and Mixed Reality. *Cinergie–Il Cinema e le altre Arti, 19*, 135-145.

Pohlmeyer, A. L., & Jones, M. A. (2009). Engaging Design: Creating Interfaces That Emotionally Connect Users to Brands. *International Journal of Design.*

Poonkuzhali, S., Archana, J. S., & Anand, T. P. P. (2023). Metaverse 3C: concept, components, and challenges in travel and tourism sector. In Lecture Notes on Data Engineering and Communications Technologies (Vol. 171, pp. 699-713). doi:10.1007/978-981-99-1767-9_51

Poulios, I. (2019). On the greatest challenge in the management of living religious heritage: Linking the authenticity of heritage and the authenticity of tourist experiences to the authenticity of religious tradition. *Communications in Computer and Information Science, 962*, 262–271. Advance online publication. doi:10.1007/978-3-030-12960-6_17

Pratt, M. (2022). *Metaverse pros and cons: Top benefits and challenges.* Retrieved from https://www.techtarget.com/searchcio/tip/Metaverse-pros-and-cons-Top-benefits-and-challenges

Proctor, A. (1997). Museum Space and the Exploration of Difference. *Museum & Society.*

Prodinger, B., & Neuhofer, B. (2023). *Never-ending tourism: tourism experience scenarios for 2030.* Springer Proceedings in Business and Economics.

Qadir, A. M. A., & Fatah, A. O. (2023). Platformization and the Metaverse: Opportunities and Challenges for Urban Sustainability and Economic Development. *EAI Endorsed Transactions on Energy Web, 10*(1).

Qin, H. X., Wang, Y., & Hui, P. (2022). *Identity, crimes, and law enforcement in the Metaverse.* arXiv preprint arXiv:2210.06134.

Queirós, A., Faria, D., & Almeida, F. (2017). Strengths and Limitations of Qualitative and Quantitative Research Methods. *European Journal of Education Studies*, *3*(9), 369–383.

Rahman, S. (2016). The Advantages and Disadvantages of Using Qualitative and Quantitative Approaches and Methods in Language "Testing and Assessment" Research: A Literature Review. *Journal of Education and Learning*, *6*(1), 102–108. doi:10.5539/jel.v6n1p102

Raimundo, R., & Rosário, A. T. (2022). Cybersecurity in the Internet of Things in Industrial Management. *Applied Sciences (Basel, Switzerland)*, *12*(3), 1598. doi:10.3390/app12031598

Rameshwar, J. R., & King, G. S. (2023). Analysis of Caribbean XR Survey Creates an XR Development Strategy as a Path to the Regional Metaverse Evolution. *Journal of Metaverse*, *3*(1), 43–65. doi:10.57019/jmv.1179104

Ramos, C. M. Q., & Mafé-García, A. (2018). Analysis of the contribution of ICT to cultural and religious tourism: In communicating religious heritage to visitors and tourists. In Handbook of Research on Socio-Economic Impacts of Religious Tourism and Pilgrimage. doi:10.4018/978-1-5225-5730-2.ch010

Rancati, E., & D'Agata, A. (2022). Metaverse in Tourism and Hospitality: Empirical Evidence on Generation Z from Italy. *European Scientific Journal*, *18*(34), 122. Advance online publication. doi:10.19044/esj.2022.v18n34p122

Rankohi, S., & Waugh, L. (2014). Review and analysis of augmented reality literature for construction industry. *Visualization in Engineering*, *1*(1), 1–18.

Rather, R. A. (2023). Metaverse marketing and consumer research: Theoretical framework and future research agenda in tourism and hospitality industry. *Tourism Recreation Research*, 1–9. Advance online publication. doi:10.1080/02508281.2023.2216525

Ratnawati, I. I., Prasetyo, A. R., & Sidyawati, L. (2023). *Using Virtual Reality Video Development as Educational and Tourist Promotional Media*. KnE Social Sciences. doi:10.18502/kss.v8i15.13933

Rauschnabel, P. (2022). XR in tourism marketing. In D. Buhalis (Ed.), Encyclopedia of tourism management and marketing. Edward Elgar Publishing. doi:10.4337/9781800377486.xr.in.tourism

Regalado, J. A. (2017). *Virtual Reality's Missing Ingredient: Other People*. MIT Technology Review.

Rejeb, A., & Rejeb, K. (2019) Blockchain Technology in Tourism: Applications and Possibilities. *World Scientific News–An International Scientific Journal, 137*, 119-144. ww.worldscientificnews.com

Rejeb, A., Rejeb, K., & Treiblmaier, H. (2023). Mapping metaverse research: Identifying future research areas based on bibliometric and topic modeling techniques. *Information (Basel)*, *14*(7), 356. Advance online publication. doi:10.3390/info14070356

Research, S. (n.d.). *Ecotourism Market Size, Share and Forecast to 2030*. StRAiTs Research. https://straitsresearch.com/report/ecotourism-market

Ribeiro, R., Ramos, J., Safadinho, D., Reis, A., Rabadão, C., Barroso, J., & Pereira, A. (2021). Web AR Solution for UAV Pilot Training and Usability Testing. *Sensors (Basel), 21*(4), 1456. doi:10.3390/s21041456 PMID:33669733

Richardson, S. (2016). The Globalization of Tourism: A Long View. *Journal of Tourism History*.

Rinschede, G. (1992). Forms of religious tourism. *Annals of Tourism Research, 19*(1), 51–67. Advance online publication. doi:10.1016/0160-7383(92)90106-Y

Roche, D. J., & Long, A. D. (2007). Tourism and Terrorism: A Holistic Approach. *Tourism Geographies*.

Rosário, A. T., & Dias, J. C. (2023). How Industry 4.0 and Sensors Can Leverage Product Design: Opportunities and Challenges. *Sensors (Basel), 23*(3), 1165. doi:10.3390/s23031165 PMID:36772206

Rosário, A. T., Lopes, P. R., & Rosário, F. S. (2023). Metaverse in Marketing: Challenges and Opportunities. In A. Khang, V. Shah, & S. Rani (Eds.), *Handbook of Research on AI-Based Technologies and Applications in the Era of the Metaverse* (pp. 204–227). IGI Global. doi:10.4018/978-1-6684-8851-5.ch010

Rouibah, K., Lowry, P. B., & Hwang, Y. (2016). The effects of perceived enjoyment and perceived risks on trust formation and intentions to use online payment systems: New perspectives from an Arab country. *Electronic Commerce Research and Applications, 19*, 33–43. doi:10.1016/j.elerap.2016.07.001

Ruan, J., & Xie, D. (2021). Networked VR: State of the Art, Solutions, and Challenges. *Electronics (Basel), 10*(2), 166. doi:10.3390/electronics10020166

Ryan, G. (2018). Introduction to positivism, interpretivism and critical theory. *Nurse Researchers, 25*(4), 41-49.

Salau, O. P., Falola, H. O., & Akinbode, J. O. (2014). Induction and Staff Attitude towards Retention and Organizational Effectiveness. *IOSR Journal of Business and Management, 16*(4), 47–52. doi:10.9790/487X-16464752

Sánchez-Amboage, E., Enrique Membiela-Pollán, M., Martínez-Fernández, V. A., & Molinillo, S. (2023). Tourism marketing in a metaverse context: The new reality of European museums on meta. *Museum Management and Curatorship, 38*(4), 468–489. doi:10.1080/09647775.2023.2209841

Santi, G. M., Ceruti, A., Liverani, A., & Osti, F. (2021). Augmented Reality in Industry 4.0 and Future Innovation Programs. *Technologies, 9*(2), 33. doi:10.3390/technologies9020033

Schmidt, M., Kafka, J. X., Kothgassner, O. D., Hlavacs, H., Beutl, L., & Felnhofer, A. (2013). Why Does It Always Rain on Me? Influence of Gender and Environmental Factors on Usability, Technology Related Anxiety and Immersion in Virtual Environments. In D. Reidsma, H. Katayose, & A. Nijholt (Eds.), *Advances in Computer Entertainment* (pp. 392–402). Springer. doi:10.1007/978-3-319-03161-3_29

Scholars@Duke publication: Reliability and validity of a brief measure of sensation seeking. (n.d.). https://scholars.duke.edu/publication/777353

Schroeder, R. (2012). *The Social Life of Avatars: Presence and Interaction in Shared Virtual Environments*. Springer Science & Business Media.

Schuemie, M. J., Van Der Straaten, P., Krijn, M., & Van Der Mast, C. A. (2001). Research on presence in virtual reality: A survey. *Cyberpsychology & Behavior*, *4*(2), 183–201. doi:10.1089/109493101300117884 PMID:11710246

Sergi, B. S., Ključnikov, A., Popkova, E. G., Bogoviz, A. V., & Lobova, S. V. (2022). Creative abilities and digital competencies to transitioning to Business 4.0. *Journal of Business Research*, *153*, 401–411. doi:10.1016/j.jbusres.2022.08.026

Sezgin, E., & Yolal, M. (2012). Golden age of mass tourism: Its history and development. In M. Kasimoglu (Ed.), *Visions for global tourism industry-creating and sustaining competitive strategies*. IntechOpe. doi:10.5772/37283

Shakeel, J., Mardani, A., Chofreh, A. G., Goni, F. A., & Klemeš, J. J. (2020). Anatomy of sustainable business model innovation. *Journal of Cleaner Production*, *261*, 121201. doi:10.1016/j.jclepro.2020.121201

Shaygani, F., Marzaleh, M. A., & Peyravi, M. (2022). Metaverse: A Modern Approach to Medical Tourism Industry. *Iranian Journal of Public Health*, *51*(12), 2844–2845. doi:10.18502/ijph.v51i12.11480 PMID:36742228

Shinde, K. A. (2020). Managing the environment in religious tourism destinations: a conceptual model. In Religious tourism and the environment. doi:10.1079/9781789241600.0042

Sica, E., Sisto, R., Bianchi, P., & Cappelletti, G. (2021). Inclusivity and responsible tourism: Designing a trademark for a national park area. *Sustainability (Basel)*, *13*(1), 13. Advance online publication. doi:10.3390/su13010013

Singh, L., & Dhankhar, D. (2020). Use of social media by tourists at religious tourism destinations in India. In Global Development of Religious Tourism. doi:10.4018/978-1-7998-5792-1.ch015

Singh, V., & Singh, A. (2024). Digital Health Revolution: Enhancing Well-Being Through Technology. In V. Nadda, P. Tyagi, R. Moniz Vieira, & P. Tyagi (Eds.), *Implementing Sustainable Development Goals in the Service Sector* (pp. 213–219). IGI Global. doi:10.4018/979-8-3693-2065-5.ch016

Sivathanu, B., & Pillai, R. (2018). Smart HR 4.0 – how industry 4.0 is disrupting HR. *Human Resource Management International Digest*, *26*(4), 7–11. doi:10.1108/HRMID-04-2018-0059

SmartSurvey. (2020). *Primary Research Methods Explained.* Retrieved January 9, 2023, from https://www.smartsurvey.co.uk/articles/primary-research-methods

Statista. (2023c, November 7). *Travel and tourism employment worldwide 2019-2033*. https://www.statista.com/statistics/1268465/number-of-travel-and-tourism-jobs-worldwide /

Štefko, R., Kiráľová, A., & Mudrík, M. (2015). Strategic Marketing Communication in Pilgrimage Tourism. *Procedia: Social and Behavioral Sciences*, *175*, 423–430. Advance online publication. doi:10.1016/j.sbspro.2015.01.1219

Stejskal, J., Hájek, P., & Prokop, V. (2021, July 5). The role of library user preferences in the willingness to read and pay for e-books: Case of the Czech Republic. *The Electronic Library*, *39*(4), 639–660. Advance online publication. doi:10.1108/EL-01-2021-0001

Studio, A. (2021). *Microsoft Flight Simulator*. Available: https://www.flightsimulator.com/

Suanpang, P., Niamsorn, C., Pothipassa, P., Chunhapataragul, T., Netwong, T., & Jermsittiparsert, K. (2022). Extensible Metaverse Implication for a Smart Tourism City. *Sustainability (Basel)*, *14*(21), 14027. Advance online publication. doi:10.3390/su142114027

Subasinghe, M., Magalage, D., Amadoru, N., Amarathunga, L., Bhanupriya, N., & Wijekoon, J. L. (2020). Effectiveness of artificial intelligence, decentralized and distributed systems for prediction and secure channelling for Medical Tourism. *11th Annual IEEE Information Technology, Electronics and Mobile Communication Conference, IEMCON 2020*, 314–319. 10.1109/IEMCON51383.2020.9284898

Suh, W., & Ahn, S. (2022). Utilizing the Metaverse for Learner-Centered Constructivist Education in the Post-Pandemic Era: An Analysis of Elementary School Students. *Journal of Intelligence*, *10*(1), 17. Advance online publication. doi:10.3390/jintelligence10010017 PMID:35324573

Sun, J., Gan, W., Chao, H. C., & Yu, P. S. (2022). *Metaverse: Survey, applications, security, and opportunities.* https://doi.org//arXiv.2210.07990 doi:10.48550

Sun, Y., Chen, L., Sun, H., & Taghizadeh-Hesary, F. (2020b.) *Low-carbon financial.*. doi:10.1016/j.frl.2020.10149

Su, P. Y., Hsiao, P. W., & Fan, K. K. (2023). Investigating the relationship between users' behavioral intentions and learning effects of VR system for sustainable tourism development. *Sustainability (Basel)*, *15*(9), 7277. Advance online publication. doi:10.3390/su15097277

Sustainable Tourism market. (2022, June 17). https://www.futuremarketinsights.com/reports/sustainable-tourism-sector-overview-and-analysis

TATA Consultancy Services. (2019, March 28). *Understanding Business 4.0™:The New-Age Transformation Paradigm.* Retrieved November 13, 2022, from https://www.business4.tcs.com/content/dam/tcs_b4/pdf/About%20Business%204.0.pdf

Telecoms. (2018). *A new reality awaits: AR and VR the next big platforms in Telecoms?* https://www.deltapartnersgroup.com/new-reality-awaits-are-ar-and-vr-next-big-platforms

Thomas, L. D. W., & Tee, R. (2022). Generativity: A systematic review and conceptual framework. *International Journal of Management Reviews*, *24*(2), 255–278. doi:10.1111/ijmr.12277

Times of India. (n.d.). Mass tourism hits Hallstatt in Austria; locals protest. *Times of India Travel.* https://timesofindia.indiatimes.com/travel/travel-news/mass-tourism-hits-hallstatt-in-austria-locals-protest/articleshow /103173755.cms

Tiwari, A., Dhiman, V., Iesa, M. A. M., Alsarhan, H., Mehbodniya, A., & Shabaz, M. (2021). Patient Behavioral Analysis with Smart Healthcare and IoT. *Behavioural Neurology*, *2021*, 1–9. Advance online publication. doi:10.1155/2021/4028761 PMID:34900023

Tomljenović, R., & Dukić, L. (2018). *Religious Tourism - from a Tourism Product to an Agent of Societal Transformation.* doi:10.15308/Sitcon-2017-1-8

Tone, S. R. J. (2000). Haptic feedback: A brief history from telepresence to virtual reality. In *International Workshop on Haptic Human-Computer Interaction* (pp. 1-16). Springer.

Tosto, C., Hasegawa, T., Mangina, E., Chifari, A., Treacy, R., Merlo, G., & Chiazzese, G. (2021). Exploring the effect of an augmented reality literacy programme for reading and spelling difficulties for children diagnosed with ADHD. *Virtual Reality (Waltham Cross)*, *25*(3), 879–894. doi:10.1007/s10055-020-00485-z

Toubes, D. R., Vila, N. A., & Fraiz Brea, J. A. (2021). Changes in consumption patterns and tourist promotion after the covid-19 pandemic. *Journal of Theoretical and Applied Electronic Commerce Research*, *16*(5), 1332–1352. Advance online publication. doi:10.3390/jtaer16050075

Trono, A., & Castronuovo, V. (2023). Pilgrimage Tourism, Accessibility and Local Communities in Western Countries. The Camino de Santiago de Compostela and the via Francigena for All. In Perspectives on Asian Tourism: Vol. Part F191. doi:10.1007/978-981-19-9677-1_9

Tsai, S. P. (2022). Investigating metaverse marketing for travel and tourism. *Journal of Vacation Marketing*. Advance online publication. doi:10.1177/13567667221145715

Tsironis, C. N. (2022). Pilgrimage and Religious Tourism in Society, in the Wake of the COVID-19 Pandemic: A Paradigmatic Focus on 'St. Paul's Route' in the Central Macedonia Region, Greece. *Religions*, *13*(10), 887. Advance online publication. doi:10.3390/rel13100887

Tussyadiah, I. (2020). A review of research into automation in tourism: Launching the annals oftourism research curated collection on artificial intelligence and robotics in tourism. *Annals of Tourism Research*, *81*, 102883. doi:10.1016/j.annals.2020.102883

Ud Din, I., & Almogren, A. (2023). Exploring the psychological effects of Metaverse on mental health and well-being. *Information Technology & Tourism*, *25*(3), 367–389. Advance online publication. doi:10.1007/s40558-023-00259-8

Um, T., Kim, H., Kim, H., Lee, J., Koo, C., & Chung, N. (2022). Travel Incheon as a Metaverse: Smart Tourism Cities Development Case in Korea. In Information and Communication Technologies in Tourism 2022. doi:10.1007/978-3-030-94751-4_20

Umrani, F., & Ghadially, R. (2008). Gender and decision-making in technology adoption among youth. *Psychology and Developing Societies*, *20*(2), 209–227. doi:10.1177/097133360802000204

Undale, S., Kulkarni, A., Mude, G., Patil, H., Raut, N., Banswal, D., & Undale, G. (2023). A bibliometric analysis of citations and publications on metaverse. *Proceedings of the 17th INDIACom; 2023 10th International Conference on Computing for Sustainable Global Development, INDIACom 2023.*

UNWTO. (2016). *World Tourism Day 2016 "Tourism for All-promoting universal accessibility" Good Practices in the Accessible Tourism Supply Chain.* World Tourism Organization (UNWTO).

Uppot, R. N., Laguna, B., McCarthy, C. J., De Novi, G., Phelps, A., Siegel, E., & Courtier, J. (2019). Implementing virtual and augmented reality tools for radiology education and training, communication, and clinical care.". *Radiology*, *291*(3), 570–580. doi:10.1148/radiol.2019182210 PMID:30990383

Venkatesh, V., Morris, M. G., & Ackerman, P. L. (2000). A longitudinal field investigation of gender differences in individual technology adoption decision-making processes. *Organizational Behavior and Human Decision Processes*, *83*(1), 33–60. doi:10.1006/obhd.2000.2896 PMID:10973782

Vergel, R. S., Tena, P. M., Yrurzum, S. C., & Cruz-Neira, C. (2020). A comparative evaluation of a virtual reality table and a HoloLens-based augmented reality system for anatomy training. *IEEE Transactions on Human-Machine Systems*, *50*(4), 337–348. doi:10.1109/THMS.2020.2984746

Virtual reality, presence, and attitude change: Empirical evidence from tourism. Tourism Management, 66, 140–154. doi:10.1016/j.tourman.2017.12.003

Volchek, K., & Brysch, A. (2023). *Metaverse and tourism: from a new niche to a transformation.* Springer Proceedings in Business and Economics.

Volchek, K., & Brysch, A. (2023). *Metaverse and Tourism: From a New Niche to a Transformation.* Springer Proceedings in Business and Economics. doi:10.1007/978-3-031-25752-0_32

Volo, S. (2017). Emotions in tourism: from exploration to design. In D. R. Fesenmaier & Z. Xiang (Eds.), *Design science in tourism* (pp. 31–40). Springer. doi:10.1007/978-3-319-42773-7_3

Wang, X., Shi, T., Bai, W., Peng, K., Li, J., & Shi, Y. (2022). The research of metaverse application in intelligent railway passenger station. Lecture Notes in Computer Science (including subseries Lecture Notes in Artificial Intelligence and Lecture Notes in Bioinformatics). doi:10.1007/978-3-031-23518-4_10

Wang, D., Xiang, Z., & Fesenmaier, D. R. (2016). Smartphone use in everyday life and travel. *Journal of Travel Research*, *55*(1), 52–63. doi:10.1177/0047287514535847

Wang, Y., Su, Z., Zhang, N., Xing, R., Liu, D., Luan, T. H., & Shen, X. (2023). A Survey on Metaverse: Fundamentals, Security, and Privacy. *IEEE Communications Surveys and Tutorials*, *25*(1), 319–352. Advance online publication. doi:10.1109/COMST.2022.3202047

Web 3D simulation-based application in tourism education: A case study with Second Life | Scholars Portal Journals. (n.d.). https://journals.scholarsportal.info/details/14738376/v11i0002/113_w3saitacswsl.xml&sub=all

Wei, W. (2023). A buzzword, a phase or the next chapter for the Internet? The status and possibilities of the metaverse for tourism. *Journal of Hospitality and Tourism Insights*. doi:10.1108/JHTI-11-2022-0568

Wei, D. (2022). Gemiverse: The blockchain-based professional certification and tourism platform with its own ecosystem in the metaverse. *International Journal of Geoheritage and Parks*, *10*(2), 322–336. doi:10.1016/j.ijgeop.2022.05.004

Weiler, B., & Ham, S. H. (2001). Tour guides and interpretation. In *The encyclopedia of ecotourism* (pp. 549–563). CABI publishing. doi:10.1079/9780851993683.0549

Werthner, H., & Klein, S. (1999). *Information technology and tourism: a challenging ralationship*. Springer-Verlag Wien. doi:10.1007/978-3-7091-6363-4

Westmattelmann, D., Grotenhermen, J. G., Sprenger, M., Rand, W., & Schewe, G. (2021). Apart we ride together: The motivations behind users of mixed-reality sports. *Journal of Business Research*, *134*, 316–328. doi:10.1016/j.jbusres.2021.05.044

What Is Ecotourism. (2019, January 11). The International Ecotourism Society. https://ecotourism.org/what-is-ecotourism /

Wight, P. (1993). Ecotourism: Ethics or eco-sell? *Journal of Travel Research*, *31*(3), 3–9. doi:10.1177/004728759303100301

Wight, P. A. (2001). Ecotourists: Not a homogeneous market segment. In D. B. Weaver (Ed.), *The Encyclopedia of Ecotourism* (pp. 37–62). CAB International. doi:10.1079/9780851993683.0037

Williams, T. (2021). *Why Is Quantitative Research Important?* Retrieved January 9, 2023, from https://www.gcu.edu/blog/doctoral-journey/why-quantitative-research-important

Williams, A. M. (2010). Mass tourism, culture, and the historic city: Theoretical perspectives. *Rivista di Scienze del Turismo Ambiente Cultura Diritto Economia*, *1*(2), 9–29.

Xiang, Z., & Fesenmaier, D. R. (2017a). Big data analytics, tourism design and smart tourism. In Z. Xiang & D. Fesenmaier (Eds.), *Analytics in smart tourism design. Tourism on the Verge* (pp. 299–307). Springer. doi:10.1007/978-3-319-44263-1_17

Xu, F., & Buhalis, D. (2021). *Gamification for Tourism. Bristol*. Channel View Publications.

Xu, F., Buhalis, D., & Weber, J. (2017). Serious games and the gamification of tourism. *Tourism Management*, *60*, 244–256. doi:10.1016/j.tourman.2016.11.020

Xu, F., Tian, F., Buhalis, D., Weber, J., & Zhang, H. (2016). Tourists as mobile gamers –gamification for tourism marketing. *Journal of Travel & Tourism Marketing*, *33*(8), 1124–1142. doi:10.1080/10548408.2015.1093999

Yang, F. X., & Wang, Y. (2023). Rethinking Metaverse Tourism: A Taxonomy and an Agenda for Future Research. *Journal of Hospitality & Tourism Research (Washington, D.C.)*. Advance online publication. doi:10.1177/10963480231163509

Yaqoob, I., Salah, K., Jayaraman, R., & Omar, M. (2023). Metaverse applications in smart cities: Enabling technologies, opportunities, challenges, and future directions. *Internet of Things : Engineering Cyber Physical Human Systems*, *23*, 100884. doi:10.1016/j.iot.2023.100884

Yersüren, S., & Özel, Ç. H. (2023). The effect of virtual reality experience quality on destination visit intention and virtual reality travel intention. *Journal of Hospitality and Tourism Technology*. doi:10.1108/JHTT-02-2023-0046

Yoon, T. H., Do, J. K., & Jeong, S. C. (2022). Developing Songjeong Metaverse Surfing Village: Development of Metaverse-based Platform Specialized for Marine Tourism. *Proceedings - 2022 IEEE/ACIS 7th International Conference on Big Data, Cloud Computing, and Data Science, BCD 2022*. 10.1109/BCD54882.2022.9900793

Yoon, S. Y., Choi, Y. J., & Oh, H. (2015). User attributes in processing 3D VR-enabled showroom: Gender, visual cognitive styles, and the sense of presence. *International Journal of Human-Computer Studies*, *82*, 1–10. doi:10.1016/j.ijhcs.2015.04.002

Young, D., & Gerard, M. (2023, August 9). *Four Steps to Sustainable Business Model Innovation*. BCG Global. https://www.bcg.com/publications/2021/four-strategies-for-sustainable-business-model-innovation

Yuan, Y., & Yang, Y. (2022). Embracing the Metaverse: Mechanism and logic of a new digital economy. *Metaverse*, *3*(2), 15. Advance online publication. doi:10.54517/m.v3i2.1814

Yung, R., & Khoo-Lattimore, C. (2017). New realities: A systematic literature review on virtual reality and augmented reality in tourism research. *Current Issues in Tourism*, •••, 1–26.

Zaman, U., Koo, I., Abbasi, S., Raza, S. H., & Qureshi, M. G. (2022). Meet your digital twin in space? profiling international expat's readiness for metaverse space travel, tech-savviness, covid-19 travel anxiety, and travel fear of missing out. *Sustainability (Basel)*, *14*(11), 6441. Advance online publication. doi:10.3390/su14116441

Zareei, A., & Namjoo, A. (2018). *The Role of Theatre, Rituals and Religious Ceremonies in Improving the Concept of Spiritual Tourism (Case Study: Iran)*. doi:10.22133/IJTS.2018.69312

Zarrouk, I., & El Aidouni, A. (2023). The digital marketing practiced by the Moroccan tourism sector: national-scale communication actions and environmental management. *E3S Web of Conferences*.

Zeithaml, V. A., Parasuraman, A., & Malhotra, A. (2002). Service quality delivery through web sites: Acritical review of extant knowledge. *Journal of the Academy of Marketing Science*, *30*(4), 362–375. doi:10.1177/009207002236911

Zeng, Y., Liu, L., & Xu, R. (2022). The Effects of a Virtual Reality Tourism Experience on Tourist's Cultural Dissemination Behavior. *Tourism and Hospitality*, *3*(1), 314–329. Advance online publication. doi:10.3390/tourhosp3010021

Zhang, J., & Ye, J. (2021). *Alibaba to test gaming potential of Metaverse as Big Tech firms stampede into virtual world.* Retrieved from https://www.scmp.com/tech/bigtech/article/3159691/alibaba-test-gaming-potential-Metaverse-big-tech-firms-stampede

Zhang, G. (2021). Bridging the intention–behaviour gap: Effect of altruistic motives on developers' action towards green redevelopment of industrial brownfields. *Sustainability*, *13*(2). Advance online publication. doi:10.3390/su13020977

Zhang, W., & Wang, Y. (2023). An empirical study of the impact of metaverse storytelling on intentions to visit. *Information Technology & Tourism*, *25*(3), 411–432. Advance online publication. doi:10.1007/s40558-023-00261-0

Zhang, X., Yang, D., Yow, C. H., Huang, L., Wu, X., Huang, X., Guo, J., Zhou, S., & Cai, Y. (2022). Metaverse for Cultural Heritages. *Electronics (Basel)*, *11*(22), 3730. Advance online publication. doi:10.3390/electronics11223730

Zhu, C., Wu, D. C. W., Hall, C. M., Fong, L. H. N., Koupaei, S. N., & Lin, F. (2023). Exploring non-immersive virtual reality experiences in tourism: Empirical evidence from a world heritage site. *International Journal of Tourism Research*, *25*(3), 372–383. doi:10.1002/jtr.2574

Zuhal, E. (2023). Naplozz Revolutionises the Hospitality Industry with Blockchain Technology. *The Crypto Basic*. https://thecryptobasic.com/2023/04/12/naplozz-revolutionizes-the-hospitality-industry

Žukauskas, P., Vveinhardt, J., & Andriukaitienė, R. (2018). Philosophy and Paradigm of Scientific Research. In *Management Culture and Social Responsibility* (pp. 122–135). IntechOpen.

About the Contributors

Surabhi Singh is an accomplished academic professional with a passion for Marketing, holding a PhD degree in the area of Marketing from AMU, she brings a wealth of knowledge and experience to her work. With over 23 years of experience in academia, Dr Singh has established herself as a leading expert in Digital Marketing and Neuromarketing. She has published extensively in reputable journals and has presented her research at numerous national and international conferences. In addition to her research accomplishments, Dr Surabhi Singh is dedicated to excellence in teaching and mentorship. She has developed and taught courses on Marketing and has supervised around 50 PGDM students and also PhD students in their research endeavours. Her commitment to service is evident through her active participation in professional organizations in various administrative, and editorial roles for academic journals, and engagement with the broader community. She strives to promote diversity, equity, and inclusion in all aspects of her work.

* * *

Simon Abou Fayad is an assistant professor at the Lebanese University faculty of tourism and hospitality management. He holds a PhD in Tourism from the Lebanese University. Dr. Simon Abou Fayad pursued his college studies and holds a BS in business management from Sagesse University. Prior to joining the Lebanese university, he worked as a lecturer in several universities in Lebanon, where he led modules at the graduate and undergraduate levels. He supervised masters students to completion in areas related to the hospitality and tourism industry. His research interests are focused on tourism, hospitality branding and food service.

Munir Ahmad, Ph.D. in Computer Science, brings over 24 years of invaluable expertise in the realm of spatial data development, management, processing, visualization, and quality assurance. His unwavering commitment to open data, crowdsourced data, volunteered geographic information, and spatial data infrastructure has solidified him as a seasoned professional and a trusted trainer in cutting-edge spatial technologies.

With a profound passion for research, Munir has authored more than 30 publications in his field, culminating in the award of his Ph.D. in Computer Science from Preston University Pakistan in 2022. His dedication to propelling the industry forward and sharing his extensive knowledge defines his mission. Connect with Munir to delve into the world of Spatial Data, GIS, and GeoTech. #SpatialData #GIS #GeoTech.

Muhammad Akram is a PhD scholar passionate about safeguarding privacy and enabling accurate location services in mobile networks. Their research delves into the intricate dance between user privacy and the power of location data. During their BS (Hons) and MS studies, Muhammad Akram explored innovative techniques for location estimation, laying the groundwork for their current doctoral research, which focuses on Location Privacy in Social Networks.

Shakeel Basheer is a researcher at Lovely professional university. About my qualification i have done bachelors in business administration from public university namely Kashmir university and an MBA in tourism management from central university of Kashmir My interest revolves around E-marketing, Ethical marketing, Ethical Tourism, JK tourism, Sustainability, E Tourism, social media, consumer psychology, organisation behaviour, and digital learning. He is proficient in using Vos viewer, Smart-PLS, AMOS, SPSS, LIWC, NVIVO, ATLAS.ti, and Mendeley. Beginner in Python and R.

Karishma Desai is an Associate Professor, Associate Program Director and Ph.D. Supervisor at Atlas Skilltech University with 12 years teaching experience. She has pursued her MCom, PGDBA (Symbiosis), UGC NET, Ph.D (Commerce) in the subject of Business Policy and Administration. She is a passionate teacher, researcher, author, soft skills trainer and PoSH enabler . She has published around 20 research papers in ABDC and UGC peer reviewed journals and over 50 students have published their research papers in peer reviewed journals under her able guidance. Her latest book chapter publication in the Emerald book series on "The Adoption of Artificial Intelligence on Human Resources Management" is her latest feat. She is a peer reviewer for Emerald studies in Finance and Insurance Management. She has been the convenor and co- convenor of many National and International Seminars and has presented her papers in International Conferences and has also chaired sessions for International conferences. She won the National award for the best Enactus faculty leader sponsored by Mahindra and Mahindra in the year 2016 and has won the best Faculty award at her previous Educational Institution NMIMS in the year 2022. She is passionate about using various pedagogical innovations to migrate from teaching to learning, she actively involved herself in Covid vaccination drive initiative, She is an environment and fitness enthusiast.

Joana Carmo Dias has a PhD in Management, with specialization in Marketing, by the Nova School of Business and Economics and a Master in Marketing at Universidade Católica Portuguesa. She is an assistant professor at IPAM Porto, in the scientific areas of management and marketing and supervises several master's dissertations. She is an integrated researcher at COMEGI and her focus of research are the areas of services marketing, healthcare, consumer experience and branding. Until 2017 she developed her professional career as marketing manager.

Amit Dutt is a Professor and Associate Dean, in Lovely Professional University. As a tenured professor at Lovely Professional University, he has made indelible contributions to the academic landscape. His research spans a wide array of topics within operations management, His work has been published in prestigious journals. His research is characterized by its innovative thinking, rigorous empirical methodologies, and real-world applicability. Their publications have not only advanced theoretical frameworks but have also provided actionable insights for organizations seeking to enhance their operational efficiency and effectiveness.

Shuaibu Chiroma Hassan is working as senior lecturer at Isa Kaita College of education, Dutsinma, Katsina State - Nigeria. He is the Students' Work Experience Scheme Coordinator; formerly HoD Home Economics. He is graduate of university of Bedfordshire (MSc International tourism and hospitality management, Higher National Diploma in Catering and Hotel Management from Kaduna Polytechnic, National Diploma in Catering and Hotel Management from Katsina Polytechnic, I have a Postgraduate Diploma in education from Usmanu Danfodiyo University, Sokoto, with Teachers' Registration Council of Nigeria. He has published some Book Chapters with Routledge, authored some papers in conferences and journals hospitality and tourism and co-authored a book on nutrition.

Viana Hassan is actively involved in academic and research work in Tourism & Cultural Management in Lebanon and Malta. She got her Ph.D. in Tourism Management and Cultural from Saint Joseph University, Beirut. Her Thesis was entitled "Medical Tourism in Lebanon". She has more than 19 years of tourism experience in many related Travel and Tourism Fields, varying from airline sales experience (MEA), to Co-management several Lebanese Travel agencies. She is an Experienced Lecturer with more than 16 years' experience at several universities in Lebanon (Lebanese University, A.U. L, Lebanese International University, Islamic University), the Institute of Tourism Studies, STC higher education and University of Malta (Malta), Scholars School system (UK) with a demonstrated history of working in the Higher education industry, Skilled in Tourism Management, Customer service, Branding, Event Management, Airline Business Management, Niche Tourism, Business operations management, Customer acquisition and Medical Tourism. Dr. Viana has participated in international conferences (Expo Dubai 2020, 7th Medical Tourism World Summit, etc...) including Athens, Paris, Vienna, Dubai, Beirut, Valencia, Amman, Lisbon, Istanbul and has published papers in peer review journals.

Dr. Preeti Mehra is a Business Faculty with Campbell College working in collaboration with Portage College Continuing Education, Alberta, Canada and is focussed on providing the definitive educational experience for international learners. She is a doctorate from Guru Nanak Dev University, Amritsar, India and her specialisation is marketing. She has an experience of 15 years in Corporate and Academics and was a professor in marketing with a leading private university in India. She is dedicated to imparting knowledge and is passionate about research and e-content development. She has an expertise in public speaking, academic instruction, and research management. She offers an history of delivering marketing advancements and developing substantial university curricula and is devoted to creating future field leaders through education and mentoring. She specialises in Micro Branding, Sachet Marketing, Gesture Recognition, Rural Marketing Strategy, Services Marketing and Brand Management. Her research work focusses on expressively enriching organizational reach and market share through the application of robust strategies, effective pricing and excellent client relationship management. She has contributed towards distinguished journals of national and international repute like Emerald, Sage and has participated and presented in many national and international conferences. She has acted as editor of several books and has contributed towards many book chapters in the field of marketing. She has acted as an external trainer in many workshops and Faculty Development Programmes related to marketing and research methodology. She has several copyrights and patents to her credit and has supervised several doctorate students.

Faizan Ashraf Mir is an alumnus of The Business School, University of Kashmir. He has a Masters degree in Management as well as in Tourism and has qualified UGC-NET. He pursued his Ph.d oin Central University of in the field of Strategic Tourism Management . He also has a Post-graduate Diploma in Business Administration from University of Kashmir. He has served in the banking sector for a while and has attended training programs in service sector. His academic interests are in the area of Organisational behaviour, HR. Strategic Tourism Management and Entrepreneurship Development. He has participated in national and international conferences, seminars, workshops and has many research papers to his credit and is presently heading the Department of Tourism as Coordinator. He also holds additional Adminsitrative assignments of Deputy Director (GC)- Department of Students Welfare, Deputy Director, DIQA and I/c Extension Lectures in the University.

Albérico Travassos Rosário is Ph.D. Marketing and Strategy of the Universities of Aveiro (UA), Minho (UM) and Beira Interior (UBI). With affiliation to the GOVCOPP research center of the University of Aveiro. Master in Marketing and Degree in Marketing, Advertising and Public Relations, degree from ISLA Campus Lisbon-European University I Laureate International Universities. Has the title of Marketing Specialist and teaches with the category of Assistant Professor at IADE-Faculty of Design, Technology and Communication of the European University and as a visiting Associate Professor at the Santarém Higher School of Management and Technology (ESGTS) of the Polytechnic Institute of Santarém. He taught at IPAM-School of Marketing I Laureate International Universities, ISLA- Higher Institute of Management and Administration of Santarém (ISLA-Santarém), was Director of the Commercial Management Course, Director of the Professional Technical Course (TeSP) of Sales and Commercial Management, Chairman of the Pedagogical Council and Member of the Technical Council and ISLA-Santarém Scientific Researcher. He is also a marketing and strategy consultant for SMEs.

Sunetra Saha is an Assistant Professor of Marketing & Retail Management with Amity Business School, Amity University, Noida (Ranked one of the Best Management Universities in India) from August 2009 till date. A wealth of talent in the development and implementation of educational technology tools and applications in the classroom. In-depth knowledge of Marketing, Retail and Strategic management adept in creative teaching strategies that fully engage students in the learning process. Deeply invested in achieving tenure through administrative service, committee contributions, and an accomplishment-oriented approach to teaching.

Amrik Singh is working as Professor in the School of Hotel Management and Tourism at Lovely Professional University, Punjab, India. He obtained his Ph.D. degree in Hotel Management from Kurukshetra University, Kurukshetra. He started his academic career at Lovely Professional University, Punjab, India in the year 2007. He has published more than 25 research publications in Scopus/Web of Science) journals. He has published 12 patents and 01 patent has been granted in the inter-disciplinary domain. Dr. Amrik Singh participated and acted as a resource person in various national and international conferences, seminars, research workshops, and industry talks. His area of research interest is accommodation management, ergonomics, green practices, human resource management in hospitality, waste management, AR VR in hospitality, etc. He is currently guiding 8Ph.D. scholars and 2 Ph.D. scholars have been awarded Ph.D.

Arpita Srivastava is a seasoned professional with a cumulative work experience of 22 years, featuring a noteworthy corporate tenure of 7 years dedicated to Marketing, Product, and Brand Management in well renowned companies like Dr Reddy's Lab, Panacea Biotech and Win Medicare. Currently serving as a Professor at the GL Baja Institute of Management and Research in Greater Noida, Dr. Arpita brings a wealth of knowledge and expertise to the academic realm. Her research focus spans diverse areas such as consumer behavior, brand management, artificial intelligence, gamification and sustainability, showcasing a broad and multidimensional understanding of contemporary marketing dynamics. Dr. Arpita has significantly contributed to the academic discourse with the publication of over 30 papers in reputable journals indexed by ABDC and Scopus. Demonstrating a passion for advancing the field of marketing, Dr. Arpita actively explores new avenues and methodologies. Her commitment to staying at the forefront of her field is evident in her consistent achievements, including being the top performer in NPTEL courses on Integrated Marketing Communication (IMC) and Product and Brand Management for the past two years. Beyond her academic pursuits, Dr. Arpita has played a pivotal role in the professional development of individuals and organizations through the execution of Management Development Programs (MDPs). Her expertise has been shared with notable entities such as Anmol Industries, KRIBHCO, HAIER, and Agarwal Movers and Packers, where she has conducted impactful programs. Dr. Arpita Srivastava's multifaceted career is marked by a blend of academic rigor, industry acumen and a genuine enthusiasm for pushing the boundaries of marketing knowledge. Her contributions, both in the https://orcid.org/0000-0002-9734-8008.53bcf380-8c6d-4b63-98d2-d40774c0b3a4

Nidhi Srivastava is a competent and dynamic academician offering rich experience in teaching and development of academic infrastructure. Ph.D holder and Masters in Finance & Control from Lucknow University with numerous publications and articles across national and international journals. Strives for academic excellence and providing quality education. Possesses strong teaching skills with excellent ability to identify talent and potential of each individual.

Saadia Ureeb is a PhD scholar working on collaborative pan Industrial Studies and exploring the Information technology advancement impact on various financial industries. The aim is to minimize the operational losses while working on data analytics. She has a diverse experience in Banking and Risk Management. A graduate from IIUI researched in MS(CS) on computer networking and security. During her studies, she worked on Artificial Intelligence, Congestion issues and Migrating inputs. Currently her scope is exploring the operational risk and financial losses due to inadequate processes and Knowledge Management.

Index

P

R

S

T

V

www.ingramcontent.com/pod-product-compliance
Lightning Source LLC
LaVergne TN
LVHW080642011026
849160LV00014B/1300